States, markets, and just growth

# States, markets, and just growth: Development in the twenty-first century

Edited by Atul Kohli, Chung-in Moon, and George Sørensen

 United Nations
University Press

TOKYO · NEW YORK · PARIS

0 7 2 3 9 5

The views expressed in this publication are those of the authors and do not necessarily reflect the views of the United Nations University.

United Nations University Press
The United Nations University, 53-70, Jingumae 5-chome,
Shibuya-ku, Tokyo, 150-8925, Japan
Tel: +81-3-3499-2811   Fax: +81-3-3406-7345
E-mail: sales@hq.unu.edu (general enquiries): press@hq.unu.edu
http://www.unu.edu

United Nations University Office in North America
2 United Nations Plaza, Room DC2-2062, New York, NY 10017, USA
Tel: +1-212-963-6387   Fax: +1-212-371-9454
E-mail: unuona@ony.unu.edu

United Nations University Press is the publishing division of the United Nations University.

Cover design by Jean-Marie Antenen

Printed in the United States of America

UNUP-1076
ISBN 92-808-1076-6

Library of Congress Cataloging-in-Publication Data

States, markets and just growth : development in the twenty-first
century / edited by Atul Kohli, Chung-in Moon, and George Sørensen.
    p.   cm.
Includes bibliographical references and index.
ISBN 92-808-1076-6
1. Developing countries—Economic conditions. I. Kohli, Atul.
II. Moon, Chung-in. III. Sørensen, George.
HC59.7 .S7585 2003
330.9172'4—dc21                                      2002154101

# Contents

# List of tables and figures

# Note on measurements

In this volume:

1 billion = 1,000 million
1 trillion = 1,000 billion
1$ = 1 US dollar

# Introduction

*Atul Kohli*

Third world countries enter the twenty-first century with four to five decades of experience along a variety of developmental pathways. Although much has been achieved, the results have also been sobering. Long gone are the heady days of anticolonial nationalism and of hopes of the "South" seeking coordinated concessions from the "North." Even the "Washington Consensus" on development that emerged following the debt crisis of the 1980s has faded. If judged against the criteria of reconciling robust economic growth with fair distribution and democracy, hardly any developing country is an unequivocal success. East Asian countries are often considered "successful developers" but they reconciled impressive economic growth with distribution under authoritarian regimes. Communist countries of the region may have eliminated basic poverty but their embrace of markets to facilitate higher growth has also proceeded without political pluralism. By contrast, a country such as India has maintained its democracy, but sluggish growth and stubborn poverty continue to mar its performance. The Middle East continues to be characterized by nearly antiquated states. Sharp income-inequalities of South American countries have survived both fluctuating regime types and fluctuating rates of economic growth. Finally, countries of sub-Saharan Africa have performed poorly on nearly all the dimensions that one may deem desirable.

What are the prospects that developing countries will reconcile economic growth, fair distribution, and democracy in the twenty-first century? We label the goal of growth with distribution and democracy as the goal of just growth. A central purpose of this volume is to analyse the obstacles to achieving just growth in the developing world in the recent past and to point to more promising pathways in the near future. The patterns of state–market interactions within developing countries provide the focus for assessing the prospects of just growth. The main themes of the volume, then, are how have states and markets interacted to produce a range of developmental outcomes, and how may one improve on the past performance?

As one looks to the twenty-first century, the pursuit of just growth not only will raise the old and enduring issues of roles of states versus markets and of potential trade-offs between growth and distribution but also important new issues will include the changing global parameters within which development efforts will unfold in the near future. The most significant of these may be grouped under the heading of "globalization." Not only have cross-national economic interactions gained in significance, but the end of the cold war and the victory of the West – especially of the USA – has created a near-hegemony of pro-market development ideas. Will such global changes help or hinder the prospects of just growth? Relatedly, governments in most developing countries – if currently not democratic – will, in the near future, experience pressure to democratize. Will democratic governments in developing countries be more or less capable than their predecessors in reconciling economic growth and fair distribution?

Within common global conditions, it is also clear by now that developing countries appear to exhibit not common outcomes but development patterns that are distinctive by regions. These patterns not only raise questions about the uniform significance of global constraints but also point to such other determinants of development as varying roles of states. East Asia, for example, is broadly characterized by "strong" states and rapid, export-oriented, economic growth; sub-Saharan Africa, by contrast, has been plagued by failed states and poor economic performance. Latin American countries appear to move through political and economic transitions in unison, from democracy to authoritarianism and back to democracy, and from severe debt crisis to modest economic growth. Security threats and "rentier" states have provided broad parameters of development in the Middle East. Finally, South Asian countries seem to muddle along a common path of fragmented polities and middling economic performance.

Such regional variations provide an organizing principle for the volume: whereas third world countries share some common problems, critical development issues vary from region to region. The pressing need in many African countries is for coherent states and resumption of economic growth; East Asian countries, by contrast, face the challenge of maintaining their high economic growth rates under conditions of "globalization." Similarly, Latin American countries need to manage their international economic links but under conditions of low domestic savings, sharp income-inequalities, and fragile democracies; South Asian states must somehow "insulate" their economies from nearly excessive politics so that the challenges of growth and poverty can be met head-on; and the countries of the Middle East must find ways to reform their antiquated state systems so that a more inclusionary pattern of development may unfold. The suggestion at the outset is not that these challenges are really the key challenges for each region; rather, the more modest suggestion is that, in between the two extremes of "all countries are different" and "one cookie-cutter development model fits all," regional variations within common constraints provide a useful organizing focus for discussing development issues.

This volume, then, explores the common concerns of all developing countries, while simultaneously emphasizing special regional needs. Five synthetic chapters that follow analyse the record of different regions and countries in achieving just growth, and three chapters provide overviews of pressing shared concerns of globalization, democracy, and poverty and inequality. In order to facilitate coherence, each of the chapter authors was asked to address the following themes.

## States, markets, and growth

To what extent states should intervene in markets to promote growth is an old and perennial debate in development studies – probably the master debate. The general views on this have swung back and forth in the scholarly and policy communities. There was a near-consensus during the 1950s and the 1960s that pervasive "market imperfections" necessitated state intervention for promoting growth. Over time, the focus shifted to "state imperfections," and the "Washington Consensus" of the 1980s argued for getting prices right, openness, and minimal state intervention. More recently, the pendulum has again swung back, at least somewhat: on the one hand there is continuing recognition of the importance of macroeconomic stability and of getting some prices right, such as the exchange rate and food prices; on the other hand, there is a growing recognition not only that sound policy-making and implementation require an effective state but also that effective state intervention is further needed to promote economic growth. The latter is important both for supporting emerging producers and for helping to build such basic economic capabilities as infrastructure, an educated and healthy workforce, and technological know-how. The real issues for discussion, then, may not be states versus markets but how states and markets can work together to promote growth, as well as the quality of state intervention. The authors of all the following chapters, especially those on regional perspectives, examine this theme of how state intervention has helped or hurt economic growth in the recent past and how one may improve on past performance in the future.

## States, markets, and distribution

How much emphasis should be placed by development strategies on deliberate redistribution and/or on poverty alleviation are, again, old and enduring questions. Tolerance of poverty and inequality also appears to wax and wane in the scholarly and policy communities, not to mention within regions and countries. If one distinguishes between issues of poverty and of inequality (as one should), current evidence on their relationship with economic growth is more conclusive concerning the former than the latter. We know by now that steady economic growth helps alleviate poverty; however, there are also major exceptions to this association – as periodically highlighted by the *Human Development Report* of the United Nations Development Programme (UNDP) – suggesting that patterns of growth matter and that public policy intervention for structuring growth patterns will remain significant in translating gains in national production into better living conditions for all.

The relationship of growth to levels of inequality, by contrast, remains indeterminate. The old fears that rapid growth accentuates inequalities have proved unfounded. The reverse causation offers intriguing possibilities for just growth: an emphasis on more egalitarian development may not necessarily hurt growth. The underlying issue, of when a redistributive emphasis scares producers and when the two may be compatible, may be a function of irresponsible populist rulers versus better-organized social democratic rulers. Whatever the deeper causes, each of the authors was also asked to address the issues of poverty and inequality and, given the importance of the subject, a separate chapter (chap. 3) is devoted exclusively to it in this volume.

## Globalization

Globalization is a new buzzword in the lexicon of development discussions, which has taken on an ideological quality. Of course, those familiar with dependency theory of the 1950s and the 1960s will experience some sense of *déjà vu*, but with a considerable and ironic twist. Champions of globalization suggest that intensified cross-national economic interactions are pervasive, are inevitable, and – unlike dependency claims – offer benign opportunities for all but those who refuse to accept this forward march of history. When one cuts through the ideological verbiage, however, only some claims are more serious than others: two important themes especially stand out. First, in terms of what has really changed with "globalization," international trade and direct foreign-investment issues faced by most developing countries have not altered all that dramatically in the last couple of decades. Instead, the really significant changes are in the realm of international finance and, related to that, in the area of rapid movement of money in the form of portfolio investments. Second, some regions of the developing world – for example, the more prosperous regions of Asia and Latin America – are more likely to be in a position to take advantage of this form of globalization than are the poorer regions of sub-Saharan Africa or South Asia.

Given globalization, how constrained are developing-country states while choosing their development paths? The answer is again likely to vary from region to region. Regions with well-organized states that preside over sound, growing economies and with a high rate of domestic savings may feel less constrained than regions that are cursed either by poorly functioning states or by low domestic-savings rates, or both. In order to investigate such issues, the opening chapter in this volume provides an overview of globalization trends, and subsequent chapters incorporate such queries in their more specific analyses.

## Democracy

Although democracy is a valued end in the process of development, the contribution of democratic government in facilitating high rates of economic growth with distribution remains unclear. Democracy's value is mainly political: it facilitates freedom of expression and association, minimizes arbitrary and dictatorial rule, and holds the ruling élite accountable for their actions. The "third wave" of democracy has thus been fuelled by the political urge of citizens worldwide to have some say in how they are governed. Nevertheless, some parts of the developing world, such as the Middle East, have not shared in the spread of democracy. Why? Furthermore, newly democratized governments in other parts of the developing world have not always provided good government and in some countries – such as Pakistan – authoritarian rule has returned.

In addition, the capacity of democratic governments in the developing world to reconcile economic growth with distribution is not necessarily superior to that of a variety of non-democratic governments. Best research continues to show that democracy has no statistically discernable impact on economic growth. The impact of democratic governments in moderating inequalities and helping the poor is also far from clear. The underlying reasons are not hard to understand: on the one hand, stable democracy may create secure property rights and a favourable investment climate facilitating higher economic growth; on the other hand, however, new democracies are not always stable and, more important, they also enable numerous interest groups to mould policies that may not be the most desirable from the standpoint of economic growth. As far as economic distribution is concerned, the democratic form of government again provides something of a double-edged sword: although democracy may enable the empowerment of popular groups, property-owning classes are also well organized and powerful in nearly all democracies.

Given the importance of democracy in the pursuit of just growth, one of the following chapters (chap. 2) discusses related issues in detail and all the authors of regional chapters address either the role of democratic governments or the obstacles to (and prospects for) democracy in their respective regions. A theme of special importance here is the possible role of political parties in stabilizing new democratic governments and in facilitating economic development: can well-organized social democratic parties help facilitate just growth?

In sum, this volume investigates roles of state and markets in facilitating just growth in the developing world. How states should intervene in markets to facilitate growth and benign distributional patterns is an old and enduring issue. The fact that democracy, robust economic growth, and modest redistribution have rarely been accomplished simultaneously in the developing world gives such issues renewed vigour. Globalization of the economies and democratization of political power adds new dimensions to old struggles. This volume, then, aims at highlighting the proposition that well-organized states that systematically incorporate popular groups will remain important in the pursuit of just growth in the twenty-first century.

# Globalization, democracy, and just growth: Some emerging general concerns

# 1

# Globalization and liberalization: The impact on developing countries

*Barbara Stallings*

Globalization is one of the most controversial topics of the early twenty-first century.[1] Academic debates currently raging about globalization include whether it even exists (Unger 1997), whether it is more important now than at some earlier date (Bordo, Eichengreen, and Irwin 1999), whether it is displacing the nation-state (Strange 1996; Wade 1996), and whether it is more important than regionalism (Fishlow and Haggard 1992; Oman 1994) or localism (Rosenau 1997a). Also, of course, there are extensive analyses as well as polemics about whether the results are good or bad and for whom (especially Rodrik 1997 and 1999). Recently, such controversies have spilled over from academic journals to street demonstrations in locations as diverse as Seattle, Washington, Montreal, and Genoa.

This chapter takes for granted that globalization exists and that it is a very important phenomenon, without entering into the various comparisons with the past or other parallel processes.[2] The main objective is to analyse the impact of globalization over the past several decades, particularly in terms of its effects on developing countries. To what extent has globalization constrained decision-making in developing countries, and how has it affected the potential for growth and equity – the "just growth" that is the overall topic of the book? Although the focus is on the globalization of finance – arguably the most important aspect of the multifaceted process – we first take a broader look at the globalization phenomenon. This is followed by data on new trends in finance for developing countries, an analysis of the impact of the new pattern of financial flows, and some conclusions with respect to policy recommendations.

Four basic arguments are developed in the chapter with respect to the impact of financial globalization. First, globalization has increased the capital available to developing countries, which potentially increases their ability to grow more rapidly than if they had to rely exclusively on their own resources. Not all capital flows contribute equally to growth, however: short-term flows and the purchase of existing assets are less valuable than investment in new facilities. At the same time, the increasing mobility of capital can also lead to greater volatility, which is very costly for growth. Second, capital flows are unequally distributed by region and country, thus skewing the patterns of growth. There is also an unequal distribution of capital within countries by geographic area, sector, type of firm, and social group, creating a division between winners and losers. Third, government attempts to extract the benefits from the globalization of capital, while limiting the costs, are more possible than usually thought. The source of many problems is local rather than global, and the experience of several countries indicates that "heterodox" policies can be followed. Finally, policy changes at the global, regional, and national levels could improve the picture outlined above.

## Components and mechanisms of globalization

There is no generally accepted definition of globalization: most attempts concentrate on the economic components. An exception is that of James Rosenau, who says: "Globalization [is] a label that is presently in vogue to account for peoples, activities, norms, ideas, goods, services, and currencies that are decreasingly confined to a particular geographic space and its local and established practices" (Rosenau 1997b: 360). From this vast array, four separable (but interrelated) sets of issues are especially relevant for the topic of this book: (a) macroeconomics (trade and finance); (b) microeconomics (the technological revolution and the production process); (c) culture and the media; and (d) pressures for democracy and human rights. We briefly comment on the most important aspects of each, always with a focus on their implications for developing countries.

The macroeconomic components of globalization are perhaps the best known. Thus, the dramatic increase in the value of international trade (and the fact that trade has grown much faster than production in the post-war period) is frequently cited as evidence of globalization. The World Trade Organization (WTO) reports that world merchandise exports in 1948 totalled $58 billion, whereas in 1997 the figure had bal-

Table 1.1  Developing-country share of world trade and capital flows, 1980–1998

|                          | 1980–1982 | 1987–1990 | 1996–1998 |
|--------------------------|-----------|-----------|-----------|
| Exports (%)              | 34.3      | 28.5      | 33.0      |
| Imports (%)              | 31.9      | 27.3      | 34.0      |
| Total[a] (billions of $) | 1,890     | 2,905     | 5,415     |
| Direct investment (%)    | 32.7      | 14.3      | 43.5      |
| Portfolio investment (%) | 7.7       | 3.1       | 12.5      |
| Total[a] (billions of $) | 107       | 355       | 1,300     |

Source: Calculated from IMF, *Direction of Trade Statistics Yearbook* and *Balance of Payments Statistics Yearbook*, various issues.
a. Total for developing and industrial countries.

looned to $5,300 billion. In 1990 dollars, the figures were $304 billion and $5,223 billion, respectively. Trade in services was growing at an even faster rate, such that the combined exports of goods and services rose from 8 per cent of world gross domestic product (GDP) in 1950 to 26 per cent in 1997 (WTO 1998: 120). Data on capital flows do not go back as far, but the growth rates in the past two decades have outstripped those of trade. Private capital flows rose from an average of $107 billion in the period 1980–1982 to $1,319 billion in 1996–1997 [International Monetary Fund (IMF) *Balance of Payments Statistics Yearbook*, various issues].

Developing countries as a group, including the former communist countries of Central and Eastern Europe, have become more integrated into these economic flows in the past twenty years. Table 1.1 provides a rough idea of the changes. In terms of world imports, developing countries' share fell during the 1980s (from 30 to 25 per cent) and then jumped to 34 per cent by the late 1990s. A similar situation was found with exports from developing countries to the world, although the trend was more muted. In both cases, however, the changing importance of trade in oil masks the degree of increasing integration.[3] Another way of thinking about the rising importance of trade is to look at the change in export and import coefficients (i.e. trade as a share of countries' own output). By this measure, too, international integration has increased as coefficients for developing countries followed a pattern similar to that just seen: a decline from 24 per cent in 1980 to 22 per cent in 1990, then an increase to 28 per cent in 1997 (calculated from World Bank 1999).

Financial trends were more dramatic than those for trade, declining more abruptly in the 1980s and rising faster in the 1990s. For example, the developing-country share of foreign direct investment (FDI) plummeted from 33 per cent in 1980–1982, before the debt crisis hit, to only

14 per cent by the end of the decade. It then more than recovered to 44 per cent by 1996–1998. Portfolio trends were similar but the numbers were much smaller: 8, 3, and 13 per cent, respectively. While the private flows shown in table 1.1 increasingly dominate total flows, official loans (both bilateral and multilateral) remain important in two ways: they are the main type of international financing available to poor countries, and the conditionality that accompanies them is an important channel for promoting particular types of economic policies.

The microeconomics of globalization has to do with the technological revolution, which is reflected in the increasing dominance of transnational corporations (TNCs) with their privileged access to the latest advances in new technologies. Whether these be in transportation, communications, electronics, robotization of production lines, or "soft" areas such as "just in time" management techniques, the developments of the past few decades have enabled TNCs to increase their share of global output and trade. Despite the difficulties in measuring such trends, the United Nations Conference on Trade and Development (UNCTAD) estimates that the sales of foreign affiliates of TNCs increased from around 10–15 per cent of world GDP in the early 1970s to around 25 per cent in the late 1990s. Likewise, World Bank data suggest that overseas affiliates' output as a share of world private GDP rose from 8 per cent in 1982 to 11 per cent in 1995 (Held et. al. 1999: 246).

The increased role of TNCs is significant but not overwhelming in quantitative terms; to appreciate the phenomenon fully it is necessary to take account of qualitative shifts as well. In particular, the globalization of production has resulted in new ways in which TNCs can expand their networks to take advantage of the lowest costs and greatest flexibility. Indeed, many of the new forms of "value chains" do not involve overseas investment at all but, rather, buying agreements with foreign producers whereby the TNCs specify the characteristics of goods and the time schedule for subcontractors in many parts of the developing world. Services, ranging from billing to accounting to online support, are also increasingly outsourced to developing countries. If they are to participate in these new types of investment, as well as in the more traditional types, developing countries must be ready and able to meet the requirements of investors (Gereffi 1995).

The globalization of culture and the media has been strongly stimulated by the expansion of TNCs in general and the communications revolution in particular [Herman and McChesney 1997; Organization for Economic Co-operation and Development (OECD) 1997]. The same products have become available throughout the world, whether they be food, clothing, music, or television programmes. In the cultural realm, these trends have fostered the identification of the middle classes – and, increasingly, the lower classes – in developing countries with their counterparts in the United States, Europe, and Japan. Policies that might limit access to desired goods and services, including travel, have thus become increasingly difficult to carry out. On a more directly political level, the growing presence of Western-educated leaders (both politicians and technocrats) who espouse economic policies in vogue in the industrial countries limits the range of policy options that are considered legitimate in developing countries. This trend is complemented by global sources of news, first through the cable channels and more recently through the Internet (Held et al. 1999: chap. 7).

Finally, and closely related to the cultural channels above, it is not only economic policies that have spread throughout the globe but also political values and institutions. Under certain conditions, the multilateral institutions have begun to include political as well as economic conditions as the counterpart to their loans; these typically involve a minimal recognition of human rights and democratic forms of governance (Gwin and Nelson 1997; Nelson and Eglinton 1993). More direct have been bilateral and regional demands for democracy and human rights, both as a condition for loans and also for membership in regional organizations. Thus, the democratic clause in the European Union charter is an important influence on potential members, while in the Western Hemisphere the Organization of American States and Mercosur (Southern Common Market) have similar requirements. Even Japan, initially reluctant to intervene in the internal affairs of its neighbours, has begun to include political criteria in its large-scale economic aid packages (Fawcett and Hurrell 1995; Stallings and Sakurai 1993).

How have these various types of globalization been propagated? The most important way is by spontaneous, market-based mechanisms whereby corporations and other economic actors engage in their own preferred activities and, in the process, create links between groups, nations, and regions. The microeconomic and cultural elements of globalization are clear examples of this type of process, as are the financial aspects of the macroeconomic link. The globalization of trade, by contrast, is an example of a second kind of mechanism, which is based on planning and negotiation. It has thus been closely related to the activities of the WTO [formerly the General Agreement on Tariffs and Trade (GATT)], which is one of the main institutions that promotes globalization. The move toward greater support for democracy and human rights has also been negotiated, in this case through the Development Assistance Committee of the OECD and the regional integration institutions. Finally, there have been attempts, not very successful hitherto, to negotiate rules for capital flows through the IMF and World Bank. It is important to note that, although these organizations have a strong impact on the behaviour and performance of the developing countries, the latter are generally not well represented in the decision-making bodies of the organizations; thus, the legitimacy of their decisions can be called into question.

A final distinction needs to be drawn between globalization and liberalization. Developing countries themselves had to take some important steps before the full impact of globalization could be felt. Specifically, they had to open their economies, to lower the barriers to trade and capital flows that had been an essential component of the import-substitution industrialization model that almost all had followed for some period. Without these policy shifts, globalization would be much less relevant than it is today, especially in the developing world. Liberalization, then, is the other side of globalization.

At the same time, liberalization is also a creature of globalization. Looking back to the four aspects of globalization discussed above, several linkages stand out as helping to promote liberalization in developing countries. One was the need to open economies as a prerequisite of membership in the GATT/WTO or as part of the conditionality accompanying loans from the IMF or World Bank. Also important was the increased cultural homogeneity of the world that stimulated demands for imports and travel on the part of local populations in developing countries. Finally, a key mechanism was the fact that many political leaders in developing countries came to agree with the types of policies that were advocated by the international financial institutions and private-sector investors. As the cold war ended, the influence of alternative ideologies waned and democratic elections frequently returned leaders who favoured such policies.

## Developing countries in a world of globalized finance

Of all of the economic trends involved in globalization, the globalization of finance has been the most dynamic; it has also had the strongest impact on the behaviour and performance of developing countries. Thus, we concentrate on this topic in the rest of this chapter and look in more detail at the changes that have come about in the post-war period, especially in the last decade, and at their impact.

The total volume of capital flows increased substantially during the period. According to the World Bank, total net long-term resource flows to all developing countries (including Eastern Europe and Central Asia) rose from $11 billion in 1970 to $75 billion in 1980. The flows stagnated or declined for many (but not all) developing regions in the 1980s, then surged again during the 1990s. They increased from $99 billion in 1990 to

Table 1.2 Net long-term resource flows and net transfers to developing countries, 1970–2000 (billions of dollars)[a]

| Type of flow | 1970 | 1980 | 1990 | 1997 | 1999 | 2000 |
|---|---|---|---|---|---|---|
| Net resource flows | 11 | 75 | 99 | 340 | 265 | 295 |
| Long-term debt flows[b] | 7 | 57 | 43 | 110 | 16 | 39 |
| Foreign direct investment | 2 | 4 | 24 | 173 | 185 | 178 |
| Portfolio equity flows | 0 | 0 | 4 | 30 | 34 | 48 |
| Grants | 2 | 13 | 28 | 26 | 29 | 30 |
| Net transfers | 3 | 20 | 27 | 221 | 125 | 136 |
| Interest on long-term debt | 2 | 32 | 55 | 87 | 100 | 108 |
| Profit remittance on FDI | 5 | 23 | 18 | 32 | 40 | 50 |

Source: Calculated from World Bank, *Global Development Finance 2001*, CD Rom version.
*a.* Values do not always add up to totals, owing to rounding errors.
*b.* Excludes IMF loans.

$340 billion in 1997, before falling off as a result of the Asian crisis. Trends in net transfers (which subtract interest payments and profit re-mittances from net flows) were even more dramatic (see table 1.2).

Short-term flows, frequently referred to as "hot money," are not in-cluded in table 1.2. As these flows have become the most controversial type of foreign capital in the 1990s, it is important to try to get some idea of their magnitude and their volatility. One of the controversies includes the very definition of short-term flows. The World Bank limits its defini-tion to short-term bank credits (less than one year). The Bank for Inter-national Settlements (BIS) also focuses on bank credit, but it includes all loans with less than a year to maturity, whereas the World Bank includes only loans with an original maturity of less than a year. UNCTAD adds another variant since it defines short-term flows to include much of the portfolio investment category. Despite these differences, there is general agreement that short-term capital has become more prevalent and that it is highly volatile (BIS 1999: 146–150; UNCTAD 1999a: 112–115; World Bank 2000: chap. 4).

Drawing on the minimalist definition of the World Bank, table 1.3 shows the trends in short- versus long-term finance during the 1990s. Short-term flows built up through 1996, fell sharply in 1997, and then became negative in 1998–1999. Long-term flows showed a similar pattern but the year-on-year changes were more gradual and the net flows re-mained positive. The broader UNCTAD data, which go only through 1997, show a negative net short-term flow for 1997 and, presumably, a larger negative flow in 1998–1999. The BIS shows a positive figure for 1997 ($43.5 billion) and a negative one ($85.0 billion) for 1998.

Table 1.3 Short-term versus long-term finance to developing countries, 1991–2000 (billions of dollars)

| Type of flow | 1991 | 1992 | 1996 | 1997 | 1998 | 1999 | 2000 |
|---|---|---|---|---|---|---|---|
| Net long-term flows | 123 | 156 | 311 | 343 | 335 | 265 | 296 |
| Net short-term flows | 20 | 38 | 43 | 16 | −51 | −18 | 4 |
| Total net flows | 143 | 194 | 354 | 359 | 284 | 246 | 299 |
| Capital outflows plus errors and omissions | −17 | −93 | −150 | −228 | −189 | −247 | −307 |
| Net external finance | 126 | 101 | 204 | 130 | 95 | −1 | −7 |

Source: World Bank, 2001: 34.

Together with changes in the volume of external finance, the composition also shifted in important ways over the last two decades. The most important change was the increased role of private finance in comparison to that of public funds. Overall, the former rose much more than the latter, although there were some indications of a trade-off as public funds came in when private finance fell off. Among sources of private finance, the commercial bank creditors (which, in 1980, had been responsible for nearly 90 per cent of all private finance and over one-half of total long-term debt flows) had almost disappeared from the scene by the early 1990s. Moreover, debt flows themselves had become less significant, as FDI had come to represent about one-quarter of net resource flows, and official flows (including grants) had again risen as a share of the total.

During the course of the 1990s the composition shift continued. The most dramatic element was FDI, which represented 48 per cent of total private flows in 1997 and 80 per cent in 1999. FDI had been considered the least desirable kind of foreign capital in the 1970s because of its negative impact on the balance of payments and the restrictions it placed on internal decision-making in developing countries; this was one reason for the shift toward bank loans. Now, as a reflection of the change in economic model, FDI is considered the most valuable kind of foreign capital, because it not only is more stable than other flows but also brings access to markets and technology. Much more unstable are portfolio equity investment, bonds, and bank loans, together with short-term flows as discussed above.[4] Table 1.4 shows these changes in the context of the earlier post-war period.

Closely related to the shift in composition of capital flows was the change in borrowers within the developing countries. In the 1970s and the 1980s, borrowers had mainly been central governments and state-owned enterprises; in the 1990s, by contrast, borrowers were increasingly large private-sector firms. FDI was, (almost) by definition, an element of

Table 1.4 Composition of net long-term finance to developing countries, 1970–2000 (billions of dollars)

| Type of flow | 1970 | 1980 | 1990 | 1997 | 1999 | 2000 |
|---|---|---|---|---|---|---|
| Official flows | 5.4 | 33.9 | 55.7 | 40.5 | 45.7 | 37.6 |
| Multilateral loans[a] | 0.8 | 7.7 | 15.0 | 21.2 | 18.9 | 10.4 |
| Bilateral loans | 2.6 | 13.1 | 12.4 | −6.8 | −2.0 | −2.4 |
| Grants | 2.0 | 13.1 | 28.2 | 26.1 | 28.8 | 29.6 |
| Private flows | 5.5 | 40.7 | 43.6 | 299.8 | 219.2 | 257.2 |
| International capital markets | 3.6 | 36.3 | 19.4 | 127.2 | 33.7 | 79.2 |
| Debt flows | 3.6 | 36.3 | 15.6 | 97.0 | −0.7 | 31.3 |
| Bank loans | 2.4 | 28.9 | 3.2 | 45.2 | −24.6 | 0.7 |
| Bonds | 0.0 | 1.1 | 1.2 | 49.0 | 25.4 | 30.3 |
| Other | 1.2 | 6.3 | 11.3 | 2.7 | −1.6 | 0.3 |
| Equity purchases | 0.0 | 0.0 | 3.7 | 30.2 | 34.5 | 47.9 |
| Foreign direct investment | 1.9 | 4.4 | 24.3 | 172.6 | 185.4 | 178.0 |
| Total | 10.8 | 74.5 | 99.3 | 340.3 | 264.9 | 294.8 |

Source: Calculated from World Bank, *Global Development Finance 2001*, CD Rom version.
a. Excludes IMF loans.

the private sector.[5] In addition, private non-guaranteed debt flows as a share of total debt flows increased from 15 per cent in 1980 to 22 per cent in 1990 to 60 per cent in 1997 before falling to 40 per cent in 1998 and 18 per cent in 2000. (Part of the sharp decline appears to have had as a counterpart the expansion of private debt with government guarantees.)

Finally, there were important changes in the allocation of capital flows among developing-country regions. During the 1980s, Latin America in particular had been starved for funds from the private sector, leading to an increased role for the multilateral agencies; East and South-East Asia, by contrast, continued to have access to private funds. In the 1990s, Latin America regained access to private finance and Eastern Europe also became an active borrower, sharing the expanding pie with East/South-East Asia; sub-Saharan Africa continued to draw primarily on official sources, while South Asia and the Middle East had limited access to external finance of any type (table 1.5).

After the international financial crisis that began in Asia in 1997, some changes occurred in the pattern just described. The most important was the decline in capital flows to Asia in 1998–1999, which was both the cause and the effect of the crisis. Latin America and Eastern Europe held their own, or increased their access to funds in 1998, but saw these flows drop off somewhat at the end of the decade. The other three regions,

Table 1.5 Regional patterns of net long-term capital flows to developing countries, 1970–2000 (billions of dollars)

| | 1970 | 1980 | 1990 | 1997 | 1999 | 2000 |
|---|---|---|---|---|---|---|
| **East Asia Pacific** | | | | | | |
| Grants | 0.7 | 1.2 | 2.1 | 2.3 | 2.7 | 2.8 |
| Official loans[a] | 0.6 | 2.8 | 6.2 | 16.0 | 11.6 | 8.5 |
| Private flows | 0.8 | 7.2 | 19.4 | 110.9 | 51.1 | 81.6 |
| International capital markets[b] | 0.5 | 5.9 | 8.3 | 45.3 | −5.0 | 23.6 |
| FDI | 0.3 | 1.3 | 11.1 | 65.6 | 56.0 | 58.0 |
| Total | 2.1 | 11.2 | 27.7 | 129.2 | 65.4 | 92.9 |
| **Europe and Central Asia** | | | | | | |
| Grants | 0.1 | 0.3 | 1.0 | 5.1 | 7.5 | 7.6 |
| Official loans | 0.2 | 2.4 | 3.8 | 4.1 | 1.8 | 2.1 |
| Private flows | 0.3 | 4.5 | 7.7 | 45.6 | 43.2 | 45.2 |
| International capital markets | 0.2 | 4.5 | 6.6 | 22.1 | 16.6 | 16.4 |
| FDI | 0.1 | 0.0 | 1.1 | 23.5 | 26.5 | 28.8 |
| Total | 0.6 | 7.2 | 12.5 | 54.8 | 52.5 | 54.9 |
| **Latin America and Caribbean** | | | | | | |
| Grants | 0.2 | 0.6 | 2.3 | 2.7 | 2.9 | 3.1 |
| Official loans | 0.8 | 4.7 | 6.8 | −4.4 | 2.3 | −2.7 |
| Private flows | 3.3 | 24.6 | 12.6 | 115.4 | 111.4 | 102.0 |
| International capital markets | 2.2 | 18.5 | 4.4 | 50.3 | 21.0 | 25.8 |
| FDI | 1.1 | 6.1 | 8.2 | 65.1 | 90.4 | 76.2 |
| Total | 4.3 | 29.9 | 21.7 | 113.7 | 116.6 | 102.4 |
| **Middle East and North Africa** | | | | | | |
| Grants | 0.4 | 4.7 | 8.3 | 4.0 | 3.3 | 3.4 |
| Official loans | 0.2 | 4.9 | 1.4 | −4.3 | −1.9 | −1.9 |
| Private flows | 0.6 | −1.0 | 0.4 | 8.1 | 1.1 | 7.8 |
| International capital markets | 0.3 | 2.3 | −2.1 | 3.0 | −0.4 | 3.3 |
| FDI | 0.3 | −3.3 | 2.5 | 5.1 | 1.5 | 4.5 |
| Total | 1.2 | 8.6 | 10.1 | 7.8 | 2.5 | 9.3 |
| **South Asia** | | | | | | |
| Grants | 0.3 | 2.8 | 2.4 | 2.4 | 2.4 | 2.5 |
| Official loans | 1.0 | 2.4 | 4.6 | 1.1 | 2.6 | 1.5 |
| Private flows | 0.1 | 1.3 | 2.2 | 9.7 | 2.2 | 12.2 |
| International capital markets | 0.0 | 1.1 | 1.7 | 4.8 | −0.9 | 9.0 |
| FDI | 0.1 | 0.2 | 0.5 | 4.9 | 3.1 | 3.2 |
| Total | 1.3 | 6.5 | 9.2 | 13.2 | 7.2 | 16.2 |
| **Sub-Saharan Africa** | | | | | | |
| Grants | 0.4 | 3.6 | 12.2 | 9.6 | 10.0 | 10.2 |
| Official loans | 0.5 | 3.6 | 4.6 | 2.0 | 0.5 | 0.5 |
| Private flows | 0.5 | 4.3 | 1.4 | 10.0 | 10.4 | 8.4 |
| International capital markets | 0.4 | 4.2 | 0.5 | 1.6 | 2.5 | 1.0 |
| FDI | 0.1 | 0.1 | 0.9 | 8.3 | 7.9 | 7.3 |
| Total | 1.4 | 11.5 | 18.2 | 21.6 | 20.9 | 19.1 |

Table 1.5 (cont.)

| | 1970 | 1980 | 1990 | 1997 | 1999 | 2000 |
|---|---|---|---|---|---|---|
| Developing countries | | | | | | |
| Grants | 2.0 | 13.1 | 28.2 | 26.1 | 28.8 | 29.6 |
| Official loans | 3.4 | 20.7 | 27.5 | 14.4 | 16.8 | 8.0 |
| Private flows | 5.5 | 40.7 | 43.7 | 299.8 | 219.2 | 257.2 |
| International capital markets | 3.6 | 36.3 | 19.4 | 127.2 | 33.8 | 79.2 |
| FDI | 1.9 | 4.4 | 24.3 | 172.6 | 185.4 | 178.0 |
| Total | 10.9 | 74.5 | 99.4 | 340.3 | 264.8 | 294.8 |

Source: Calculated from World Bank, *Global Development Finance 2001*, CD Rom version.
a. Excludes IMF loans.
b. Portfolio investment, bonds, bank loans, and "other" flows.

which had been less privileged by foreign capital in the past, were correspondingly less affected by the crisis.

Other insights about the nature of globalization can be obtained by noting with whom developing countries trade and from where investment comes. On the basis of data for the first half of the 1990s, a clear distinction can be made (Stallings and Streeck 1995). Asian developing countries mainly traded among themselves and with Japan, and a growing share of their investment also came from within the region. In Latin America, in contrast, trade and investment were heavily weighted toward the United States, especially in the northern tier of countries. In Africa and Eastern Europe, economic transactions focused on Western Europe.

What was then referred to as the "tetrahedron" meant that different developing regions were tied into the global economy in different ways through their main trading and investment partners. Since the respective industrial countries featured different "models" of capitalism, this led to somewhat different policies in the developing countries themselves. Growth rates of the industrial countries also differed. In the 1980s and early 1990s, these differences contributed to the great economic dynamism in the Asian region, but the decline of the Japanese economy exacerbated the later problems of its Asian neighbours, and the high level of interaction within the region propelled the contagion effect once the crisis there began in 1997. The lagging US economy, which had appeared to be a drag on Latin America in the 1980s and early 1990s, proved a boon to its neighbours – particularly Mexico and Central America – later in the decade. In the early years of the new century, however, the simultaneous downturn in the United States, Europe, and Japan has had a negative impact throughout the developing world.

## The impact of the new pattern of financial flows

Given the overall focus of this book on "just growth," the main thrust of this section is on how the globalization of capital has affected growth rates and equity. In addition, we want to ask whether (and, if so, how) global finance has limited the autonomy of governmental decision-making with respect to these two topics. It should be emphasized that these questions are extremely difficult to answer. Many other events and processes were occurring simultaneously, including other aspects of globalization, and it is impossible to separate the individual contribution of each. None the less, we can draw some tentative conclusions with the help of comparative regional experiences and secondary analysis by other authors.

### Capital flows and growth

At the aggregate level, growth is related to capital flows in two main ways. One involves the impact on investment, the crucial determinant of growth in the medium and long run. In the short run, of course, higher growth can result from fuller use of existing capacity. The other main link between growth and capital flows centres on cycles and sustainability. If capital flows are extremely volatile they can stimulate growth in the short run; however, such growth will be offset by recessions due in part to capital flight. Capital flows also make it more difficult for governments to carry out stable macroeconomic policies, which in turn contributes to the volatility of growth.

The foreign capital-investment relation has two components, as reflected in the classic "two-gap" model. The first gap has to do with the lack of adequate savings in developing countries to finance the investment required to attain a desired growth rate. This situation can arise through either large fiscal deficits (which absorb available credit and thus "crowd out" the private sector), or insufficient savings by households and businesses, or both. Under these circumstances, foreign savings (capital) can help to fill the gap, although evidence suggests that foreign savings comprise partially a substitute for domestic savings rather than being totally complementary. The parameters may vary between countries and regions: in Latin America in recent years, approximately 50 per cent of foreign savings was offset by lower domestic savings [United Nations Economic Commission for Latin America and the Caribbean (ECLAC) 2000a].

The second gap involves lack of foreign exchange. Even where there are adequate domestic savings, much of the machinery and equipment needed for investment in developing countries comes from abroad and must be paid for in foreign currency (usually dollars). The foreign exchange can come from a trade surplus, but if exports are insufficient then foreign capital is necessary. Foreign capital can also serve to extend the maturity structure of domestic savings, since local capital markets frequently lack a long-term segment.

The sustainability of growth is also related to capital flows. In so far as capital flows are necessary for investment in developing countries, this implies a long-term stable type of flow to enable investment projects to be designed, implemented, and put into production. If the flows come in for only a short period (for example, to take advantage of interest-rate or exchange-rate imbalances), then they are not very useful from the investment perspective. The same is true if they are likely to leave as soon as any negative indicators appear in the domestic or international environments.

One mechanism through which capital inflows and outflows create volatility in the "real"economy (i.e. income and employment) is by shifting the capacity of local firms to import. With more capital inflows they can operate at a higher capacity level, but when capital leaves they have to cut back. Another mechanism involves the impact of capital flows on macroeconomic policies of developing-country governments. One sequence of events, which was more common in the 1970s than the 1990s, is for foreign capital to finance government budget deficits. Thus, if the capital pulls out, the deficits must be rapidly cut, leading to a fall in growth rates. A more recent problem is that capital inflows can lead to the overvaluation of exchange rates and thus to large current-account deficits that require measures to cool down the economy. Large inflows can also expand the money supply unless they are "sterilized," which creates additional problems for central banks.[6]

As it happens, there is a link between the impact of capital flows on investment, on the one hand, and sustainability, on the other. It has to do with the composition of flows, which we began to discuss earlier in the chapter. Although there is some disagreement on this topic, most experts agree that FDI is more stable than other types of capital flow.[7] Moreover, a substantial share goes directly to increase investment in the recipient country. This share refers to FDI that is used to set up new plants or to expand existing facilities ("greenfield" investment). FDI that comes in to acquire existing assets, either through privatization or through mergers and acquisitions, is investment from the point of view of the firm but not the local economy. Of course, there is the possibility that the asset transfer will be followed by greenfield investment, either as part of a privatization agreement or because the new owner wants to modernize or expand a newly acquired firm.

Even in the absence of greenfield investment, however, foreign capital can provide important benefits to developing economies. In the increasingly globalized world, one of the main challenges for all countries is to increase their competitiveness. Often this involves access to state-of-the-art technology, which (as discussed previously) is most characteristic of large transnational corporations. With such technology it is possible to lower unit costs and raise quality at the same time. Thus, it is not surprising that TNCs are major exporters in the world economy, which is one of their attractions to developing countries.

What does the empirical evidence show? At the most general level, there appears to be a positive link between access to foreign capital and higher growth rates. The decline in growth rates in Africa and (especially) Latin America in the 1980s was closely connected to the debt crisis and resulting closure of capital markets to those regions. Likewise, the return of foreign capital in the early 1990s was part of the explanation for renewed growth. In contrast, the Asian countries where capital flows continued during the 1980s saw no such halt to growth. Certainly, foreign capital was not the only variable in play: domestic economic policies were important, as were cultural and other factors that led to higher domestic savings in Asia than in other regions. None the less, the access to foreign capital makes it possible for developing countries to grow faster than if they had to rely totally on their own resources.[8]

In the return of foreign capital in the 1990s, FDI came to represent an ever-larger share of capital inflows that themselves increased in developing countries. In 1970, FDI represented around 20 per cent of all long-term capital inflows, falling to 5 per cent by 1980; by 1990, it was nearly one-quarter of all long-term flows and over 65 per cent by the end of the decade. Although we can assume that virtually all FDI was of the greenfield type in the 1970s and early 1980s, the liberalization policies (privatization and the elimination of restrictions on FDI) in the late 1980s and the 1990s require additional information on the destination of FDI in recent years. For developing countries as a whole, the share of FDI devoted to acquiring existing assets (whether through privatization or mergers and acquisitions in the private sector itself) is quite low, but it has been rising and there are differences across regions. Latin America has the highest ratio, between 20 and 40 per cent in the period 1995–1999; for Asia, the share rose from an average of 5 per cent in 1991–1996 to 12 per cent in 1997 and 16 per cent in 1998 as a consequence of the financial crisis at the end of the decade.[9]

Whereas most governments consider FDI to be an attractive kind of foreign capital that, on balance, provides significant advantages to developing economies, other kinds of foreign capital can be more problematic. In particular, short-term capital flows frequently lead to volatile growth rates and even to crises in extreme cases. Some of the mechanisms through which this can occur were discussed earlier.

Two prominent cases of such problems occurred during the 1990s. The first was a fairly contained situation that centred on two Latin American countries. In 1992–1994, Mexico had been running a very large current-account deficit, partly caused by a pegged exchange rate as an instrument to lower inflation. The government did not expect serious problems, as much of the deficit was caused by the import of capital goods, which would eventually result in higher growth and more exports. None the less, a series of political shocks during the election year of 1994 undermined investor confidence. When the incoming government tried to bring about a controlled devaluation of the peso, investors (both domestic and foreign) began to withdraw their capital. A full-blown crisis was averted only by a large rescue package led by the IMF and the US Treasury.

For Mexico, the result was a sharp contraction of GDP in 1995 and a fall in real wages that have yet to recover their pre-crisis level. In addition, the banking sector was left in a very weak state that further compounded problems of recovery. Argentina was also affected by the Mexican crisis, because the financial markets came to believe that it, too, might have to devalue its fixed exchange rate; although Argentina suffered less than Mexico, it also required an international rescue package. For the rest of the emerging markets there was a brief increase in interest rates but little lasting impact. (On the Mexican crisis, see Calvo and Mendoza 1996 and Sachs, Tornell, and Velasco 1996.)

The other case, much more widespread and long lived, began in Thailand in mid-1997. Sharing some characteristics with Mexico in 1994, Thailand was also forced to devalue its currency and, again, the decline in value went well beyond government expectations and was accompanied by extensive capital flight. In this instance, however, the crisis quickly spread to other countries in the region, especially Indonesia, the Philippines, and Korea. IMF-led rescue packages were again put together. The accompanying conditionality centred on cutting government expenditure and closing troubled financial institutions, which led to severe economic contractions. These policies led to an ongoing debate about their appropriateness, with many experts arguing that the "remedy" only made the problem worse.

After a brief recovery in the first half of 1998, the crisis spread to Russia. At this point it severely disrupted international capital markets, even in the industrial countries. It also reached Latin American shores, initially through a speculative attack on the Brazilian currency. Since the still-suffering Asia was an important market for commodities exported by Latin America and other developing countries, trade shocks compounded the financial shocks that virtually shut developing countries out of access to external finance. (On the "Asian" financial crisis and the impact in various regions, see Herman 1999.)

Table 1.6 Net short-term capital flows during recent financial crises (billions of dollars)

| Type of flow | Latin America[a] | | East Asia[b] | |
|---|---|---|---|---|
| | 1993–1994 | 1995–1996 | 1995–1996 | 1997–1998 |
| Liabilities to banks | 14.9 | −0.1 | 51.3 | −60.4 |
| Debt securities issued abroad | 5.6 | 1.3 | 5.2 | 4.3 |
| Total | 20.5 | 1.4 | 56.4 | −56.2 |

Source: BIS-IMF-OECD-World Bank, Joint Statistics on External Debt, online database.
a. Argentina and Mexico.
b. Malaysia, Philippines, Republic of Korea, and Thailand.

Despite the differences between the two cases, short-term capital flows were generally seen to be an important causal factor in both. Data jointly produced by the BIS, IMF, OECD, and the World Bank give an idea of the behaviour of short-term capital flows during the two experiences (table 1.6). In both, net short-term external flows fell dramatically after significant positive flows preceding the crises, with almost all of the drop due to bank credits. In the Latin American case, net flows to the two countries most affected fell by nearly $20 billion when comparing pre- and post-crisis years, but still remained slightly positive. In Asia, the drop in the four crisis countries was over $100 billion, and flows became strongly negative.

These similar trends mask the different mechanisms at work in the two cases. In Mexico, the large short-term debt consisted mainly of government obligations that had been converted from local-currency debt when investors became nervous following the assassination of the main presidential candidate and an increase in interest rates in the United States. In Asia, much of the short-term debt was held by the private non-financial sector that took advantage of liberalized regulations to borrow abroad.

The similarity was that investors were unwilling to roll over the short-term debt when it fell due, thus requiring either a moratorium or a rescue package. Since moratoria were not considered legitimate, even by the affected governments, rescue packages with the attached conditionality were the answer.[10] Another similarity that has been noted by some observers is that most of the countries involved in these crises had previously been considered outstanding examples of successful development models. This held for Mexico in Latin America as well as Korea and the second-tier newly industrialized economies (NIEs) in Asia. The argument is that foreign investors want to participate in these successful markets

Table 1.7 Percentage share of net long-term capital flows to developing countries by region, 1970–2000[a]

| Region | 1970 | 1980 | 1990 | 1997 | 1999 | 2000 |
|---|---|---|---|---|---|---|
| Total flows | | | | | | |
| East Asia Pacific[b] | 19.9 | 15.0 | 27.9 | 38.0 | 24.7 | 31.5 |
| Europe and Central Asia | 5.4 | 9.5 | 12.6 | 16.1 | 19.8 | 18.6 |
| Latin America/Caribbean | 39.1 | 40.1 | 21.9 | 33.4 | 44.0 | 34.7 |
| Middle East/North Africa | 10.6 | 11.5 | 10.2 | 2.3 | 0.9 | 3.2 |
| South Asia | 12.6 | 8.7 | 9.2 | 3.9 | 2.7 | 5.5 |
| Sub-Saharan Africa | 12.3 | 15.3 | 18.1 | 6.3 | 7.9 | 6.5 |
| Total | 100.0 | 100.0 | 100.0 | 100.0 | 100.0 | 100.0 |
| Foreign direct investment | | | | | | |
| East Asia Pacific[b] | 14.4 | 29.9 | 45.9 | 38.0 | 30.2 | 32.6 |
| Europe and Central Asia | 3.1 | 0.4 | 4.3 | 13.6 | 14.3 | 16.2 |
| Latin America/Caribbean | 58.8 | 138.9 | 33.7 | 37.7 | 48.7 | 42.8 |
| Middle East/North Africa | 15.0 | −74.6 | 10.3 | 3.0 | 0.8 | 2.5 |
| South Asia | 3.7 | 4.2 | 1.9 | 2.8 | 1.7 | 1.8 |
| Sub-Saharan Africa | 5.0 | 1.2 | 3.8 | 4.8 | 4.3 | 4.1 |
| Total | 100.0 | 100.0 | 100.0 | 100.0 | 100.0 | 100.0 |

Source: Calculated from table 1.5.
a. Percentage shares do not always total 100, because of rounding errors.
b. Developing countries only.

and thus capital surges appear, fostered by the so-called herd behaviour of investors. The sudden access to large amounts of capital leads to overheating and eventually worrisome signs that cause the "herd" to leave and crises to result (see Ffrench-Davis 2001).

## Capital flows and equity

Although the globalization of finance can stimulate growth under some conditions, it also has a profound impact on the distribution of the fruits of that growth. In some cases the link between growth and indicators of equity is positive; in others the relation is more ambiguous. Overall, the picture that emerges is one of great and perhaps increasing heterogeneity, with some regions, countries, sectors, and social groups taking advantage of the opportunities provided by globalization, while others fall ever further behind.

As we have already seen, there was great diversity in the distribution of capital flows across regions over the last two decades. Table 1.7 summarizes the pattern, showing clear winners and losers in the period 1970–2000. East Asia and the Pacific were the main winners up to and including 1997, more than doubling their share of total capital flows to developing countries; the Middle East, South Asia, and sub-Saharan Africa were equally clear losers, especially in the 1990s. Latin America and Europe and Central Asia saw their share decline between 1980 and 1990, but they more or less regained it by 1997. During the crisis years of 1998–1999, the main change was the presumably temporary decline in capital flows to Asia.[11]

Within the category of FDI, capital was even more concentrated than for total flows, especially in the 1990s. Thus, while East Asia and Latin America together accounted for 50–70 per cent of total flows, their share of FDI was nearly 80 per cent. Conversely, South Asia and sub-Saharan Africa together received only about 5 per cent of FDI flows compared with 10–20 per cent of the total. In so far as we have argued that FDI is the most important type of capital for investment (and, therefore, growth), these differences have a significant impact. Beyond the regional differences, there is additional evidence of concentration at the country level. According to UNCTAD (1999a: 115–120), in the period 1990–1997 the top ten emerging market economies accounted for over three-quarters of all FDI to developing countries; China, Brazil, and Mexico alone received almost one-half of such investment. Calculating FDI in per capita terms also shows great inequality: sub-Saharan Africa received less than $5 a year, the Association of South-East Asian Nations (ASEAN) $31, and Latin America $62. Among the highest individual recipients on this measure were Malaysia ($223 per capita), Chile ($170), Mexico ($79), Brazil ($35), and China ($21). The two sub-Saharan African countries with the largest amount of FDI were Ghana ($6 per capita) and Uganda ($3).

The private capital markets (banks and institutional investors such as insurance companies, pension funds, and mutual funds) have an even stronger preference than direct investors for the most advanced developing countries, commonly referred to as "emerging markets." This is because much of their investment is channelled to the private sector through the local or international stock markets, and these are present in only a limited number of countries. Another instrument is bonds, issued by both private and public borrowers; however, again, only a limited number of countries can meet the requirements for access to the major bond markets. It should be noted that, although these preferences limit poorer countries' access to foreign capital, the result is that they have also been less afflicted by the international financial crises of the 1990s, because stock and bonds markets were a major channel of contagion.

Poorer countries, then, must rely mainly on official flows – both loans and grants. Although these sources of finance have the advantage of low interest rates and long maturities (or no repayment at all in the case of grants), the volume of official development assistance (ODA) has lagged

Table 1.8 Net concessional flows to developing countries, 1990–2000

|  | 1990 | 1997 | 1998 | 1999 | 2000 |
|---|---|---|---|---|---|
| **Type of flow (billions of dollars)** | | | | | |
| Concessional finance | 43.7 | 33.5 | 37.3 | 40.7 | 40.6 |
| Grants (excl. technical cooperation) | 28.2 | 26.1 | 27.3 | 28.8 | 29.6 |
| Loans | 15.5 | 7.3 | 10.3 | 11.9 | 11.0 |
| Bilateral concessional | 9.5 | −0.1 | 3.4 | 5.2 | 4.9 |
| Multilateral concessional | 5.9 | 7.4 | 6.9 | 6.7 | 6.1 |
| **Memo item** | | | | | |
| Technical cooperation grants | 14.1 | 15.7 | 16.2 | 16.6 | 17.1 |
| **Regional allocation (per cent)** | | | | | |
| East Asia Pacific | 17.0 | 14.2 | 18.2 | 23.4 | 21.2 |
| Europe and Central Asia | 3.5 | 17.3 | 16.1 | 20.4 | 20.7 |
| Latin America/Caribbean | 10.2 | 9.2 | 9.5 | 8.2 | 8.0 |
| Middle East/North Africa | 19.9 | 13.5 | 11.3 | 8.4 | 9.2 |
| South Asia | 12.1 | 8.2 | 12.1 | 10.5 | 11.3 |
| Sub-Saharan Africa | 37.3 | 37.5 | 32.8 | 29.1 | 29.6 |
| All developing countries | 100.0 | 100.0 | 100.0 | 100.0 | 100.0 |
| **Percentage of regional GNP** | | | | | |
| East Asia Pacific | 0.8 | 0.2 | 0.4 | 0.5 | 0.4 |
| Europe and Central Asia | 0.1 | 0.5 | 0.6 | 0.8 | 0.8 |
| Latin America/Caribbean | 0.4 | 0.2 | 0.2 | 0.2 | 0.2 |
| Middle East/North Africa | 2.2 | 0.8 | 0.7 | 0.6 | 0.6 |
| South Asia | 1.3 | 0.5 | 0.8 | 0.7 | 0.7 |
| Sub-Saharan Africa | 5.8 | 3.8 | 4.0 | 3.9 | 3.9 |
| All developing countries | 0.9 | 0.5 | 0.6 | 0.6 | 0.6 |

Source: Calculated from World Bank, *Global Development Finance 2001*, CD Rom version.

behind that of private flows. Bilateral aid, in particular, fell during the 1990s, from 0.33 per cent of the GDP of industrial countries in 1990 to 0.22 per cent in 1998, before rising slightly to 0.24 per cent in 1999 (OECD, *Development Co-operation*, various issues). Although multilateral funds increased somewhat in nominal terms during the decade, a significant share of these funds was concentrated in a few large countries that were hit by financial crises.[12]

Table 1.8 shows the volume of total concessional flows and their allocation during the 1990s. Total funds dropped from $44 billion in 1990 to only $34 billion in 1997, rising to $40 billion in 1999 and 2000 as a consequence of the crisis. The main decline was in bilateral loans, but multilateral loans and grants were also stagnant or falling. In the regional allocation of these funds, the share going to East Asia rose, especially between 1997 and 1999, while South Asia and Latin America more or less maintained their share and that of the Middle East and sub-Saharan

Africa fell. The largest increase was in Eastern Europe and Central Asia. As a share of GNP, all regions lost out during the decade with the exception of Europe and Central Asia – although, once again, we see some recovery in 1998–2000.

One issue of concern, then, is the failure of concessional funds (which go mainly to the poorest countries) to keep up with the private funds that are directed primarily toward middle-income countries. A related problem has to do with the high level of debt that characterizes the poorest countries: as a percentage of GDP, the levels are much higher than for wealthier developing countries. The particular mechanism designed to deal with this problem – the so-called Highly Indebted Poor Countries (HIPC) Initiative – has made some progress. None the less, the terms are onerous and the speed slow. Perhaps the most important element is the new link between the HIPC debt negotiations and the World Bank/IMF Poverty Reduction Strategy Papers. The latter are poverty-reduction programmes that are designed jointly by governments and various elements of civil society in the respective countries; although potentially very positive, they have not been in operation long enough for their effectiveness to have been evaluated.[13]

Globalization and liberalization seem to have increased the inequality of external savings across regions and individual countries; in addition, they have contributed to raising inequality within countries. Identifying indicators of domestic inequality is not a simple task. One possibility would be to calculate Gini coefficients to estimate inequality in data from the household-income surveys that are now carried out in most countries. The problem is that the surveys do not capture the income of the wealthiest groups in society, who are precisely those most likely to have benefited from globalization.[14]

An alternative indicator is employment and wage patterns, which is our main focus here. Almost all empirical evidence shows that expansion of GDP is a necessary condition for employment creation, although it is not usually a sufficient condition. Thus, in so far as financial globalization promotes economic growth, this is good for employment, and increased employment opportunities are positively related to equity. Tight labour markets drive up wages and provide opportunities to those with lower skill levels. That said, there is, nevertheless, a widespread view that globalization has damaged employment prospects (for example, Rodrick 1997; Kapstein 1999). What is the basis for this opinion, and what does the evidence say? Much of the controversy centres on the shifting sectoral composition of employment, deriving from the sectoral composition of investment and growth. As employment creation is shifting from relatively well-paid jobs in industry and the public sector to low-productivity services, the quality of jobs may be negatively affected.

It is difficult to deal with this topic at the level of developing countries as a whole because of the lack of adequate data, but some insights can be obtained from a recent study of nine countries in Latin America and the Caribbean (Stallings and Peres 2000). A clear finding is that investment in the 1990s was concentrated in a relatively small number of sectors. Among tradeables, mining and natural gas stood out, as did a few branches of manufacturing (cement, steel, petrochemicals, and chemicals). Among non-tradeables, telecommunications was by far the most dynamic. The key point is that all of these sectors are capital intensive: that is, the most dynamic sectors in terms of investment, and thus long-term growth potential, are not producing many jobs. A related finding is that large firms were the most dynamic investors and, among large firms, transnational corporations gained ground *vis-à-vis* their domestic competitors.

Employment generation was jointly determined by secular trends and the impact of globalization and liberalization. Agriculture continued its long-term decline in total employment, and manufacturing generally lost share, except for the assembly plants (*maquila*). In manufacturing, most new jobs were created by small firms and microenterprises. These were the only firms that increased employment in Argentina, Brazil, Chile, and Costa Rica, where they accounted for more than 100 per cent of net job creation because larger firms posted a net job loss as a result of the downsizing that accompanied modernization.

Within sectors, the branches that grew most rapidly were capital intensive, such as natural-resource-based commodities and automobiles. Changes also occurred across sectors: specifically, activities that had traditionally produced the largest volume of employment, such as textiles and garments, declined across the board; only the *maquila* assembly plants, operating under conditions that differ from those of the rest of the economy, provided strong growth in highly labour-intensive activities.

When the fast-growing capital-intensive activities created few jobs, services became the residual source of employment. Services had a heterogeneous performance: high-quality jobs were created in telecommunications, banking, and finance, but most were in low-skill services, leading to slow growth in the overall productivity of the sector. Microenterprises offered the greatest number of jobs, with most of them operating on what the International Labour Organization (ILO) calls the "informal sector."

The heterogeneity in job creation was closely associated with another indicator of equity that centres on wages. Specifically, the 1990s saw a widening wage differential in most countries, developed and developing. Jobs in the large, modern, capital-intensive firms were well paid and offered good fringe benefits (especially health care and social security). Jobs in the small, traditional, labour-intensive shops tended to be poorly paid and often without benefits; this was especially true in the informal sector. Although the wage gap can be measured in a variety of ways, the most common is according to educational characteristics as a proxy for skills. In the study mentioned above of nine Latin American and Caribbean countries, there was a widening gap in seven of the nine during the 1990s. For the group as a whole, the gap grew by 11 per cent when university graduates were compared with those earning the average wage and by 25 per cent when university graduates were compared with those with 7–9 years of schooling (Stallings and Peres 2000: 127).

## Capital flows and government autonomy

One explanation for the particular pattern of resource flows that has emerged in the last two decades, with respect to both type of capital and its distribution, is that globalization limits the power of governments to follow desired policies. According to this argument, for example, governments can no longer use capital controls, which would restrict the entry or departure of all or certain types of capital. Nor can they follow the kinds of redistributive policies they would prefer. The constraints are said to come from the international financial institutions (IFIs) or "the markets."[15]

There is certainly some truth in these allegations, but perhaps less than is often believed. To begin with the question of macroeconomic policies, deficits – fiscal and current account – are what the markets (and the IFIs) most object to. A large deficit is seen as an indicator that government policies are inadequate and that serious problems may be in the offing. Confronted by such a deficit, and if no policies are in place to reduce it, investors may withdraw their funds. Although this action can have the effect of inducing the very crisis that is feared, it is logical from the microeconomic viewpoint, because those who wait are more likely to lose the money they have invested. The issue of deficits, however, should be seen in another light. Experience has shown that large deficits are not a desirable policy outcome (except perhaps as a Keynesian response to a situation of deep recession), so the inability to maintain them is not a result that should be lamented. Redistributive policies are better pursued within the context of reasonable macroeconomic equilibrium.

Capital controls present a different set of issues. The old style of controls aimed to prevent capital from leaving a country, often to enable loose macroeconomic policies to be followed. More recently, the emphasis has been on restrictions on the entry of capital to avoid surges that can then leave as rapidly as they arrived and cause both recessions and banking problems in the process. Although the IMF was initially against such controls, some countries used them in any case. Chile is the best-known example, but Colombia and Brazil followed a similar policy through different instruments. Malaysia later applied temporary controls on capital leaving the country. After the Asian crisis, and increasing evidence that large amounts of "hot money" can move around the globe very rapidly and overwhelm the economies of even well-managed developing countries, opinion began to change. There is now more openness to some type of controls, but as a complement, not a substitute, for sound macroeconomic policy (Herman and Stallings 1999). This area thus offers an example of when well-designed domestic policies can influence international thinking.

The third set of policies that is relevant to the topic of policy autonomy concerns redistributive measures – ranging from taxes and expenditures, to subsidies for certain groups, to redistribution of assets. This is where governments encounter the greatest resistance to policy initiatives, but it comes as much or more from domestic groups as from foreign investors. Clearly, foreign investors like to have low taxes and subsidies for infrastructure and so on, but other factors are also important in investment decisions. Certainty about the rules and predictability about policy in general are major considerations; other factors of importance depend on the sector and the target market (Maxfield 1999). In all cases, however, for both domestic and foreign investors, property safeguards are crucial. Here, globalization (especially the ability to move money rapidly from one place to another) indeed limits the autonomy of governments and has taken certain issues virtually off the agenda. Examples include land reform or expropriations of any kind, unless they are fully compensated. Nevertheless, as with deficits, attempts to redistribute through this type of policy have not produced very good results in the past, so the constraint may actually be beneficial in the long run if it leads governments to design and implement more effective redistributive measures.

## Conclusions: Recommendations for policy change

To summarize, we have argued that the globalization of finance can provide important support for higher growth rates in developing countries, but that the composition of capital flows is crucial. FDI is positive through its impact on investment, whereas short-term flows may well have a negative effect by increasing volatility. At the same time, financial globalization has led to increased inequality as poorer countries are reliant on declining official flows, whereas middle-income countries are beneficiaries of expanding private flows. As the latter are more volatile, however, the benefits are offset to some extent. Inequality has also increased within countries, owing in part to the employment patterns generated by international investors. Finally, globalization has constrained government action to some extent, although less than is sometimes believed. The main constraints are the requirement for certainty about rules and the inviolability of private property, so that governments must find ways to offset the inequality generated by globalization without transgressing in these two areas.

Both international and domestic policy changes are needed if developing countries are to maximize the benefits and minimize the costs from the new world environment created by globalization. Unfortunately, these countries have little voice with respect to international policies, which are mainly determined by the major developed countries together with the IFIs. They can, however, largely determine their own policies, as we have argued previously. In this final section we outline both international and domestic policies that would improve the functioning of the global system from the point of view of the developing countries. We also make some suggestions on policy initiatives at the regional level that can usefully complement the other two.[16]

## International policies

Much has been said since the Asian crisis began in 1997 about the need for a "new international financial architecture," but little has actually been accomplished. Among the agenda items that are under discussion, we can identify five that would be particularly important for developing countries in terms of lowering the chances of destructive international crises and establishing adequate mechanisms for dealing with them when they do arise.

- *Consistent macroeconomic policies at the global level*: The lack of a commitment to maintain adequate and stable growth rates in the developed countries is a major problem. The resulting boom–bust cycles are transferred to developing countries through trade as well as financial channels, and their impact is much more serious.
- *Enhanced financial supervision and regulation and improved information flows*: The international financial system, which is dominated by institutions from the developed countries, needs to increase its transparency and coordinate its regulatory frameworks as another way to limit the tendency to boom–bust behaviour and to create a more "level playing field."
- *Reform of the IMF in order to provide adequate international liquidity in times of crisis*: When crises do occur, international liquidity must be maintained. The IMF is the institution that has been designated for this role, but it currently lacks both the funds and an adequate mandate.

- *Sharing the costs of adjustment*: Another measure to deal with crises has to do with ensuring that the lenders share in the costs, rather than leaving borrowers to cope with all of the consequences (the equivalent of international bankruptcy procedures). For this to happen, internationally sanctioned stand-still provisions must be included in loan documents to avoid legal difficulties and free-riding among creditors.
- *Debt alleviation for the least-developed countries*: The lack of speed with which the HIPC negotiations have proceeded has further increased the burden on the poorest of the developing countries. Debt alleviation is the most efficient way of offsetting the disadvantages that currently face them.

## Domestic policies

Given their limited ability to affect international decision-making, developing countries must put priority on designing and implementing domestic policies that protect themselves from crises. The intent is not to return to the closed economies of the earlier post-war period but to improve the operation of the more open system of the twenty-first century. Five areas are of special importance.

- *Anticyclical macroeconomic policies*: Just as it is important to avoid boom–bust cycles at the international level, this aim should also be pursued within developing economies. Experience indicates that procyclical policies slow average growth in the long run because they deter investment, both foreign and domestic.
- *Control of foreign capital surges*: One of the main ways that boom–bust cycles have originated or been exacerbated is through large amounts of capital entering a country at the same time (the so-called herd behaviour). As these flows tend to exit in the same way, it may be sensible to slow down the original entry. This is also important because capital surges can interfere with the maintenance of stable domestic macroeconomic policy.
- *Policies to encourage domestic savings*: As one of the main reasons why developing countries rely heavily on external resources is lack of domestic savings, policies to stimulate the latter should be included as an element of macroeconomic policy. Of course, high growth rates are the best way to increase savings, so there is necessarily a problem of cause and effect in this area.
- *Improved regulation and supervision of the financial sector*: International financial crises can wreak havoc on the local banking sector in developing countries, which compounds the difficulties of returning to a new growth path afterwards. The best way for developing countries to protect themselves is through strong regulation and supervision of

local financial institutions; this may involve higher standards than are required internationally.

- *Policies to offset the inequality that frequently results from financial globalization*: Because developing countries are part of the global system that tends to increase inequality, domestic policies must counteract this trend as far as possible. In particular, the domestic inequality across economic sectors and social groups must be moderated, but the policies must not simultaneously cut investment and thus growth. One of the best examples of policies that will promote both growth and greater equality is support for small firms. Others include labour-intensive growth strategies, with a special emphasis on infrastructure, and efficient social spending, especially on education.

### Regional policies

Although most attention has centred on the international or domestic levels, regional arrangements can help to strengthen domestic policy initiatives, especially in the absence of movement on the international front. Four areas should be the focus of attention.

- *Peer review of policies*: Because neighbouring countries will suffer when one country in a region follows irresponsible policies, one of the most effective ways to avoid the latter is to establish a system whereby neighbours monitor each other's performance.
- *Regional schemes to increase liquidity in times of crisis*: International sources of liquidity may be delayed in arriving in times of crisis, because of bureaucratic inertia or disagreements over conditionality. To avoid long delays in which a crisis can worsen seriously, regional financial institutions can help to plug the gap.
- *Regional integration policies to encourage trade and investment*: Increasingly, both in the developed and developing worlds, economic interactions are centred on regional integration groupings. Experience in Asia as well as Europe suggests that promoting regional integration is a useful way to raise growth rates.
- *Joint negotiations at the international level*: As mentioned earlier, one of the main problems that developing countries face is lack of influence in determining how the global economy operates. Even the largest developing countries have little international clout but, if they negotiate as regional groups, they can magnify the weight of their opinions.

## Notes

1. The author wishes to acknowledge helpful comments from the editors and from participants in the project seminar held in New York in December 1999 as well as those at the

Secretary of State's Roundtable, held at the Institute for Development Studies, University of Sussex, in July 2000, as part of the preparation for the UK White Paper on Globalisation and Development. In addition, the assistance of Guillermo Mundt at ECLAC is appreciated.

2. For an excellent analysis that does address comparative issues, see Held et al. (1999).

3. As oil prices rose and then fell, this had a strong impact on trade patterns, especially with respect to the Middle East. The value of that region's trade was very high in 1980 and then fell steadily through the end of the 1990s. Thus, excluding the Middle East from the calculations in table 1.1 would show a larger increase in developing countries' share of world trade.

4. Although long-term bonds would also appear to be a stable form of finance, they were increasingly issued with options that allow a lender to pull out before the official maturity date; see Griffith-Jones (1998).

5. The possible exception is the purchase of former state-owned enterprises in developing countries by state firms in Europe or the remaining socialist countries, especially China.

6. Sterilization refers to a central bank buying foreign exchange and then engaging in open-market operations (selling bonds in the domestic market) to offset the liquidity represented by the foreign exchange. Because the interest rate on the bonds will typically exceed that earned by central bank assets, the result is a decapitalization of the institution.

7. UNCTAD (1999a: 162–163) compares coefficients of variation for FDI and other flows. On average, the latter are two or three times higher than the former. For a different view, see Claessens, Dooley, and Warner (1995).

8. Econometric evidence on this question is mixed. UNCTAD (1999a: 341) presents a set of regressions relating FDI to per capita growth: although the coefficients are generally positive, they are significant only for the 1990s. Other studies have shown a positive relationship for Latin America (de Gregorio 1992; Ffrench-Davis and Reisen 1998), but a recent cross-regional study of determinants of growth in developing countries (de Gregorio and Lee 1999) did not find a significant relationship.

9. ECLAC (2000b: 71) and UNCTAD (1999b: 57). It is important to note, as these publications make clear, that the data for FDI and for mergers and acquisitions are of very different sorts and thus not directly comparable.

10. An interesting exception was Malaysia, which imposed controls on capital outflows and refused to request assistance from the IMF. Later analysis suggests that Malaysia may have been helped by this policy and did not suffer the isolation that was initially expected.

11. When viewed on a per capita basis, the regional distribution of capital flows shifts somewhat, but not dramatically. The main difference is that East Asia falls to third place, owing to the very large population of China. Using population figures for the mid-1990s (World Bank 1997) and total capital flows for 1997 (table 1.5), the per capita figures are Latin America and the Caribbean $236, Europe and Central Asia $123, East Asia Pacific $75, sub-Saharan Africa $36, Middle East and North Africa $17, and South Asia $10.

12. For an analysis of trends in aid, see World Bank (1999: chap. 4; 2000: chap. 3).

13. On the Poverty Reduction Strategy Papers and debt reduction, see IDS (2000) and IMF (2000). Information on the World Bank's own evaluation of the PRSP process can be found on its Web site: ⟨http://www.worldbank.org/poverty/strategies/index.htm⟩

14. Not surprisingly, then, the most reliable set of cross-national income distribution data shows little change over the past several decades and even some decline in inequality. The main exception is Eastern Europe, where inequality rose markedly between the 1980s and the 1990s. See Deininger and Squire (1996).

15. For a sophisticated version of these arguments, see Held et al. (1999: 227–234).

16. This section draws heavily on the policy recommendations that several United Nations units have put forward recently. See especially United Nations (1999), Herman (1999), UNCTAD (1999a), and the documents related to the international meeting on "Financing for Development" (http://www.un.org/esa/analysis/ffd) that was held in March 2002 in Mexico City.

## REFERENCES

BIS (Bank for International Settlements). 1999. *69th Annual Report.* Basle: BIS.

BIS/IMF (International Monetary Fund)/OECD (Organization for International Cooperation and Development)/World Bank. Joint BIS-IMF-OECD-World Bank Statistics on External Debt. Online database (http://www.oecd.org/dac/debt/index.htm).

Bordo, Michael D., Barry Eichengreen, and Douglas A. Irwin. 1999. "Is Globalization Today Really Different than Globalization a Hundred Years Ago?" National Bureau for Economic Research (NBER) Working Paper 7195.

Calvo, Guillermo and Enrique Mendoza. 1996. "Mexico's Balance of Payments: A Chronicle of Death Foretold." *Journal of International Economics* 41(3–4) (special issue).

Claessens, Stijn, Michael P. Dooley, and Andrew Warner. 1995. "Portfolio Capital Flows: Hot or Cold?" *World Bank Economic Review* 7(1).

De Gregorio, José. 1992. "Economic Growth in Latin America." *Journal of Development Economics* (39).

De Gregorio, José and Jong-Wha Lee. 1999. "Economic Growth in Latin America: Sources and Prospects." Paper presented at the annual meeting of the Latin American and Caribbean Economics Association (LACEA), Santiago, Chile.

Deininger, Klaus and Lyn Squire. 1996. "A New Data Set for Measuring Income Inequality." *World Bank Economic Review* 10(3).

ECLAC (United Nations Economic Commission for Latin America and the Caribbean). 2000a. *Finance for Development: Challenges that Face the Region.* Santiago: ECLAC.

ECLAC (2000b). *Foreign Investment in Latin America and the Caribbean, 1999 edition.* Santiago: ECLAC.

Fawcett, Louise and Andrew Hurrell, eds. 1995. *Regionalism in World Politics: Regional Organization and International Order.* Oxford: Oxford University Press.

Ffrench-Davis, Ricardo, ed. 2001. *Financial Crisis in "Successful" Emerging Economies.* Washington, DC: The Brookings Institution Press.

Ffrench-Davis, Ricardo and Helmut Reisen, eds. 1998. *Capital Flows and Investment Performance: Lessons from Latin America.* Paris: OECD.

Fishlow, Albert and Stephan Haggard. 1992. *The United States and the Regionalisation of the World Economy.* Paris: OECD Development Centre.

Gereffi, Gary. 1995. "Global Production Systems and Third World Development." In *Global Change, Regional Response: The New International Context of Development*, ed. Barbara Stallings. New York: Cambridge University Press.

Griffith-Jones, Stephany. 1998. *Global Capital Flows*. London: Macmillan.

Gwin, Catherine and Joan Nelson, eds. 1997. *Perspectives on Aid and Development*. Washington, DC: Overseas Development Council.

Held, David, Anthony McGrew, David Goldblatt, and Jonathan Perraton. 1999. *Global Transformation: Politics, Economics, and Culture*. Stanford: Stanford University Press.

Herman, Barry, ed. 1999. *Global Financial Turmoil and Reform: A United Nations Perspective*. Tokyo: United Nations University Press.

Herman, Barry and Barbara Stallings. 1999. "International Finance and the Developing Countries: Liberalization, Crisis, and the Reform Agenda." In *Global Financial Turmoil and Reform: A United Nations Perspective*, ed. B. Herman. Tokyo: United Nations University Press.

Herman, E. S. and R. W. McChesney. 1997. *The Global Media: The New Missionaries of Corporate Capitalism*. London: Cassell.

IDS (Institute for Development Studies). 2000. "Poverty Reduction Strategies: A Part for the Poor." *IDS Policy Briefing* (13).

IMF (International Monetary Fund). 2000. "Progress Report on Poverty Reduction Strategy Papers." (http://www.imf.org/external/np/pdr/prsp/2000/0411400.htm).

IMF. (Various years). *Balance of Payments Statistics Yearbook*. Washington, DC: IMF.

IMF. (Various years). *Direction of Trade Statistics Yearbook*. Washington, DC: IMF.

Kapstein, Ethan B. 1999. *Sharing the Wealth: Workers and the World Economy*. New York: W. W. Norton.

Maxfield, Sylvia. 1999. "Financial Reform and Market Democracy in East Asia and Latin America." Paper presented at National Endowment for Democracy conference on The State, Market, and Democracy in East Asia and Latin America, Santiago, Chile.

Nelson, Joan and Stephanie Eglinton. 1993. *Global Goals, Contentious Means: Issues of Multiple Aid Conditionality*. Washington, DC: Overseas Development Council.

OECD. 1997. *Communications Outlook*. Paris: OECD.

OECD (Organization for Economic Co-operation and Development). (Various years). *Development Co-operation*. Paris: OECD.

Oman, Charles. 1994. *Globalisation and Regionalisation: The Challenge for Developing Countries*. Paris: OECD Development Centre.

Rodrik, Dani. 1997. *Has Globalization Gone Too Far?* Washington, DC: Institute for International Economics.

Rodrik, Dani. 1999. *The New Global Economy and Developing Countries: Making Openness Work*. Washington, DC: Overseas Development Council.

Rosenau, James N. 1997a. *Along the Domestic–Foreign Frontier: Exploring Government in a Turbulent World*. New York: Cambridge University Press.

Rosenau, James N. 1997b. "The Complexities and Contradictions of Globalization." *Current History* 96(613).

Sachs, Jeffrey, Alfredo Tornell, and Andrés Velasco. 1996. "The Collapse of the Mexican Peso: Sudden Death or Death Foretold?" *Journal of International Economics* 41(3–4) (special issue).

Stallings, Barbara and Wilson Peres. 2000. *Growth, Employment, and Equity: The Impact of the Economic Reforms in Latin America and the Caribbean.* Washington, DC: The Brookings Institution.

Stallings, Barbara and Makoto Sakurai. 1993. *Common Vision, Different Paths: The United States and Japan in the Developing World.* Washington, DC: Overseas Development Council.

Stallings, Barbara and Wolfgang Streeck. 1995. "Capitalisms in Conflict? The United States, Europe, and Japan in the Post-Cold War World." In *Global Change, Regional Response: The New International Context of Development,* ed. Barbara Stallings. New York: Cambridge University Press.

Strange, Susan. 1996. *The Retreat of the State: The Diffusion of Power in the World Economy.* New York: Cambridge University Press.

UNCTAD (United Nations Conference on Trade and Development). 1999a. *Trade and Development Report.* Geneva: UNCTAD.

UNCTAD. 1999b. *World Investment Report.* Geneva: UNCTAD.

Unger, Roberto Mangebeira. 1997. "Globalization as an Instrument of Exploitation." Paper presented at a conference on Globalization, University of São Paulo, Brazil.

United Nations. 1999. *Towards a New International Financial Architecture. Report of the Task Force of the Executive Committee on Economic and Social Affairs of the United Nations.* Santiago: ECLAC.

Wade, Robert. 1996. "Globalization and its Limits: Reports of the Death of the National Economy Are Greatly Exaggerated." In *National Diversity and Global Capitalism,* eds. Suzanne Berger and Ronald Dore. Ithaca, NY: Cornell University Press.

World Bank. 1997. *World Development Report.* Washington, DC: World Bank.

World Bank. 1999. *Global Development Finance, 1999.* Washington, DC: World Bank.

World Bank. 2000. *Global Development Finance, 2000.* Washington, DC: World Bank.

World Bank. 2001. *Global Development Finance, 2001.* Washington, DC: World Bank.

WTO (World Trade Organization). 1998. *Annual Report,* 2 vols. Geneva: WTO.

# 2

# Democracy and development: Trends and prospects

*Atul Kohli*

This chapter analyses both the successes and failures of building democracy in the developing world. While taking stock of the major political trends over the last few decades, an attempt is also made to assess the performance of developing-country democracies in facilitating such valued goals as stable governance and economic growth with equity. Finally, some suggestions are made as to the political and economic strategies that may encourage continued democratization.

Since the intellectual terrain is large and complex, the focus below is quite selective in terms of both the themes and the cases discussed. The general argument is that, although democratization in the developing world has made some progress – at times even significant progress – there is still a long way to go. Numerous developing countries continue to be ruled by authoritarian rulers of one type or another. Where democratically elected governments exist, governmental performance is often less than satisfactory: stable governance remains elusive, as does economic growth with equity. The "democratic revolution" of the 1980s ran into snags in the 1990s; new ruling élite and veto groups rapidly emerged and are now attempting to block the spread of power and wealth in these countries; relatedly, there is growing disillusionment among the popular sectors with the process of "economic liberalization" from above. As the "Washington Consensus" fades and the myth that "all good things go together" takes a beating, the path to just growth in the developing world remains fraught with obstacles.

## Democracy and democratization

Democracy as a form of government is distinguishable from democratization as a political process. A democratic government emerges when all
adult citizens of a country are free to participate in periodic elections and
where these elections help select that country's political-office holders,
including the highest leaders. By contrast, democratization as a political
process refers to a genuine spread of power in society, leading to enhanced popular control over national choices. The point that needs to be
underlined at the outset is that a democratic government, although necessary, is not sufficient to facilitate democratization of power in society;
the latter requires political struggles and deliberate crafting of new institutions within the frame of a democratic government. More specifically, among the conditions facilitating democratization are accessibility
of political offices within the nation to members of diverse social and
ethnic groups; attempts to neutralize the disproportionate power that
business and other monied groups enjoy in most polities; and continued
participation of government in policy areas that influence the life-chances
of the majority, and, in the case of developing countries, enhanced national self-determination.

It should also be noted at the outset that democracy as a form of government has no direct and necessary bearing on a more egalitarian distribution of wealth and status in society, i.e. a democratic government
does not necessarily facilitate socio-economic democracy. On the contrary, some authoritarian-socialist polities have done considerably better
at economic distribution than comparable democracies, although often at
the expense of other cherished values. When power in a democracy is
democratized it may have more of a direct impact on the distribution of
wealth. Even this, however, tends to occur mainly on the margins and is
certainly not a strong relationship; for example, distribution of wealth via
property redistribution is legally insulated from the purview of legislative
politics in many well-established democracies. In sum, democracy as a
form of government, democratization of power as a political process, and
socio-economic democracy as a possible goal, are analytically and empirically distinguishable; there is no linear or automatic trend from a democratic government to democratization of power and on to a more egalitarian democracy.

Those who value democracy must thus be clear about why they value
democracy. A democratic government is an improvement over many authoritarian governments because most people in most countries prefer a
predictable to an arbitrary government, value the freedoms of expression
and association as ends in themselves, and increasingly hold that it is
their right to have some say in the selection of their political leaders. An

established democracy also institutionalizes hope for excluded groups that they may get to share power in the future. Beyond that, however, the significance of democracy for achieving such other valued social goals as economic growth or income redistribution is far from clear, with the possibility of significant trade-offs always present.

## Democracy in developing countries: An overview

Democracy as a modern form of government originated in parts of Western Europe and subsequently – via some combination of imposition, diffusion, and emulation – spread to other parts of the world. The experience with this governmental form in countries of Asia, Africa, and Latin America has been, at best, mixed. Since the Second World War, democracy's vicissitudes in the developing world can be broadly divided into three periods. The first period, which lasted about a decade (from the late 1940s to the late 1950s and early 1960s), was characterized by political experimentation and an optimism about the prospects of stable democratic rule in the "new states." Although there were many early failures, democracy remained the optimistic ideal during much of this period, obliging nearly every new state to experiment with elections and parliaments. As failures mounted, however, the developing world settled into a long, second phase of authoritarianism (with prominent exceptions, of course) that lasted well into the late 1970s. From early 1980s onwards we have been in a third phase, wherein numerous countries have again moved away from authoritarian regimes and are experimenting with democracy.

What factors help explain these vicissitudes? This major question can be answered by addressing two sub-questions: why did so many early attempts at creating democracies in the 1950s fail, and why did so many authoritarian regimes "transit" to more open polities in the 1980s? While synthesizing a large body of scholarly literature that exists on such themes, the answer outlined below takes account of both national and global forces on the one hand and the significance of cross-regional variations within the developing world on the other hand (Huntington 1968; Haggard and Kaufman 1995).

It is clear in retrospect that, following the Second World War, neither the state–society relations within nor the global context of developing countries was conducive to consolidation of democratic regimes. While developing countries were quite diverse, especially across regions, they also shared some common characteristics: low per capita incomes with relatively small urban middle classes; an influential, traditional élite with roots in landed wealth; a considerable élite–mass gap; and non-existent or weak political institutions, such as political parties. These circumstances encouraged the political élite in a few countries to reconsolidate traditional polities (as, for example, in some Middle Eastern countries), and in a few others (such as China or Cuba) to undertake revolutionary overthrow of the *ancien régime*. By contrast, in a majority of developing countries, democratic experiments of one type or another were tried but without much success. One typical pattern was that new leaders, wanting legitimacy and attempting to consolidate state power, undertook popular mobilization along anti-imperialist and socialist symbols. Without institutions to channel this mobilization, however, the resulting nationalist–populist upsurge readily threatened the property-owning élite who, in turn, allied with the armed forces and/or with external actors to re-establish the socio-economic status quo with the help of the authoritarian élite. Another pattern was that both the sense of a nation and institutions of the state were so weak that the introduction of democracy readily accentuated ethnic and other forms of identity politics, leading to democratic breakdowns. Mobilization of class or ethnic identities thus readily overwhelmed fragile democratic institutions.

The global context of the cold war also hindered consolidation of democratic experiments in the developing world. Both the Soviet Union and the United States mainly sought friendly allies in the third world. As a challenging power, the Soviet Union fished in troubled waters and encouraged anti-status quo forces; if and when these forces were victorious, they often turned out to be antidemocratic. While the United States espoused support for democracy, it also often breached this commitment in practice. Given the cold war mind-set, the United States was deeply suspicious of left-leaning, nationalist forces within the developing world. Since open politics in these countries would frequently bring left-leaning, nationalist leaders to the forefront – i.e. democratic politics would open up the possibility of rapid democratization of power – the United States, in order to checkmate such developments, often ended up supporting pro-American authoritarian leaders in various parts of the developing world.

Within these broad commonalties there were considerable variations across regions. A brief discussion of some of these may help to fill out the picture of why democracy had such a difficult start in much of the developing world.

- In much of East Asia, indigenous political traditions were deeply authoritarian. Colonial impact often reinforced these tendencies – as, for example, in the case of Japanese colonial influence in Korea and Taiwan, that of the Dutch in Indonesia, or the French role in Indo-China. The national political forces that survived these experiences and thus came to the fore in the post-colonial period were hardly ever a

cohesive, reform-oriented group with strong commitment to democracy; such groups were generally squeezed out, and what survived instead were more extreme groups with a variety of non-democratic political inclinations.

Moreover, the cold war was fought bitterly in this part of the world,
particularly in Korea and Viet Nam. The case of Korea helps to exemplify some broader regional tendencies (Cumings 1981). After the Japanese defeat in the Second World War, Korea experienced a brief moment of national euphoria and political opening. Although they were
far from cohesive, a variety of national political leaders attempted to
put together a left-of-centre, nationalist coalition. Whether this would
have evolved into a reform-oriented, democratic regime will never be
known. What happened instead was that major powers intervened,
leading to a division of the country that encouraged non-democratic
alternatives in both halves. In the North, the Soviet Union encouraged
the nationalist revolution to unfold, but also at the same time tilted
the outcome towards the establishment of a communist dictatorship.
American occupation forces in the South were profoundly distrustful of
the left-leaning nationalists, taking them to be communist stooges, and
thus encouraged the establishment of a right-wing dictatorship under
Syngman Rhee. Variations on this basic theme subsequently emerged
in several parts of East and South-East Asia.

• As much of Africa emerged from colonialism in the late 1950s and
early 1960s, its political forms were characterized by incomplete state
formation. "Left–right" politics and the cold war played a less significant role in this part of the world; instead, political problems had
deeper historical origins. Decolonization left a legacy of weak central
and civil authority and of poorly established public spheres in most
African countries. Democratic experiments under such conditions
quickly evolved into sectional social conflicts over distribution of state
power leading to military coups. The case of Nigeria helps to exemplify
some of these dynamics (Diamond 1988).

Nigeria was an artificial colonial construction and it emerged from
British colonial rule in 1960 with a fairly weak central state structure.
The main component groups of the body politic – the Yoruba, the
Ibo, and the Hausa-Fulani – were extremely sensitive to their relative
shares in any effort to centralize authority. Introduction of democracy
in this setting thus further politicized community identities, generating
strong centrifugal tendencies around ethnic politics. Absence of any
national social groups, such as a national middle class, and of strong
national political institutions, further contributed to a political crisis,
including a civil war, that was "resolved" only by the imposition of
military rule.

- Democratic experiments after the Second World War lasted somewhat longer in parts of Latin America but also eventually succumbed to military rule of one type or another in the 1960s. Democratic politics under conditions of deep inequalities and dependence encouraged the emergence of nationalist–populist leaders (and, on occasion, socialist leaders). Established business and landed interests, as well as US-sponsored cold war politics in the region, combined to oppose these popular trends. Political polarization, a problem in its own right, also made it difficult to overcome a variety of economic bottlenecks that had resulted from early successes via import-substitution industrialization (ISI). Growing polarization and economic bottlenecks were, once again, "resolved" only by military coups – as, for example, in the case of Brazil (Skidmore 1967).

Brazil sided with the allies during the Second World War and, in the aftermath, sought to distance itself from its authoritarian past, while experimenting with democracy. Unfortunately, a national consensus on the nature and the role of the state never developed. The political situation increasingly came to be polarized: on the one side were the "internationalists," who argued for closer political and economic relations with the United States and for a minimal role of the state in the Brazilian economy, and who were deeply distrustful of the anti-imperialist, pro-labour stance of Brazilian populists; on the other side were the "nationalists," who wanted to minimize dependence on the United States, favoured the use of the Brazilian state as a motor of protected industrialization, and who championed such "social" questions as the rights of labour and the peasantry. When the economy was growing in the 1950s these tensions remained manageable. However, as the "easy" phase of import substitution became exhausted, and growth decelerated in the early 1960s, major debates on the future direction of the national political economy came to the fore. The political situation became increasingly polarized: the United States, worried about Cuban socialism as a potential model in Latin America, was hostile to the seemingly left-leaning, Brazilian nationalist rulers; as the latter gained in popularity and pushed the political spectrum further to the left, the military – openly nudged by Brazilian propertied classes and with silent approval from the United States – stepped in, terminating the first Brazilian democratic experiment in 1964.

Similar examples from such other regions as the Middle East, South Asia, or Central America could be multiplied. However, the general conclusion concerning why so many democratic experiments in the developing countries failed in the first period can be summarized. Although the deeper reasons for these failures varied – certainly from region to region but, on occasion, even from country to country – at a proximate level of causation, the main factors were both the failure to generate a modicum of domestic political cohesion and an unfavourable global environment. The few exceptional developing countries in which democracy took root further buttress this general conclusion. Take, for example, the case of India: within the framework of British colonialism, Indians developed a fairly cohesive nationalist movement. Leaders of this movement participated in electoral politics before independence and, while vying for power with each other, came to conduct their power struggles by democratic means. This moderately cohesive and democratic nationalist movement, in turn, came to the fore in the post-colonial period, providing the core of the sovereign state. Leaders such as Nehru, with considerable popular support behind them, also steered the new nation in a "non-aligned" direction, in effect keeping cold war politics at arm's length from Indian domestic politics. Whereas a fuller discussion would reveal layers of complexity, the general fact is that an element of domestic political cohesion and a degree of insulation from global political forces provided the framework within which democracy, in the exceptional case of India, took root.

By the mid-1960s, most developing countries had become sovereign; many had experimented with democracy and, as failed democratic experiments accumulated, there was a growing sense that democracy may well be ill-suited to the needs and circumstances of low-income countries. Many authoritarian leaders thus settled in to rule, seemingly for the long haul. Their main claims to rule were that they provided a bulwark against "political disorder" (i.e. against the lack of any working consensus among the civilian political élite, corruption, and the threat of a mobilized left) and that they were likely to be superior facilitators of "economic development." With rapid economic growth in areas such as South Korea and Brazil, the case for authoritarianism received a boost. Although I suggest below that systematic relationship of regime type to economic growth is nearly non-existent, association of authoritarianism with high growth in a few prominent cases created its own popular "demonstration effect," with real-world legitimizing consequences. Those sympathetic to communist experiments could also maintain that, whatever the problems of communism, communist rulers in cases as diverse as China and Cuba were successful at creating more egalitarian societies and at eliminating bottom-level poverty. Performance-based legitimacy claims (rather than the procedural legitimacy of democracy) thus enhanced the support for regimes both on the left and the right; the 1970s, as a result, turned out to be a bad decade for democracy in the developing world.

How did all this change? What factors help to explain the crisis of authoritarianism in the 1980s? From the perspective of the 1970s, it would be very difficult indeed to explain why, by the end of the century, numerous developing countries were actually experimenting with democracy and that numerous others were experiencing some pressure to democratize. By now, however, numerous scholarly accounts exist that help explain this "global transition" to democracy.[1] Some of these insights can be usefully synthesized by first delineating some broad national and international forces that provided the overall context of the "transition," and then by pointing to specific regional or country-level variations.

The economic and political performance of many authoritarian regimes came to be increasingly questioned over the 1980s, leading to major political changes. Part of this was nearly "normal" in so far as, in modern times, citizens in most countries tire of most governments after they have been in power for a while and demand periodic political change; when systematic avenues for governmental change do not exist, citizen demands can readily escalate into demands for a change in type of regime that may enable some citizen participation in the selection of a new government. Beyond these "normal" forces, specific developments further undermined the performance-based legitimacy of numerous authoritarian rulers. On the economic front, the 1974 increase in oil prices set the stage for global economic contraction. Wary of the political consequences of slow economic growth, numerous authoritarian rulers sought to "borrow-and-grow" their way out of adverse global circumstances. Although this strategy seemed to work over the short run – and for some East Asian countries, who had continued access to foreign finance from Japan and who succeeded in pushing their exports, it even worked over a longish run – it had also, by the early 1980s, contributed to a severe debt crisis and relatedly to a deceleration of economic growth in most Latin American and African countries. As a consequence, the rulers who presided over this economic downturn found themselves in growing political difficulty.

On the political front also, the threat of "political disorder," which may have initially provided some support for non-democratic rulers, increasingly fell into the background. Instead, the "success" of brutal regimes in eliminating leftist and other dissenting forces became the new focus of political ire. Growing troubles of international communism over the 1980s also made the perceived threat from the left less pressing, undermining one of the elements in the overall *raison d'être* of some authoritarian regimes. Lastly, many authoritarian rulers (Marcos and Mobutu, for example) turned out to be no less corrupt, nepotistic, and personalistic than their predecessors; instead of "saviours" from chaos and disorder, therefore, many authoritarian rulers by the 1980s came to appear as obstacles to more desirable forms of government.

One final socio-political development that occurred in many developing countries and that ought to be noted because it had considerable bearing on democratic transitions, was the slow but steady shift in rural–urban power balance: the power of the traditional élite groups declined and there was a simultaneous emergence of a new urban middle class of sorts across the developing world. Although the process has been uneven (varying with rates of economic progress), most developing countries by the 1980s had a much greater concentration of businessmen, professionals, traders, civil servants, and those with higher education – employed or unemployed – in their cities than in the 1950s. Although this was a politically heterogeneous group, some of the political preferences of its members nevertheless aggregated and added distinctive political tendencies, as follows.

- This new middle class was less nationalist than its smaller, post-colonial counterpart of the 1950s.
- Relatedly, its members were more attuned to global political and economic trends, creating pressure for democracy and economic opening (although identity-based politics, with sharp reactions to these global trends, have also emerged from within this political stratum in some countries).
- A variety of political groups that opposed the authoritarian rulers (e.g. lawyers' associations, women's groups, university students, and even, in some instances, businessmen's political organizations) emerged from within this growing "middle class".
- The presence of a sizeable number of educated groups, often concentrated in the capital city, increased the scrutiny of (and thus the pressures for accountability on) unsavoury rulers.

Within the context set by these economic and political changes – a context that slowly but surely helped to undermine numerous authoritarian rulers – there were considerable regional and even country-specific variations. A brief reference to some of these will once again help fill out the broad-brush account of political "transitions" in the 1980s.

- The most dramatic set of democratic transitions in the developing world (excluding Eastern Europe) occurred in Latin America. The example of Brazil again helps to demonstrate how the broader forces mentioned above played themselves out in a specific context (Stephan 1989). The democratic transition in Brazil resulted from a combination of two proximate set of causes: these were, first, a divided authoritarian élite that, for a number of reasons, was willing to yield to a democratic opening and, second, growing popular pressures for such an opening from below. Although these processes fed each other, the role of a yielding élite was probably more significant in the case of the Brazilian transition (whereas that of growing pressures on the ruling élite was more significant in some other Latin American countries, such as Chile).

Brazil's military rulers pushed the economy very hard in the 1970s, refusing to adjust downwards, hoping to borrow and grow. At the same time, however, worried about their domestic political standing, the military rulers also made numerous economic concessions to business groups (e.g. low interest rates on investment credit, when economic logic would have indicated a reverse trend) and to the more "traditional" regional élite groups who could drum up some political support. Whereas the economy grew at very high rates over the 1970s, by the second oil-price increase in the early 1980s macroeconomic disequilibrium had become severe, with the pressures to maintain payments on foreign debt leading to austerity and sharp deceleration of economic growth.

As economic growth faltered, the ruling élite came to be more and more divided among themselves over the issue of the best future economic path. Hoping to shore up sagging political support, the military rulers also allowed some political expression of dissent. As often happens in such cases, the opening only encouraged further discontent. Throughout the military period Brazil's Catholic Church provided a political forum for various discontented groups, including rural groups. Over time, labour, lawyers', and women's groups also got into the political act, demanding full democracy. By the mid-1980s, after ruling for nearly two decades, the Brazilian military thus decided to step aside in favour of an elected civilian regime.

• Democratic transitions in such East Asian countries as South Korea were partial exceptions to the overall trend, inasmuch as they were propelled more by economic success than by economic difficulties. Nevertheless, what South Korea shared with a country like Brazil was the role of the new middle class. A buoyant middle class, which emerged along with spectacular economic growth, was instrumental in pushing for reforms in South Korea. Additionally, the political performance of South Korean rulers came to be increasingly questioned, especially because, over time, the communist threat appeared to be less imminent. Korean students especially pushed the regime authorities hard, demanding investigation of political repression, demanding investigation of corruption in high places and, more generally, demanding accountability. With significant external pressures – as, for example, from the "demonstration effect" of successful democratization in the neighbouring Philippines – and desperately wanting to join the ranks of the more-developed nations, Korean authorities finally succumbed to electoral politics in the late 1980s.

- There have been some moves towards democracy in Africa as well. Global pressures operate on this region, as they do on all other regions. However, legacies of poorly formed neo-patrimonial state structures, group conflicts, corrupt and personalistic rulers, along with severe economic difficulties have made the process, at best, halting (Bratton and Walle 1997).

Take again, for example, the case of Nigeria. After the first failure of democracy in the mid-1960s, and after the civil war and considerable, deliberate state construction (e.g. centralization of authority and breaking up of the larger ethnic groups into smaller federal units), the second attempt at democracy (1979–1983) again failed. The underlying causes were partly economic and partly political: throughout the 1970s, Nigerian rulers failed to put that country's enormous oil wealth to good use; much of it was squandered on imported consumption, poor investment choices that were also heavily import-intensive, and personalistic corruption; economic problems in the 1980s were compounded as oil prices fell. The politics of scarcity worsened the politics of ethnicity – which, in any case, is a persistent theme in Nigerian politics and had re-emerged under open political competition (Joseph 1987).

Following the coup in 1983, Nigeria was ruled by military leaders for more than 15 years. Promises to hold elections were repeatedly unfulfilled. Unlike the case of Brazil, therefore, it is clear that neither were the Nigerian military élite ready to relinquish power nor were the pressures from the "civil society" decisive (Forrest 1995). When democracy eventually came in the late 1990s, it was more a result of growing international pressures: a heavily indebted country that needed to attract foreign resources simply could not go on and on as a "pariah state." As this realization seeped in, the reluctant military rulers stepped aside and opened the way for what is likely to prove to be another tumultuous democratic phase in Nigeria's difficult political evolution.

What generalizations can one then make concerning this incomplete process of democratic transition in developing countries? It is clear from the brief discussion above that there are considerable variations across regions and countries. Nevertheless, the few common contextual conditions discussed above can also be re-specified. First and foremost, performance-based legitimacy of numerous authoritarian regimes declined over the 1980s and the 1990s, paving the way for mounting challenges and eventual transitions. Many authoritarian rulers, when they took power in earlier decades, had made themselves minimally acceptable to their citizens by promising superior performance at establishing political order and at facilitating economic dynamism. Over time, however, these claims began to appear hollow. Since coercion seldom provides infinite resources to maintain rule, declining legitimacy and growing opposition reinforced each other, contributing to eventual changes in regime. Additionally, the growing political significance of urban middle and lower-middle income groups in most developing countries and, relatedly, greater integration of these countries into a world in which communism has been discredited and where Western models of markets and democracy have gained ascendancy, facilitated the process of democratic transitions.

It is important to emphasize that major exceptions to the democratic trend remain within the developing world: these include China, North Korea, Indo-China, and much of South-East Asia, in Asia; much of the Middle East; a significant number of North and sub-Saharan African countries; and even pockets in Central America. How have these areas resisted the pressures delineated above? Although the specific and detailed answers will, again, vary from area to area, the general factors at work help to reinforce the argument developed above: major countries such as China have resisted a democratic opening, in part simply by the use of well-organized coercion but also by presiding over a buoyant economy (thus by maintaining some performance-based legitimacy) in a largely agrarian society (i.e. in a society with a relatively small urban middle class); others, such as North Korea and some Middle East countries (e.g. Saudi Arabia) have heavily insulated themselves from global cultural influences; the urban middle classes, especially entrepreneurial groups, in yet other countries (especially in some African countries), remain relatively weak and thus unable to pose a major challenge to personalistic, coercive rulers; and finally, countries remain where conditions for stable rule of any type – authoritarian or democratic – are simply non-existent.

## Democracy and governability

As one looks ahead, what are the prospects that new democracies will facilitate effective governance and economic growth with distribution, or that just growth will unfold? The issue of democracy and governance is discussed in this section and that of democracy and economic development in the next. Unlike the optimistic view entertained in some policy circles that democracy provides a ready solution to problems of governance, the argument developed below is less sanguine.

Most new democracies in the developing world will continue to find the tasks of consolidating these democracies and providing effective governance difficult. Some of the causes of these difficulties are deep and structural, whereas others are a result of policy choices. Moreover, some difficulties are short term and are already evident, whereas others are likely to emerge over the next few decades of democratic experimentation. The following brief review of both institutional and policy issues may help to explain, at least in part, why the politics of so many new democracies are, and are likely to remain, turbulent.

## Institutional issues

The manner in which most recent "transitions" have occurred has not been the most auspicious from the standpoint of future consolidation. Disintegration of authoritarian regimes was often relatively rapid (rapid, at least, on the scale of "political time" over which new institutions take root) and left in its wake a divided élite, a mobilized populace with heightened expectations, and weak links between the élite and the masses.

Given weak democratic institutions, a typical outcome followed: irrespective of the levels of civil-society activism during the anti-authoritarian phase, power in many new democracies came to rest in the hands of a few individuals, if not a single leader. A further recurring consequence was that, whenever the ruling élite were threatened, further centralization and personalization of power was a readily available alternative. Because centralization of power in individuals nearly always further emasculates fragile institutions (strong institutions do constrain the power of individuals), there is a built-in incentive in new democracies for leaders to undertake periodic deinstitutionalization. Weak institutions and personalistic rule thus become vicious and mutually reinforcing processes. As long as a democracy remains more an affair of a few élite and less an established framework that dwarfs the leaders, only exceptional leaders are likely to resist the tendency to maintain personal power at the expense of institutional development.

An élite-dominated democracy, without such constraining institutions as parties, parliaments, or legal systems, also structures patterns of political mobilization perversely. Leaders in these settings mobilize socio-economic groups more as power resources in intra-élite struggles and less to satisfy group aspirations. While a fair amount of this is "normal" politics, what is not always appreciated is that mobilized but unorganized groups that are ignored by politicians once they have served their political purposes add considerable volatility to the polity. When "real groups" with "real interests" (such as labour) are mobilized, there is a realistic chance that the mobilization will be accompanied by organization and that group demands can be accommodated after negotiations. By contrast, mobilization from above often attracts demagogues. Because it remains unorganized and really does not have concrete (even if incremental) gains for the mobilized groups as its priority, such mobilization periodically tends to generate political turmoil.

Particularly in new democracies, causes and consequences of the weakness of political parties need to be better understood. One hypothesis that would fit a number of countries is that strong parties – parties with well-developed political identification, programmatic goals, and organization – develop mainly as vehicles for gaining power. Conversely, leaders who acquire power because of personal appeal have little incentive to encourage the development of parties from above; on the contrary, parties as institutions often constrain the individual discretion and personalistic power of towering leaders. Thus, well-developed parties often emerge from below rather than from above and, just as often, take time and require sustained open political spaces. If this proposition is valid, significant policy implications follow: the typical resort to personalistic, concentrated executive power as a post-transition, stabilizing measure only postpones the deeper need to work out a society's power conflicts.

As to the consequences of party organization, well-organized parties can perform several important political tasks: they can help to train and socialize new leaders, minimize factional conflict among existing leaders, and clarify lines of authority. To repeat, mobilization undertaken by parties rather than by individuals is also more likely to be accompanied by organization: not only are new participants brought into the political arena but also their political energies are simultaneously harnessed to accomplish specific goals. More important, well-organized parties tend to have long-term programmes and a stable core of membership to support those programmes. When such parties come to power, they help to narrow the gap between the state's representative and developmental goals. The coalition that such a party brings to power is likely to favour the policies that the new government wishes to pursue. It thus stands to reason that the absence of strong parties is likely to remain a major source of political problems for new democracies. The resulting organizational vacuum will continue to be a root cause of the growing gap in these countries between how power is won and how power is used – or between personalization of power, on the one hand, and the inability to use that power to solve pressing problems, on the other.

A related but separate institutional issue concerns the political problems generated by misdirected state intervention. While the issue of state intervention is generally discussed in connection with problems of economic development and/or "rent seeking," the political consequences of an interventionist state at low levels of development – a characteristic that is rather widespread in the developing world – are not fully understood; two of these deserve our attention.

- First, an interventionist state in the early stages of development has difficulty in establishing a separation between the public and private spheres in social life. This has several consequences, the most important of which, from the standpoint of democratic consolidation, is that an interventionist state cannot claim that distributive problems are social and not political problems. The coexistence of political equality with considerable economic inequality facilitated the establishment of proto-democracies in parts of nineteenth-century Europe. The interventionist welfare state developed only under resource-abundant, mature capitalism. In much of the developing world, however, a highly interventionist state is inherent to the overall design of state-led development. This could change with waves of "liberalization," but not dramatically. Moreover, once democracy is introduced to the brew, the combination of democracy, a low-income economy, substantial inequities, and state intervention tends to politicize numerous societal cleavages – old versus new, social, and economic. A fair amount of what looks like a "new wave" of ethnic or religious conflict is actually a result of this dynamics of the politicization of old identities for the sake of new "secular" gains of power and wealth. Thus, the accumulating distributive claims on the state partly reflect the state's attempt to penetrate and reorganize socio-economic life.
- Second, an interventionist developing state typically controls a substantial proportion of a poor economy. Thus, many of the society's free-floating economic resources are controlled by politicians and bureaucrats. Who should have access to those resources? Unlike situations involving the products of private endeavour, the legitimacy of claims on public resources is not easy to establish. Given the scarcities in a poor economy, moreover, the competitive energies of many individuals and groups seeking economic improvements tend to get focused on the state. Thus, competition over the state's resources often results in intense conflict, contributing to problems of democratic consolidation.

## Policy issues

A second set of critical issues that require attention in understanding governance concerns the economic policies being pursued by many new democracies. This issue is critical, not only because of the impact of economic decisions on politics but also because this is one area where there is some room for choice.

Many new democracies in the developing world have been pushed to implement economic liberalization. Note the logic of change: regime change brought new élite groups to power; the interests and ideology of these élite groups led them into various degrees of cooperation (collusion?) with external centres of power; and the new internationalized locus of state power, involving national and international decision makers, pressed for economic liberalization. In this sequence of change, free-market capitalism is no longer an economic system that emerges spontaneously and influences society and politics; it is, instead, a political goal, an end-point of an ideology that the newly elected élite are supposed to impose on their societies. It must be underlined that the logic of a state élite imposing their ideological vision on the society (especially if there is social resistance) is rather antidemocratic, with predictable consequences for the legitimacy of such regimes. As a process, it has more in common with states creating socialism than with democracy and capitalism evolving as aspects of a new social order.

The economic liberalization programmes, despite varying considerably across countries, have tended to involve both macroeconomic stabilization and promotion of competitiveness via microeconomic reform, or structural adjustment. Stabilization measures are expected to have a relatively immediate impact on the economy, whereas improvements in efficiency are expected to take somewhat longer. Whatever the medium-term consequences, short-term impact makes most members of a society worse off. One leading scholar of these issues documents why this should be so:

... stabilization and, in particular, structural reforms, necessarily cause a temporary decline of consumption. To be sustained, stabilization must entail a transitional reduction of demand, due to a combination of reduced public spending, increased taxation and high interest rates. Trade liberalization, anti-monopoly measures, reductions of subsidies to industries and prices inevitably cause temporary unemployment of capital and labor. Privatization implies reorganization: again a costly transition. Moreover, market-oriented reforms are often undertaken when the effects of the original shock are still present and while some important markets are still missing. Finally, architects of reforms make mistakes, and mistakes are costly. Hence, the effect of economic reforms on growth must be negative in the short run. (Przeworski 1992)

If stabilization tends to be recessionary, expectations of societies flush with democratic victories run in nearly the opposite direction: most citizens expect the new era to deliver material improvements. Until (and unless) robust economic growth resumes, the gap between expectations and the reform-induced reality is likely to exacerbate the problems of managing fragile new democracies.

The most common "resolution" of the conundrum unleashed by simultaneous democratization and economic liberalization is a rather disturbing tendency to move towards two-track polities (i.e. polities with a democratic and a not-so-democratic track). More specifically, many new democracies are likely to want to restrict democratic practices to the political arena, with periodic elections bestowing legitimacy upon new rulers. After that, however, once in power, these rulers want government decision-making to be as free of political pressures – especially from the popular sectors – as possible. This decision-making autonomy is deemed essential for pursuing the not-so-popular economic reform programmes. If institutionalized, this two-track polity – democracy in politics but not in government – would offer the best chance of "reconciling" the contradictory goals of democracy and strong executives capable of sustaining "economic rationality."

What are the prospects that such two-track political arrangements will find a firm foothold in post-transition countries? On the basis of logic, one would have to say that attempts to move in this direction will definitely be made but that, at the same time, the prospects of institutionalization are not good. There is always some gap between what citizens vote for and what elected governments do; however, this gap can not be simultaneously large, permanent, and stable. Well-established Western democracies manage to maintain popular support for the not-so-popular, pro-efficiency, economic policies during some phases, especially when coalitions that champion efficiency over redistribution are in power. However, this phase is tolerated because there exists in society the hope – and the reality – that, sooner or later, a more distributive coalition will come back to power. Without institutional memory that generates such expectations, and without any institutions in place that would build up hopes of future shifts in a state's priorities, continuing demand for sacrifices in new developing-country democracies is not a recipe for democratic consolidation.

Nevertheless, given the limited options, many new democracies will attempt to create two-track arrangements. Several political implications follow. If a two-track polity is to function, economic policy will come to be made more and more behind closed doors, as exercises in technical efficiency devoid of social content. Social groups, unions, parties, parliaments, and maybe even ministers will be kept out of the inner policy-making circle. Will they all accept this exclusion? Maybe for a while, and mainly in the name of efficiency, pragmatism, external pressures, and the need to correct mistakes of the past.

Severe tests of two-track arrangements will come whenever elections approach. Elections will be the critical moment when the not-so-democratic state must account for itself in the more democratic political arena. This will not be easy; rapid turnover in incumbents is likely. Incumbents, with their newly acquired "pragmatism," will prefer to keep economic policy issues (especially redistributive issues) off the electoral agenda. Depending on whether the opposition obliges or not, one of two outcomes is possible, neither of which is highly desirable: if the opposition chooses to champion distributive issues, incumbents will also feel the pressure to join in, with competitive populism as the most likely outcome; conversely if, owing to its own understanding of "constraints," the opposition cooperates with the incumbents to keep distributive claims off the political agenda (implicitly, of course), attention may shift to non-economic appeals as mobilizational tools. Religion, ethnicity, and other forms of sub-national tensions provide prime candidates. As is widely recognized, these can prove to be as destabilizing as, (or more destabilizing than) class issues. Corruption and personality issues, by contrast, provide safer political subjects. It is quite likely, therefore, that many an election will be waged mainly around such "safe" issues. However, corruption and personality issues, although they may raise some short-term passions, do not generate mandates to demand sacrifices from society.

In sum, it will not be easy to create and reproduce two-track polities that are both stable and efficacious. Meanwhile, it is important to recognize the attempts to create such polities – often implicitly, rather than explicitly – as an important new political trend. In one form or another, these efforts are under way in many developing countries (O'Donnell 1994). The underlying logic is comprehensible: the driving force is the need to "resolve" a political impasse. To repeat, democratization has created expectations that cannot be easily satisfied without sustained economic growth and some redistribution. Many economic doctors suggest that this is not possible without a "lean and mean" interregnum. An impasse of sorts is thus created because citizens are suspicious of whether "leanness and meanness" will be evenly distributed or whether prosperity will indeed follow the "lean and mean" phase.

The existence of a near-impasse in many new democracies suggests two final conclusions. First, contrary to the neo-liberal orthodoxy, forces of democracy and of market-oriented reforms are in considerable tension in the contemporary developing world; vigorous pursuit of economic reforms in these cases will succeed – if it succeeds – only at the expense of the popular forces unleashed by democratic movements. Second, a number of political pathologies in the new democracies result from the contradiction between expansive expectations, on the one hand, and the contractionary consequences of economic reforms, on the other hand. Especially noteworthy are the pressures to reduce democracies to two-track semi-democracies, with democracy in politics but not in government. Hence, the recurring irony of democratization: those who demand democratic changes expect further spread of power in society, whereas the managers of new democracies aim to "stabilize" the system, often by limiting the scope of democracy. These trends now threaten a central

goal motivating the democratic revolution of the 1980s – further redistribution of power in society.

In sum, countries that discarded authoritarianism in the 1980s or 1990s
face numerous obstacles on their way to consolidating a new political
system. There are such short-term problems as implementing economic
reforms; the choice of reform strategy will continue to be of considerable
significance for consolidation efforts. Short- to medium-term problems –
especially those concerning the political consequences of democracy
under developing-world conditions of weak political institutions, divided
societies, and heavy state intervention – are also quite significant. As
leadership is always an additional variable in evolution of democracies,
some countries will clearly deal with these problems better than others.
Overall, however, consolidation of many new democracies will remain a
path full of hurdles. A few will certainly fall and may even revert back to
authoritarianism of one sort or another; more likely, many will continue
to struggle – stumbling, regaining balance, but only to hit yet another
obstacle, muddling through at fairly low levels of political performance.

## Democracy, economic growth, and equity

The final major question that needs to be addressed concerns less the
short-term prospects of democratic consolidation than (assuming democracy) the medium-term issue of effectiveness of new developing-country
democracies in facilitating economic growth and equity. One way to begin
to address this complex and futuristic question is to ask what we do (or
do not) know about the record of democracies in general and of democracies in developing countries in particular, as agents of economic growth
and distribution. The unfortunate fact is that we do not know very much.

Cross-national evidence on the impact of democracy on economic
growth, and of democracy on equity, is highly inconclusive. On the
growth issue, for example, several studies have found a positive relationship, whereas others argue a negative relationship, and still others con-
tend that there is no relationship. Studies on the impact of democracy on
distributional issues also discover a range of possible outcomes. It is not
surprising, therefore, that there are few established relationships between
democracy, on the one hand, and economic growth and the pattern of
income distribution, on the other.

Where does that leave scholars and analysts who still need to worry
about policy issues, based presumably on some means–ends knowledge
of the real world? The first thing to note is that, just because cross-
national quantitative studies fail to capture a relationship, does not nec-

essarily mean that the relationship does not exist in the real world; it may mean instead that the relationship is difficult to capture by such studies. There are enormous difficulties, for example, in measuring democracy as a variable and then in systematically relating it, through a long and complex chain of causation, to such outcomes as economic growth – the dynamics of which are not well understood, even by economists.

Whereas all democracies may share some political traits that are economically consequential, non-democracies do not. The latter – authoritarianism – is a residual category that includes highly diverse political forms. For example, communist regimes, personalistic dictators such as Mobutu of Zaire, bureaucratic–authoritarian rulers such as the Brazilian junta in the 1970s and Park Chung Hee of South Korea, and monarchies such as those in Saudi Arabia are all authoritarians. The only thing that such diverse regimes share is that they are not democracies. This is consequential, both from the standpoint of liberal values and (in so far as labelling them all non-democracies captures real political differences on some such dimensions) as freedom of expression and association, the right to vote and elect one's own leaders, and, often, protection of human rights. However, the economic impact of diverse types of authoritarian rules is highly variable: if the scholarly attempt is to relate regime types to economic outcomes, Mobutu's Zaire, the Saudi monarchy, Maoist China, and Park Chung Hee's Korea have very little in common; in this context, there is no intellectual justification for treating them as one type of polity. Any attempt to create a single measurement of democracy to authoritarianism, therefore, that can be used to relate governmental types systematically to economic outcomes is bound to remain problematic.

Similarly, economic outcomes are the product of a host of factors. Take economic growth, for example. One sensible review of theories of economic growth has suggested that, among the proximate variables that influence growth, six are especially significant: these are rates of investment, infrastructure, quality of human capital, level of research and production of knowledge, quality of organization and management, and balance of intersectoral investments (especially agriculture versus industry) (Stern 1991). It is even difficult to assign relative weights to these proximate determinants of growth. Now imagine trying to determine systematically whether democracies or non-democracies are better at facilitating these intermediate conditions (the proximate determinants) that, in turn, influence economic growth. It is no wonder that cross-national, quantitative studies, attempting to relate democracy systematically to growth, remain highly inconclusive.

The real issue, then, is whether any limited and modest claims can be made about the impact of democracy on growth and equity and, if so, what the implications of such claims may be for developing-country democracies. One way to proceed intellectually is by the process of exclusion (i.e. by excluding the economic outcomes with which democracies are not likely to be compatible). On the growth issue, for example, the cases of very high growth rates (say, 8–9 per cent per annum or more for more than a decade) are generally rare and, in the twentieth century, would include the Stalinist Soviet Union, pre-War Japan, South Korea, Taiwan, Brazil under the military Junta, and contemporary China. Although it would be difficult to generalize about the underlying political and economic links in these diverse cases – and that is why it is difficult to treat authoritarian regimes as a single category – one thing is evident: none of these cases of very high growth were democracies. Why should this be so? It appears that extremely rapid social change either requires considerable controlled mobilization of all societal resources from above or unleashes forces that need to be contained by tightly controlled regimes – or probably both. Whatever the reasons, one conclusion that is worth entertaining seriously is that democracies and very high growth rates of the type suggested above are not likely to go together.

There are also some reasons to believe that stable democracy and very low rates of economic growth (say, below 2 per cent per annum for over a decade) are not readily compatible. The causal arrows here go in both directions. To the extent that low growth performance results from poor political leadership and corrupt and predatory states, one presumes that democracy provides some check on how long poorly performing leaders can stay in power. However, low economic growth can obviously be a result of numerous other factors besides poor leadership and policies. In that case, sustained low growth rates may create sufficient discontent to threaten any type of political regime, but especially a democracy. One does not want to overstate the case for this relationship because, once again, survivability of a democracy is a function of more than economic performance. Nevertheless, sustained low growth can create problems for many democracies, especially developing-country democracies. Take, for example, the case of India: democracy has clearly survived in India, in spite of low rates of economic growth (although the overall growth rates have not been all that low; they have averaged between 4 and 5 per cent per annum). What is notable about India, however, is that every time the monsoons fail in that country and agricultural production (and thus the overall growth rate) declines, resulting inflation becomes a source of such political troubles as demonstrations, riots, and the declining popularity of incumbents. Even in a relatively institutionalized developing-country democracy such as India, therefore, low growth rates are a ready source of political turbulence.

In sum, it appears that the marriage of democracy with extremes of growth performance is not very comfortable. Of the two extremes, the incompatibility of democracy with very high growth rates is a relatively strong relationship. By contrast, well-institutionalized democracies can muddle through, in spite of low growth rates; even they, however, become strained when the performance is too low or when the low performance is sustained for too long. A reasonable proposition thus emerges: on the issue of economic growth, stable developing-country democracies are likely to fall in the "middle" range (i.e. growth rates in most of them are likely to be in the range of 3–7 per cent per annum). This is roughly borne out by the examples of stable developing-country democracies (i.e. where the democratic experiment lasted for at least a decade) listed in table 2.1.

Table 2.1 Annual GDP growth in major developing countries with at least 10 years of democracy[a]

| Country (years of democracy)[b] | "Democratic Years"[c] | Average annual GDP growth (%) |
|---|---|---|
| Argentina (1983–present)[e] | 1983–1998 (16)[d] | 3.0 |
| Bangladesh (1991–present) | 1991–1998 (8) | 4.7 |
| Brazil (1945–1964, 1985–present) | 1961–1964 (4) | 5.0 |
| | 1985–1998 (14) | 2.5 |
| Chile (1989–present) | 1989–1998 (10) | 7.6 |
| Colombia (1957–present) | 1961–1998 (38) | 4.5 |
| India (1947–present) | 1961–1998 (38) | 4.6 |
| Republic of Korea (1987–present) | 1987–1998 (12) | 6.8 |
| Malaysia (1963–present) | 1963–1998 (36) | 6.7 |
| Nepal (1991–present) | 1991–1998 (8) | 4.8 |
| Peru (1980–present) | 1980–1998 (19) | 2.0 |
| Philippines (1961–1972, 1986–present) | 1961–1972 (12) | 5.0 |
| | 1986–1998 (13) | 3.2 |
| Sri Lanka (1948–present) | 1961–1998 (38) | 4.6 |
| Turkey (1950–1960, 1961–1971, 1973–present) | 1973–1998 (16) | 4.5 |
| Venezuela (1959–present) | 1961–1998 (38) | 3.0 |

a. Includes "major" countries only, with population of more than 10 million.
b. Coding of years of democracy drawn from: *The World Almanac and Book of Facts* (Mahwah, New Jersey: World Almanac Books, 2001); and *Political Handbook of the World* (Binghamton, New York: CSA Publications, 1999).
c. Indicates years of democracy for which World Bank GDP growth data are readily available.
d. Values in parentheses are no. of years.
e. Note that "present" generally refers to the late 1990s.
GDP Data Source: World Bank, *World Development Indicators* (1961–1998)
This table was prepared by Jason Brownlee, a graduate student at Princeton University.

A somewhat similar case for "middling" performance can be made for democracies on the equity front. Once again, at one extreme, we know that democracies are not likely to undertake radical property redistribution. Contemporary democracies exist mainly in private-property economies and protection of such property is written into their constitutions; failure to protect private property as a matter of fact is likely to lead to a failure of democracy itself. These strictures put limits on how much equity can be achieved within a democracy. Some land redistribution (but often with compensation) and a variety of income transfers and social services can create more-or-less egalitarian democracies – but within a "middling" range. The type of extreme equality that comes from radical property redistribution has been implemented mainly by communist regimes or in some such exceptional communist-threatened cases as South Korea and Taiwan under American military occupation following the Second World War; democracy and radical equality are thus not a likely pair.

At the other extreme, democracies can clearly exist with considerable inequality. Worse, democracies can even sharpen inequalities in some cases when right-of-centre rulers rule by appeal to non-economic symbols (e.g. appeals to race, ethnicity, or nation), while all along tilting the political process in favour of the wealthy. Nevertheless, there are some reasons to believe that democracy and sharp inequalities are not readily compatible. First, we know that sharp and sustained inequalities create problems for stabilizing developing-country democracies. This does not imply that democratic rulers will necessarily undertake egalitarian measures in order to stabilize the political system; what it does suggest, instead, is that (as in the case of contemporary Brazil) sharp wealth and income inequalities will continue to be a source of political pressure on fledgling democracies. Reversing the causal arrows, the impact of sustained democracy on equality is more problematic. As noted above, there is no linear trend from democracy to democratization of power and on to socio-economic democracy. However, over time, if democratic politics leads to democratization of power (an outcome more likely in social democracies than in the laissez-faire type of capitalist democracies), then democracies may generate some pressures towards greater equalization. We know this to be the case in advanced industrial democracies; however, for most developing-country democracies these are issues of the future. The policy implication, however, is clear: improvements in equity may be compatible with democracy if, and only if, the design of new democracies consciously aims to strengthen social-democratic institutions such as social-democratic parties, peasant and labour associations, careful decentralization, and restructuring of the role of governments away from unnecessary intervention and towards those policy areas that directly influence the life-chances of the majority.

## Conclusions

Democracy as a form of government is ultimately valuable as an end in itself. Basic democratic freedoms are something that all those who are exposed to the modern world increasingly want. Democracy thus does not need to be justified as a facilitator of other values, such as stable government, economic growth, and equity. Nevertheless, to the extent possible, one wants to know the implications of a turn to democracy for these other values and, if possible, to undertake actions that will enhance their compatibility. Our discussion of these issues leads to a mixed picture: if new democracies can be stabilized, there is no inherent reason that they are not compatible with moderate rates of economic growth. On the equity front, the picture is more complex: new democracies will have to be consciously tilted towards social democracies to make progress on this dimension. The short-term problem, however, is of a different order: most new democracies are likely to remain turbulent. Although many of the underlying reasons are structural, it is also the case that the political problems are worsened by sharp attempts at economic "liberalization" and the associated short-term economic contraction and growing maldistribution of economic opportunities that has come to characterize these "liberalizing" democracies. If sustained democracy is a valuable goal, this is one area of international policy choice wherein there is some room for manoeuvre. In conclusion, therefore, the goal of just growth (that is, of reconciling democracy, sustained economic growth, and some redistribution) is internally not inconsistent, on the one hand; however, on the other hand, it will require deliberate national and international effort towards creating social democracies – an effort that would be a departure from the "Washington Consensus" of the recent years.

## Note

1. For example, see O'Donnell and Schmitter (1986); Huntington (1991), and Haggard and Kaufman (1995).

## REFERENCES

Bratton, Michael and Nicolas van de Walle. 1997. *Democratic Experiments in Africa: Regime Transitions in Comparative Perspective.* Cambridge: Cambridge University Press.
Cumings, Bruce. 1981. *The Origins of the Korean War: Liberation and the Emergence of Separate Regimes, 1945–1947.* New Jersey: Princeton University Press.

Diamond, Larry. 1988. *Class Ethnicity and Democracy in Nigeria: The Failure of the First Republic*. Syracuse: Syracuse University Press.

Forrest, Tom. 1995. *Political and Economic Development in Nigeria*. Boulder: Westview Press, updated edition.

Haggard, Stephan and Robert Kaufman. 1995. *The Political Economy of Democratic Transitions*. New Jersey: Princeton University Press.

Huntington, Samuel H. 1968. *Political Order in Changing Societies*. New Haven: Yale University Press.

Huntington, Samuel H. 1991. *Third Wave: Democratization in the Late-Twentieth Century*. Oklahoma: University of Oklahoma Press.

Joseph, Richard. 1987. *Democracy and Prebendal Politics in Nigeria*. Cambridge: Cambridge University Press.

O'Donnell, Guillermo. 1994. "Delegative Democracy." *Journal of Democracy*.

O'Donnell, Guillermo and Phillipe C. Schmitter, eds. 1986. *Transitions from Authoritarian Rule, Vols. 1–4*. Baltimore, MD: Johns Hopkins University Press.

Przeworski, Adam. 1992. "Ideology Theory and Reality: A note of caution about Neo-Liberal policies" (mimeo). Paper presented at conference on "Capitalism, Socialism, and Democracy," organized by the *Journal of Democracy*, Washington DC, on 13 April 1992.

Skidmore, Thomas. 1967. *Politics in Brazil, 1930–1964: An Experiment in Democracy*. Oxford: Oxford University Press.

Stephan, Alfred, ed. 1989. *Democratizing Brazil: Problems of Transition and Consolidation*. Oxford: Oxford University Press.

Stern, Nicholas. 1991. "The Determinants of Growth." *Economic Journal* January.

# 3

# Meeting the challenge of poverty and inequality

*Mick Moore and Howard White*

## Introduction: Discourses on poverty and inequality

There is little that genuinely is new in moral, philosophical, conceptual, and political debates about poverty and inequality. These debates have long been intense because they are central to alternative conceptualizations of the actual or proper constitution of society. For example, Slack argues that, in sixteenth- and seventeenth-century England, there were three distinct understandings of how the poor, as a social category, were related to the rich:

In the first place, the poor could be seen as objects of charity: targets for the pity, sympathy, generosity and sometimes admiration of their betters. Secondly, they might appear as a threat: they must be excluded from sympathy and aid, if not eliminated altogether, in order to preserve public order, public morality, and public health. Thirdly, they might be viewed as a potentially productive resource: needing only the proper training in labour to yield profits for the general good. (Slack 1988: 17)

Add to the first point the notion of the poor as objects of state as well as private welfarism, and this list encapsulates neatly the contradictory attitudes to poverty of Britain's New Labour Party. It also has powerful echoes in policy and discourse in many countries. Similarly, there is a great deal of continuity in the core debates on the nature and causes of poverty. Much the same questions were asked in the seventeenth century as today. How far is poverty purely a material phenomenon? What else is implied in the term? Is material assistance the best or only way of alleviating the problem? Or should one begin somewhere else entirely? It is difficult to see much that is intrinsically new in today's debates, even in some of the most useful new jargon, such as Amartya Sen's concept of "capabilities" (Sen 1999).

Although far from original, the discourse on poverty in contemporary international development differs from that in, say, nineteenth-century Europe, in two senses: first, it is suffused with a concern for numbers; second, it is remarkably devoid of explicit moralistic content;[1] notions of "undeserving poor" are almost unheard. Part of the reason is that, in the development arena, the term "poverty" has two different referents: (a) as a condition that affects virtually the entire population of the poor or developing countries ("poor countries"); or (b) as an affliction visited only on a particular segment of each national population. It is because of this ambiguity that the development business spawns terms such as "the poorest of the poor" and "the extreme poor" to focus more precisely on the latter category. This difference in the underlying concept of poverty intersects with contrasting approaches to public policy. The national (macro) conception of poverty implies a policy emphasis on boosting overall economic growth in poor countries, with little regard for distributional issues and their political implications. Conversely, the (micro) "poorest of the poor" conception of poverty implies more focused public interventions.

Attitudes toward inequality have been rather more ambivalent. Although there have always been strains of both political economy and political philosophy concerned with inequality, the periods in which promoting equity has been a central policy concern have been relatively few and far between. In the development arena, the 1970s were one such period. There was concern over the possible existence of a generic "Kuznets inverted-U curve" (Kuznets 1963): in poor countries, income inequality would initially increase as a result of economic growth, and be reversed only after a certain threshold level of national income was reached. Following empirical analysis by Ahluwalia (1976), the existence of such an inverted-U became an accepted, stylized, fact of development; it was used by the World Bank to project likely future income shares. However, critics in the 1990s (notably Anand and Kanbur 1993 and Deininger and Squire 1996) demolished the notion of the Kuznets curve to their own satisfaction and to that of the international community who wished to focus on poverty rather than inequality. The intellectual paradigm may be shifting even further, towards the idea that there is an intrinsic and positive connection between income equality and economic growth. The *World Development Report 2000/1* accepts the argument that there is no systematic relationship from growth to distribution – but it argues that better income distribution is good for economic growth; hence, redistribution reduces poverty both by redirecting resources to the poor and by promoting growth. However, this apparently powerful argument has not fed through to the policy arena (see below).

Our own views on these debates, and the argument of this chapter, can be summarized under four points:

- Any realistic concept of poverty, which addresses the actual causes of deprivation and ill-being, is relatively broad. It encompasses more than measures of household or individual consumption or purchasing power and takes into account concerns such as freedom from famine and undernutrition, and access to basic health services and education.
- The evidence available on the linkages between poverty, inequality, and economic growth supports the "synergistic" case: the argument that, in poor countries with high levels of inequality, a policy emphasis on reducing poverty and inequality is very unlikely to reduce rates of economic growth, and may enhance them.
- Governments and other public authorities necessarily play a substantial role in poverty reduction.
- There is, however, a major question about the role that public authorities should play. This issue is, in current development jargon, debated in terms of the nature of the linkage between governance and poverty reduction. A range of ideas, including "democracy," "empowerment," and "participation," have been very much in vogue. There are, however, a range of questions about whether these ideas help to generate effective interventions. We suggest that effective poverty-reducing governance lies principally in attention to the "basics": in the creation and preservation of states that can (a) themselves deliver basic services and (b) have sufficient stability and coherence to encourage the creation of political parties and movements that embody and advance the interests of the poor, and hence a domestic political basis for redistributive policies.

In the course of making these arguments, we have quite a lot to say about facts and trends in poverty. We concentrate to some degree on sub-Saharan Africa. On current trends, sub-Saharan Africa exemplifies the worst regional case scenario – low rates of economic growth, a very high degree of income inequality, fast rates of population growth, weak provision of basic antipoverty services by national governments, and a dearth of political forces embodying antipoverty concerns.

We begin by looking at the debate, sketched out above, between those who advocate prime concentration on economic growth as a solution to poverty, with little or no direct attention to poverty reduction, and those sympathetic to a more interventionist or targeted approach. In the section on pages 67–70 we summarize the evidence that the "going-for-growth" strategy may, in some circumstances, make it difficult to redistribute resources and achieve social goals at a later stage. In the section on pages 70–72 we illustrate how, in some parts of the world, it will be very difficult to achieve the high rates of economic growth needed to reduce the number of people in poverty unless the process of economic growth is (or is made to be) pro-poor and additional measures are taken to tackle the non-income dimensions of poverty. Africa is presented as an "extreme case" in the section on pages 72–76. That on pages 76–81 deals with recent changes in perceptions of poverty reduction in the international development community: contrary to the situation only a few years ago, a neo-liberal focus on "pro-poor" economic growth as the prime solution to poverty has been replaced by a more activist attitude – a view that almost everything and anything that could be done to reduce poverty should be tried. However, such sentiments stop short of endorsing meaningful redistributive policies. Within the World Bank, this more activist orientation extends to a new emphasis on organizations of the poor as a key component of the solution to poverty. We question whether this is a viable or honest position for international agencies and consider three important issues linking governance with poverty reduction: these are the role of democracy (pp. 82–87); representing the voice of the poor in politics through participatory exercises (pp. 87–89); and accountable states (pp. 89–90). Our conclusions follow (pp. 90–91).

## Go all out for growth?

A strong statement of the pro-growth position comes from Martin Ravallion: "arguably the biggest problem facing the world's poor today is not 'low-quality growth' ... but too little growth of even quite normal quality" (Ravallion 1997: 637). He argues that UNDP, through its *Human Development Reports*, focuses on the residuals at the expense of the relationship that explains most of the improvement in social indicators – increases in income per capita. What this means is explained in figure 3.1, which depicts a stylized version of the relationship between human development and income. The graph shows the estimated regression line between a measure of social welfare, such as the Human Development Index (HDI), and income per capita.[2] The *Human Development Reports* focus on comparisons between countries such as A and B. Given their average income levels, country A performs worse than expected in terms of human development indicators (of longevity, education, and literacy), and country B better than expected; hence there should be some set of

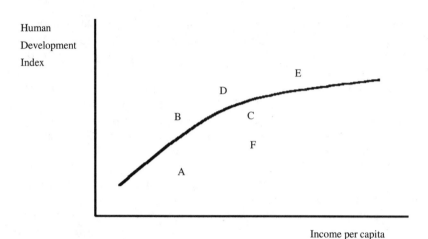

Figure 3.1  Relationship between income and human development

policies that would allow country A to move to the position of country B. This is the focus on the residual: how countries deviate from the expected (fitted) value from the regression. Ravallion argues that the emphasis should, instead, be on the expected (i.e. average) value. If country A were to invest in growth, then it could move to position C and thus enjoy the same level of human development as if it had invested in human development, despite still having lower human development scores than one would predict on the basis of income levels. Ravallion argues that (a) economic growth improves human development, both because it reduces poverty (i.e. increases private expenditures) and as it raises social spending; and (b) policies that attempt merely to promote human development may do so at the expense of economic growth.

Ranis, Stewart, and Ramirez (2000) argue that there are links both from growth to human development and the other way round. This fact would seem to support the case for balanced development to encourage a virtuous circle. They find that the links can be strengthened by policy intervention; to the extent that a country emphasizes either growth or human development, they suggest that it should be the latter. This case is based on the analysis summarized in figure 3.2, which plots the change in human development against economic growth, dividing the figure into four quadrants by mean values for each variable.[3] The top right quadrant is the virtuous circle of high human development and high growth and the bottom left quadrant represents a vicious circle. The off-diagonal quadrants are lopsided to either economic growth (EG) or human development (HD). Ranis and colleagues plotted the position of 67 countries

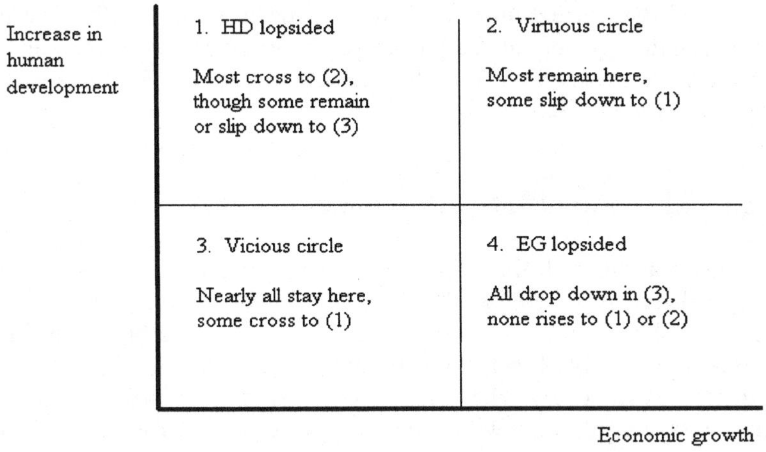

| Increase in human development | 1. HD lopsided<br><br>Most cross to (2), though some remain or slip down to (3) | 2. Virtuous circle<br><br>Most remain here, some slip down to (1) |
|---|---|---|
| | 3. Vicious circle<br><br>Nearly all stay here, some cross to (1) | 4. EG lopsided<br><br>All drop down in (3), none rises to (1) or (2) |

Economic growth

Figure 3.2 Virtuous and vicious circles in economic growth (EG) and human development (HD)

in this figure using average values for three periods (the 1960s, the 1970s, and 1980–1992). The main findings are that, once they reached one of the "circle" quadrants (whether virtuous or vicious), many countries stayed there, whereas the other two (lopsided) quadrants tended to be temporary addresses. However, whereas some countries shifted from the HD lopsided quadrant (i.e. an "excess" of human development in relation to income) to the virtuous circle, no country shifted from the EG lopsided quadrant to the virtuous circle. Further, no country moved from the virtuous circle into the EG lopsided quadrant, and countries in the EG lopsided quadrant *all* fell back into the vicious circle.[4]

This argument can be translated back to figure 3.1: a country starting from point A that invests in human development is not likely to move just to point B: it is likely also to move right, possibly reaching a point such as D and thence onto E. Again, a country investing in growth alone may not reach C at all but may reach a point such as F and then stay there – or, at best, move only sluggishly to the right from that point.

Economic growth is, indeed, necessary for poverty reduction: the regression line does, indeed, slope upward. However, going for growth alone is not enough: a sizeable empirical literature verifies the link from human development (investing in human capital) to economic growth. For example, no country has sustained high growth rates over any substantial period of time with literacy rates at the levels observed in most African countries today. Economic growth itself is likely to be both more rapid and more robust (as will be gains in human development) if policies are pursued to ensure a more equitable distribution of benefits. We turn to consider in more detail the nature of the growth–poverty linkage. In particular, we stress the role that redistribution plays in translating growth into poverty reduction.

## When will economic growth reduce poverty?

No one can argue with the principle of pro-poor growth; the problem is how to achieve it in reality. The 1990 *World Development Report* proposed the related concept of broad-based growth as the first plank of its poverty-reduction platform. Unfortunately, the meaning of broad-based growth has never been defined: it is most usually equated with labour-intensive growth but also with the spread of growth across geographical regions, productive sectors, and income quintiles. In recent years, the expression "broad-based growth" has been replaced with that of "pro-poor growth" – this is also undefined, though economists could probably at least agree on what should be the set of rival definitions (White and Anderson 2000). The modest evolution in terminology has not been accompanied by any advance in creating an agenda around policies to achieve such growth. No set of policy instruments is being advocated by the international community to promote pro-poor growth that can be distinguished from the existing set of policies for growth *per se*; moreover, the record of experience is at least as much that of anti-poor growth as pro-poor.

In the typical situation of many poor countries – where incomes are very unequally distributed, populations are growing rapidly, and the pattern of economic growth is, at best, distributionally neutral – quite substantial rates of economic growth are required if the absolute number of people living below a given poverty line is to fall. The link between income, poverty, and economic growth is captured in the poverty elasticity ($\varepsilon$), which measures the impact of GDP growth on a poverty measure, most usually the poverty headcount. With distributionally neutral growth (i.e. growth that leaves income distribution unchanged), then the rate of economic growth ($g$) required to reduce the absolute number of poor is given by:

$$g = (1 - 1/\varepsilon)p$$

where $p$ is population growth. Table 3.1 thus shows, for a given poverty elasticity and rate of population growth, the annual rate of economic growth required to reduce the absolute number of poor people.

Hanmer and Naschold (2000) report that the poverty elasticity for

Table 3.1 Annual rate of economic growth required to reduce the number of poor (assuming distribution-neutral growth)

| Poverty elasticity | Rate of population growth | | | |
|---|---|---|---|---|
| | 1.5 | 2.0 | 2.5 | 3.0 |
| −0.5 | 4.5 | 6.0 | 7.5 | 9.0 |
| −1.0 | 3.0 | 4.0 | 5.0 | 6.0 |
| −1.5 | 2.5 | 3.3 | 4.2 | 5.0 |
| −2.0 | 2.3 | 3.0 | 3.8 | 4.5 |

countries with a low level of income inequality (defined as a Gini coefficient of less than 0.43) has a value of −0.93, whereas for countries with high inequality it is −0.34. In other words, economies with high rates of income inequality and typical rates of population growth of about 2.5 per cent per year would have to grow at close to 7 per cent per annum to begin to reduce the numbers of people below the poverty line.

Incomes are distributed far more equally in Asia than in Latin America and Africa. The Gini coefficient of income inequality ranges between 0.31 and 0.38 in the various regions of Asia; in Latin America and sub-Saharan Africa it is close to 0.50. Inequality is perhaps greater in sub-Saharan Africa than in any other region of the world, and appears to have increased from the 1980s to the 1990s. The figure of 47 given for sub-Saharan Africa in table 3.2 is almost certainly an underestimate. The figures in the table are based on a mixture of data series relating to income and expenditure or consumption. The distribution of expenditure or consumption in any population is less unequal than the distribution of income: the poor save less. The figures for sub-Saharan Africa are, to an unusual degree, based on expenditure and consumption surveys; to make the figures more comparable, it is advised to add about 0.05 to the African figures. Because of these very high levels of inequality, poverty elas-

Table 3.2 Inequality (Gini coefficient) by region, 1960s–1990s

| Region | 1960s | 1970s | 1980s | 1990s |
|---|---|---|---|---|
| Latin America and the Caribbean | 53 | 49 | 50 | 49 |
| Sub-Saharan Africa | 50 | 48 | 44 | 47 |
| Middle East and North Africa | 41 | 42 | 41 | 38 |
| East Africa and the Pacific | 37 | 40 | 39 | 38 |
| South Asia | 36 | 34 | 35 | 31 |
| High-income countries | 35 | 35 | 33 | 34 |
| Eastern Europe | 25 | 25 | 25 | 29 |

Source: Deininger and Squire 1996: 565.

ticities in sub-Saharan Africa tend to be low.[5] Given population growth rates of around 3 per cent, GDP growth of 6–9 per cent is required to reduce the number of African poor. This figure far exceeds the achievements of all but a small number of countries, and the problem is exacerbated by the fact that income distribution is actually worsening in many African countries; even a 9 per cent rate of economic growth may not be enough. If poverty is to be reduced, not only must economic growth be more pro-poor but also governments must intervene more directly.

Some simple arithmetic illustrates this argument. It is, of course, the income of the poor that must increase to reduce poverty; what happens to the income of the non-poor does not matter directly. The income of the poor ($Y_P$) can be written as the product of their share in total income ($\phi$) and total income ($Y$). From this it follows that

$$\hat{Y}_P = \hat{\phi} + \hat{Y}$$

where the circumflex ($\hat{\ }$) denotes percentage change.

Suppose that total income is growing at 4 per cent per year. To achieve the desired growth rate in the income of the poor of 8 per cent, then their income share must also increase by 4 per cent. The income share of the bottom 20 per cent is typically around 6 per cent. An increased share of 4 per cent takes this figure to 6.24 per cent. That is, a redistribution of just 0.24 per cent – less than one-quarter of 1 per cent – of national income will double income growth amongst the poor from 4 to 8 per cent. A little redistribution goes a long way to reducing poverty.

Finally, it is self-evident that distributionally neutral growth will reduce absolute poverty; however, it is equally self-evident that it will do nothing to reduce relative poverty. If the poor are identified as the bottom 20 or 40 per cent of the income distribution, then they will always be there in the absence of perfect equality. Less trivially, if the poverty line is defined (as it commonly is) as a percentage (say two-thirds) of mean income, then the percentage of people living in poverty is unaffected by distributionally neutral growth. Whereas the international community may be concerned with absolute poverty, relative poverty is equally likely to be a policy concern. Tackling relative poverty necessarily requires redistributive policies.

## Sub-Saharan Africa: The extreme case

We pay particular attention here to sub-Saharan Africa because it is emerging as the most problematic region of the world from the perspective of issues of poverty and inequality. Economic growth has been low (or even negative) for a long time in many countries. Current forecasts are for a very slow rate of increase in average per capita incomes.over the coming decade. Contrary to common perceptions, income inequality may be higher in sub-Saharan Africa than in any other region of the world (above). Moreover, there is some evidence that income inequality is worsening in a continent where the conventional explanations of increasing inequality – economic globalization or the collapse of central planning systems – would not seem very applicable. Sub-Saharan Africa has not participated heavily in recent processes of economic globalization; indeed, the region is increasingly marginalized from the global economy. Its share of international private capital flows has fallen from around 20 per cent in the early 1970s to just 3 per cent by the later 1990s, and its share of world exports from 5 per cent in the 1950s to less than 2 per cent in the 1990s.

On top of all this, African states are underperforming in antipoverty activities. African political-economic systems convert economic resources into welfare for their populations less efficiently than do, for example, the south Asian states that suffer from similarly low average income levels: although the proportion of the population of sub-Saharan Africa who are below the $1 per day poverty line is a little greater in sub-Saharan Africa than in South Asia (table 3.3), the incidence of infant and overall undernourishment is much higher in sub-Saharan Africa (table 3.4, fig. 3.3). The greater degree of income inequality in sub-Saharan Africa may explain part of this difference; however, a range of other data indicate that there is some more fundamental explanation. As shown in figure 3.1, in general, life expectancy and levels of education and literacy increase with income. We can learn a great deal by examining the residuals from this relationship on a cross-national basis – the extent to which life expectancy and levels of education and literacy in a country are higher or lower than one would predict on the basis of average per capita income. For sub-Saharan Africa they are consistently lower. This is demonstrated visually in figure 3.4 in relation to life expectancy. We have recently undertaken cross-national regression analysis that illustrates the same phenomena in relation to both life expectancy and measures of education and literacy (Moore, Leavy, and White, 1999). In that analysis, location in West Africa, to a greater extent than location in sub-Saharan Africa generally, was a powerful predictor of the failure of longevity and education/literacy measures to match up to the levels predicted on the basis of per capita incomes. On the other hand, the incidence of undernourishment in West Africa is low by African standards (table 3.4). Both of these factors may be explained, to some extent, by tropical environmental conditions which make the likelihood of food shortage less but that of disease high; child (rather than infant) mortality rates are particularly high in the region.

Table 3.3 Income poverty by region

| Year | East Asia and the Pacific | | Eastern Europe and Central Asia | Latin America and the Caribbean | Middle East and North Africa | South Asia | Sub-Saharan Africa | Total | Total, excluding China |
|---|---|---|---|---|---|---|---|---|---|
| | Total | Excluding China | | | | | | | |
| Millions of people | | | | | | | | | |
| 1987 | 415.1 | 109.2 | 1.1 | 63.7 | 25.0 | 474.4 | 217.2 | 1,196.5 | 890.6 |
| 1990 | 452.4 | 76.0 | 7.1 | 73.8 | 22.0 | 495.1 | 242.3 | 1,292.7 | 916.3 |
| 1993 | 431.9 | 66.0 | 18.3 | 70.8 | 21.5 | 505.1 | 273.3 | 1,320.9 | 955.0 |
| 1996 | 265.0 | 45.2 | 23.8 | 76.0 | 21.3 | 504.7 | 289.0 | 1,179.9 | 960.1 |
| 1998 | 278.3 | 55.6 | 24.0 | 78.2 | 20.9 | 522.0 | 290.9 | 1,214.2 | 991.5 |
| Headcount (percentage of population) | | | | | | | | | |
| 1987 | 26.6 | 22.9 | 0.2 | 15.3 | 11.5 | 44.9 | 46.6 | 28.7 | 29.6 |
| 1990 | 27.6 | 15.0 | 1.6 | 16.8 | 9.3 | 44.0 | 47.7 | 29.3 | 29.3 |
| 1993 | 25.2 | 12.4 | 4.0 | 15.3 | 8.4 | 42.4 | 49.6 | 28.5 | 28.5 |
| 1996 | 14.9 | 8.1 | 5.1 | 15.6 | 7.8 | 40.1 | 48.5 | 24.3 | 27.3 |
| 1998 | 15.3 | 9.6 | 5.1 | 15.6 | 7.3 | 40.0 | 46.3 | 24.3 | 27.3 |

Source: World Bank (www.worldbank.org/poverty)

Table 3.4 Prevalence of undernourishment in developing countries (percentage of population)

| Region/country | 1979/81 | 1990/92 | 1995/97 |
|---|---|---|---|
| Asia and Pacific | 32 | 21 | 17 |
| Oceania | 31 | 27 | 24 |
| South-East Asia | 27 | 17 | 13 |
| South Asia | 38 | 26 | 23 |
| Latin America and Caribbean | 13 | 13 | 11 |
| Caribbean | 19 | 25 | 31 |
| Central America | 20 | 17 | 17 |
| South America | 14 | 14 | 10 |
| Near East and North Africa | 9 | 8 | 9 |
| Near East | 10 | 10 | 12 |
| North Africa | 8 | 4 | 4 |
| Sub-Saharan Africa | 37 | 35 | 33 |
| Central Africa | 36 | 37 | 48 |
| East Africa | 35 | 45 | 42 |
| Southern Africa | 32 | 45 | 44 |
| West Africa | 40 | 21 | 16 |
| All developing countries | 29 | 20 | 18 |

Source: FAO 1999: table 1.

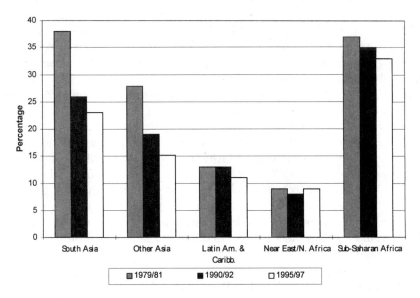

Figure 3.3 Proportion of children under 5 years of age who are undernourished (Source: FAO 1999)

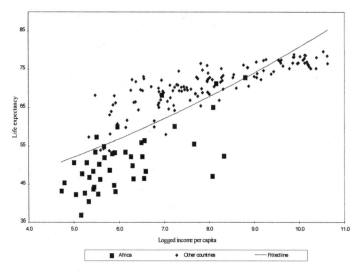

Figure 3.4 Social indicators improve with income – but Africa underperforms (scatter plot of life expectancy against income per capita) (Source: World Bank 1999)

Some indication of the underlying reasons for this poor performance, in relation to longevity at least, can be gleaned from recent statistics on immunization coverage (although these data are incomplete and not fully reliable). They indicate, first, that overall coverage is lower in sub-Saharan Africa than in other regions of the world: sub-Saharan Africa is the only region where coverage is typically below the 80 per cent level generally assumed necessary to prevent contagion for major diseases and therefore the outbreak of epidemics. In consequence, contagious diseases account for about 70 per cent of the burden of disease in Africa, compared with only 50 per cent in most other developing regions and only 25 per cent in China (White et al. 2001: 78). Second, in contrast to other regions, immunization coverage levels in sub-Saharan Africa have not increased during the 1990s, and may have fallen a little during that period. This kind of evidence reinforces our argument that the path to poverty reduction relies at least as much on public action as on private enterprise. This thinking is, of course, not new and, as we now document, the current orthodoxy has swung rapidly in the same direction.

## From neo-liberalism to international activism?

Until very recently, the orthodox position in international development policy institutions was the one we have critiqued above: that solutions to poverty lay mainly in markets and economic growth. This was one manifestation of the neo-liberal doctrine that appeared dominant at all levels. There was a Washington Consensus. Markets, price signals, and competition were the keywords. The state was to do less and concentrate on doing well the basics (which were very narrowly defined). Market-oriented economic growth would be "pro-poor," for it was state intervention and market distortions that both stifled economic growth and biased it in favour of the influential and well connected; inequality, by inference, was not a significant problem.[6]

Things have changed fast. There has, over recent years, been a reassertion of the importance of effective states and of state action in development policy generally. This is reflected especially in the 1997 *World Development Report*, in responses to the 1997/8 Asian crisis, and in calls for greater regulation of financial markets, environmental issues, and the activities of newly privatized enterprises. There is widespread agreement that the Washington Consensus has been replaced by the post-Washington Consensus – although there is little consensus as to the nature of this more recent "consensus."

In relation to poverty, the pace of change in dominant ideas has been especially fast. However, the change is more attitudinal than doctrinal: there has been no swing of the pendulum back to the ideological left; states are not again viewed as *the* solution; the neo-liberal emphases on markets and competition have not been rejected. It is laissez-faire – the attitude that a relaxed, hands-off style of managing public affairs produces the better outcomes – that has gone out of the window; it has been replaced by a high level of international public *activism* about poverty/inequality issues. These problems are imbued with a sense of urgency. The major aid donors have committed themselves to precise quantitative targets for reducing income-poverty, mortality, and HIV/AIDS, notably to halving the incidence of extreme poverty by the year 2015. They have followed up this commitment with a plethora of supporting activities. The neo-liberal emphasis on choosing the right means to tackle poverty has been replaced by an emphasis on mobilizing all available means. Governments, citizens, firms, markets, civil society, non-governmental organizations (NGOs), networks, coalitions – all have a role to play under the embracing concept of *partnership*. The *World Development Report 2000/1* (World Bank 2000a) on poverty will embody this concern and activism which was already articulated in less complete form in the UK's 1997 White Paper on international development (Department for International Development 1997). First the White Paper explicitly rejected either state-led or market-led models of development in favour of a third way which combined the two; second, there is considerable emphasis on forging partnerships with a range of stakeholders in the development process. Since that paper was written, the rhetoric of the development community increasingly has emphasized the political dimensions of poverty reduction.

This evolution is exemplified by the following sections from a speech by James Wolfensohn, President of the World Bank:

What is it, Mr Chairman, that the poor reply when asked what might make the greatest difference to their lives? They say, organizations of their own so that they may negotiate with government, with traders and with non-governmental organizations ... They want non-governmental organizations and governments to be accountable to them ... It will take strong local institutions to bring government closer to the poor. It will take empowering local people to design and implement their own programs because far less is lost in corruption when a community manages its own resources.

Whether you look at it at the government or the community level, whether you look through the prism of financial crisis, or human need; whether you speak to investors, bankers, or the dispossessed, governance and capacity are key. With poverty reduction front and center of our agenda, our work at the rockface must be governance, institutions, and capacity building ... bad governance – lack of accountability and transparency, corruption, and crime – is the number-one impediment to development and poverty reduction. (World Bank 2000b)

Poverty alleviation is not here conceived as a piece of routine social mechanics – extending a helping hand to pull the poor out of the mire onto the solid ground occupied by the rest of society; the imagery is more radical and transformative: poverty is seen as deeply embedded in poor governance, and vice versa. The President of the World Bank is not simply calling for more direct state action to reduce poverty, he is first asserting that such a strategy cannot be effective without transforming the nature of the state itself. That message, phrased differently, is consistent with the neo-liberal emphasis on the rent-seeking nature of states and of public action. However, he goes well beyond neo-liberalism in his plea that the organized poor should somehow be at the centre of decision-making in poor states. This is an endorsement of an idealized image of governance that is very much at odds with the traditions and image of the World Bank.

Why has the international development community become so activist in relation to poverty, at least at the declaratory level? Because we have a poor general understanding of the reasons for changes in intellectual fashions, we are unlikely to reach full agreement on the answer to this question. The most pessimistic interpretation may be that this new activism does not extend beyond the international aid and development institutions. Their leaders have taken this position because they are urgently searching for new legitimations for development aid now that the cold war no longer performs this role and the attempt to use the good government and democracy agenda for this purpose has not been very successful. On this reading, these concerns about poverty and inequality are not shared by governments, rich or poor, or by the most influential societal forces. Aid and development agencies are writing the tune themselves and trying to persuade governments of poor countries to dance to it.

A more positive interpretation is that global financial instability and a perception of growing inequality have stimulated genuine concerns, whether altruistic or instrumental, about the long-term implications of current policy trends. Those who support a greater degree of state activism can cite some new evidence and ideas in support of their stance.

In the realm of evidence, there is now enough information to make plausible the claim that growing inequality is a global trend, both inter- and intra-nationally. Whether intra-national inequality really is a general, long-term trend is not entirely clear. It is particularly unclear in the poorest countries: they have the worst statistics, but there are enough cases of fast-growing intra-national inequality to make credible the argument that there is something generic and global going on here. These areas of fast-growing inequality include "traditionally" relatively unequal societies such as the United States and the United Kingdom, and countries such as China, Viet Nam, and the former Comecon countries, which started from relatively egalitarian positions and have experienced dramatic increases in their Gini coefficients, measuring income inequality. These apparently general trends toward growing intra-national inequality are congruent with a range of arguments about the unequalizing tendencies inherent in economic globalization – above all, the shift of bargaining power away from both governments and organized labour, toward increasingly mobile capital. These same causal factors might underlie another dimension of growing inequality to which UNCTAD in particular has drawn attention – the shrinking of the middle-class household economy. Prior to 1980 there was a shift in the distribution of income from the rich to the middle classes in many countries; since 1980, the trend has been reversed (UNCTAD 1997: 111–115).

The international picture appears more clear-cut. Aggregate global statistics on poverty reduction are somewhat encouraging. Between 1970 and 1996, infant-mortality rates in the least-developed countries fell from 107 to 59 per 1,000 live births. Between 1987 and 1998, the proportion of the population of the developing world living on less than $1 a day (constant real values) declined from 29 to 24 per cent. However, global differentiation is very marked, especially in relation to these income measures of poverty. The reduction in the global number of households living in poverty reflects, above all, a major shift out of poverty in East Asia. The absolute numbers of the poor increased in Eastern Europe and Central Asia, in Latin America and the Caribbean, in South Asia and in sub-

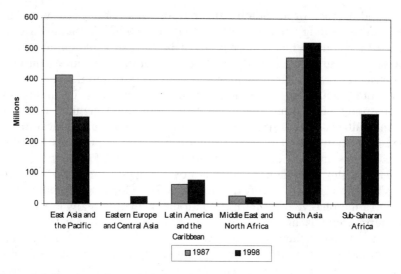

Figure 3.5 Number of people below the poverty line (Source: World Bank Web site: http://www.worldbank.org/poverty/data/trends/income.htm)

Saharan Africa (figure 3.5). The proportion of the population living in poverty fell in most regions but increased sharply from almost nothing in Eastern Europe and Central Asia and remained stationary in sub-Saharan Africa (table 3.3).

In the realm of ideas, it is increasingly accepted that meaningful definitions of poverty – i.e. definitions that are likely to contribute to the action that will lead to an improvement in the conditions of the poor – should extend beyond the core notion of poverty as an issue of income or consumption. The issues here are complex. They involve ethics, semantics, and politics, as well as more pragmatic concerns such as what is actually measurable. It is on the latter grounds that most organizations, especially those with an international remit, still use some measure of private (family or individual) income, expressed in monetary terms, as the core measure of poverty. It remains true that the only relatively reliable and comprehensive international data series we have on poverty are those that indicate the proportion of national populations that live on less than $1 (or $2) per person per day. Data are, however, improving: we are close to a situation where we could produce fairly reliable data series based on the following concepts of poverty (or ill-being, deprivation), which are listed in ascending order, starting with the most basic (i.e. the most direct threat to basic human needs):

• "Famine" (we use this word reluctantly, for lack of a more elegant term to describe the situations in which the lives of large numbers of people in a single location are suddenly at acute risk from some combination of hunger and disease).[7]

- Undernutrition.
- Income (understood here as a shorthand term for some broad concept encompassing both consumption and the inputs (income, expenditure) that are required to make consumption possible).
- Longevity/mortality.
- Education/literacy.

Most of these concepts of poverty can be defined in a variety of ways and all can be measured in a variety of ways. The list is not comprehensive, in the sense that it does not include everything that we would wish to include in a list of even the basic dimensions of well-being and ill-being, as experienced by poor people in poor countries. In particular, we have not included (because it is not yet measurable) any concept of freedom from physical violence, crime, and oppression. We know that these are serious concerns. The important point about the list for present purposes is that it immediately and directly, once again, draws attention to the essential role of public action in reducing poverty. Only if poverty is defined solely in terms of income do we face the credible prospect that there is a serious alternative to the state (i.e. the market) as the prime instrument for poverty reduction. Once we think of poverty in terms of famine, undernutrition, early mortality, ill-health, or lack of education and literacy, then it is impossible not to give public action a central role; further, once we add the need to tackle inequality to the policy menu it is even clear that we cannot rely on market forces alone.

The big question is not so much the relative roles of public action and the market as the type of public action that is needed. In particular, is the President of the World Bank right in emphasizing governance concerns as the number one issue on the poverty-reduction agenda? Certainly, there is good reason to believe that African underperformance in poverty reduction is due in large part to what are conventionally called governance problems. These are especially acute in (but not confined) to sub-Saharan Africa. On those points we can find wide agreement; the dissent begins when we try to specify in more detail what exactly these governance problems are, why they exist, and what might be done about them. One issue not treated here is the realism of the notion that international aid and development agencies could play a direct and significant role in empowering or mobilizing the poor in poor countries. In brief, they lack both competence and legitimacy (Moore 2001). We examine below three alternative approaches to the linkages between governance and poverty reduction, labelled "democracy," "participation," and "accountable states," respectively.

## The governance–poverty connection in democracy

Democracy is desirable for many reasons. However, the democracies among contemporary developing countries are no better than the non-democracies at poverty reduction. This finding is not new: it was replicated in a number of recent pieces of work that each used a different operational definition of "pro-poor" (see Moore and Putzel 1999 for a summary of these conclusions). Ashutosh Varshney (1999) examined the record of countries at reducing the numbers of people below the poverty line, defined in terms of income or consumption. Kimberly Niles (1999) measured the effort that governments put into protecting the poor against the adverse effects of economic adjustment. Mick Moore and colleagues (Moore, Leavy, and White, 1999) explored the extent to which national political-economic systems converted national income into longevity, literacy, and education for the mass of citizens (see table 3.5). White and Anderson (2000) examine how political orientation affects the share of incremental national income accruing to poor people. All concluded that there was no consistent connection between pro-poorness and democracy: although the very worst performers tend not to be democracies – democracy does provide some kind of safety net – there are non-democracies among the best performers. Over relatively long periods of time some authoritarian regimes, such as that which existed in Indonesia for over thirty-five years, made faster progress in reducing

Table 3.5 Distribution of countries according to poverty-reduction performance[a] and degree of democracy

| Poverty-reduction performance | No. of countries with degree of democracy[b] | | | |
| | More democratic | Less democratic | Undemocratic | Total |
| --- | --- | --- | --- | --- |
| High | 5 | 5 | 9 | 19 |
| Modest | 2 | 10 | 12 | 24 |
| Low | 4 | 3 | 11 | 18 |
| Total | 11 | 18 | 32 | 61 |

a. Poverty-reduction performance is conceived as the efficiency of national political-economic systems at converting national income into longevity, literacy, and education for the mass of the population. For more details on the measures used here, and the sample of countries, see Moore, Leavy, and White (1999). The measures of poverty-reduction performance relate to 1995.

b. The measures of the degree of democracy are from the POLITY III database. An average was calculated for the period 1980–1989, on the basis of annual scores on a scale of 0–10. "More democratic countries" scored 8 or more; "undemocratic countries" scored 0.

poverty than other states which have enjoyed long periods of democracy – such as the Philippines, where the rate of poverty reduction has been much more modest. Table 3.5 illustrates the kind of inconclusive patterns that result when we classify poor countries according to their poverty-reduction performance and degree of democracy.

What is going on here? Democracy does offer more voice and influence to the poor than most non-democratic systems. Why does this not result in a clear association between democracy and good performance in poverty reduction? There are two main answers to that question. The first is that the statistics from which we draw our conclusions reflect the effects of the cold war. Some of the best performers in poverty reduction over the past half-century have been the (former) socialist states, which were undemocratic by conventional criteria but highly focused on improving mass welfare for reasons of ideology and politics. The positive impacts of these histories of pro-poor mobilization are still evident in the poverty and welfare statistics for China, Cuba, and Viet Nam. The impacts have faded in the case of most of the countries of the former Soviet Bloc after their transition to market economies and have turned grotesque in North Korea. The residual effects of this experience of non-democratic but pro-poor socialist regimes is one reason why democracy is not associated with poverty reduction in the cross-national statistics. There is probably also another side to the same coin: democracies may have been less pro-poor than expected because, even in formally democratic regimes, the cold war encouraged and legitimated the repression of leftist movements. This relates to the other reason for a weak connection between democratic regimes and poverty-reduction strategies – wide variations in the substantive content of formal, electoral democracy.

If democratic politics were mainly about organizing people to vote according to their broadly defined economic interests, one would expect the poor to have considerably more influence and voice than they do. There are three important reasons why democracy does not work in this way.

- The actual participation of the poor, particularly women, does not reflect their numbers in society. Many poor people are excluded from, or do not participate actively in, the political process.
- When the poor do participate, their "class" identities (as poor people in general or, specifically, as small farmers, landless, wage workers, tenants, recipients of food subsidies, squatters, etc.) are not the only influences on the way they vote or on the politicians, parties, or programmes that they support: the forces that move them are often more tangible, short-term, direct, and local than relatively abstract notions about income group, class, or occupational position – individual "patronage" ties to politicians who promise something immediate in return; the ethnic, linguistic, or regional identities that often prove so effective

in creating emotional attachments to political ideas and programmes; or the opportunity to sell a vote.

• Poverty in developing countries is especially acute in rural areas, where, except at the very local level, it is particularly difficult to sustain effective organizations that involve poor people on a continuous basis. Communication and travel are difficult; information is scarce. Poor rural populations rarely sustain coherent, encompassing, political organizations. They tend to be responsive rather than proactive in politics.

In sum, in many democracies the poor are often badly organized and ill-served by the organizations that mobilize their votes and claim to represent their interests.

Nevertheless, some democracies in developing countries perform well in terms of poverty reduction. This can be traced in part to differences in the quality of organizations in political and civil society and the ways in which the poor realize a voice within them. In every democratic system, different kinds of organizations mediate between various poor sections of the population and the state. Civil society is made up of a wide range of associations rooted in – and cutting across – class, gender, income, and other identities. Some of these emerge out of poor communities, or are organized explicitly to interact with and promote the interests of those communities. They include religious, community, and non-governmental organizations (NGOs). Groups within civil society, whether aligned with the poor or with élite groups, such as business or professional associations, often serve as points of mobilization and advocacy in relation to the state.

Whereas civil-society organizations are important sources of assistance and mobilization for specific groups among the poor, it is the organizations of political society within democratic systems that are crucial to the character and conduct of public policy. Chief among these are political parties. These can range from temporary alliances of powerful individuals; through more stable organizations constructed around regional, patronage, ethnic, or religious networks; to organizations based on clearly defined ideologies and programmes and run by committed voluntary members operating through a democratic institutional structure. The more that parties are located towards this latter end of the spectrum, the more likely they are to represent the poor effectively.

Where there are political parties actually competing for the votes of the poor, the poor have a better chance of influencing policy or seeing policy formed that addresses their needs. Kimberly Niles (1999) explains the way in which the pattern of party competition affects the extent and way in which parties compete for the votes of the poor. She compares countries in terms of the extent to which parties are stable or fluid and fragmented. Where parties are stable, elections are generally dominated by two or three competing programmatic parties with a degree of party discipline. Each party needs to win a high proportion of votes to enter government. Parties operate with relatively long time horizons; they accumulate a great deal of information about potential voters and the potential pay-offs to different political strategies; each tries to appeal to a broad constituency of voters. The system tends to produce parties and governments with a high degree of commitment to the poor. In fragmented systems, politics are personalistic; there are many poorly disciplined parties, which do not need to obtain a large proportion of votes to have a chance of entering government. They have shorter time horizons and face higher information costs because politicians are continually engaging in new activities, with new allies or opponents, and seeking the support of different voters. These systems tend to produce governments with low degrees of commitment to the poor. Niles (1999) found that "semi-authoritarian" regimes that used elections to test their popular support and to discipline their own cadres and supporters (e.g. South Korea, Taiwan, Indonesia), made more efforts to tackle poverty than did regimes that were democratic but plagued by fragmented party systems.

Many developing-country democracies remain characterized by just such fragmented party systems. This is certainly the case in sub-Saharan Africa: contested elections have become the norm there over the past decade. However, it is rare to find coherent and stable party systems in which two or three large parties of blocs compete for power. Individual elections are generally characterized by the dominance of one party and the fragmentation of the opposition, or fragmentation more generally; in addition, there is often a great deal of change in the party line-up and membership between elections.

It is possible that, freed of the tyranny of cold war geopolitics, democracy in many poor countries will lead to a greater interest in pro-poor agendas; however, the process is likely to be very gradual. The instability and fragmentation of party systems reflects a number of underlying features of society and polity that are especially pronounced in sub-Saharan Africa, but characteristic of much of the poor world.

One such feature is the weak development of the national-level class and occupational identities that provide the essential basis for stable and encompassing social organizations and political parties in most contexts. There has been little industrialization in sub-Saharan Africa: mining has, in the past, provided some basis for an organized urban proletariat, but only in South Africa and Zimbabwe is there a significant urban industrial working class. Only there do we find significant encompassing political parties and movements of a class and programmatic character. Low levels of industrialization are, of course, characteristic of much of Asia and Latin America. Many countries in those regions have, however, contained

– and sometimes been ruled by – landlord groups that have the characteristics of a distinct social class. Opposition to these groups has provided
some basis for encompassing popular mobilization and programmatic
political parties in much of Asia and Latin America.

The other characteristic of sub-Saharan Africa that militates against
encompassing social organizations and movements and programmatic
political parties is the character of states. Patterns of socio-political organization to a large extent reflect the character of states. People try to
create the political organizations that will be most effective in the policy
arena where they wish to have influence. An important feature of that
arena is the pattern of organization of the groups with whom they are
likely to ally or compete. National employers' organizations emerged in
most industrial countries in response to the creation of national trade-
union federations. National farmers' movements emerged only after
governments began to intervene consistently in agricultural markets and
there was a perceived need to deal with government at a national level.
Conversely, the mass-based civil-rights movements that emerged to challenge so many authoritarian Latin American and Central European regimes in the 1970s and 1980s fell apart once democracy had triumphed
and the focus of such movements – a consistently oppressive state – had
disappeared. Where the state is fragmented, social and political organizations, especially organizations that involve the poor, are either weak,
or are fragmented, or are the creation of external actors such as international aid donors and NGOs. The modern state eliminates rival centres
of authority within society. This provides the basis for social groups to
organize on a national scale and to create collective identities that cut
across geographic regions and ethnic identities. Whether social groups
organize to influence the state depends on whether they believe the state
has the authority and capacity to meet their demands. If the national
state has little authority, why bother to organize at the national level?
Better to concentrate limited political resources (and political resources
are always limited) on exercising influence in different ways: negotiating
an acceptable level of informal taxes with the guerrilla movement in this
region; using ethnic linkages with a minister to remove oppressive po-
licemen from this town; building up connections with the aid of donors
who might provide money for local NGOs in that district. Building large
membership movements of the poor is unlikely to be the most efficient
means of exercising influence through these kinds of channels. Global
maps of effective states and effective social movements (and mass or
programmatic political parties) would look very similar. Where the state
is ineffective, social and political movements are rare, weak, exclusive,
localized, and often closely connected with armed secessionists and

smugglers. Where states are ineffective, improving their capacity may be the best way to stimulate effective organizations of the poor.

## The governance–poverty connection: "Participation"

The comments above about the obstacles to the creation of effective, encompassing, programmatic political parties and social movements in many poor countries (including especially much of sub-Saharan Africa) provide a suitably sceptical introduction to the "participation" strategy that is now finding great favour within the World Bank and other aid agencies. To call it a *strategy* may be to exaggerate the coherence. There is nevertheless a strong affinity between (a) the emphasis on creating organizations of the poor in Wolfensohn's recent speech (p. 78) and (b) the extent to which poverty specialists in the World Bank have viewed participatory poverty assessments (PPAs) as *the* instrument for permitting the poor to influence national policies.

An illustration of how the Bank conceives of the voice of the poor influencing policy in practice is given by the recent World Bank publication by Caroline Robb (1999) *Can the Poor Influence Poverty? Participatory Poverty Assessments in the Developing World*. The book is largely devoted to the design and use of PPAs by the World Bank. We are not questioning that PPAs have helped broaden the conception and understanding of poverty; we are more sceptical that they are an adequate weapon with which to enter the political arena.

Robb identifies three contributions of PPAs: (1) deepening understanding of poverty; (2) influencing policy of the government and World Bank (other "partners" are not mentioned); and (3) strengthening policy implementation. Consistent with our own impressions, the material presented suggests that PPAs have been most effective in deepening understanding of poverty. Robb's subjective assessment (table 3.6) is that one-

Table 3.6 Subjective rating of PPA influence on policy

| Influence | None | Low | Medium | High |
|---|---|---|---|---|
| Deepening understanding | 0 | 28 | 48 | 24 |
| Influencing policy | | | | |
|   at World Bank | 38 | 33 | 19 | 10 |
|   at country level | 43 | 28 | 19 | 10 |
| Increasing implementation capacity | 62 | 14 | 14 | 10 |

Source: Robb 1999: 32.
PPA: participatory poverty assessment.

quarter have had a high impact in this area and that none has made zero impact. By her own assessment, the picture with respect to policy influence is far less impressive – high in only 10 per cent and zero in two-thirds of cases.

However, even these results can overstate the extent to which PPAs allow the voice of the poor to influence policy. This opinion is based on two grounds, namely (1) methodological problems in the practice of PPAs resulting in a selective reading of evidence, and (2) the depoliticization of policy-making implicit in the Bank's approach to this issue.

The idea that PPAs can represent the "voice of the poor" has been criticized from a variety of perspectives. More-quantitatively based social scientists question the lack of sampling to ensure the representativeness of the findings. This is not a case of the "case study versus survey" argument, because some participatory exercises have been very extensive in coverage of both communities and households. Sociologists and anthropologists (for example, Mosse 1994) point out that the arrival of a PPA "team" is an event in a community that is hardly likely to elicit normal behaviour and can well be subject to élite capture. Even if the fieldwork is conducted well, there are dangers of selective readings of the evidence at various stages. In the absence of a structured questionnaire, facilitators impose their own social constructions on the evidence with which they are presented; in the absence of a systematic technique for analysing the data, researchers use their own implicit conceptual framework to organize the material (for example, Moore, Chaudhary, and Singh, 1998). Finally, people advising policy makers may choose which points to highlight and which to ignore. Hanmer, Pyatt, and White (1997) compared policy recommendations from PPAs from those in the World Bank's routine poverty assessments, and found that those PPA findings that were consistent with the general arguments in the poverty assessments were included, whereas others were not.

The depoliticization of policy is evident from Robb's discussion of how PPAs influence policy. First, influence on government policy and implementation capacity receives only two pages of her 120-page book. Second, concrete examples of how PPAs have influenced policy more often refer to influence on the World Bank than to influence on national governments. Third and most striking, Robb discusses only the insights into potential poverty policy provided by PPAs and not the processes by which PPAs have (or could have) affected policy outcomes. The implicit concept of policy-making is idealist, with technocratic policy makers simply waiting for better ideas on how to reduce poverty. The role of PPAs is thus to provide these better ideas. The reality is, of course, that policy-making is inherently political. The President of the World Bank is thus nearer the nub of the issue when he advocates creating organizations of the poor. However, effective organizations are not created through will-power and external resources; there are fundamental reasons, sketched out above, why organizations that might encourage and support active antipoverty policies are weak in poor countries.

## The governance–poverty connection: Accountable states

The international community has made a bid to develop accountability through the promotion of the International Development Targets (IDTs). Drawing on a rights-based approach to poverty reduction, donors encourage ("require" would be too strong a word for current practice) developing country governments to accept these (or their own similar targets) against which they may be held accountable. This begs the question of accountable to whom? In the past, the international community has held developing-country governments to account, creating a wedge between governments and the population. Because aid funds are more discretionary than tax revenue, governments have found it advantageous to bend at least the rhetoric of their policies to the will of the donors. What are the structures of domestic accountability most relevant to poverty reduction? We look particularly at sub-Saharan Africa.

Accountability through the formal political structure in party-based democracies needs the sort of programmatic government and opposition system that (we argued above) is lacking in many developing countries and certainly in Africa. It can often be difficult to discern genuine differences in policy platforms (and less so between the policies they would pursue in power) between different parties, and it is not these policies that are the root of the political struggle. Policy issues are not openly debated before the government establishes its position, nor do the mechanisms exist for widespread discussion and lobbying from different quarters of society over implementation issues. We are not suggesting that these things do not happen at all. Some groups – large farmers, the chambers of commerce – may be well placed to lobby (mostly on an informal basis), but systems do not exist for this to happen on a wider basis. In the United Kingdom, for example, the Labour government announced its own poverty-reduction plan in the summer of 1999. The concept of poverty used, and the policies proposed to tackle it, became the subject of intense debate in the media, with attacks from the opposition and groups such as the Child Poverty Action Group. Similar activities do not surround the launch of such plans in African countries. One immediate reason is the character of the mass media.

For many years the media were government controlled and reported mainly official "news." Although this is still commonplace, there has been a growth of an independent press (but not radio) that can be critical of the government and may well highlight an issue such as corruption. These independent presses rarely provide analysis of the kind that will inform a general policy debate and they may often fail to provide the information needed for independent organizations to put effective pressure on government. Sen (1999) has argued the importance of a free press in famine prevention. In India, the ability and the willingness of the media to report on the threat of famine put the concern in the wider public domain and politicized the issue so that government had to act. De Waal (1997) has questioned how far Sen's argument is valid, but even he agrees that the absence of a free press in Africa is a principal reason for the persistence of preventable famine. Much the same may be true of other aspects of poverty and deprivation, such as infant mortality (which is rising in several African countries) or the increasing number of street children. Nevertheless, although the media can play a key role here, it is unlikely that they can drive the process of policy change in the absence of supportive political context.

One important dimension of a supportive political context is a set of societal organizations that vocalize concerns about poverty. As indicated above, African political parties fail to do this very consistently or effectively. Furthermore, as argued in the section on pages 82–87, the poor may fail to mobilize as groups of the poor, so that organizations of the poor will not exist to take this role. In other contexts, such as nineteenth-century Britain, middle-class groups played a very active role in publicizing the facts of poverty and mobilizing public support for more activist government policies: Joseph Rowntree and Charles Booth became historical figures for this kind of activity. In contemporary sub-Saharan Africa there are few signs of a "concerned middle class," with individuals taking a career option to working on poverty programmes, moving to poor regions and working with groups of the poor, and, through their networks, mobilizing some political action. Although the number of development NGOs has grown fast, they are heavily driven by donors' funds and the emphasis on "partnership" creates a rather complacent consensus around government plans, rather than critical attention to government (in)action.

## Concluding comments

Poverty reduction will require a substantial degree of public action.
- Economic growth alone – which is, itself, at best an unreliable outcome of market-based policies – will be insufficient to eliminate even income poverty.

- Once the non-income dimensions of poverty (such as freedom from eradicable disease, illiteracy, and famine) are taken into account, then the importance of public action is clear. It is even more so once the importance of tackling inequality is taken into account.

From where will that public action spring? The international community addresses such issues through the lens of "governance." At its worst, this is presented as the missing ingredient that explains relatively poor performance (especially in Africa) in reducing poverty over the last decades, and provides the key to improved performance; however, there is no credible consensus about what good governance means in relation to poverty and inequality and how it may be brought about. The kind of democracy found in most poor countries does not seem to contribute much to putting poverty and inequality high on policy agendas. The (extra-electoral) participatory processes that are now so popular with aid donors – especially PPAs and, now, participation-based Poverty Reduction Strategy Papers – appear largely artificial and formal and (even if "genuine") would not themselves do much to change the underlying politics. Aid donors are now very much in favour of "empowering the poor," but have little sense of what this might mean in practice – and especially for their own practices; they can do little directly to further this objective.

This is not a counsel of despair. There are plenty of exceptions not only to all the generalizations that we make but also to many organizations, movements, political parties, and governance mechanisms in the countries of the South that are actively or potentially pro-poor. Our attention has been on the more problematic cases. For them, the most general conclusion that we can draw is that effective poverty-reducing governance lies principally in attention to the "basics" – in the creation and preservation of states that can (a) themselves deliver basic services and (b) have sufficient stability and coherence that they encourage the creation of political parties and movements that embody and advance the interests of the poor, and hence a domestic political basis for pro-poor and redistributive public policies.

## Notes

1. This may not be an entirely welcome phenomenon; see Toye (1999).
2. The relationship between most social indicators and income per capita is log-linear with an $R^2$ of around 0.7.
3. A version of this analysis was also presented in the *1996 Human Development Report* (UNDP 1996).
4. There are regional patterns in these findings. All of Africa, with two exceptions, has either remained in the vicious circle or had a period EG lopsided before falling back into

the vicious circle. The exceptions are Botswana (which had moved from vicious to virtuous), South Africa, (which has moved from virtuous to vicious), and Niger (which moved from HD to EG lopsided). In contrast to Africa, five East Asian countries have remained in the virtuous circle and three moved into there from being HD lopsided.

5. There is also a positive relationship between the elasticity and mean income which also serves to make elasticities low in Africa.

6. The *1990 World Development Report* on poverty (World Bank 1990) exemplifies this general position.

7. It is important not to see famine purely in terms of hunger; the main cause of death in situations we describe as famine is often epidemic disease.

## REFERENCES

Ahluwalia, M. 1976. "Inequality, Poverty and Development." *Journal of Development Economics* 3: 307–342.

Anand, Sudhir and Ravi Kanbur. 1993. "The Kuznets Process and the Inequality–Development Relationship." *Journal of Development Economics* 40(1): 25–52.

Deininger, K. and L. Squire. 1996. "A New Data Set Measuring Income Inequality." *World Bank Economic Review* 10(3): 565–591. September.

De Waal, Alex. 1997. *Famine Crisis: Politics and the Disaster Relief Industry in Africa*. Oxford: James Currey and Bloomington: Indiana University Press in association with African Rights and International African Institute.

Department for International Development (DFID). 1997. *Eliminating World Poverty: A Challenge for the 21st Century: White Paper on International Development*. London: DFID.

Food and Agricultural Organization of the United Nations (FAO). 1999. *The State of Food Insecurity in the World*. Rome: FAO.

Hanmer, Lucia and Felix Naschold. 2000. "Attaining the international development targets: will growth be enough?" *Development Policy Review* 18(1), March. London: Overseas Development Institute.

Hanmer, Lucia, Graham Pyatt, and Howard White. 1997. *Poverty in Sub-Saharan Africa: What Can We Learn from the World Bank's Poverty Assessments?* The Hague: ISS.

Kuznets, S. 1963. "Quantitative Aspects of the Economic Growth of Nations: VIII. Distribution of income by size." *Economic Development and Cultural Change* II(2).

Moore, Mick. 2001. "Empowerment at Last?" *Journal of International Development* 13(3): 321–329, May.

Moore, Mick and James Putzel. 1999. "Thinking Strategically about Politics and Poverty." *IDS Working Paper No. 101*. Brighton: IDS.

Moore, Mick, Madhulika Chaudhary, and Neelam Singh. 1998. "How Can We Know What They Want? Understanding Local Perceptions of Poverty and Ill-Being in Asia." *IDS Working Paper No. 80*, December. Brighton: IDS.

Moore, Mick, Jennifer Leavy, and Howard White. 1999. "Polity Qualities: How governance affects poverty." *IDS Working Paper No. 99*, December. Brighton: IDS.

Mosse, David. 1994. "Authority, Gender and Knowledge: Theoretical Reflections on the Practice of Participatory Rural Appraisal." *Development and Change* 25(3): 497–526.

Niles, Kimberly. 1999. "Economic Adjustment and Targeted Social Spending: The Role of Political Institutions (Indonesia, Mexico and Ghana)." Paper presented at IDS–DFID meeting, Castle Donnington, UK, 16 and 17 August 1999, on the Responsiveness of Political Systems to Poverty Reduction.

Ranis, Gustav, Frances Stewart, and Alejandro Ramirez. 2000. "Economic Growth and Human Development." *World Development* 28(2): 197–219.

Ravallion, Martin. 1997. "Good and Bad Growth: the Human Development Reports." *World Development* 25(5): 627–830.

Robb, Caroline. 1999. *Can the Poor Influence Poverty? Participatory Poverty Assessments in the Developing World.* Washington DC: World Bank.

Sen, Amartya. 1999. *Development as Freedom.* Oxford: Oxford University Press.

Slack, Paul. 1988. *Poverty and Policy in Tudor and Stuart England.* London: Longman.

Toye, John. 1999. "Nationalising the Anti-poverty Agenda." *IDS Bulletin* 30(2): 6–12, April. Brighton: IDS.

United Nations Conference on Trade and Development (UNCTAD). 1997. *Trade and Development Report 1997.* New York: United Nations.

United Nations Development Programme (UNDP). 1996. *Human Development Report 1996.* New York: Oxford University Press.

Varshney, Ashutosh. 1999. "Democracy and Poverty." Paper presented at IDS–DFID meeting, Castle Donnington, UK, 16 and 17 August 1999, on the Responsiveness of Political Systems to Poverty Reduction.

White, Howard and Tony Killick, with Steve Kayizzi-Mugerwa, and Marie-Angelique Savane. 2001. *African Poverty at the Millennium.* Washington DC: World Bank.

White, Howard and Edward Anderson. 2000. "Growth vs. Distribution: Does The Pattern Of Growth Matter?" Background paper for DFID White Paper on Eliminating World Poverty: Making Globalisation Work for the Poor. ⟨www.globalisation.gov.uk⟩

World Bank. 1990. *Poverty: World Development Report 1990.* Washington DC: World Bank.

World Bank. 1997. *The State in a Changing World: World Development Report 1997.* Washington DC: World Bank.

World Bank. 1999. *World Development Indicators 1999.* Washington DC: World Bank.

World Bank. 2000a. *Attacking World Poverty. World Development Report 2000/1.* Washington DC: World Bank.

World Bank. 2000b. "Coalitions for Change." Address by James D. Wolfensohn (President, The World Bank Group) to the Board of Governors, 28 September 1999, Washington DC.

# Regional perspectives

# 4

# Latin America in the global economy: Macroeconomic policy, social welfare, and political democracy

*Robert R. Kaufman*

## Introduction

We are living in dangerous times. Although the expansion of international trade and capital markets (i.e. "globalization") has created new opportunities for growth in developing countries it has also left large segments of the world's population increasingly vulnerable to uncertainties and crises in trade and financial markets. This became vividly apparent during the summer of 1998, a period in which the Russian economy collapsed, a major US hedge fund barely staved off bankruptcy, and Brazil teetered on the edge of a financial meltdown. For much of the international financial and policy élite, the world economy appeared closer to a global collapse than at any time since 1929.

These fears ebbed during the following year, particularly after timely interest-rate reductions by the US Federal Reserve. Brazil, a flashpoint of the crisis, was impelled to accept a costly devaluation of its currency in January 1999, but it then began to bounce back more quickly than expected, thanks in part to a rescue package rapidly assembled by the IMF and the US government. By the fall of 1999, emerging markets were on the rebound and financial analysts were again forecasting a resumption of growth for Latin America. Given the experience of the past decade, however, it seems unlikely that we have seen the last of major international crises, in either Latin America or other parts of the developing world.

Since long before the current problems in Brazil, Latin America has been very much at the centre of these global cross-currents. During the past twenty years, and particularly since the early 1990s, the region has become increasingly integrated into the global economy, both through expanding trade in goods and services and through the liberalization of capital accounts. Intraregional variation persists, of course. Nevertheless, the changes that have swept through Latin America as a whole contrast sharply with the past period of import-substitution industrialization (ISI). Compared with middle-income countries in other regions, moreover, Latin America appears distinctive in its embrace of "neoliberalism." Unlike the East Asian economies, Latin American states have played a relatively limited role in fostering export competitiveness, and most of the countries of the region are well ahead of most African countries in terms of market-oriented reforms. Unlike Eastern Europe, finally, there appears to be less concern in Latin America with reproducing some of the features of the "social market" economies that characterized many countries of the European Union.

In this chapter I examine social and political aspects of this structural transformation. The section on pages 99–103 reviews the scope and extent of the adjustments taking place in the 1980s and 1990s. I then discuss the long-term implications of the Brazil crisis, particularly the expanded macroeconomic policy debates that have emerged as a consequence. The section on pages 108–115 focuses on the social impacts of the transformations and the options available for social spending and welfare policies. In the last section (pp. 115–123) I review some of the political implications, particularly some of the issues related to the political crafting of development and welfare bargains.

In dealing with these issues, it is important to take into account major differences within the region. To a great extent, the long-term future of the region as a whole is a "tale of two countries" – Brazil and Mexico. Developmental prospects for many South American countries hinge closely on whether the Brazilian giant can continue to recover from its current crisis and resume high rates of growth. On the other hand, Mexico's NAFTA (North Atlantic Free Trade Agreement) membership has pulled that country in another direction. Its economic performance as well as its tentative movement towards a more democratic polity in turn is likely to have an important impact on Central America and the Caribbean.

Both for these countries and for the region as a whole, the crises of 1998 and 1999 raised new questions about macroeconomic policy and underlined the important role of social welfare measures in promoting social cohesion and long-term growth. This chapter highlights, however, the paradoxical relation between social policy and growth – namely, interdependence and mutual reinforcement over the long run and trade-offs in the short run (especially during difficult periods of adjustment). Representative institutions, particularly political parties, are crucial variables in determining the capacity of societies to manage these trade-offs.


## Macroeconomic policy and structural change: The transformation of the 1990s and the choices ahead

### International and historical influences on Latin American development

The dramatic and distinctive "neoliberal" transformation of Latin American economies during the past two decades can be explained in terms of a combination of international influences and historical legacies. Perhaps the most important of the international influences is the overwhelming role of the United States as a regional (as well as a global) hegemon. As Barbara Stallings has written, a substantial part of this influence is based on trade ties and capital flows: in the early 1990s, over 40 per cent of Latin America's trade was with the United States (with an additional 17 per cent intraregional; Stallings 1995: 357). Similar regional tendencies are reflected in capital flows: the United States is still the largest single source of portfolio and FDI in Latin America, whereas Japan and the European Union (EU) weigh more heavily in Asia and Eastern Europe, respectively.

These structural patterns provide an important underpinning for international ideological and financial roles played by IFIs. In Asia, the Japanese model (at least until very recently) provided an important counterweight to policy recommendations coming from the IMF and World Bank. In Eastern and Central Europe, the "social-market" approaches of the EU played a similar role. Although the IMF and World Bank have also been highly influential in both regions, the influence of Japan and the EU have offered relatively coherent alternative strategies which place greater emphasis on the coordination of market economies through state intervention or interfirm cooperation (Hart 1994; Soskice 1999). IFIs have arguably exerted much greater financial power in Africa than in Asia or Eastern Europe; nevertheless, even there, the influence of American-inspired models has been muted by "special" financial and diplomatic ties to former colonial powers, especially to France and Britain. Compared with the countries in these other regions, then, Latin American societies have been more "exposed" to the intellectual and financial influences of so-called neoliberal doctrines that prioritize market competition over the use of public or private networks of coordination and cooperation.

These influences were reinforced throughout Latin America by the apparent success of Chile, one of the first countries in the region to initiate market reforms. In reality, the Chilean experience was characterized by some notable departures from "pure" market policies – including continued state ownership of the copper sector, selective forms of export promotion, and regulations on the capital account (Meller 1996). Nevertheless, the "lessons" drawn from that experience generally bolstered the market-oriented prescriptions emanating from the US policy community and from the IMF and World Bank.

Finally, to understand the distinction between Latin America and other regions during the 1980s and 1990s, it is important to take into account the legacy of earlier developmental models. In Latin America, earlier ISI models – which had survived largely on debt during the 1970s – became unsustainable by the early 1980s. Efforts to find "heterodox" routes out of the ensuing crisis proved disastrous in Brazil, Peru, and Argentina. By the 1990s, therefore, radical adjustment of some kind was difficult to avoid.

In several other regions, developmental legacies had quite different effects. In East Asia, coordinated market economies tended to work quite well through most of the last two decades. Under pressure from the West, many of these countries did open their capital accounts during the 1980s and undertook some degree of trade liberalization; nevertheless, the pace of structural reform was considerably slower than in Latin America (Haggard 1990; Wade 1990). In Eastern Europe and the USSR, socialist economies collapsed even more quickly than did the ISI models in Latin America. Nevertheless, the huge size of the state sector and the broad expectations about protection from market forces operated as important deterrents on a full-scale turn to neoliberal approaches. In countries such as Russia, big public enterprises continued to provide some minimal degree of social services for sectors of the population. Where market reforms had proceeded more rapidly – as in Hungary and Poland – such arrangements were replaced by pension, health, and disability transfers that were inefficient and costly but relatively comprehensive (Cook, Orenstein, and Rueschemeyer 1999).

## The great transformation: 1982–1999

The structural changes that transformed Latin America did not proceed smoothly or uniformly throughout the region; on the contrary, they were controversial and painful almost everywhere. The two leaders in reform – Chile and Mexico – were both autocratic regimes that deployed political resources to repress or co-opt opposition. Many democratic regimes, such as Argentina or Bolivia, initiated reforms only after costly policy stalemate or heterodox experiments had resulted in a virtual collapse of their economies. Some countries – most notably Brazil, Ecuador, and Venezuela – either were significantly slower to reform their economies or experienced a good deal of backsliding (Haggard and Kaufman 1995).

Notwithstanding these important cross-national differences, however, there is little doubt about the overall direction and depth of the changes that have occurred over the last two decades. By the early 1990s, almost every country in the region had taken significant steps to liberalize trade by lowering tariffs and eliminating quantitative restrictions. Between 1985 and 1995, the average tariff was reduced from 46 per cent to only 12 per cent and average variance among products had been reduced from 20 per cent to 6.4 per cent (Morley, Machado, and Pettinato 1999). Although Latin American countries continued to trade less than their Asian counterparts, trade as a percentage of GDP increased from just over 20 per cent in the 1970s to almost 30 per cent in the 1990s (World Bank 2000: 52). Privatization also accelerated during the 1990s, with Chile and Mexico leading the way but being followed in the 1990s by Bolivia, Argentina, Peru, and Jamaica (Morley, Machado, and Pettinato 1999).

Finally, by the early 1990s, many countries in the region had undertaken liberalization of their capital accounts, and even those that retained some controls (Chile, Brazil, Colombia, and Mexico) experienced a virtual explosion of incoming portfolio and direct foreign investment. Table 4.1 compares the capital flows and stock-market capitalization in Latin America with those of East Asia between the early and late 1990s. By 1997, Latin America had overtaken Asia in net capital flows, after having been one-third lower in 1990. Changes in stock-market capitalization tell a similar story: in 1990, the totals in Asia were 2.5 times higher than those in Latin America; by 1998, emerging markets in Latin America had exploded to more than 608 billion dollars as contrasted with 426 billion in Asia. Significantly, about one-half of these flows went to Brazil and Mexico, with Chile and Argentina adding another 16 per cent.

A recent study by Morley, Machado, and Pettinato (1999) provides a useful summary index of the degree of structural change that has occurred in Latin America over the past two decades. Each country in the region is assigned annual scores of zero to one on five reform policies (trade reform, domestic financial market reform, privatization, tax reform, and capital account liberalization) from 1970 to 1995. Although reforms occurred at different paces and times throughout the region, Morley and colleagues found that, between 1990 and 1995, there was a substantial convergence in at least three of the policy areas (trade, financial reform, and capital account liberalization) and that there was also

Table 4.1 Net private capital flows and stock-market capitalization, 1990–1998 (millions of dollars)

| | Net private capital flows[a] | | Stock-market capitalization[b] | |
|---|---|---|---|---|
| | 1990 | 1997 | 1990 | 1998 |
| Argentina | −203 | 19,834 | 3,268 | 45,332 |
| Bolivia | 3 | 812 | | 344 |
| Brazil | 562 | 43,377 | 16,354 | 160,887 |
| Chile | 2,098 | 9,637 | 13,645 | 51,866 |
| Colombia | 345 | 10,151 | 1,416 | 13,357 |
| Costa Rica | 23 | 104 | 475 | 820 |
| Dominican Republic | 130 | 401 | | 140 |
| Ecuador | 183 | 829 | | 1,527 |
| El Salvador | 8 | 61 | 69 | 499 |
| Guatemala | 44 | 166 | | 139 |
| Haiti | 8 | 3 | | |
| Honduras | 72 | 124 | | |
| Jamaica | 92 | 377 | 911 | 2,139 |
| Mexico | 8,253 | 20,533 | 32,725 | 91,746 |
| Nicaragua | 21 | 157 | | |
| Panama | 127 | 1,443 | 276 | 2,175 |
| Paraguay | 67 | 273 | | 389 |
| Peru | 59 | 3,094 | 812 | 11,645 |
| Uruguay | −192 | 632 | | 212 |
| Venezuela | −126 | 6,282 | 8,361 | 7,587 |
| Latin America | 12,411 | 118,918 | 78,470 | 608,395 |
| East Asia | 18,720 | 104,257 | 197,109 | 426,006 |

a. Source for net private capital flows: World Bank 2000: 270–271.
b. Source for stock-market capitalization: World Bank 2000: 260–261.

substantial privatization among countries where the state sector was relatively large. Tax reform was the only item on which countries continued to vary widely during the 1990s.

Table 4.2 shows the changes between 1970, 1980, 1990, and 1995 in the composite index that summarizes reform in the five issue areas. The table shows that all countries of the region liberalized over time, with the biggest "jump" coming between 1990 and 1995. In 1970, dispersion of scores on the index was limited, because most economies of the region remained relatively closed. Between 1980 and 1990, cross-national differences widened, a reflection of markedly varied responses to the debt crisis. By 1995, however, these differences had again narrowed substantially, as most of the "laggard" countries of the region introduced liberal reforms. The high score assigned to Uruguay comes as something of a surprise, but the low scores for Venezuela during the 1980s and 1990s

Table 4.2  Index of market reform in Latin America, 1970–1995

|  | High score (a) | Low score (b) | (a) minus (b) | Region average |
|---|---|---|---|---|
| 1970 | 0.569 (Argentina) | 0.347 (Chile) | 0.222 | 0.472 |
| 1980 | 0.759 (Uruguay) | 0.343 (Dominican Republic) | 0.416 | 0.548 |
| 1990 | 0.844 (Uruguay) | 0.472 (Venezuela) | 0.428 | 0.683 |
| 1995 | 0.891 (Uruguay) | 0.667 (Venezuela) | 0.224 | 0.821 |

Source:  Morley, Machado, and Pettinato 1999.

and for Chile in 1970 fits well with conventional expectations. Other high-ranking countries (Argentina, Peru, Bolivia) during the 1990s are also in accordance with conventional expectations. Mexico also ranks well above average for most of the years during the 1990s, although it fell somewhat during the crisis of 1995. Brazil's score for 1995 (0.805) ranks slightly below the regional average but is still significantly higher than in earlier years. Overall, then, the index underscores the dramatic convergence to liberal market economies taking place throughout the region.

## Economic growth and crises during the 1990s: The Brazil crisis and the new policy debate

How have these transformations affected economic growth in the region? Although it is not possible here to trace the causal connection between policy adjustments and performance, it was clear by the end of the 1990s that the overall growth record was quite mixed (table 4.3). During the first half of the decade, many countries did make substantial recoveries from the bleak recession of the 1980s. These recoveries were spurred, at least in part, by structural reforms, Brady bond agreements, and a renewed inflow of finance capital and direct foreign investment. Argentina, Mexico, and Peru all experienced several years of high growth during the early 1990s, along with significant reductions in poverty levels. Meanwhile, the Chilean economy sustained the strong macroeconomic performance that had begun under Pinochet.

Performance during the second half of the 1990s, on the other hand, was more disappointing: aggregate and per capita GDP growth rates declined in seven of the nine largest economies, and Brazil remained

Table 4.3  Growth in GDP and GDP per capita, 1990–1994 and 1995–1999

(a) Nine largest economies

| Country | GDP per capita | | GDP | |
|---|---|---|---|---|
| | 1990–1994 | 1995–1999 | 1990–1994 | 1995–1999 |
| Argentina | 4.7 | 0.9 | 6.1 | 2.2 |
| Brazil | −0.2 | 0.8 | −1.3 | 2.3 |
| Chile | 4.9 | 3.4 | 6.7 | 4.9 |
| Colombia | 2.2 | −0.8 | 4.2 | 1.1 |
| Ecuador | 1.2 | −1.4 | 3.6 | 0.6 |
| Mexico | 2.0 | 1.1 | 3.9 | 2.8 |
| Peru | 1.3 | 2.7 | 3.1 | 4.5 |
| Uruguay | 3.2 | 1.3 | 3.9 | 2.0 |
| Venezuela | 1.7 | −1.1 | 4.1 | 1.0 |
| Average | 2.3 | 0.8 | 3.8 | 2.2 |

(b) Smaller economies

| Country | GDP per capita | | GDP | |
|---|---|---|---|---|
| | 1990–1994 | 1995–1999 | 1990–1994 | 1995–1999 |
| Bolivia | 1.7 | 1.3 | 4.1 | 3.8 |
| Costa Rica | 1.4 | 1.0 | 4.6 | 3.6 |
| El Salvador | 3.4 | 1.4 | 5.5 | 3.6 |
| Guatemala | 1.2 | 1.5 | 3.9 | 4.2 |
| Honduras | −0.4 | 0.1 | 2.6 | 2.9 |
| Nicaragua | −2.0 | 2.2 | 0.8 | 5.0 |
| Panama | 4.7 | 1.6 | 6.7 | 3.3 |
| Paraguay | 0.0 | −1.2 | 2.8 | 1.5 |
| Dominican Republic | −0.3 | 4.5 | 1.7 | 6.3 |
| Average | 1.1 | 1.4 | 3.6 | 3.8 |

Source: Economic Commission for Latin America and the Caribbean (ECLAC) 1999.

virtually stagnant in per capita terms through the entire decade. Some of the smaller economies of Central America and the Caribbean did experience a significant upsurge in growth during the late 1990s – notably, El Salvador, Guatemala, Nicaragua, Panama, and the Dominican Republic. Growth slowed in many of the others, however, and the general average of per capita growth for the smaller economies reached only 1.4 per cent in the last part of the decade.

Many factors worked to limit growth in the late 1990s, but the financial crises in Mexico in 1994–1995 and in Brazil in 1998–1999 were important parts of the regional story; each of these events had crippling fallouts in other countries of the region. Prior to their respective crises (it should be noted), both countries had taken substantial steps to bring down inflation, to liberalize trade, and to privatize state enterprises. Nevertheless, several factors left each vulnerable to exogenous shocks: these factors included large current accounts and fiscal deficits in Mexico and Brazil, respectively, as well as currency appreciation and a large volume of maturing dollar debt in both countries.

The exogenous shocks that set off the Mexican crisis took the form of political turbulence experienced during the 1994 election campaign, which triggered massive capital flight and a painful devaluation at the end of that year. In Brazil, the shocks came from the Asian and Russian crises of 1997–1998, combined with continuing difficulties in coordinating the finances of state and local governments and implementing a fiscal adjustment. An important turning point in that story came with the devaluation of the real in January 1999, undertaken in response to growing pressure on hard-currency reserves. As in Mexico a few years earlier, the government was impelled to tighten monetary policy in order to contain inflationary pressures and to redouble its efforts at fiscal reform. Although the resulting economic slow-down proved far milder than many had originally feared, it had a significant impact on the economies of neighbouring countries and posed serious threats to the future of Mercosur, the most important regional trading block of the southern hemisphere.

From a short-run perspective, it is significant that both the Mexican and Brazilian governments responded to these crises in ways that were very much in line with prevailing market orthodoxies. Both governments placed a high priority on regaining credibility in financial markets through stabilization initiatives backed by the IMF. In Mexico, the wisdom of this course seemed reaffirmed by a rapid economic rebound in 1996 and 1997. In Brazil, the outcome remained unclear, but the willingness of the Cardoso administration to impose painfully high interest rates in order to contain inflation was quite noteworthy; it represented a major change from previous orientations that tended to view inflation as a necessary and acceptable price of continued growth.

Over the longer term, as I suggest at more length in due course, a frontal attempt to roll back earlier transformations also seemed unlikely. These transformations have created new stakeholders, who could impose significant costs on those political leaders who seek radical changes in the current policies orientations.

Within these parameters, however, the shocks encountered during the second half of the 1990s – and, particularly, the Brazilian crisis – are likely to have important long-term implications for debates over macroeconomic policy and economic growth in the region. One major reason is that the cascading sequence of crises in Asia, Russia, and Brazil has had an important impact on opinion within the international centres of economic power. The credibility and political support for the IMF have been seriously weakened within the Washington and New York "policy communities," and have impacted its capacity to play a stabilizing role within the international system. Just as important, the "Washington Consensus" has been deeply shaken by sharp divisions over exchange-rate policy and liberalization of the capital account, over problems of moral hazard in the behaviour of international investors, and – more broadly still – over the dangers and limits of "globalization."

Within Latin America itself, the spaces opened by the cracks in the Washington Consensus, combined with the direct fallout of the Mexican and Brazilian crises, is also likely to widen conflicts over macroeconomic policy alternatives. Within Brazil, the period immediately preceding the devaluation was marked by sharp disputes over exchange-rate policy. Advocates of "holding the line" – or, more accurately, of continuing a very gradual depreciation of the currency – feared that, without a prior fiscal adjustment, a major devaluation would lead to an uncontrolled stampede of dollars out of the country. Such views were held by officials in the Brazilian Finance Ministry and the US Treasury, as well as by international financial actors with a strong economic stake in the stability of the currency. Advocates of a greater devaluation argued that the current exchange rate was unsustainable and that high interest rates imposed in attempts to maintain it would drive up the fiscal deficit and reduce exports. This position was articulated by a number of influential economists within the Brazilian government such as Jose Serra, as well as by "mainstream" US economists such as Rudiger Dornbusch. Distributive interests were at play as well: the case for devaluation and lower interest rates was pushed hard by exporters and industrialists, represented in the powerful Industrial Federation of São Paulo.

Notwithstanding the less-than-expected costs of Brazil's eventual devaluation, the lessons to be drawn from the experience remain ambiguous, both for Brazil and for Latin America more generally. This is not only because the Brazilian recovery is still fragile but also because the causes of the crisis and the appropriate responses are subject to debate over counterfactuals. Would Brazil have been better off if it had widened its exchange-rate band much earlier? Could the dislocations of devaluation have been avoided by more rapid fiscal-adjustment measures? Or was an effective fiscal adjustment precluded by the high interest rates necessary to defend the real?

One general conclusion that does appear to have emerged from the current situation is that attempts to maintain pegged exchange rates lead eventually to overvaluation, currency speculation, and disruptive devaluations. After the experiences in Asia and Brazil, not to mention the collapse of the Argentine convertibility regime, even the IMF appears to have come round to this position; there continue to be strong disagreements, however, about the alternatives.

One possibility is to substitute the US dollar for local currency, a step recently taken in Ecuador and a number of Central American countries. "Dollarization," however, is a very risky measure: it eliminates exchange-rate instability but also takes away the capacity to use monetary policy to cushion external shocks. It has thus become a serious policy alternative only in countries such as Ecuador or Argentina, where chronic high inflation and policy instability has undermined the credibility of government policy makers. It is doubtful that such an arrangement could be implemented successfully in countries such as Mexico or Brazil, where many economic and political groups resist attempts to relinquish control over monetary policy.

The other main alternative – a floating currency – is more politically acceptable in the other countries but must be accompanied by strict (and, typically, controversial) fiscal and monetary policies if severe disruptions in trade are to be avoided.

A related issue involves national regulation of transnational capital flows. In this area there has been considerable interest in Chile's interest-free deposit requirements for incoming portfolio investment. This arrangement was often credited with helping to insulate Chile from financial-market turbulence. Nevertheless, the Chilean government itself has suspended the deposit requirements on the grounds that it discouraged needed capital inflows. On this issue, the Malaysian experience with capital controls will undoubtedly also figure in the policy debates.

These macroeconomic policies, of course, will not be the only determinants of growth during coming decades; a very long list of other policy issues of significant consequence remains on the agenda as well, including labour-market reform, competitiveness policies, restructuring and regulation of domestic banking systems, tax reform, and social policy. Moreover, a number of developments crucial to growth unfold more or less independently of policy choices taken at the national level of government. Much of the flow of FDI, for example, responds to the distribution of skills or of raw materials within subnational regions, or to the integration of local firms in transnational production chains (Gereffi and Korzeniewicz 1994). It is also obvious that the policy and performance of the American, European, and Japanese economies will have a decisive impact in coming years.

On the other hand, the issues of capital controls and exchange-rate management highlighted by the Mexican and Brazilian crises raise core questions about the links between Latin America and the international economy. Even before the collapse of Argentina's currency board, it was unlikely that Mercosur could survive for long in a context where one major trading partner relied on a currency board and the other on a floating exchange rate. This anomalous situation gave rise to discussions about the possibility of macroeconomic convergence and the establishment of a common currency within the trading bloc. At least in the medium term, however, the conditions that might allow for this level of coordination do not appear to be present, particularly in Brazil, where party fragmentation and robust federalism remain significant impediments to coherent fiscal policy.

The broader issue, of course, concerns the policies that Latin American countries will adopt in their relation to the broader global economy – how they can respond to the opportunities and challenges of trade and capital flows in ways that maintain macroeconomic stability and maximize opportunities for growth. The stakes of debates over macroeconomic policy are likely to be very high. In a recent study, Dani Rodrik (1999: 17) shows that the ability to maintain macroeconomic stability was the "single most important factor accounting for the diversity of post-1975 performance in the developing world." Conversely, countries unable to maintain macroeconomic policy in the face of exogenous shocks suffered dramatic collapses of productivity.

## Social impacts and welfare reform

It is increasingly part of the conventional wisdom that sustainable and coherent responses to these macroeconomic challenges require the construction of social safety nets that cushion shocks to vulnerable sectors of the population. In Latin America, however, economic crises and structural transformations have undermined the "social bargains" that once characterized the relation between some social sectors and the state. Until the early 1980s, these bargains were closely linked to import-substitution strategies and relied heavily on subsidized employment in the public sector, ISI industries, and strategic export and transport sectors of the economy. Unions organized in these sectors were often able to secure substantial protections and welfare benefits for their rank and file. With some important exceptions (such as Uruguay and Costa Rica), however, these generally came at the cost of substantial rigidities and the exclusion of people in the rural sector and the large urban informal economy (Mesa-Lago 1978).

As a result of the shocks of the 1980s, the countries of the region experienced a substantial increase in both poverty levels and inequality, while governments faced much tighter fiscal constraints. This combination of fiscal constraint and sharply deteriorating social conditions has given rise to a significant policy debate about how limited public resources should be deployed in order to minimize the social dislocations. To what extent should public benefits be available to all citizens, or targeted to those most in need? To what extent should they be linked to individual contributions and to what extent to general taxes based on solidaristic or redistributive norms?

To analyse this debate, it is important to underline the significance of the two-way causal relationship between growth and structural change, on the one hand, and opportunities for welfare reform, on the other. Sustained and equitable economic growth eases the conflict over welfare reform, because there are fewer demands on the system and more resources available to meet these demands. On the other hand, as noted, compensation and social insurance may contribute to growth by encouraging consent to market-oriented policies and maintaining social cohesion. Given this relationship, it is important to review some of the questions involving both the broad social impacts of the current social transformations, before turning directly to the issues of social policy and welfare reform.

## Social impacts of the crisis and adjustment

The social impact of the 1980s recession and the resulting efforts at structural adjustment have been the subject of major controversy, precisely because it has been very difficult to sort out the effects of the crisis from those of the response. Although a full discussion of these issues is well beyond the scope of this chapter, it is possible to underline a number of general points.

First, overall macroeconomic performance has had a major impact on poverty levels in the region. Studies of the social impact of the crisis of the 1980s show that both the recessions and high inflations of that period had devastating impacts on the poor (Lustig 1995; Morley 1995). Conversely, the picture began to change somewhat during the 1990s as the region began to recover. Disinflation had a major positive impact on the real wages of the low-income population, and growth allowed more family members to enter the workforce and augment family income. A recent study by the Economic Commission for Latin America and the Caribbean (ECLAC) shows that, between 1990 and 1997, the number of households below the poverty line dropped from 41 per cent to 36 per cent, with the most substantial declines in Chile, Brazil, Panama, Costa Rica, Peru, and Columbia (ECLAC 1999). The connection was stronger in some countries than in others: for example, in Argentina the decline in poverty was small, relative to high growth rates achieved in the early 1990s. Nevertheless, on the basis of the general evidence, there is good reason to believe that poverty will decline if countries can maintain macroeconomic stability and economic growth.

There is considerably less reason for hope about the prospects of reducing high levels of inequality. Income gaps widened substantially during the 1980s, but continued to grow as well in many countries during the 1990s or, at best, showed only limited improvement. The ECLAC (1999) studies show worsening income distributions in six countries (Argentina, Brazil, Costa Rica, Ecuador, Panama, and Venezuela); they improved in Bolivia, Honduras, Mexico, and Uruguay and remained about the same in Chile. This raises major questions about whether structural reforms introduced at the end of the decade have alleviated or added to the crippling social effects of the earlier crisis; this issue, needless to say, is hotly contested.

Samuel Morley (1995) has placed the primary blame for increasing inequality on the effects of the crisis, but has argued as well that the distributive impact of adjustment depended on cross-national differences in the relative weight of the traded and non-traded sectors of the economy and in the relations of the poor to those sectors. Where the traded-goods sector was relatively small (Argentina or Venezuela), and/or where it employed relatively limited numbers of workers, recovery has been slow and the social impact has been harsh, relative to that in other countries in the region. Devaluations hurt the poor as consumers as well as workers in the non-traded sectors, and these losses were not offset by new employment opportunities in the export sector. On the other hand, countries with the largest export sectors responded most quickly to devaluations and thus recovered most rapidly from crises. Where the export sector was relatively labour intensive, increased employment opportunities tended to offset employment losses in the sheltered sectors, muting the negative effects of economic adjustment on income inequality.

Other studies attempting to disentangle the effects of the crisis from those of structural adjustment focus on similar variables but reach somewhat more pessimistic conclusions about the region as a whole. A collection of works edited by Victor Bulmer-Thomas (1996) attempts to disaggregate the effects of specific adjustment policies. In addition to the negative effects of trade reform on employment in the sheltered sectors, liberalization of domestic financial markets has led to higher interest rates and greater concentration of wealth. Fiscal reforms are more ambiguous, because they have helped to reduce inflation but have also involved cuts in social programmes. The only aspect of reform that is found to have positive effects is the opening of capital accounts, which lowers interest rates and broadens access to financial markets.

As with Morley, the key question for contributors to the Bulmer-

Thomas study is whether reforms will generate sustainable high growth, which can potentially offset the negative short- and medium-run impact of reform. There is considerable scepticism, however, that this will happen. Empirically, as already implied, growth rates have been uneven (Bulmer-Thomas 1996: 308). More important, it is argued that equity losses during the first phase of reform were so severe that subsequent recoveries cannot be expected to be high enough to reverse their impact (Bulmer-Thomas 1996: 310).

## Implications for welfare reform

Even if growth alone cannot be expected to ensure a significant improvement in distribution and social welfare, it will have an important impact on the viability of social programmes directed toward these ends. Studies by the Economic and Social Commission on Latin America also show that per capita social spending on health and education increased markedly during the economic recoveries of the 1990s (table 4.4). In the

Table 4.4 Social expenditures in Latin America, 1990/1991–1996/1997 (1997 dollars)

| | Expenditure per capita | | | Social expenditure/ total expenditure | |
|---|---|---|---|---|---|
| | 1990–1991 | 1996–1997 | Change (%) | 1990–1991 | 1996–1997 |
| Argentina | 1,222 | 1,570 | 28.5 | 62.2 | 65.1 |
| Uruguay | 929 | 1,371 | 47.6 | 62.3 | 69.8 |
| Brazil | 821 | 951 | 15.8 | 59.5 | 59.1 |
| Chile | 451 | 725 | 60.8 | 60.8 | 65.9 |
| Panama | 494 | 683 | 38.3 | 40.0 | 39.9 |
| Costa Rica | 445 | 550 | 23.6 | 64.4 | 65.1 |
| Colombia | 181 | 391 | 116.0 | 29.7 | 38.2 |
| Mexico | 283 | 352 | 24.4 | 41.6 | 52.9 |
| Venezuela | 328 | 317 | −3.4 | 33.9 | 39.0 |
| Peru | 51 | 169 | 231.4 | 16.7 | 40.9 |
| Paraguay | 55 | 148 | 169.1 | 39.9 | 47.1 |
| El Salvador | 87 | 147 | 69.1 | 21.9 | 26.5 |
| Bolivia | 55 | 119 | 116.4 | 25.8 | 44.2 |
| Dominican Republic | 66 | 107 | 62.1 | 36.9 | 39.0 |
| Guatemala | 52 | 71 | 36.6 | 29.8 | 42.1 |
| Honduras | 59 | 58 | −1.7 | 33.1 | 31.9 |
| Nicaragua | 48 | 49 | 2.1 | 38.3 | 35.6 |
| Latin America | 331 | 457 | 38.1 | 41 | 47.2 |

Source: ECLAC 1999: 97.

region as a whole, the increase was 38 per cent between 1990/91 and 1997/98, about the same as the per capita rate of growth. Of the 17 Latin American countries examined by ECLAC, 14 experienced such increases; this allowed three-quarters of the countries to surpass pre-crisis spending levels (reached prior to 1980). On the other hand, the study also indicates that many of these gains were seriously threatened by the recession of 1999. Particularly with respect to countries where per capita spending has been relatively high, "the most pressing challenge may be to consolidate levels that have now been reached, especially in view of current signs that growth may be dampened by the crises of the last few years" (ECLAC 1999: 105).

In the light both of continuing fiscal constraints and of the uncertain prospects for growth over the medium run, much of the debate over welfare reform has centred on how to redeploy resources in ways that will maximize their impact on "social capital" and socially vulnerable sectors of the population. With respect to welfare reform, two issues are central to this policy debate.

- *Universalism versus targeted poverty relief.* One question is whether the government seeks to institutionalize a more inclusive or universal system of social insurance or whether it remains targeted, either to the poor and vulnerable or to the politically salient. For governments in the region, the targeting of resources toward vulnerable groups offers some relief from the fiscal pressures they now face. On the other hand, targeted assistance also involves high administrative costs and is susceptible to political corruption. To the extent that it focuses on the poor, targeted aid does not address the insecurities of other low-income sectors and risks backlash from those citizens who are not eligible for benefits (Huber 1996).
- *Social or individual financing and provision.* A second critical question concerns the extent to which the government should be directly involved in the financing and provision of social insurance – funding its commitments through taxation on the grounds of some solidaristic or redistributive principles and providing services directly. Alternatively, governments can establish and mandate private savings vehicles of various sorts and can rely to a greater extent on the market for service provision. Such conflicts are likely to be particularly sharp where fiscal pressures are intense while at the same time "social rights" have been strongly embedded in the culture of blue-collar and middle-income sectors of the population (Pierson 1996).

Social spending in health and education reflects similar dilemmas. In education, the most pressing needs are to allocate more resources to primary and secondary education, which have historically received much fewer resources than have universities. In health, as in social insurance more generally, the allocation of individual and social responsibilities for costs is a key question, as is the distribution of pay-offs between primary and preventive care and treatment of more complex diseases. An additional issue in both of these areas is the need to win the cooperation of the skilled service providers (especially health workers and teachers), who are essential for the effective delivery of services (Nelson 1997).

As is the case with adjustment policies, IFIs have played a crucial role in setting the agenda for debates over welfare reform. Although projects are not uniform across countries or time, the general pattern has been to press for (a) targeted assistance to low-income groups, (b) privatization and and/or decentralization of health and education services, (c) the encouragement of competition among service providers. In pension reform, the Chilean system of private investment funds has provided an important policy template: the model has had widespread influence throughout the region, despite high management costs that cut deeply into the returns generated by the investment funds.

Again, as was the case in macroeconomic adjustment, alternative international models such as that provided by the EU have been less influential in Latin America than in Eastern Europe, although the Inter-American Development Bank has at times adopted perspectives differing from those of the World Bank or the IMF. The Latin American exposure to neo-liberal influences is also greater than in Asia, where a tradition of very limited public commitments to welfare has left a good deal of room for expansion; most Latin American governments (as indicated) face tighter fiscal constraints.

It should not be surprising, therefore, that welfare-reform policies of many countries in the region have adopted reforms that move along liberal lines. This appears quite evident, for example, in the case of pension reform: since 1990, at least seven countries have transferred part or all of their pension contributions from pay-as-you-go public funds to private funds. According to estimates provided by Sarah Brooks (1999), five countries (Chile, Colombia, El Salvador, Mexico, and Peru) have switched entirely to private pension funds; the other cases of partial privatization are Argentina (49 per cent), Bolivia (79 per cent), and Uruguay (39 per cent).

Notwithstanding these trends, however, it may well be the case that convergence around international reform templates within Latin America will be slower and less complete in the area of social policy than it was in the case of macroeconomic reform. In part (as has been observed elsewhere), this is because social policy tends on the whole to be less salient to international markets than macroeconomic policy and performance and because the administrative complexity in social-policy areas such as health and education provides more opportunities for service providers and other stakeholders to force compromises in the policy reform (Nelson 1997).

In the specific case of pension reform, the overhang of commitments to existing pensioners places significant financial limits on privatization, because the shift of contributions into private funds reduces the tax revenues that fund existing liabilities. These constraints are greatest, of course, where coverage of the old system was most extensive: thus, in her cross-national study of pension reform, Brooks (1999) finds a significant negative relation between privatization and the size of the pre-existing system.

In the case of welfare reform more generally, there are strong political as well as financial impediments to radical reform. As in Europe, prior welfare entitlements have created constituencies in unions, pensioners, and other beneficiaries that provide strong political constraints to targeting and other liberal reforms (Pierson 1996). Such groups are likely to be especially powerful in countries such as Uruguay and Costa Rica, where pre-crisis coverage of the welfare system was quite extensive. In Uruguay, the ECLAC Social Panorama argues that the extensive social-service network and broad coverage of retirement benefits and transfer payments helps to account for a reduction in income inequality during the course of the 1990s. It did so without a negative impact on growth rates, although the causal connections remain unclear.

In systems where coverage was more limited, and/or in those facing substantial fiscal constraints, the politics of welfare reform may be more complex. On the one hand, as noted above, many of these systems do involve extensive commitments to constituencies represented by well-organized unions and associations and, at times, popularly-based political parties. Notwithstanding extensive fiscal pressures, such groups may be inclined to mount a strong defence of the existing system and to resist attempts to redeploy resources toward more targeted assistance. On the other hand, given the inequities and rigidities in existing systems, they lack the legitimacy of their counterparts in Europe. Under such circumstances, support for welfare provision that would address the interests of marginal groups has at times come from social movements and NGOs, in some instances with support from the World Bank and other IFIs.

In the aftermath of democratic transitions, politicians also have stronger incentives to appeal to a broader electorate, providing some incentives for a widening of the social safety net. In Mexico, for example, the National Solidarity Program (Programa Nacional de Solidaridad; PRONASOL) was a widely popular programme during the Salinas period: although electoral interests had a strong influence on how resources were allocated, these did reach poor communities in cases such as Chile (Graham 1994). Kurt Weyland (1998) has documented similar effects in Peru and Argentina.

A key issue – still unresolved in most countries, however – is whether such reforms can be combined with compensation for other groups disadvantaged by market conditions in ways that are economically sustainable and politically viable. Compromises that might accommodate existing stakeholders and formerly excluded groups are not inconceivable; they may depend, however, on mechanisms of party and interest-group representation that can forge the bargains necessary for a stable political equilibrium. These channels of representation remain weak in most countries, even those that have actually taken steps to initiate welfare reform. Where socio-political compromises elude politicians, policy stalemate may increase political alienation and magnify political pressures on other aspects of the market transformation.

## The politics of development: Brazil and Mexico

In view of the difficulties sketched above, it should not be at all surprising that we see signs of popular protest and disaffection throughout the region. Such signs were clearly evident in the round of national elections occurring in the late 1990s. In a number of countries, criticisms of neo-liberal strategies were important campaign themes of major presidential candidates: the most visible example was Hugo Chavez, whose overwhelming victory in Venezuela was based on sweeping criticisms of both the political system and the market reforms undertaken by previous presidents. Chavez's victory, however, was not the only sign of electoral protest: in Uruguay, dissaffection with the traditional Colorado and Blanco parties allowed Tabare Vasquez of the left-of-centre Frente Amplio to emerge as the leading candidate in the first round of the 1999 presidential elections. In Mexico, Labastida, the candidate of the Partido Revolucionario Institucional (PRI; Institutional Revolutionary Party), has attempted to distance himself from the "technocratic" approaches of his predecessors. In Argentina, although the winning candidate promised continuity with the basic economic policies of Carlos Saul Menem, it was also clear that much of his support came from voters who were profoundly dissatisfied with deteriorating economic conditions. Disaffection has deepened dramatically, of course, with the financial crisis of 2001–2002.

Even more significant than the vote for critics of prevailing market policies are indications that voters in many countries are becoming more alienated from representative institutions themselves – particularly from the established political parties. Parties, to be sure, have always been weakly rooted in most Latin American countries; nevertheless, contemporary trends indicate deterioration even in those countries where parties had previously been important parts of the political landscape. The major parties in Peru and Venezuela have virtually disappeared as significant political forces, and have been on the defensive in Uruguay. Between the late 1980s and mid-1990s, the percentage of voters identifying with a political party also declined sharply in Argentina (44.4 to 24.6), Chile (80.0 to 50.0), and Mexico (62.0 to 49.0) (Hagopian 1998: 116). Party identification, to be sure, has declined throughout Western democracies, in part as a consequence of the impact of television campaigning and post-industrial "issue voting." Hagopian notes, however, that in contrast to most Latin American countries, voters who continue to identify parties in Germany, England, and Sweden still constitute between 65 and 75 per cent of the electorate (Hagopian 1998: 116).

Combined with increasing voter absention in many countries and highly volatile swings in the support for political parties, these trends constitute strong evidence of electoral dealignment and alienation in most, if not all, countries in the region. Although this vacuum might be filled in part by NGOs, civic organizations, and policy networks, it is difficult to see how they can substitute for political parties as agents of interest aggregation and policy negotiation. This implies that most countries will face continuing difficulties in arriving at stable and broadly based social compromises over development and welfare strategies. Some countries – as in Venezuela – will remain vulnerable as well to the rise of political strongmen who rise to power on the basis of populist and antidemocratic appeals.

On the other side of the political ledger, it is important to emphasize that the market reforms themselves have altered the economic and political balance of power in many countries. New stakeholders have been created by the changes themselves, and their reaction would be costly to any politician seeking to reverse reforms.

In a number of countries, liberalization has significantly increased the export-orientation of the private sector. In Mexico, this is reinforced by NAFTA. Privatization has also created a powerful class of new owners that would strongly resist attempts at reversal: these interests include not only domestic private groups but also foreign buyers. As the privatization process has gone forward, it has also weakened the capacity of public-sector unions to resist.

Most important in many countries has been the strong positive reaction to successful stabilization of high-inflation economies. Although anti-inflation policies were extraordinarily controversial in the 1980s and early 1990s, they have proved enormously popular once implemented, particularly among low-income sectors that were hit hardest by inflation. Successful stabilizations were instrumental in the electoral support for Menem in Argentina and, in both 1992 and 1995 (a depression year), polls indicated that majorities were willing to accept deficit reduction and cutbacks in social programmes in exchange for price stability. In Brazil, the success of the Real Plan also accounts for Cardoso's victory over the left candidate, Lula, in the presidential elections of 1994 and 1998. In the absence of further growth and economic improvement, the political gains from these measures eventually faded. Nevertheless, a resurgence of inflation would also clearly impose major political costs on any incumbent government.

More generally, it seems plausible that experiences of past decades – including events both inside the region and in other parts of the world – have led to a basic change in "world views" and a greater general acceptance of market principles. This shift seems clearest among policy élite groups, where both incumbent officials and most of their opponents seem willing to work within the framework of structural changes instituted during the preceding decade, but there also appear to be changes in mass opinion. In a Latino barometer survey of 14 Latin American countries in 1998, 65 per cent of the respondents agreed that a market economy was best for their country, whereas only 21 per cent disagreed (reported in the *Wall Street Journal*). These opinions vary substantially from country to country; however, earlier surveys in Argentina and Peru pointed in similar directions. In 1992 a survey of Argentine opinion, for example, showed that 59 per cent of the public agreed that free competition was likely to lead to development, in contrast to 35 per cent who argued for state planning. In 1995 the percentage favouring a "free market without state intervention" dropped to 49 per cent, but this was still quite substantial in a depression year and only 33 per cent disagreed (Stokes 1998). In Mexico, opposition to the government's reform programme rose substantially between 1992 and 1995, from 9.4 to 47.1 per cent; nevertheless, even in 1995, over 50 per cent of the population surveyed continued to support reform packages pursued by the market-oriented government (Kaufman and Zuckermann 1998).

Venezuela, it should be noted, constitutes an important exception to this broader picture. Expectations in that country have been shaped by a long history of petroleum wealth and public welfare and they are unlikely to fade quickly. Around 70 per cent of Venezuelans surveyed in 1993 expressed support for the maintenance of social programmes and the subsidization of food prices, and 52 per cent opposed the idea that prices should be freed to stimulate production (Stokes 1998).

Of course, there is no guarantee that, in other countries, opinion will not also shift against reform in the event of continued poor performance.

It seems plausible that, at most, "pro-market" opinions reported in the general surveys reflect resignation and the lack of perceived alternatives, rather than strong, positive support for the reforms of earlier decades. Even taking these cautions into account, however, political officials in most countries continue to have considerable political space to search for ways to broaden social policies and increase equity within the context of a basic market framework.

To explore fully the long-term implications of these contradictory political pressures it would be necessary to undertake a country-by-country analysis. The variance in the current context ranges from Chile's relatively solid economic and democratic system, to the financial meltdown in Argentina, to the near-collapse of the state in Colombia. Such variations may well increase in future years.

For the region as a whole, however, developments in the two largest economies – Brazil and Mexico – appear to be crucial. The former has emerged as the core economy of South America, and its performance over the coming decade will have a substantial impact on neighbouring countries. Evolving ties between Mexico and the United States, on the other hand, will be critical not only for Mexico, but also for the US economy and for other countries in Central America and the Caribbean. I thus conclude this chapter by discussing the critical junctures which these countries appear to be facing at the start of the twenty-first century.

## Brazil

In evaluating prospects for a recovery and long-term expansion, it must be emphasized that Brazil has unique underlying advantages, including a huge domestic economy, a dynamic export sector, and a large inflow of direct foreign investment which will begin to pay off in coming years. Moreover, during the first half of the 1990s there were significant steps towards both trade liberalization and privatization. During the Cardoso presidency, the sell-off of major portions of the state sector brought in billions of dollars in new direct foreign investment and reduced pressure on fiscal and external accounts. In response to the fallout from the 1994 peso crisis, moreover, the federal government also restructured and privatized several major state and private banks – a move which substantially reduced its vulnerability in the current financial crisis. Politically, the government's most important achievement was the implementation of the Real Plan – the disinflation programme that was started while Cardoso was Finance Minister in 1993. Stabilization was based on a combination of a tough monetary policy and reliance on an exchange-rate anchor; it was, clearly, the most popular achievement of the Cardoso government.

On the other hand, Brazil's loosely organized parties and highly decentralized federal system have made it difficult for its political leaders to address a number of pressing issues discussed in the preceding sections, including both fiscal and tax reform (Mainwaring 1999). Recent studies have, it is true, shown that legislative parties are more cohesive than previously believed, at least with respect to roll-call votes (Limongi and Figueiredo 1998). Throughout most of his term, moreover, President Cardoso was able to cobble together a fractious but durable majority coalition in the Congress. Nevertheless, legislative politicians are highly dependent on personal appeals to local constituents and are far more concerned with access to patronage for their districts than with macroeconomic policy. Recalcitrant back-benchers and powerful state governors have made it extremely difficult for Cardoso to obtain legislative backing for proposed reforms, or to coordinate fiscal transfers between federal and local governments.

These difficulties were very much in evidence in the response to the shocks of the Russian meltdown in the summer and fall of 1998. Notwithstanding the dangers of a currency collapse, legislators delayed action on a series of reforms that the government had negotiated as part of an IMF rescue package. For part of that period, the presidential and congressional election campaign diverted the attention of the political leadership, but delays continued well after the elections had passed. The bubble finally burst in January 1999 after Itamar Franco, the governor of a major state (and Cardoso's predecessor as president), declared a moratorium on the state's debt to the federal government. This dealt a psychological blow to the government's attempt to maintain the credibility of its exchange rate. With dollar reserves rapidly declining, the government first attempted a controlled devaluation, then turned quickly to a float; in less than twenty-four hours, the real depreciated by over 40 per cent against the dollar.

As noted, this event did not produce the financial meltdown that some had anticipated, but it did ratchet up to a new level the difficulties faced by Brazil and by the region as a whole. The negotiation of a new IMF agreement in February contributed to an easing of the run on the currency, and tight monetary policies helped to fend off inflationary pressures. It might even be the case that – in abandoning its attempt to defend the currency – Brazil chose the "least bad" of the available options. Nevertheless, Brazil remained in recession throughout 1999 – hardly an exit from the crisis that one might have wished for in the best of all possible worlds.

More important for the long term is that there is still much that could go wrong in coming years. The perverse political incentives and underlying social pressures that led to the crisis in the first place remain in place.

Although the government appeared set to meet IMF targets for fiscal retrenchment in 1999, Cardoso's undisciplined legislative coalition continued to delay the passage of key measures such as social security and tax reform. A precipitous decline in the popularity of the President, moreover, significantly weakened his hand *vis-à-vis* the congress. Thus, the Brazilian economy remains extremely vulnerable to a new round of shocks over the medium term, and this, in turn, poses significant threats to sustained recovery in the rest of South America.

The ongoing macroeconomic difficulties, as noted, also have serious implications for efforts to deal with welfare reform within the region. As indicated, the issues of education and health reforms were beginning to emerge from the second-class status that they had endured during the 1980s, as a result of pressure from assorted domestic groups and from IFIs such as the World Bank and the Inter-American Development Bank (IDB). Although demands for social reform are likely to continue in coming years, the need for tight fiscal and monetary policy will seriously constrain the capacity of Brazil and other Latin American governments to respond over the medium run.

Reforms in representative and party institutions are also urgent. Proposals are on the table for electoral reforms that would strengthen incentives to form larger and more disciplined parties, but it is far from clear that legislative politicians with stakes in the existing system will be willing to pass such reforms. Given the underlying strengths of the economy, it is still quite possible that Brazil can muddle its way back to recovery over the next few years, particularly if there is no new exogenous shock to push it off track again. However, the political and social vulnerabilities that led to the crisis of 1998–1999 are structural and institutional, not conjunctural. The campaign for the October 2000 presidential election increased the political uncertainly and, in the absence of reforms of political institutions, the government will continue to face serious difficulties in coordinating either macroeconomic or social policy.

## Mexico

Like Brazil, Mexico faces daunting economic and political challenges. Until the defeat of the PRI in the presidential election of 2000, Mexico was the only large country besides Cuba not to have completed a transition to electoral democracy and, despite the landmark victory of Vicente Fox, there is great uncertainty about how politics will evolve over the next six years. After so many decades of dominant-party rule, Fox faces a state apparatus, police, and courts permeated with clientelistic networks and corruption. This has increased in recent decades as a consequence of the drug trade. As in Brazil, there are pervasive problems of poverty, severe regional disparities and social inequalities, and widespread political alienation.

Notwithstanding such problems, there are grounds for optimism about developments in Mexico in the medium-term future. Restructuring the Mexican economy started earlier and proceeded further than in Brazil. Even before the signing of the NAFTA agreement, an extensive process of trade liberalization and deregulation had opened the economy to international market forces. In 1994–1995, to be sure, this proved to be a mixed blessing, as heavy dollar indebtedness and political upheaval combined to produce the peso crisis. Nevertheless, with the assistance of a United States–IMF rescue package, recovery came quite quickly and, by 1997, Mexico appeared to be back on a growth track.

Public finances in Mexico also appear to be in better shape than those in Brazil. The fiscal picture is clouded, it is true, by the huge costs of bailing out the fragile banking system; this has yet to recover from the hasty privatization in the early 1990s and from the blows of the 1994 financial crisis. However, the dangers that this problem poses are offset to an important extent not only by the very cautious fiscal and monetary policies that the government has adopted throughout most of the 1990s but also by steps to strengthen significantly the independence of the Central Bank. Moreover, under Zedillo, the government has moved steadily toward systematic reorganization of banking liabilities and the establishment of a regulatory financial framework.

Finally, integration through NAFTA into the North American trading system has served not only to "lock in" earlier reforms but also to consolidate Mexico's position as a major site for export-bound investment. This has come at the cost of serious social dislocations and regional inequalities, particularly in the agricultural south. Nevertheless, the close links to the vast North American markets insulated Mexico from the economic turbulence that hit Brazil and the rest of South America at the end of the 1990s: growth rates reached well over 3 per cent in both 1998 and 1999. Although the Mexican economy is certainly more vulnerable than Brazil to cyclical downturns in the United States, its ties to the developed North American economies can be expected to provide the conditions for sustained expansion over the longer term. If this occurs, we can expect poverty rates to decline, as they have elsewhere during periods of growth.

In many respects, the greatest opportunities and the most serious challenges come in the political and social realms, rather than the economy. On the positive side, even before the 2000 presidential election, Mexico had made substantial progress towards the establishment of a competitive multiparty system. Although the PRI remains the largest single party and may well win the presidency again in 2000, it must now compete at every level of the federal system with oppositions of the Partido Acción Nacional (PAN) on the right and the Partido de Revolucion Democratico (Party of Democratic Revolution; PRD) on the left. With the decline of the hegemonic party has come a diminution of the overweening power of the president, who is no longer in a position to "appoint" state governors or mayors by controlling dominant-party nominations, or to dictate to a rubber-stamp federal congress. As is the case with economic reforms, domestic impulses toward political reform are reinforced by Mexico's deepening ties with Canada and the United States.

The major political question in Mexico – as in Brazil and most other Latin American countries – is whether it can evolve a system of representation that provides the basis for the negotiation of stable compromises over development and welfare policies and that allows citizens to hold governments accountable for their implementation. Moving in that direction, in turn, will depend on whether Mexican politicians and citizens can deal with several key issues that have arisen in the course of the political transition.

A fundamental question – and one that is emphasized throughout the theoretical literature on democratic transitions – is whether contending party and interest-group leaders can converge around shared interests in the establishment of a credible legal–constitutional framework for electoral competition and policy decisions. Mutual accommodation, however, will depend at a minimum on further reductions of the PRI's privileged access to the resources and authority of the state. This process is bound to be fraught with conflicts between the government and opposition and within the PRI itself.

As in other transitions, however, it is far from impossible to imagine a scenario of confidence-building accommodations that move the system in a positive direction; indeed, there have already been a number of such steps of considerable importance. These include, for example, a series of institutional reforms that have gone far to establish the honesty and credibility of the electoral process. By the late 1990s, the PRI had lost majority control of the federal congress as well as 5 of the 31 state governorships and the mayorality of Mexico City. Opposition-party victories at the state and federal levels have both increased their credibility as alternatives to the PRI and have loosened the latter's historical grip on public resources. Since the loss of the PRI's congressional majority in 1997, legislative cooperation in framing bank reforms and sustaining a cautious fiscal policy has demonstrated the capacity of the executives and congressional leaders to reach policy compromises across party lines.

Within the context of these developments, a key issue concerns the shape and viability of the party system that emerges as electoral politics become more competitive. At the end of the 1990s, as noted, the trend appeared to be toward three large parties of the centre, centre-right, and centre-left – an arrangement that can potentially represent a fairly wide spectrum of opinion and provide stable governing majorities. However, electoral and organizational realignment is likely in coming decades, and incentives of politicians to offer viable alternatives to the electorate will depend in part on the evolution of rules governing nominations and election. A major question on the reform agenda is whether to end the constitutional ban on the immediate re-election of governors and legislators – a provision that has reduced politicians' accountability to territorial constituencies and allowed their superiors to determine the "next step" in their careers. Party structures will also be affected by evolving intergovernmental division of authority and fiscal resources within the Mexican federal system. On the one hand, these structures have been strengthened in many localities by the establishment of cleaner and more participatory electoral politics. On the other hand, an excessive decentralization of power – as in the Brazilian case – can impede parties' capacity for coordination at the federal level and lead in some areas to the entrenchment of local bosses and drug Mafiosi.

In the background, of course, are even deeper questions related to citizenship, rule of law, and social rights. At best, these will remain on the social agenda for decades; at worst, one can imagine a scenario of state failure characterized by the privatization of violence and a collapse of legal control over entire regions, with effective central governance restricted to the northern tier or states on the US border. Against these possibilities, however, it will be a major accomplishment if the institutional framework is rebuilt in a way that encourages accountability and compromise and avoids some of the perverse incentives that impede political coordination in the Brazilian system. This will not, in itself, eliminate the myriad problems that persist within Mexican society, but it may increase the opportunities to search for solutions.

## Conclusions

Mexico, Brazil, and the other countries of Latin America face important crossroads at the beginning of the twenty-first century. Indeed, the choices made by citizens and governments may be more important than at any time since the debt crisis of the early 1980s. These choices continue to involve macroeconomic policy – as they have throughout the past decades. Moreover, disappointing social effects of the "first round" of market reforms also place welfare policies high on the reform agenda.

Coherent macroeconomic policies and viable welfare systems are mutually interdependent and tend to reinforce each other over the long run. At any given moment, however, policy choices involve tensions and trade-offs that can have important and lasting consequences. Development strategies that ignore investment in "human capital" and vulnerable social sectors can be undermined by distributive pressures and political and economic uncertainty. However, social investments are also placed at risk if they are undertaken at the cost of coherent macroeconomic policies that lead to disequilibria and recessions. The social effects of poor economic performance, as I have suggested, may well offset the gains that derive from social spending.

The severity of the trade-offs between macroeconomic caution and social investment will be determined in part by macroeconomic and international conditions at the time that choices are made. The choices themselves, however, are inevitably political, rather than technical or economic in nature: this is so both because the full risks of "bad" choices can never be known with certainty and because contending groups will have different degrees of tolerance for these risks. There is every reason to believe, therefore, that the specific balances between the competing objectives can (and should) be shaped at the margins by ongoing contestation between political forces on the "left" and the "right."

In many Latin American countries, however, fiscal pressures and the need to maintain credibility in international markets mean that the margin of error is relatively narrow and that policy stalemates or polarized positions are likely to have heavy costs. Under such circumstances, the institutional organization of democracies – and particularly of the party system – can play a critical role in structuring incentives for compromise and providing resources for policy coordination. Where party politicians remain unaccountable to their constituencies and are unable to offer meaningful programmatic alternatives, the dangers of policy "slippage" increase: incremental compromises, in other words, can cumulate in incoherent and unsustainable decisions. Given the pervasive "reform fatigue" evident throughout the region, this is a distinct possibility in a fairly large number of countries. In some instances, failures of representation can lead to even more costly attempts to roll back market-oriented reforms of past decades. Such backlashes will themselves be reversed as they encounter the realities of international markets – but, perhaps, not before inflicting severe damage on the economy and the polity.

## REFERENCES

Brooks, Sara M. 1999. "Social Protection and the Market: Pension Reform in the Era of Capital Mobility." Paper presented at the Annual Meeting of the American Political Science Association, Atlanta, Georgia, 1–5 September 1999.

Bulmer-Thomas, Victor, ed. 1996. *The New Economic Model in Latin America and its Impact on Income Distribution and Poverty*. New York: St Martin's Press.

Cook, Linda J., Mitchell A. Orenstein, and Marilyn Rueschemeyer, eds. 1999. *Left Parties and Social Policy in Postcommunist Europe*. Boulder: Westview Press.

Economic Commission for Latin America and the Caribbean (ECLAC). 1999. *Social Panorama of Latin America*. Santiago: ECLAC.

Gereffi, Gary and Miguel Korzeniewicz, eds. 1994. *Commodity Chains and Global Capitalism*. Connecticut: Praeger.

Graham, Carol. 1994. *Safety Nets, Politics, and the Poor: Transitions to Market Economies*. Washington, DC: Brookings Institution.

Haggard, Stephan. 1990. *Pathways from the Periphery: The Politics of Growth in Newly Industrializing Countries*. Ithaca: Cornell University Press.

Haggard, Stephan and Robert R. Kaufman. 1995. *The Political Economy of Democratic Transitions*. New Jersey: Princeton University Press.

Hagopian, Frances. 1998. "Democracy and Political Representation in Latin America in the 1990s: Pause, Reorganization, or Decline?" In *Fault Lines of Democracy in Post-Transition Latin America*, eds Filipe Aguero and Jeffrey Stark. Florida: North-South Center Press.

Hart, Jeffrey. 1994. *Rival Capitalists: International Competitiveness in the United States, Japan, and Western Europe*. Ithaca: Cornell University Press.

Huber, Evelyne. 1996. "Options for Social Policy in Latin America: Neoliberal versus Social Democratic Models." In *Welfare States in Transition: National Adaptations in Global Economies*, ed. Gosta Esping-Andersen. London: Sage Publications.

Kaufman, Robert R. and Leo Zuckermann. 1998. "Attitudes toward Economic Reform in Mexico: The Role of Political Orientations." *American Political Science Review* 92(2): 359–375.

Limongi, Fernando and Argelina Figueiredo. 1998. "Bases institucionais do presidencialismo de coalizao." *Lua Nova* 44: 81–106.

Lustig, Nora, ed. 1995. *Coping With Austerity: Poverty and Inequality in Latin America*. Washington DC: The Brookings Institute.

Mainwaring, Scott. 1999. *Rethinking Party Systems in the Third Wave of Democratization: The Case of Brazil*. Stanford: Stanford University Press.

Meller, Patricio. 1996. "Chilean Export Growth, 1970–1990." In *Manufacturing for Export In the Developing World: Problems and Possibilities*, ed. G. K. Helleiner. London and New York: Routledge.

Mesa-Lago, Carmelo. 1978. *Social Security in Latin America: Pressure Groups, Stratification, and Inequality*. Philadelphia: University of Pittsburgh Press.

Morley, Samuel A. 1995. *Poverty and Inequality in Latin America: The Impact of Adjustment and Recovery in the 1980s*. Baltimore, MD: Johns Hopkins University Press.

Morley, Samuel A., Roberto Machado, and Stefano Pettinato. 1999. "Indexes of Structural Reform in Latin America." ECLAC Economic Development Division, LC/L.1166. Santiago: ECLAC.

Nelson, Joan M. 1997. "Social Costs, Social-Sector Reforms, and Politics in Post-Communist Transformations." In *Transforming Post-Communist Political Economies*, eds. Joan M. Nelson, Charles Tilly, and Lee Walker. Washington, DC: National Academy Press.

Pierson, Paul. 1996. "The New Politics of the Welfare State." *World Politics* 48(2): 143–179.

Rodrik, Dani. 1999. *The New Global Economy and Developing Countries: Making Openness Work*. Washington DC: The Overseas Development Council. Distributed by the Johns Hopkins University Press.

Soskice, David. 1999. "Divergent Production Regimes: Coordinated and Un-coordinated Market Economies in the 1980s and 1990s." In *Continuity and Change in Contemporary Capitalism*, eds Herbert Kitschelt, Peter Lange, Gary Marks, and John D. Stephens. London: Cambridge University Press, pp. 1–135.

Stallings, Barbara. 1995. "The New International Context of Development." In *Global Change, Regional Response: The New International Context of Development*, ed. Barbara Stallings. Cambridge: Cambridge University Press.

Stokes, Susan C. 1998. "Orientations Toward Neoliberalism in Latin America." Paper presented at the Annual Meeting of the American Political Science Association, September.

Wade, Robert. 1990. *Governing the Market: Economic Theory and the Role of Government in East Asian Industrialization*. New Jersey: Princeton University Press.

Weyland, Kurt. 1998. "Swallowing the Bitter Pill: Sources of Popular Support for Neoliberal Reform in Latin America." *Comparative Political Studies* 31(5): 37–67, October.

World Bank. 2000. *Entering the 21st Century: World Development Report 1999/2000*. Oxford: Oxford University Press.

# 5

# East Asia: Development challenges in the twenty-first century

*Yun-han Chu*

Three years after a sudden reversal of foreign capital flows had caused the collapse of the Thai baht and ushered in the regional financial melt-down, East Asian developing economies were still struggling with the challenges of structural reform and social recovery. Although the five countries most affected by the crisis – Indonesia, South Korea, Malaysia, the Philippines, and Thailand – have rebounded faster than expected, corporate and banking restructuring was by no means complete, even in South Korea (the best-performing of the crisis countries). Can the mo-mentum of economic reform at *fin de siècle* be converted into a sustained and broadly shared economic expansion in the next century? The answer depends on how East Asian developing economies respond to the epic changes in the global and regional development context as well as on their respective domestic socio-political environment.

As the region is searching for a reliable path to a new era of burgeon-ing growth and declining poverty, a litany of new development challenges awaits its policy makers and citizens – the globalization of the financial market; the emergence of a knowledge-based global economy; and the associated shift in trade, investment, and production regimes propelled by the acceleration of innovation in information and telecommunication technology, the assault of economic neo-liberalism on the ideological and institutional foundation of their existing modes of economic accumula-tion, and the imperative of broadening the scope and strengthening the institutional foundation for regional economic cooperation. In many respects, the recent crisis can be seen as a failure of many East Asian countries to cope with these changing conditions and transformative forces.

The most critical intellectual challenge facing the policy makers and citizens in the developing East Asia is how to rethink, redefine, and re-invigorate the role of the state amid the twin challenge of globalization and democratization. Forces of globalization – in particular, the integration of the world financial market; concurrent movements in trade liberalization; the trend towards increased fragmentation of the global production process; the intensity, velocity, and speed of cross-border business transactions; and the diffusion of economic neo-liberalism – have constrained the state's capacity in managing national economy and steering industrial change (Boyer and Drache 1996). It was no longer possible for the state in the East Asian NIEs to help the private sector to absorb and socialize risks through traditional policy tools such as tariff, import controls, export subsidies, and restriction on foreign participation. It also has become more difficult for the state to monitor and discipline the performance of targeted sectors and firms as the cleavage between domestic and international financial sectors broke down and national firms expanded their business organizations abroad. At the same time, the global spread of neo-liberal doctrines has everywhere reduced the legitimacy of broad state involvement in the economy and reduced governments' ability to shape or to protect against market outcomes (Schmidt 1999).

The triumph of liberal democracy as the predominant mode of legitimation has brought down many non-democratic regimes and threatened the viability of the remaining authoritarian arrangements in the region. For many East Asian developing societies, political liberalization and democratization of the 1980s and 1990s meant a realignment of the state–society relations. The frozen clarity of authoritarian order was replaced by partisan contestation and electoral uncertainty. The democratically elected regime is susceptible to the rising demand from the élite economic groups for increased participation in economic and political decision-making as well as the call for a more balanced development strategy from newly mobilized social sectors. The coherence and autonomy of the economic bureaucracy has suffered as the resourceful business élite has capitalized on the electoral opening and the strengthening of representative institutions to pursue influence buying at strategic junctures in the policy-making process. On the other hand, the acquiescence of the labour force over inhuman working conditions and low wages, of the consumers over collusive business practices, and the community over pollution can no longer be taken for granted. Even the most resilient authoritarian regimes, which have so far resisted the trend of democratization, are wrestling with the political implications of rapid economic transformation – the rapid growth of market-oriented newspapers, radio, television, and the Internet; the emergence of NGOs and social groups; and the political awakening of urban middle classes – all spawning greater demand for political participation and accountability from government institutions.

This chapter uses the recent financial crisis as a vantage point for re-examining many of the core assumptions underlying the success of East Asian export-oriented development strategy for the last three decades, and attempts to identify the policy reorientation, institutional reform, organizational adaptation, and ideational breakthrough that are required for the region to carve out a new path to sustainable economic expansion and a pattern of development that promises extensive social empowerment and equitable economic participation. This chapter is intended to be polemical, as there is clearly no intellectual consensus over the various contentious issues under investigation. Also, for an intellectual exercise with a geographical scope as sweeping and an analytical task as complex as this, one is under the constant risk of overgeneralization and under-prescription for the region.

## Developing East Asia in comparative perspective

The developing East Asia is so diversified that it defies simplistic generalization. Developing economies in the region vary greatly in size, trajectory of economic development, and level of industrialization. The region witnesses the glaring contrast between Singapore – a tiny, rich, and service-based city state enjoying a per capita income higher than a great majority of the OECD countries – with the world's most populated and predominantly rural China, which still had about 200 million people (17 per cent of the population) living on less than a dollar a day by 1998 despite its impressive record of economic transformation over the last two decades (table 5.1). For our purpose, it is useful to break down developing East Asia into at least three country groupings – the first-tier high-income NIEs (including Hong Kong, Singapore, Taiwan, and South Korea); the second-tier middle-income NIEs in South-East Asia (including primarily Malaysia, Thailand, the Philippines, and Indonesia); and the transitional economies (such as China, Viet Nam, and Myanmar).[1]

There is little dispute that developing East Asia has shared one success story of remarkable economic expansion and spectacular poverty reduction: the region registered the highest average annualized growth rate among all developing countries for the last four decades; it also succeeded in converting persistently high growth into improvement in welfare. In the last four decades, poverty – measured by the international

Table 5.1 Economic statistics of selected East Asian developing economies

| Economy/country | Population (millions) 1999 | GNP per capita (Dollars) 1999 | GNP per capita (Measured at PPP) 1998 | Human Development Index[a] 1998 | Gross Domestic Production (average annual growth rate) 1965–1980 | Gross Domestic Production (average annual growth rate) 1980–1990 | Gross Domestic Production (average annual growth rate) 1990–1998 |
|---|---|---|---|---|---|---|---|
| High-income NIEs | | | | | | | |
| Singapore | 3.9 | 29,610.0 | 28,620.0 | 0.881 | 10.0 | 6.6 | 8.0 |
| Hong Kong | 6.8 | 23,520.0 | 22,000.0 | 0.872 | 8.6 | 6.9 | 4.4 |
| Taiwan | 22.0 | 13,601.0 | – | – | 9.8 | 7.9 | 6.6 |
| South Korea | 46.9 | 8,490.0 | 12,270.0 | 0.854 | 9.9 | 9.4 | 6.2 |
| Middle-income NIEs | | | | | | | |
| Malaysia | 22.7 | 3,400.0 | 6,990.0 | 0.772 | 7.4 | 5.3 | 7.7 |
| Thailand | 61.8 | 1,960.0 | 5,840.0 | 0.745 | 7.3 | 7.6 | 7.4 |
| Philippines | 76.8 | 1,020.0 | 3,540.0 | 0.744 | 5.7 | 1.0 | 3.3 |
| Indonesia | 207.4 | 580.0 | 2,790.0 | 0.670 | 7.0 | 6.1 | 5.8 |
| Transitional economies | | | | | | | |
| China | 1,254.6 | 780.0 | 3,220.0 | 0.706 | 6.8 | 10.2 | 11.1 |
| Viet Nam | 78.0 | 370.0 | 1,690.0 | 0.671 | – | 4.6 | 8.6 |

Table 5.1 (cont.)

| Economy/country | Exports of goods and services (average annual growth rate) | | | Exports as percentage of GDP (1998) | Gini coefficient | | Population below $1 PPP/day (Percentage) | (Survey year) |
|---|---|---|---|---|---|---|---|---|
| | 1965–1980 | 1980–1990 | 1990–1998 | | 1980s | 1990s | | |
| High-income NIEs | | | | | | | | |
| Singapore | 4.7 | 8.6 | 13.3 | 198.7 | 0.41 | 0.39 | – | – |
| Hong Kong | 9.1 | 6.2 | 9.5 | 125.0 | 0.37 | 0.45 | – | – |
| Taiwan | 18.9 | 12.1 | 9.2 | 50.2 | 0.28 | 0.31 | – | – |
| South Korea | 27.2 | 12.8 | 15.7 | 38.0 | 0.39 | 0.34 | <1.0 | 1998 |
| Middle-income NIEs | | | | | | | | |
| Malaysia | 4.6 | 10.3 | 13.2 | 118.0 | 0.51 | 0.48 | 4.0 | 1995 |
| Thailand | 8.6 | 13.2 | 11.1 | 47.0 | 0.43 | 0.52 | <2.0 | 1992 |
| Philippines | 4.6 | 2.5 | 11.0 | 56.0 | 0.46 | 0.45 | 27.0 | 1994 |
| Indonesia | 9.6 | 2.8 | 8.6 | 28.0 | 0.36 | 0.32 | 8.0 | 1996 |
| Transitional economies | | | | | | | | |
| China | 4.8 | 11.0 | 14.9 | 22.0 | 0.32 | 0.38 | 17.0 | 1998 |
| Viet Nam | – | – | 27.70 | 46.0 | – | – | – | – |

Sources:

Population, Gini coefficients and population below $1 a day from *Asian Economic Outlooks 2000* (Asian Development Bank 2000);

Per capita income in dollars from Asian Development Bank on-line database;

Per capita income measured at PPP and exports as percentage of GDP from *World Development Report 2000* (World Bank 2000);

GDP growth and exports growth from *World Development Report 1992 to 2000* (World Bank, various dates);

Taiwan's GDP and exports growth rate from *Taiwan Statistical Data Book 2000* (Council for Economic Planning and Development 2000);

HDI from *Human Development Report 2000* (UNDP 2001).

a. The HDI is a composite index of longevity (as measured by life expectancy at birth), knowledge (as measured by adult literacy rate and combined enrolment ratio), and decent standard of living (as measured by the adjusted per capita income in PPP US$).

poverty line of a dollar per day (adjusted for purchasing power parity, PPP) – has been virtually eliminated in Hong Kong, Singapore, Taiwan, and Korea. The incidence of dollar-a-day poverty in China, Indonesia, Malaysia, and Thailand has also undergone dramatic reductions: overall, the region reduced the number of people living in poverty by half over the last two decades, a pace unmatched by any other region of the developing world. The number of people living with an income below a dollar a day was reduced from 720 million in 1975 to 350 million in 1995 (World Bank 1998: 2). Life expectancy at birth, infant mortality rates, nutrition intake, and literacy indicators all have improved in tandem, generating real improvement in the quality of life. Income inequality, in general, has been also lower in East Asia than in other parts of the developing world. For example, Gini indexes – the standard measure of overall income inequality – of 0.5 or more are common in Latin America and many African countries; in contrast, the Gini indexes for developing countries in East Asia generally fall in the range of 0.3–0.4 and have been fairly stable over time (see also table 5.1).

There is also little dispute that, across the region, a very similar set of factors lay behind the high growth and spectacular welfare gains over the last two decades. The miraculous growth has been largely attributable to the efficient and rapid accumulation of physical capital and market-directed allocation of new investment under an export-oriented industrialization strategy (World Bank 1993). Trade has been the engine of growth for developing East Asia, the developing economies of which have been impressively outward oriented. In most mid-sized East Asian countries, exports as a percentage of GDP ranged from 30 to 50 – much higher than the regional average of Latin America (about 14 per cent in 1998). In the region's nine main economies,[2] exports and imports of goods and non-factor services rose by 11.5 per cent per year between 1970 and 1995 – more than twice the average world trade growth of 5 per cent. At home, governments generally kept inflation low and the exchange rate competitive, invested in human capital through public expenditure in education, sustained high rates of savings by keeping real interest rate positive and by effectively protecting deposits in financial institutions, and encouraged the inflow of foreign capital and absorption of foreign technology. Most East Asian countries also benefited from their shared cultural heritage – preference for education and an emphasis on work ethics, entrepreneurship, strong family ties, and vibrant social networks (Tu 1996).

Although the developing East Asia shared one success story, major structural and systemic differences existed among the countries. The three country groupings have been engaged in the global economy to different extents, with varying scope and depth, and came into the re-gional crisis on rather different development trajectories. Over the past two decades, the economic achievement of the NIEs of South East Asia has been much more modest than that of the first-tier East Asian NIEs in several important aspects, and the sustainability of their growth, indus-trialization, and structural change was much more suspect as a con-sequence (Jomo et al. 1997). Particular historical conditions endowed the state in many of the first-tier East Asian NIEs with unusual capacity to transform its society and to pursue development-oriented economic poli-cies (Islam 1992; Rowen 1998). Industrial policy or selective state inter-vention has been of much poorer quality and less effective in the second-tier South-East Asian NIEs owing to differences in the constellation of political priorities, state structure, and government–business relations (Doner 1992; Weiss 1998). In a similar vein, the possibility for the state to acquire a more complex and strategic capacity, in the context of a highly internationalized economy and amid the trend of political liberalization and democratization, also differs significantly between the first-tier and the second-tier NIEs and, of course, among themselves (Woo-Cumings 1999). Some countries are better equipped than others to balance the risk and benefit in opening up domestic capital market to foreign portfolio investment; to motivate and enable the local firms to invest, upgrade, in-novate, internationalize, and carve out a bigger slice of value-added ac-tivities of the global production networks; to close up the digital divide between itself and the advanced industrial societies as well as within in its own border; and to resist the neo-liberal call for "one-size-fits-all" in-stitutional reform.

Furthermore, as the region became ever more integrated and inter-dependent economically, the development prospect of any of the three country groupings is inevitably enmeshed and entangled with others. Since the mid-1980s, the mode of economic accumulation in the second-tier NIEs has been significantly shaped by Japan and the first-tier NIEs, surging as the primary source of investment capital, technology, and ac-cess to the global production networks after the Plaza Accord. While China, as usual for a gigantic continental power, has slotted into the world economy under rather different conditions and has been preoccu-pied with its own development priorities, its actions have begun to have a significant impact on the rest of developing East Asia, especially after it reignited the momentum of market-oriented reform in 1992. The rise of China has exerted tremendous pressures on the second-tier NIEs as a competitor in the export market for low-end manufactured goods, in the labour-intensive segment of the global production process, as well as over the share of foreign investment flow. China's forthcoming economic ascendance, on the other hand, will redefine the parameters of regional institutional building and will significantly raise the prospect of the emergence of an East Asian economic community.

## Meeting the challenge of financial globalization

The regional crisis of 1997–1999 powerfully demonstrated that the volatility in the financial sector – with the recent proliferation of new financial instruments, institutions, and markets – has an ever-greater potential to inflict harm on the real economy and unravel the social fabric. The recent crisis has put the globalization of the financial market in the spotlight and led to its intense scrutiny. However, the prospect for the G-7 governments to make concerted efforts to address the inadequacy in the existing arrangements of global financial governance in order to avoid the recurrence of similar crises looks very dim. In the foreseeable future, East Asian developing economies have to learn to live with three dire facts.

- First, the trend of financial globalization will not be arrested, because the supply of financial resources will continue to expand with the build-up of excess liquidity in the major industrial economies, and the menu of sophisticated financial products will also continue to expand with the current pace of technological innovation.
- Second, de-globalization is not a viable option for virtually all East Asian developing economies, because attempts to disengage their economies from global financial integration, except for short-term circuit-breaking measures, will not only retard domestic financial development over the long term but also invite immediate political assault by ideological neo-liberals as well as economic ostracism by their powerful allies in the international financial centres.
- Third, the burden of controlling the volatility in exchange rate and short-term financial flow and that of containing the contagion effects will be shouldered primarily by themselves, both individually and collectively.

An important task for policy makers in all of developing East Asia is to learn the right lessons from the recent financial meltdown and to scrutinize any simplistic diagnosis and policy prescriptions. The Asian crisis was both externally induced and home-grown (Wade 1998; World Bank 1998; Jomo 1999; Pempel 1999; Haggard 2000). A number of forces interacted to leave some countries structurally vulnerable to external shocks as well as to the ensuing attack by hedge funds. Rising global liquidity fed huge amounts of short-term capital into poorly regulated institutional settings. In particular, the ready availability of the low-cost yen-denominated credit, which was in search of higher returns in the region, induced their corporate and financial sector to become unusually reliant on financing long-term investment with short-term debt. Funding options from abroad exposed highly leveraged firms to minor shocks concerning exchange rates and interest rates. At the same time, rising world excess capacity in commodity manufactured goods suppressed export price and widened the current-account deficits. The heavy inflow of short-term capital temporarily offset the macroeconomic imbalance but exposed the economies to sudden reversal of capital inflows. The heavy inflow and credit boom, in turn, channelled substantial investment into real property, creating an asset price bubble, and added to the excessive debt of already over-leveraged firms. The blame for the explosion of the crisis can be laid squarely on the financial panic of international and domestic investors, suddenly concerned about the fate of their portfolios.

In the aftermath, crisis-afflicted countries were advised by IFIs such as the IMF to implement banking reform, capital-market deregulation, and corporate restructuring. The prevailing view (which has been much shared in Washington and some East Asian capital cities) suggested that rigorous banking regulation, prudential banking practices, and orderly sequencing of capital-account liberalization would help them navigate safely through this financially integrating world. This standard prescription placed a great premium on creating environments of stability and predictability for global investors and, perhaps for that reason, it was oversold on many scores. One should question both its feasibility and adequacy. First, a "right" recipe for sequencing capital-account liberalization simply does not exist, because East Asian countries differed substantially in the nature of their legal infrastructure, corporate governance practices, banking regulation, capital-market development, and macroeconomic conditions. At the same time, the growing complexity and diversity of banking activities, especially the growth of electronic banking and non-bank institutions, are straining regulatory authorities everywhere. It is unrealistic to expect that most East Asian second-tier NIEs and transitional economies will be able to acquire the kind of judicious public and private oversight that would enable them to reap the full benefit of financial liberalization.

More importantly (as Robert Wade explained it), banking regulation, in the forms of prudential limits, capital-adequacy requirements, and currency-matching conditions for foreign assets and liabilities, cannot alone prevent excessive risk-taking by banks in the presence of an asset boom: in booms it becomes very difficult to prevent risk-taking that looks excessive after the crash, yet the ﹍ ﹍w of "hot money" commonly triggers excessive asset booms. Furthermore, domestic banking regulation cannot prevent excess non-bank private-sector borrowing abroad through an open capital account (Wade 1999); therefore, capital controls should be a legitimate instrument helping to manage a country's external liabilities. For most East Asian developing economies, prudential regulations on capital mobility – such as taxes on short-term capital inflow or the introduction of "circuit-breakers" into the foreign exchange spot market[3] – is justifiable because their financial markets are thin, their private sector's risk-management practices are underdeveloped, and their regulators' capacity to supervise the financial sector is limited.

Taiwan's experience in coping with the challenge of financial liberalization is of important relevance for other East Asian countries because not only has the island economy emerged from the regional financial crisis relatively unscathed but also its unorthodox approach poses a creditable challenge to the neo-liberal call for "one-size-fits-all" institutional reform that has perilously led policy makers in the crisis-affected East Asian countries to see their future options in terms of either maintaining the discredited status quo or embracing neo-liberalism in its entirety.

Taiwan was insulated from the external financial shock in part, because both its dependence on foreign portfolio investment and its exposure to short-term foreign borrowings have been minimal. In the past, the island's economic expansion was financed almost exclusively by domestic savings (Chu 1999). Despite the trend toward an integrated global financial market, Taiwan has chosen a sequence of financial liberalization that gave priority to deregulating the domestic capital market over internationalization (i.e. foreign participation). When the government opened up the stock market for foreign investors in 1991, it started out with a strict investment cap and raised the ceiling only gradually.[4] On the eve of the regional crisis, the actualized foreign investment totalled only $11.1 billion, which accounted for less than 4 per cent of the total market capitalization. In addition, Taiwan's central bank has been keen to safeguard its ability to set monetary targets by preventing the internationalization of its currency. In curbing the growth of an off-shore foreign-exchange market of the New Taiwan (NT) dollar, Taiwan's central bank prohibited domestic banks from offering local currency accounts for their customers abroad and restricted the outbound movement of the NT dollar; in so doing, Taiwan's monetary authority was able to retain its position as the sole market-maker of the NT dollar. Furthermore, after the government, in the late 1980s, removed most restrictions on private holdings of foreign exchange and started to nurture the growth of a foreign-exchange spot market and later futures market, the central bank has subsequently established an array of monitoring schemes and has, from time to time, intervened in the spot market to prevent excessive short-term fluctuation. Furthermore, the central bank has placed a strict cap on the domestic bank's foreign-exchange derivatives positions, as well as on their holding/

owing of foreign assets/liabilities. None of these prudential measures has conformed to the "neo-liberal" economic prescriptions.

The evolution of Taiwan's financial regulatory regime of the 1980s and 1990s did not take place in an institutional vacuum or ideological void and, therefore, it may not be readily transferable to other developing countries. Nevertheless, Taiwan's experiences did offer three valuable lessons for the rest of the region.

- A country should choose its pace of financial opening in accordance with its tolerance for short-term fluctuation and in tandem with the strengthening of its regulatory and monitoring capacity.
- Next, a prudent financial regulatory regime should place a premium on creating environments of stability and predictability for domestic savers and investors first, rather than for global investors.
- Third, a country should give priority to developing the domestic capital market, including developing a robust stock market as an alternative funding source, over its internationalization. This last point is of particular relevance to the more bank-based systems, such as Thailand and Indonesia.

Lastly, the regional crisis also led to a renewed attack, which carried a strong overtone of neo-liberal triumphalism, on the various forms of growth-oriented centralized coordination of production activities and resource allocation practised by many East Asian states – such as protection of domestic industries, investment incentives to channel capital flows into targeted sectors, implicit or explicit government guarantees on private investment projects, and, most significantly, selective allocation of subsidized credit. Such strategies allowed firms to undertake highly risky projects by relying heavily on bank credit. For instance, the average debt-to-equity ratios estimated by Claessens, Djankov, and Lang (1998) for 1996 were as high as 355 per cent in Korea and 236 per cent in Thailand. Lower, but still high ratios were to be found in Indonesia (188 per cent) and the Philippines (128 per cent); the corresponding figure for Japan is 221 per cent. The Asian miracle has occurred despite – or, as some would say, because of – significant distortions of the market mechanism in the financial sector (Chang 1994). In the presence of extensive controls and limits to foreign borrowing, however, these distortions had not been translated into high domestic vulnerability to external shocks.

These practices were vigorously de-legitimized by the Western mass media, which singled out "crony capitalism," constituted by excessive and corruption-directed government intervention, as a major home-grown cause of the financial crisis. The attack was so powerful and crippling that it prompted some to issue an obituary for the so-called "developmental state model" (Woo-Cumings 1999). It is, perhaps, true that, in some second-tier NIEs (such as Malaysia and Indonesia), state-directed policy incentives and soft loans were driven less by developmentalist considerations than by rent-seeking motivation – and such interventions bear some of the responsibility for their structural vulnerability to external financial shocks. It was also plausible to argue that South Korea's high-debt model (which was characterized by a national industrial strategy of state-mediated capital going to large firms pursuing aggressive business expansion for carving out their world-market share, rather than maximizing profit margins or return to stockholders) has run into serious trouble under the challenge of financial globalization because the South Korean government has gradually lost its capacity to monitor and discipline the business operation of Korean firms and banks, especially with respect to short-term foreign borrowing and risky financial investment in the foreign markets (Mo and Moon 1998). However, as Jomo (1999) has reminded us, neither simplistic perspective nor gross generalization recognize, or distinguish between, developmentalist rents and rentier abuse.

The case for the discretionary use of credit policy in industrial targeting is still ultimately built on three premises: (1) if the state possesses the institutional capacity to coordinate industrial change; (2) if the economic bureaucracy is protected by institutional arrangements from the undue influence of rent-seeking actors; and (3) if the long-term net social return from accelerating the creation or expansion of some strategic industries with extensive forward or backward linkage to other sectors justifies the short-term distortion.[5] Policy reforms that fail to do so will encourage throwing out the developmentalist baby with the bath water of abuse (Jomo 1999: 25).

## The long-term sustainability of export-oriented industrialization

Too sharp a focus on managing global financial integration might, however, distract the policy makers in the region from two more fundamental issues: first, did the crisis spell the exhaustion of the export-oriented industrialization (EOI) strategy, much as the import substitution in Latin America became fully exhausted during the crisis decade of the 1980s? Second, how has developing East Asia measured up to the new growth pattern centred on information and telecommunication (IT) technologies?

Trade has been the engine of growth for East Asia's thirty-year rapid expansion. There is strong agreement that the EOI strategy has benefited East Asian economies in many important ways. Competitive pressure has helped East Asian economies to improve the allocation of resources, expanding foreign demand has enabled them to reap the benefits of economies of scale as well as of specialization, and exposure to foreign markets has also facilitated technological transfer from foreign clients. There is also strong consensus over the region's success in converting the export-led growth into spectacular welfare gains. The process of EOI, supported by widespread social services, has created jobs for the poor and enormous opportunities for economic empowerment (World Bank 1998). However, the past success offers only a very qualified assurance for the long-term viability of the EOI paradigm. This is especially true for the second-tier NIEs, whose rapid EOI from the mid-1980s was partly due to a favourable conjunction – involving South-East Asian currency depreciation coinciding with Japanese and first-tier East Asian NIE currency appreciation and rising production costs – as well as liberalization of some existing regulations inimical to attracting export-oriented foreign direct investment (FDI) (Jomo et al. 1997).

The gathering cloud over the horizon has little to do with the long-term prospect of the world trading system. Despite the recent social backlash in the OECD countries against the doctrinal push for free trade, and the developing countries' strong reservation with regard to extending the agenda of multilateral trade negotiations under the WTO into labour and environmental dimensions, both the trend towards outward-oriented trade policies accelerating under the Uruguay Round negotiation and the momentum for incorporating countries further into the global trading system stand a good chance of continuing, as does the trend towards re-allocating manufacturing activities from industrial to developing countries. Thus has something to do with (but only in a limited sense) the management of the increasing new-development problems associated with export-led growth: these include migration and urban congestion, widening of economic disparity among regions, structural vulnerability to external economic shocks, strains on traditional social norms and institutions, and pollution and depletion of natural resources. These problems will, no doubt, exert tremendous pressure on the political system but should remain socially, politically, and ecologically manageable in a context of sustained economic expansion. The real challenges for the East Asian NIEs are, first, that to ensure a meaningful and equitable participation in the global economic system, the East Asian NIEs must undertake proactive strategies to cope with the constant market pressures for upgrading their industrial portfolio and level of technological sophistication. Furthermore, they must address the challenge in a new context of global industrial restructuring, which is characterized by increased fragmentation of production processes across national borders and propelled by the revolution in IT technologies (Sassen 1996).

During the 1980s and 1990s, the first-tier NIEs have managed the task of industrial upgrading with stunning success (Biggs and Yoon 1990). Despite a sharp currency appreciation during the late 1980s, and a significant rise in labour cost and land price (and growing environmental concern) throughout the last decade, the first-tier NIEs were able to keep up international competitiveness through human-resource development, technological upgrading, and overseas outsourcing (Chu 1995). Most notably, the capital- and technology-intensive industries have replaced the traditional labour-intensive industries to become the backbone of the export sector of South Korea and Taiwan, while the two city-states have consolidated themselves as the regional financial/operational centres. In addition, in their traditional export sectors, the growth of higher-value-added export activities was made possible by creating a bottom layer of international subcontracting in the region and pushing local producers to move upwards in the hierarchy of international subcontracting networks.

The second-tier NIEs, however, have not yet replicated the success of their predecessors; on the contrary, there were unambiguous signs that, in many second-tier NIEs, the EOI strategy had lost its steam by the mid-1990s. Since the early 1990s, their export sector has faced adverse terms of trade fluctuation, falling prices, falling profits, and dwindling new FDI. Since 1994, China has overtaken ASEAN as a more favourable destination for the FDI coming from the OECD countries as well as from the first-tier NIEs. The export growth hit a wall in 1996 and the current-account deficit became much worsened. These developments, by themselves, could not have precipitated the financial crisis but, nevertheless, did contribute to the build-up of their structural vulnerabilities.

The accumulation of competitive pressures began to threaten ASEAN's growth momentum from the early 1990s. First, their export performance was threatened by a general trend of excess capacity worldwide in the making of commodity manufactured goods – relatively undifferentiated products such as textiles, garments, footware, consumer electrical/electronics, major appliances, and some steels and petrochemicals. Second, their export-oriented manufacturing activities have over-concentrated on one sector – electronics – which exposed them to intensified competition and wild fluctuation in world demand as well as prices (World Bank 1998: 25–26). Third, they have lost their wage competitiveness associated with currency appreciation to the newly emerging low-cost production sites, such as China and Viet Nam. China, in particular, with a virtually unlimited supply of low-wage labour, has emerged as the major supplier of commodity manufactured goods to the world market since the mid-1990s.

To avoid the lose–lose game of competitive currency devaluation and the resultant loss in real income, the second-tier NIEs are compelled to graduate from the status of low-cost producers and to strive for an ascending position in the regional division of labour. In the game of industrial upgrading, the second-tier NIEs are facing tougher challenges than had been the case for the first-tier NIEs in the 1980s. They have to tear down the technological protectionism practised by their major foreign investors – the Japanese TNCs, Korean *Chaebols* (conglomerates), and Taiwanese investors alike. They have to overcome the downside of the trend towards increased fragmentation of the global production process, which tends to lock their specific export-oriented sector into a closely knit network of the transnational supply chain, making it a sort of "export enclave" with minimal technological externalities and spillover benefits and little forward or backward linkage with other sectors of the local economy. Most critically, they are less advantageously positioned to tackle the new challenges brought about by the revolution in IT technologies.

The new IT technologies are at the roots of new productivity sources, of new organizational forms, and of the formation of a global economy. In the next century, the widespread access to, sharing of, and use of information and knowledge in economic activities through technology are a prerequisite for economic and social development. There is little chance for a country, or region, to develop in the new economy without its incorporation into the technological system of the information age. The crucial role of informational and communication technology is a two-edged sword: rapid advances in knowledge and in information and communication technology make it possible for firms in developing East Asia to leapfrog to newer, more efficient technologies, so that East Asian developing economies can leapfrog stages of economic growth by being able to modernize their production systems and increase their competitiveness faster than in the past; on the other hand, for those developing economies that are unable to adapt to the new technological systems, their retardation becomes cumulative (Castells 1996).

The IT revolution has redefined elements of international competitiveness and carries enormous implications for the EOI strategy. A wide range of offshoot industries have overhauled their production processes, with an emphasis on flexible manufacturing and custom-made products and services and on higher-value-added, information-intensive market segments. The Internet and the information technology revolution have enhanced the predictability and reliability of the division of labour across firms. Technological advances such as computer simulation and digital codification of design specifications make it feasible for companies to outsource increasingly complex functions they once had to perform in-house, and thus shifts the advantage to "de-verticalization." Many services have also become highly tradeable (or potentially highly tradeable) – for example software, routine paperwork, design, and entertainment. Reduction of transaction costs enables the exploitation of efficiencies in specific segments of the manufacturing and distribution process. For the same reason, it also shifts the advantage to "globalization" of supply chains through the coordination of a company's value chain spread across national borders to exploit location-specific advantages. Increasingly, US firms count on using global suppliers with a set of more or less ready-made (or "turn-key") solutions, available anywhere in the world (Sturgeon 1997). The result is a "dual fragmentation" of production, with companies breaking up their research and development (R&D), production, and marketing systems and moving the component parts into new locations, and with companies breaking-off functions once carried out within vertically integrated organizations and acquiring these goods and services from networks of increasingly capable outside suppliers and service providers. The new competitive challenge will, in due course, force the Japanese TNCs (whose FDI strategy conventionally follows a product-cycle approach – low value-added products manufactured overseas, high value-added functions kept in Japan – and whose international production networks have been characterized by their intra-firm and "sticky" business relationships rather than inter-firm, arms-length relationships) to reconfigure their regional supply chains and adopt a more open and decentralized network (Tachiki 1999).

Overall, the new economic trends diminish the competitive advantage of cheap labour and place the emphasis on skill and knowledge creation. They put more pressure on East Asian NIEs to develop "location-specific advantages," especially in the areas of human capital, local supply networks, and science and technology policies to integrate themselves into the regional economy. On the other hand, opportunities arising from horizontal collaboration with OECD-based start-ups and vertical cooperation with transnational giants will allow regional small and medium-sized enterprises (SMEs) to become dynamic instigators of industrial development in many sectors and major producers for world markets. The most successful NIE-based global suppliers, who have acquired the core competence to perform a wide range of functions for a number of customers at high levels of quality and efficiency, can reap the full benefit of external economies of scale that span the globe.

For the second-tier NIEs, the established approach – constructing modern transportation and telecommunication infrastructures, liberalizing trade regimes, maintaining a competitive exchange rate, offering FDI generous fiscal incentives and a friendly business environment, etc. – to attracting EOI is no longer sufficient to sustain the export-led growth in the new century. The right ingredients for a sustainable EOI strategy must include human capital development through the expansion of higher education and vocational training/retraining programmes, the creation of an enabling environment for indigenous SMEs with provision of focused R&D support, fair trade regulation, government loan guarantees, ready access to the domestic capital market, and the expansion and deepening of domestic (or subregional) subcontracting networks and the creation of industrial clusters. In a nutshell, the second-tier NIE must follow in the footsteps of the first-tier NIEs and strive to develop "a cluster of specialization" in a series of high-growth industries. For example, in the computer industry, Taiwan specializes in the design and manufacture of custom-made integrated circuit (IC) chips, Singapore in hard-disk drives, and South Korea in memory chips and liquid-crystal display (LCD) monitors. English-speaking second-tier NIEs, such as Malaysia and the Philippines, can follow Hong Kong's successful example in the development of a few export-oriented service sectors, such as publishing, entertainment, and on-line customer service.

The challenge of industrial upgrading for the first-tier NIEs in the new century will be just as tough, because they are in competition with the major industrial economies over technological innovation and for "high-tech" talents. Acquisition of skills, productive assets, and a comparative advantage in the production and utilization of four heartland technologies – information (i.e. microelectronics and computer software), telecommunication, advanced material components, and biotechnologies – becomes critical for a successful entry into the high-tech industries. The competitive pressure from innovation in the high-tech industries is fierce because the average product cycle has been shortened from five years to between 12 and 18 months by the reduction in the time to market.

More critically, for the first-tier NIEs, excelling in the game of technological catching-up is no longer good enough because, in the transition to knowledge-based economy, the "first-move advantage" is magnified by the expanded realization of economies of scale. While only a few NIE-based high-tech firms will surge to reap the full advantage of first-mover, a majority of them have to upgrade themselves from original-equipment manufacture (OEM) suppliers to own-design manufacture (ODM) and even to own-brand manufacture (OBM).[6] Under the OEM model, the NIE firms specialize only in production, whereas the foreign TNCs undertake the development/design, marketing, distribution, and service of the product in-house. Under the ODM model, the NIE firms have to acquire the core competence to perform a range of functions, development, design, production and/or distribution, and service (Chu 2000). To be effective ODM suppliers in the high-tech industries, the NIE firms have to acquire sophisticated in-house R&D capacity so that their speed in bringing out new product development and/or design is virtually in tandem with the rate of innovation imposed by the pace-setters of the industry, such as Microsoft and Intel to the PC industry. To be competitive ODM suppliers for the high-end market segment of consumer goods, NIE firms have to coordinate their R&D activities closely with the trend-setters, such as Nike in the high-end sportsware sector. In addition, they have to prove themselves over time as indispensable turn-key suppliers to their foreign clients, because their ODM strategy may potentially threaten their strategic partners' own position in the future.

For a smooth upgrade from an OEM to ODM (or even OBM) model across a broad range of industry, the state in the first-tier NIEs must help national firms to manage the risk of integration into ever more complex transnational production networks, to increase immensely its indigenous R&D and design (or even marketing) capacity, and to accelerate the transfer of new technologies and best work practice across borders. The state must also provide the umbrella institutions, within which the acquisition, diffusion, and commercialization of these heartland technologies can take place, by reforming the education, training, banking, capital market, legal system, and trade regime. In particular, a successful pursuit of economic growth with equity under an ODM and/or OBM model depends not just on a country's ability to train and retain world-class engineers and to groom the managerial talents of those who can perform the complex function of investment and linkage but also on the capacity of the whole society to be well educated and to be able to assimilate and process complex information. All public schools in the first-tier NIEs have to live up to the task of producing the new, informational labour force by providing the overall educational, cultural, and technological environment that mirrors the dynamism of the information age (Castells 1999).

## The distributive implications of globalization and democratization

Both globalization and democratization offer new opportunities as well as challenges for a pro-poor development strategy in East Asia. The expanding market opportunities in an increasingly integrated global economy potentially enable most East Asian societies to pursue rapid, sustainable, and inclusive economic growth, which should remain the major component of a strategy for addressing the region's social challenge (Asian Development Bank; ADB 2000: 178–179). Growth is crucial because it increases the demand for labour, the asset on which the poor depend. It is also crucial because the resources for antipoverty programmes and the political feasibility of social programmes for the poor are greater when incomes and economic opportunities are expanding for all.

On the other hand, globalization necessarily breeds instability and inequality (Mittleman 1996). With the increased velocity of cross-border economic transaction and financial flows, globalization has a strong tendency to compound the human cost of economic restructuring and a country's structural vulnerability to external shocks. The adjustment costs oftentimes fell most heavily on the economically disadvantaged groups – typically, farmers, unskilled labourers, migrant workers, women, and ethnic minorities. The financial crises have shown both the region's structural vulnerabilities and the inadequacy of its domestic social-protection mechanisms. The financial crises of 1997–1998 were a costly setback for the worst-affected countries in East Asia; their spectacular progress in poverty reduction has apparently faltered. The recent financial and economic crises in East Asia may have added around 10 million more people to the ranks of those living below a dollar-a-day income between 1996 and 1998 (ADB 2000: 179). As a result, there are more people living in poverty today in East Asia than there were in the mid-1990s.

Entering the 1990s, not even the most dynamic East Asian economies (let alone the poor ones) had an adequate system of safety nets in place to protect the economically disadvantaged groups against the market outcomes. Over the last two decades, economic growth has undermined the traditional protection mechanisms for the unemployed, the sick, and the elderly. East Asia relied on high personal savings and family ties to provide security for its elderly; it came to rely on growth itself to provide an ever-more-buoyant labour market. The forces of growth – with their demand for an increasingly mobile labour force, migration, and wider scope for personal consumption – were putting strains on traditional ways of providing a social safety net (World Bank 1998: 3). In some middle-income countries, such as South Korea, lifetime employment guarantees in the corporate sector were increasingly out of tune with the demands for rapid change and flexibility.

In the coming decade, the state in developing East Asia will confront a growing demand for the establishment of effective systems to protect the socially vulnerable from external shocks and to ease the pain of structural adjustment. There will be considerable debate within the region about whether to extend formal safety nets and how to do so. These formal programmes include unemployment insurance, old-age pensions and social assistance, public works and social funds, health insurance and crop insurance, and other agriculture-stabilization measures. No single answer applies to all East Asian developing economies, however: in devising an appropriate safety-net programme, each country must consider the nature of the risks faced by its most vulnerable groups, as well as the financial and administrative capacity of the government and the nature and extent of informal social safety nets. For instance, only the high-income NIEs of East Asia have the financial and administrative capacity to introduce a comprehensive system of unemployment insurance; it is not feasible for the rest of the region. More appropriate and feasible actions for these countries might include means-tested social-assistance and public-works programmes. While most East Asian developing economies need to pay greater attention to the needs of the elderly and must introduce more comprehensive old-age pension and other social-assistance programmes such as health care, the design and financing mechanisms for these pension systems, however, need careful review. Most importantly, a system of formal safety networks must be augmented by an overall policy regime that promotes inclusive economic growth, key components of which should include investments in human capital, infrastructure, government-assisted microfinance, targeted redistributive policies, improved governance, and broadened participation of the civil-society groups representing the poor in decision-making as well as in delivering social services.

An equally challenging task for East Asia is addressing the enormous distributive implications of the revolution in IT, popularly known as the issue of closing up the "digital divide." The explosion of IT is a potentially powerful tool in Asia's efforts towards poverty reduction. On the other hand, when IT conditions power, knowledge, and productivity, it also becomes a new source of economic inequality and social segregation. In the information age, because of the individualization and extreme mobility of resources, everything and everyone who can be a source of value can easily be connected to the global production system – and anyone who ceases to be so can easily be disconnected and excluded (Castells 1999). For people who are unable to adapt to the new technological system, their backwardness becomes cumulative. If left to market forces, there is an undeniable tendency towards a polarized social structure – with the accelerated concentration of talents and investment capital in a few globalized segments of the economy while a large share of the population remain in low-end, low-skill jobs (Carnoy 1999). Thus, without an orchestrated effort by the state and civil-society groups to raise the general level of functional literacy, to promote the local content of the Internet media, and to facilitate the diffusion of informational infrastructure within the country as a whole, a significant portion of the population will be left in a technological apartheid. In countries with a large rural population, such as China and Indonesia, the market is hardly the most efficient and rational provider for extending state-of-art IT to the farmers in the vast rural areas; re-engineering the existing mechanisms of agricultural extension service administered by the state and NGOs can substantially lower the entry barriers for little-educated farmers to benefit directly from access to Internet resources.

Similarly, democracy and pluralism can bring huge potential benefits to economically disadvantaged groups but also carry risks. Historically, democracies clearly vary in their performance in achieving growth with equity. Some of the most spectacular achievements in poverty reduction have taken place in East Asian countries under authoritarian regimes; in contrast, India, essentially a democracy since its independence, has not produced an impressive record in poverty reduction. For the developing countries, one might argue that democratization at the early stage of industrialization may actually foreclose the possibility for some radical reform measures – such as land reform and affirmative action – to lift up the poorest and produce a more rational distribution of productive assets. On the other hand, it appears that democracy – with its characteristics of transparency, accountability, and consensus formation – can avoid some of the worst forms of rent-seeking and predation associated with many authoritarian regimes. In the OECD countries, political and social ideologies shape the extent to which democratic systems actually pursue a pro-poor development strategy. Configuration in organized interests and constellation of political power underlying welfare policies in OECD countries produce very different outcomes in social equity and income distribution (Garrett 1998; Kitschelt 1999).

In theory, democratization can open up possibilities for the economically disadvantaged groups to voice their concerns and affect the decisions that influence their lives. Better protection of individual freedom and civil rights under a democracy can protect the poor against the abuse of the local power élite, the state officials, and unruly employers. However, it is not clear that many of the new democracies in East Asia will live up to these promises: a majority of the new democracies in the region still lack the necessary institutional depth and auxiliary arrangements to prevent electoral politics from being hijacked by entrenched political and social élite groups and thus are unable to avert tendencies towards worsening inequities. Suffice it to say that democratic processes, by themselves, are not enough to bring about a political coalition and a prevailing social ideology in favour of an inclusive development strategy. To realize the pro-poor potential of democracy requires, among other things, the removal of social and political impediments to the participation of the poor in the political decision-making process, improvement in the quality of legal and judicial institutions, an enhancement of the state's fiscal and administrative capacity, and political entrepreneurship.

## The challenge of democratic governance

Globalization and democratization have pushed the issue of governance squarely onto the development agenda. Governance encompasses not only the institutional arrangements through which governments are chosen and replaced but also the ability of the incumbent to formulate appropriate policies and to implement them effectively. It also includes the means and scope by which ordinary people are able to voice their concerns and affect the decisions that influence their lives. Poor governance can take many different forms – a lack of accountability for state actions; a lack of voice for the governed; ineffective bureaucracy and partisan executives; political instability and violence; the absence of the rule of law; and corruption. All are detrimental to inclusive economic growth and all have adverse ramifications for the poor.

For most East Asian developing economies, their future success in achieving growth with equity will depend largely on the quality of democratic governance. At present, many East Asian newly democratized societies suffer from the same deficiencies in their constitutional designs, the administration of justice, and the restraint of executive-branch power. Lately, political gridlock and partisan strife have paralysed many democratically elected governments, from Estrada, Wahid to Chen Shui-bian. Many institutions need to be in place to ensure that mechanisms of democratic accountability function as they should – among them, independent media to monitor political processes, an independent judiciary to uphold the constitution and rule of law, strong parliamentary institutions with the capacity to oversee the executive, a robust party system to organize representation and aggregate interest, and a vibrant civil society to raise political consciousness and enrich public discourse. Building these institutions takes time and constant vigilance.

For many East Asian developing economies, a critical step towards effective democratic governance is the re-engineering of the state itself. Globalization prompts the East Asian state to pick up new socio-economic responsibilities, to upgrade its regulatory capability, to acquire a more complex and strategic capacity for effective economic governance in the context of a highly internationalized economy, and to define new tasks for state–society collaboration. In a nutshell, it entails a reinvigoration of the state's transformative capacity. Without it, the state cannot ensure its citizens a more equitable and meaningful participation in the global economy and respond effectively to the rising popular demand for a rapid, sustainable, and inclusive economic growth (Wade 1996).

An important ingredient of success in the effort to reinvigorate the state's transformative capacity is an adjustment in state–society relations through the creation and strengthening of durable and inclusive political institutions. In the past, the remarkable industrial transformation in East Asian developmental states, such as South Korea and Taiwan, was in part attributed to a strong collaboration between a meritocratic and resourceful state and a well-organized business sector within state-sanctioned policy networks, which allowed for continual negotiation and re-negotiation of goals and policies (Wade 1990; Chang 1994; Evans 1995). The incumbent élite derived its political capacity from the overall authoritarian arrangements that limited the access to economic decision-making and precluded autonomous collective actions by social actors. The state-sanctioned institutional infrastructure enabled the planning technocrats to exact improved economic performance in exchange for government assistance and protection; to keep collaborative government–business relations from degenerating into unproductive, rent-seeking collusion; and to exclude organized labour and other social groups from economic policy-making (Evans 1995). A softer version of the statist paradigm found in ASEAN also emphasized a significant role of the business sector in policy reforms of the 1980s (Doner 1992; Islam 1992).

The political liberalization and democratization of the late 1980s and 1990s have eroded the power bases of the entrenched incumbent élite and undermined the institutional autonomy of the economic bureaucracy. In all newly democratized East Asian countries, national representative bodies have emerged as an important arena of interest politics. The shadow of electoral uncertainty has constrained the ability of economic technocrats to make creditable long-term policy commitments. However, democratization may not lead to the undoing of the developmental state; this depends on how policy makers adapt the developmental state model to a democratized environment. The experiences of Western European democratic corporatism (Katzenstein 1985; Garrett 1998) have demonstrated that a strong society and a strong state can coexist under a democratic regime. A robust organizational infrastructure in the private sector and a system of extensive consultation and coordination governed by shared broad goals between the state and major economic groups may actually enhance the state's transformative capacity.

Thus, when many East Asian NIEs strive to strengthen and consolidate their new democracies, they should aspire for a vision of a "democratic developmental state," under which participatory forms of democracy and broad-based development can be mutually reinforcing under the right political and institutional circumstances (Robinson and White 1999). East Asian countries must also judiciously avoid two other possible evolutional paths. One such possibility is the marriage between "*guanxi* capitalism" and "illiberal democracy," where family-owned enterprises infiltrate the state through pre-existing particularistic ties and captured elected politicians and where meaningful political empowerment of the mass is lacking because of ill-developed political parties, a rigged electoral process, corrupt mass media, and a flawed legal system. The second possibility converges on a cramped vision of liberal democracy that abdicates its transformative role, tolerates widespread exploitation, and allows inequalities to grow. Alternatively, the well-being of the vast majority of the population of developing East Asian societies can be better served under the aegis of a democratic developmental state that seeks to combine economic growth with extensive social empowerment.

Although the thrust of democratization and globalization might generate conflicting demands on the reform of the state and adjustment in state–society relationships, it is possible for the state to reconstitute itself in such a way that its capacity in facilitating structural transformation and in responding in a meaningful way to the social and economic agenda demanded by domestic constituencies is not diminished by forces of globalization (Chang 2000). Under a democratic regime, there are two important steps by which the state may reinvigorate its transformative capacity in the area of economic development. The first is to upgrade the quality of local governance through expanding the functions and resources of sub-national governments and strengthening the mechanism of democratic accountability; an expanded role for local government in delivering social services and promoting rural industrialization would enhance the state's overall transformative capacity. Equally important is the construction of new institutional foundations that suppress the infiltration of clientelism and facilitate a more encompassing and transparent business–government collaboration. This involves the acquisition of new regulatory capacity and analytical competency on the part of the state bureaucracy; a more inclusive state–business consultative mechanism; stronger institutional foundations for effective private-sector self-governance at both industry and firm levels; and the systematic incorporation of additional social actors – such as labour unions, middle-class-based public-interest groups, local communities and mass media – whose interests are only partly compatible with those of the business community, in the formulation and implementation of development strategies.

## The challenge of sizing-up China

Among all East Asian developing economies, China has a particular claim on our attention. China is poised to become the world's largest economy and the new locomotive of growth for the region in the next century. The rise of China will, inevitably, redefine the parameters of regional economic cooperation. More importantly, China's transition from command economy is one of the greatest events of economic transformation in its own rights: in the course of just two decades, the country has undergone processes of industrial, economic, and social change that, in the West, spanned centuries (Steinfeld 1999). Between the launching of China's economic reform programme in 1978 until 1998, its transition from a command-based to a market-based economy helped to fuel a remarkable average GDP growth of 10 per cent per year – a level impressive by any standard (World Bank 1999a). Moreover, economic growth in China, especially in the early years of reform, was shared broadly among all regions and segments of society. The precipitous reduction in poverty was especially stunning: twenty years ago, China was among the world's poorest countries, with 80 per cent of the population living on incomes of less than a dollar a day and only one-third of all adults able to read or write; in 1998, only 213 million people – 17 per cent of the population – lived on less than a dollar a day (World Bank 1999a); by 1999, only about 7 per cent of the population between 15 and 25 years old is illiterate, and China's high life-expectancy and low infant-mortality rates are envied by much richer nations. Similarly, China's reforms have facilitated its progress toward integration into the world economy. By 1998, China's exports as share of world imports jumped to 4.6 per cent from less than 1 per cent in the pre-reform era. During the 1990s, China was the "number one" recipient of FDI, absorbing about one-third of all FDI flows from the OECD countries to the developing world. Moreover, it was the first transition economy to be awarded an investment-grade rating for its sovereign debt and has sold far more debt and equity in international capital markets than any other transition economy (Lardy 1998: 2).

China's gradualist approach to economic reform offered critical advantages compared with the big-bang approach (i.e. a combination of rapid privatization, overnight price reform, and wholesale dismantling of trade barriers, as initiated in several former socialist states in Eastern Europe and parts of the former Soviet Union).[7] The first distinctive element of China's gradualist approach is the "dual-track system," which is the coexistence of a traditional plan and a market channel for the allocation of goods and services. It is a reform strategy that minimized potential downside losses and hence substantially reduced economic and political risks associated with market-oriented reforms (Lau, Qian, and Roland 2000). The "vested interests" in the old system have been, by and large, protected by the adoption of a two-tier pricing system and a two-tier wage. At the same time, Chinese reformers were making a generally credible commitment to freeze the size of the traditional plan. This guaranteed a long-run dynamic process that would gradually increase the share of market transaction in the economy and which made the dual-track system into a transitional device (Naughton 1995: 8–9). The second distinctive element is the devolution of economic decision-making power to local governments and to professional management of the enterprises. The autonomy and fiscal incentives empowered, as well as motivated, the local government at all levels to undertake similar economic functions that other development-oriented East Asian states had performed at the same stage of industrialization (Oi 1995).

The state initially ended controls on many agricultural prices and then, by the mid-1980s, introduced a two-tiered pricing strategy for most industrial goods. Under this system, planned output continued to be distributed at prices fixed by the state, whereas supply and demand in the market determined the price of the above-plan output. By the mid-1990s, the share of output distributed at below-market prices had shrunk dramatically, paving the way for the elimination of fixed prices in favour of a single market price for most industrial goods. Opening the economy to foreign trade was similarly gradual and was a key part of the process by which relative domestic prices converged to world levels (Lardy 1998). De facto privatization of small state-owned enterprises (SOEs) did not get under way until the mid-1990s, and few medium and large SOEs have been fully privatized. Instead, a variety of new forms of ownership have flourished under the sponsorship of local governments. Extraordinary forces of entrepreneurship have been unleashed. These firms, typically market-oriented collectives and township and village enterprises (Oi 1999), as well as export-oriented foreign-owned firms (Lardy 1994), accounted for a significant portion of the employment growth and productivity gains. As a result, the share of output produced in the SOE sector has fallen dramatically. The trend allowed the Chinese economy gradually to "grow out of the plan" (Naughton 1995).

Looking over the horizon, China enjoys a good prospect of sustaining the growth momentum for the next two decades. The country will continue to benefit from a number of favourable factors – a relative abundance of natural resources, a potentially huge domestic market for the realization of both economies of scale and "coordination externalities," the possibility of leap-frogging traditional development in telecommunication, a favourable demographic trend that ensures an almost unlimited supply of surplus labour, a high domestic savings rate of 35–40 per cent, and a cultural preference for education. Furthermore, China's commitment to economic openness and a lock-in to the global economy will become permanent with a WTO membership, which will improve domestic economic efficiency through open global competition.

However, as China continues to manage its dual transition from plan to market-based economy and from rural agricultural to urban industrial society, it also faces enormous challenges in the new century. China's economic future hinges on successful implementation of a host of related reform agendas – enterprise restructuring in the SOE sector, rationalization of the state-owned banks, the establishment of a social safety net, reconstituting public finance, reducing regional economic disparity, closing the digital divide, and reforming the political system to increase accountability and eradicate corruption.

At the turn of the century, the economic cost of postponing fundamental transformation of the SOE sectors has become even more severe. The situation surrounding the SOE sector threatens both the fiscal integrity of the central government and the stability of the entire banking sector, while hampering both job creation and economic growth (Steinfeld 1999: 3). Throughout almost twenty years of economic reform, although the SOE sector shrank in relative importance it continued to grow in absolute terms, in both output and employment. Even though employment levels have stabilized since the mid-1990s, the SOE sector still provides the basic industrial input for the economy, employment and social welfare for the vast majority of China's urban workers, as well as the bulk of fiscal revenue for most government levels. In addition, the SOEs have continued to absorb a disproportionately large share of investment resources. The huge losses that China's state banks incurred from loans to SOEs have pushed up the ratio of non-performing loans to a staggering level. By the end of 1999, the gross stock of the non-performing loans amounted to approximately $200 billion or 20–30 per cent of the gross national product (GNP).[8]

The banking sector is badly in need of a rationalization plan that will restructure non-performing loans, strengthen bank supervision, introduce risk-management techniques in state banks, install international accounting standards and practices, and raise loan-loss provisioning. A permanent solution of the problem of non-performing loans depends on the reform of SOEs. To make the SOEs economically viable requires a successful reduction of the currently redundant labour force, assumption of the social welfare costs by other public-funded agencies, reduction of the debt–equity ratio, and ultimately some restructuring programmes involving divestment, bankruptcy, mergers, governance, and ownership reform.

Over the long term, the development of a market-oriented banking sector and a fully-fledged capital market is absolutely necessary for China's next phase of economic expansion. An efficient banking sector will help to direct China's high level of savings into more productive investment. A sophisticated capital market can diversify the funding sources of SOEs and provide an avenue for the government to dilute its holdings in state enterprises and facilitate investment. At the same time, reconstituting and reshaping public finance is crucial to the creation of an efficient modern state in China, in which governments at all levels can meet their increasing obligations for the provision of basic public services,

for support of unemployment and other SOE-related labour market reforms in urban areas, and for targeted assistance to reduce hard-core
poverty in rural and isolated areas. An important component of the fiscal
reform is the introduction of a more rule-based system of interprovincial
transfers to ensure that the benefits of growth at the national level are
spread evenly across the country and to retard the growing trend of regional inequalities of income (Wang and Hu 1999).

Despite China's impressive record of economic growth and poverty
reduction, about 130 million Chinese continued to live on less than
a dollar a day in 1997. The rural poor are concentrated in resource-
constrained remote upland areas in the interior north-west and south-
west, where the poor quality of land makes it impossible to achieve even
a subsistence level of crop production. The urban poor, estimated to
comprise about 5 per cent of all poor people in the country, are an
emerging concern. Rural–urban income disparities remain substantial
and, although they have declined somewhat in recent years, when combined with regional income-growth differentials, contribute to increased
migration pressures. If these pressures continue to build up, they will
propel a rural exodus of gigantic dimensions and will push many over-
crowded mega-cities over the edge of ecological catastrophe. To divert
this worrisome trend, the government must accelerate the diffusion of
technology and capital into the land-locked western interior and vastly
improve the infrastructure and access to education in poor and minority
areas, allowing the economic development of different regions, generally
following the so-called "flying geese pattern," with the coastal urban area
leading the way.

Finally, to ensure a stable social and political environment conducive
to long-term economic development, the Chinese leaders must confront
the issue of political reforms more seriously. Failure to implement political institutional reforms will cause a tangible loss in economic efficiency
as the costs of insecure property rights, poor contract enforcement, and
exorbitant rents will surely become more ruinous. Lack of progress in
broadening the avenue of political participation and social representation
will exacerbate social tensions and damage the legitimacy of the Communist Party, as the current system lacks credible institutional channels
for resolving state–society conflict. Failure to implement political reform
is likely to cause an increased rift within the ruling élite, as there is no
institutional mechanism to resolve the conflict within the party and the
state. A modest political reform agenda should include a stepwise introduction of competitive electoral mechanisms up from the village to the
town and county levels, upgrading the existing People's Congress at all
levels into a system of a functioning representative institution, the creation of a modern meritocratic civil service, and a vast improvement in

both the professional standard and independence of the judicial system, thus making way for the autonomous operation of the mass media and NGOs.

China's development prospect carries enormous implications for the region as a whole. At the very minimum, China exemplified the way to grow out of the plan and exerted tremendous pressure on neighbouring transition economies, such as Viet Nam, Mongolia, and Myanmar, to follow a similar path of market-oriented reform. At the same time, China has been putting tremendous competitive pressure on the entire Asian region since Beijing opened its markets significantly to incoming FDI in 1992–1993 and pegged its currency to the dollar from 1 January 1994. The competition is as much in the form of competing for market share as it is competing for inward FDI flows, as China is in a structural position in the world economy similar to that of the ASEAN countries (Tan 1995). The recent competitive challenge from Chinese consumer electric/electronic manufacturers in low-end products has also forced Japanese companies to choose either to outsource much of their value chain in order to compete or to cede this low-end market. Some argue that this competitive trend might partially account for the virulence of Asian flu (because it brought about falling profit, slower export growth, and competitive devaluation of currencies) (Krause 1998). In the foreseeable future, China will also become a formidable player in the game of technological catching-up, with its solid foundation in basic scientific research and a vast and expanding domestic market for technology-intensive products, especially IT products. In less than a decade, China has come out of nowhere to become the world's second-largest market for mobile phones (after the United States) and will soon take over, from Japan, the status of hosting Asia's largest Internet population.[9] Before long, Chinese high-tech start-ups based in the most advanced coastal urban regions, such as Shanghai and Beijing, will make a major impact on the low-end market segment and will force Taiwanese and South Korean firms to re-configure their outsourcing strategies.

China's economic ascendance also raises the prospect of the emergence of the East Asian economic community. China's imminent membership of the WTO will open up new opportunities for its neighbours to forge stronger economic ties with this emerging economic giant and to "piggy-back" their economic expansion on the growing purchasing power of China's 3.5 billion urban consumers, while proportionally reducing their reliance on the United States as "the market of last resort." A novel but potentially significant dimension of China's integration into the regional economy is the prospect of China becoming an important FDI-exporting country in East Asia, especially with the official plan to introduce capital account convertibility over the next few years. Already, since 1996, China has become the fourth largest outward investor among the developing countries, next only to Hong Kong, Singapore, and Taiwan. The regional financial crisis has brought about a marked increase in China's stature in East Asia. The regional crisis gave China an unprecedented opportunity to exert leadership in Asia, with symbolic financial aid to Thailand (one billion dollars) and Indonesia (500 million dollars), and a firm commitment to peg its currency to the dollar (Naughton 1999).

Looking to the future, there is great potential for China to have a leadership role in the responsibility vacuum in East Asia created by the abdication of Japan and the absence of any other credible economic powers. Whether China will be able to realize this potential leadership role will largely depend on whether it can reconcile its historical grievances as well as its prospective strategic conflict with Japan and, thus, remove a major geopolitical obstacle to the development of East Asian regionalism (Selden 1997).

## Conclusion

Over the last two decades, East Asia has grown into a $2.1 trillion regional economy and the home of 1.7 billion people. It is increasingly recognized as a potentially powerful force in the global economy. East Asia has also rapidly evolved into a highly integrated economic region. Levels of economic interdependence within the region have risen rapidly. By 1996, intraregional exports (excluding Japan) accounted for nearly 40 per cent of the region's exports, up from 20 per cent in 1980; if Japan is included, the share of intraregional trade rises to 49 per cent. The region has witnessed the emergence of an integrated production economy, as the increasing importance of parts, components, and other intermediates in intraregional trade clearly implies.[10]

In contrast to the European Community, the acceleration of intraregional trade and investment flows was mostly driven by the adjustment strategies of Japanese and East Asian NIE transnational corporations and was facilitated by the informal overseas Chinese business networks; it received little help from regional economic cooperative institutions or multilateral arrangements (Harris 1993). There is a range of forums for regional deliberation on economic issues, such as ASEAN, a quasi-EAEC (an East Asian Economic Caucus known as ASEAN Plus Three), the Asia-Pacific Economic Cooperation Conference (APEC), the Pacific Basin Economic Council (PBEC) and the Pacific Economic Cooperation Council (PECC), but none of them has so far acquired the necessary institutional strength and organizational coherence to foster close policy coordination or enforce binding regional accords (Higgott 1997).

The East Asian way of regional integration – building an integrated regional economy without strong cooperation and coordination – has become dysfunctional and is simply not sustainable over the long term. The regional financial crisis heightened the issue of strengthening the multilateral mechanisms for the coordination of macroeconomic and regulatory actions. The region suffered from the striking failure of leadership in the crisis from within Asia – from regional states and regional organizations. In the middle of the crisis, the American obstruction to the Japanese proposal for an Asian Monetary Fund was a wake-up call for all Asian leaders, realizing that the United States was the only powerful state able to define its interests and disinterests in regional cooperation agendas under the APEC framework and that, with continued US dominance in this geographically diverse organization, the APEC will serve little purpose in the furtherance of East Asian regional cooperation. After the crisis, there is growing awareness among the East Asian leaders that their countries' own strategies need to be complemented with regional arrangements to cope with volatile capital flows, currency crises, and contagion, and that the region as a whole is paying a higher and higher price for its retarded growth in multilateralism.

Without a regional mechanism for concerted policy actions, the dense intraregional trade and investment links can be a means of spreading economic prosperity but also a perfect channel for the financial contagion to spread swiftly throughout East Asia. It is simply beyond the capacity of any East Asian developing economy to deal with future large-scale market failure in the international financial system by itself. On the other hand, concerted monetary and regulatory actions among the principal East Asian economies would have kept the exchange rate and the associated interest-rate fluctuations and stock-market slide within manageable bounds and contained the crisis at an early stage.

The successful holding of the ASEAN Plus Three Summit in Manila in 1999 represents the beginning of a new era of regionalism. So far, there has been significant progress in the area of regional financial cooperation. The East Asian financial ministers first agreed to establish a cooperative arrangement of regional surveillance, known as the Manila Framework. In March 2000, East Asian governments created a network of bilateral repurchase agreements among central banks, known as the Chin Mai Accord, as a first step toward greater macroeconomic collaboration. There is little doubt that East Asia has the financial means to implement an effective regional liquidity fund as the central banks of ASEAN countries, together with China, Japan, Korea, Hong Kong, and Taiwan, collectively had foreign reserves of well over $900 billion (Dieter 2000).

In the future, the agenda for regional economic monitoring could include the exchange of macroeconomic and structural information on fiscal positions, monetary and exchange rate policies (including domestic and foreign assets and liabilities of central banks), capital flows, external debt, financial-system conditions, and corporate developments. With effective consultation and monitoring, the region's economies will face peer pressure to pursue disciplined policies conducive to stable currencies and external accounts. In addition, the agenda for concerted policy actions can be extended to include common policies on short-term capital flows (such as raising the cost of short-term borrowing by taxing inflows, setting higher reserve requirements, or requiring central bank fees for sovereign guarantees), a regional financial architecture to cope with the trend of "merger-and-acquisition" of local financial services companies by the American and European TNCs, and a regional agenda for a new "Millennium Round" of WTO negotiation. It is also necessary for East Asian developing countries to reform fiscal incentives and to adopt common environment and labour standards for FDI at a regional level to alleviate fears of being strategically undercut by continued major incentives and lax labour and environmental regulations in neighbouring countries.

Over the long term, the construction of a robust East Asian economic community requires not only a Sino-Japanese partnership but also the development of a multilateral institutionalization of power, in which the smaller East Asian countries are not simply silly putting in the hands of a Japanese or Chinese giant but act as parties to contractual bargains and through which the power of the two regional giants, China and Japan, is regulated and funnelled rather than being allowed to erupt in a narrow, power-defined sense of national self-interest. In a nutshell, the growth of East Asian regionalism requires the Asianization of both China and Japan, much as the post-war European integration requires the Europeanization of Germany (Katzenstein 1997). To this end, the government and NGO leaders in the region must resolve to build up the cultural, intellectual, and social infrastructure for the East Asian community through the construction of an East Asian identity, the development of a regional "episteme community" (to serve as an idea-binder and policy advocate for the regional agenda), and the emergence of a regional civil society with a dense regional network of NGOs.

On the domestic front, the most critical intellectual challenge facing policy makers and citizens in the developing East Asia is how to rethink, redefine, and reinvigorate the role of the state, given the twin challenges of globalization and democratization. East Asian countries will put themselves in grave peril if they naïvely subscribe to the "convergence school" thesis or the "neo-liberal" prescriptions at their face values. It is also totally unrealistic to leave the task of protecting human security and achieving widespread social empowerment to the unfettered market. The rewards of globalization in terms of access to markets, technology, and

capital need to be balanced by the adjustment risks, structural vulnerability, and distributional consequences for the domestic economy.

Globalization and democratization have pushed the issue of governance squarely onto the development agenda. The very task of balancing
the risk and benefit of globalization actually compels the state in the East
Asian NIEs to reinvigorate its transformative capacity and redefine the
task for state–society collaboration. Financial liberalization must be accompanied by re-regulation and the enhancement of the state's monitoring and regulatory capacity. The advances in multilateral trade negotiation and the trend towards regional economic groupings require the state
not only to acquire new administrative capacity in such areas as anti-
dumping adjudication and intellectual property-right enforcement but
also to upgrade their technical capacity in dealing with the growing
number and complexity of trade negotiations and using the dispute-
settlement mechanisms effectively. With the trend of de-verticalization
and fragmentation in the global production process and the unprecedented time compression in technological innovation, the state is called upon
to act as a guiding element in a national effort to identify trajectories of
technological diffusion and innovation and to serve as a catalyst motivating and enabling the local firms to invest, upgrade, innovate, and internationalize. Only a reinvigorated state in collaboration with both the
business and civil-society groups can effectively close the digital divide,
protect the poor against the risk of economic integration, ensure its citizens an equitable participation in the global economy, and respond in a
meaningful way to the public-policy demands of its domestic constituencies.

## Notes

1. For the sake of keeping our analysis within manageable scope, we leave out countries
   such as Brunei, Myanmar, Cambodia, East Timor, and North Korea. We also exclude
   Japan because it was part of the industrialized world before the war. Nevertheless, the
   prospect of Japan's economic restructuring and its leadership role will have profound
   consequences for the developing countries in the region.
2. The nine economies cover all the countries presented in table 5.1 except Viet Nam.
3. The two measures were suggested respectively by James Tobin and Lawrence Klein.
4. Only $50 million to each institutional investor and a quota of $2.5 billion, which represents only about 2 per cent of total market capitalization, for all foreign investors. In
   addition, each institution was allowed to buy up to 5 per cent of a single company and
   total foreign ownership of a company was limited to 10 per cent. On top of that, all
   portfolio investment capital was required to stay in Taiwan at least three months before
   remission. The three-month requirement amounted to a hidden tax on "hot money." By
   mid-1997, the capital ceiling for individual foreign institutional investors has been
   steadily raised to $600 million. The cap on ownership of individual foreign institutional

investors in any listed company was raised to 15 per cent, and no more than 30 per cent for all foreign investors

5. The long-term net social return comprises spillover effects, improvement in market co-ordination, reduction in transaction costs, and promotion of dynamic efficiency. On the economic rationality for industrial policy, see Chang (1994).

6. Under OEM, the latecomer produces a finished product to the precise specification of a foreign TNC. According to Hobday, "the term originated in the 1950s among computer makers who used sub-contractors to assemble equipment for them." This term now generally refers to "the system by which firms cooperate in sub-contracting relation-ship" (Hobday 1995: 49).

7. The distinction between the two approaches was not as stark as would appear. Chinese economic reform appeared gradualist because the planners sequenced reform by sectors – agriculture, industry, international, labour, and capital – and the population is pro-tected from shock because of the policy of "no losers." However, for each of the sectors the markets were opened instantaneously, just like "Big Bang" (Lau, Qian, and Roland 2000).

8. According to the People's Bank of China (PBOC), 20 per cent; according to interna-tional rating agencies, at least 25 per cent. Ultimately, non-recoverable non-performing loans have been estimated to be of the order of 15 per cent of all outstanding loans by non-government analysts: e.g. Moody's Investors Service estimated the total cost of cleaning-up bad loans to be $120.8 billion in 1998/1999, or 12.5 per cent of Chinese GDP (Lau 2000).

9. By the end of August 2000, China's Internet users had reached the 20 million threshold and the Internet population had doubled every six months (*International Herald Trib-une*, 14 September 2000).

10. Intraregional exports of parts and components grew by 21 per cent a year between 1984 and 1996, outpacing the 14 per cent growth of intraregional trade and the 15 per cent growth of East Asian exports of parts and components to the world at large (Yeats 1999).

## REFERENCES

Asian Development Bank. 2000. *Asian Economic Outlooks 2000*. Manila: Asian Development Bank.

Biggs, T. S. and Chang-Ho Yoon, 1990, "Market Structure and the Transition to High-end Products in Developing Countries." EEPA discussion paper No. 27. Cambridge: Harvard Institute for International Development.

Boyer, Robert and Daniel Drache, eds. 1996. *States Against Markets: The Limits of Globalization*. London: Routledge.

Carnoy, Martin. 1999. *Sustainable Flexibility: Work, Family and Community in the Information Age*. New York: Cambridge University Press.

Castells, Manuel. 1996. *The Information Age: Economy, Society and Culture – Volume 1: The Rise of Network Society*. Oxford: Blackwell.

Castells, Manuel. 1999. "Information Technology, Globalization and Social De-velopment." United Nations Research Institute for Social Development, Dis-cussion Paper, DP 116.

Chang, Ha-Joon. 1994. *The Political Economy of Industrial Policy*. New York: St Martin's Press.

Chang, Ha-Joon. 2000. "An Institutionalist Perspective on the Role of the State –

Towards an Institutionalist Political Economy." In *Institutions and the Role of the State*, L. Burlamaqui, A. Castro, and H.-J. Chang, eds. Aldershot: Edward Elgar.

Chu, Wan-wen. 2000. "The OEM Model of Development: Can the East Asian NIC Catch Up?" Paper presented at the MIT/Academia Sinica Workshop. Taipei, Taiwan, 8 July 2000.

Chu, Yun-han. 1995. "The East Asian NICs: A State-led Path to the Developed World." In *Global Change, Regional Response*, ed. Barbara Stallings. Cambridge: Cambridge University Press.

Chu, Yun-han. 1999. "Surviving the East Asian Financial Storm: The Political Foundation of Taiwan's Economic Resilience." In *The Politics of the Asian Economic Crisis*, ed. T. J. Pempel. Ithaca: Cornell University Press.

Claessens S., S. Djankov, and L. Lang. 1998. "East Asian Corporates: Growth, Financing and Risks over the Last Decades." Washington, DC: World Bank. Unpublished manuscript.

Council for Economic Planning and Development (CEPD). 2000. *Statistical Data Book 2000*. Taipei: CEPD.

Dieter, Heribert. 2000. "Asia's Monetary Regionalism." *Far Eastern Economic Review* 6 July 2000.

Doner, Richard. 1992. "Limits of State Strength: Toward an Institutionalist View of Economic Development." *World Politics* 44(4): 398–431.

Evans, Peter B. 1995. *Embedded Autonomy: States and Industrial Transformation*. New Jersey: Princeton University Press.

Garrett, Geoffrey. 1998. *Partisan Politics in the Global Economy*. Cambridge: Cambridge University Press.

Haggard, Stephen. 2000. *The Political Economy of the Asian Financial Crisis*. Washington DC: Institute for International Economics.

Harris, Stuart. 1993. "Economic Cooperation and Institutional Building in the Asia-Pacific Region." In *Pacific Economic Relations in the 1990s*, eds. R. Higgott, R. Leaver, and J. Ravenhill. Boulder: Lynne Rienner.

Higgott, Richard. 1997. "Regional Integration, Economic Cooperation, or Economic Policy Coordination in Asia Pacific? Unpacking APEC, EAEC and AFTA." In *The Regionalization of the World Economy and Consequences for Southern Africa*, ed. Heribert Dieter. Marburg: Metropolis-Verlag.

Hobday, M. 1995. *Innovation in East Asia: The Challenge to Japan*. Aldershot: Edward Elgar.

Islam, Iyanatul. 1992. "Political Economy and Economic Development." *Asian Pacific Economic Literature* 6(2): 69–191, November.

Jomo, K. S. 1999. "Introduction: Financial Governance, Liberalization and Crises in East Asia." In *Tigers in Trouble*, ed. K. S. Jomo. New York: St Martin's Press.

Jomo, K. S., Chen Yun Chung, Brian C. Folk, Irfan Ul-Haque, Pasuk Phongpaichit, Batara Simatupang, and Mayuri Tateishi. 1997. *Southeast Asia's Misunderstood Miracle: Industrial Policy and Economic Development in Thailand, Malaysia and Indonesia*. Boulder: Westview Press.

Katzenstein, Peter. 1985. *Small States in World Markets*. Ithaca: Cornell University Press.

Katzenstein, Peter, ed. 1997. *Tamed Power: Germany in Europe*. Ithaca: Cornell University Press.

162   CHU

Kitschelt, Herbert, ed. 1999. *Continuity and Change in Contemporary Capitalism.* Cambridge: Cambridge University Press.

Krause, Lawrence. 1998. *The Economics and Politics of the Asian Financial Crisis of 1997–1998.* New York: Council on Foreign Relations.

Lardy, Nicholas. 1994. *China in the World Economy.* Washington DC: Institute for International Economics.

Lardy, Nicholas. 1998. *China's Unfinished Economic Revolution.* Washington DC: Brookings Institution Press.

Lau, Lawrence. 2000. "The State of the Chinese Economy: A View From Outside." Presentation at Conference on China at the Crossroads, Institute for International Studies, Stanford University, 19 May 2000.

Lau, Lawrence, Ying-Yi Qian, and Gerard Roland. 2000. "Reform without Losers: An Interpretation of China's Dual-Track Approach to Transition." *Journal of Political Economy* 108(1): 120–143, February.

Mittelman. J. H. ed. 1996. *Globalization: Critical Reflections.* Boulder: Lynne Rienner.

Mo, Jongryn and Chung-in Moon. 1998. "Democracy and the Origins of the 1997 Korean Economic Crisis." In *Democracy and Korean Economy*, eds Chung-in Moon and Jongryn Mo. Stanford: Hoover Institution Press.

Naughton, Barry. 1995. *Growing out of the Plan.* Cambridge: Cambridge University Press.

Naughton, Barry. 1999. "China: Economic Restructuring and a New Role in East Asia." In *The Politics of the Asian Economic Crisis*, ed. T. J. Pempel. Ithaca: Cornell University Press.

Oi, Jean. 1995. "The Role of the Local State in China's Transitional Economy." *China Quarterly* No. 144: 1132–1149, December.

Oi, Jean. 1999. *Rural China Takes Off: The Institutional Foundations of Economic Reform.* Berkeley: University of California Press.

Pempel, T. J. 1999. "Introduction." In *The Politics of the Asian Economic Crisis*, ed. T. J. Pempel. Ithaca: Cornell University Press.

Robinson, Mark and Gordon White, eds. 1999. *The Democratic Developmental State: Politics and Institutional Design.* Oxford: Oxford University Press.

Rowen, Henry, ed. 1998. *Behind East Asian Growth: The Political and Social Foundations of Prosperity.* London: Routledge.

Sassen, Saskia. 1996. "The Spatial Organization of Information Industries: Implications for the Role of the State." In *Globalization: Critical Reflection*, ed. James Mittelman. Boulder: Lynne Rienner.

Schmidt, Vivien. 1999. "Convergence Pressures, Divergent Responses: France, Great Britain, and Germany between Globalization and Europeanization." In *State and Sovereignty in the Global Economy*, eds D. Smith, D. Solinger and S. Topik. London: Routledge.

Selden, Mark. 1997. "China, Japan and the Regional Political Economy of East Asia, 1945–1995." In *Network Power: Japan and Asia*, eds Peter Katzenstein and Takashi Shiraishi. Ithaca: Cornell University Press.

Steinfeld, Edward. 1999. *Forging Reform in China: The Fate of State-Owned Industry.* Cambridge: Cambridge University Press.

Sturgeon, Timothy. 1997. *Turn-key Production Networks: A New American*

*Model of Industrial Organization?* Berkeley: University of California at Berkeley, Berkeley Roundtable on the International Economy. Working Paper 92A, August.

Tachiki, Dennis S. 1999. "The Business Strategies of Japanese Production Networks in Asia." In *Japanese Multinationals in Asia: Regional Operations in Comparative Perspective*, ed. Dennis J. Encarnation. Oxford: Oxford University Press.

Tan, Kong Yan. 1995. "China and ASEAN: Competitive Industrialization Thorough Foreign Direct Investment." In *The China Circle: Economics and Technology in the PRC, Taiwan and Hong Kong*, ed. Barry Naughton. Washington: Brookings Institution.

Tu, Wei-ming, ed. 1996. *Confucian Traditions in East Asian Modernity*. Cambridge: Harvard University Press.

United Nations Development Programme (UNDP). 2001. *Human Development Report 2000*. Oxford: Oxford University Press.

Wade, Robert. 1990. *Governing The Market: Economic Theory and the Role of Government in East Asian Industrialization*. New Jersey: Princeton University Press.

Wade, Robert. 1996. "Globalization and Its Limits: Reports of the Death of the National Economy are Greatly Exaggerated." In *National Diversity and Global Capitalism*, eds Susan Berger and Ronald Dore. Ithaca: Cornell University Press.

Wade, Robert. 1998. "The Asian Debt and Development Crisis of 1997–?: Causes and Consequences." *World Development* 26(8): 1535–1553.

Wade, Robert. 1999. "Is This the End of the Asian Model?" Paper presented at Seminar held on the occasion of the 32nd Annual Meeting of the Asian Development Bank, Manila, 30 April 1999.

Wang, Shaoguang and Angang Hu. 1999. *The Political Economy of Uneven Development: The Case of China*. New York: M. E. Sharpe.

Weiss, Linda. 1998. *The Myth of the Powerless State*. Ithaca: Cornell University Press.

Woo-Cumings, Meredith, ed. 1999. *The Developmental State*. Ithaca: Cornell University Press.

World Bank. 1993. *The East Asian Miracle: Economic Growth and Public Policy*. Oxford: Oxford University Press.

World Bank. 1998. *East Asia: The Road to Recovery*. Washington DC: World Bank.

World Bank. 1999a. *China: Weathering the Storm and Learning the Lessons. A World Bank Country Study*. Washington DC: World Bank.

World Bank. 1999b. *World Development Report 1999/2000: Entering the 21st Century*. Oxford: Oxford University Press.

World Bank. 2000. *World Development Report 2000/2001: Attacking Poverty*. Oxford: Oxford University Press.

Yeats, Alexander. 1999. *The East Asian Economic Crisis: Was the Region's Export Performance a Factor?* Trade Team, Development Research Group. October. Washington: World Bank.

# 6

# States, markets, and the limits of equitable growth: The Middle Eastern NICs in comparative perspective

*Ziya Öniş*

## Introduction

The Middle East and North Africa (MENA) has been confronted with the common challenges facing all regions of the developing world – namely, the impact of neo-liberal globalization and the associated pressures of economic liberalization, deregulation, and reform designed to accomplish greater integration into the international economy as well as enhancing competitiveness in external markets. Similar challenges have been evident, although perhaps to a lesser extent, in the political realm, with pressures building up for some degree of political liberalization and democratic opening. One of the striking features of MENA compared with other regions of the world, however, is the enormous degree of intraregional variation that characterizes the countries of the region judged in terms of size, natural resources, socio-economic indicators, type of economic indicators, type of political regime, economic performance, and levels of per capita income. Hence, an investigator is immediately confronted with the daunting question of whether it is sensible to treat MENA as a homogeneous entity that could meaningfully be compared with other regional entities in the global political economy such as "East Asia" or "Latin America."

None the less, a major contention of the present study is that there are enough characteristics or challenges common to all or most of the countries in the region to justify a focus on MENA as a highly distinct region from a broad comparative perspective. The first part of the study involves an attempt to identify and highlight these common regional characteristics. In the second part, the focus shifts to a more detailed consideration of three "Middle Eastern newly industrialized countries (NICs)" – Turkey, Egypt, and Morocco – from a comparative standpoint. The so-called Middle Eastern NICs represent an interesting spectrum of cases, ranging from Turkey to Egypt, with Morocco in many ways constituting an intermediate case, in terms of the depth of private-sector development; degree of orientation towards Europe; and steps taken in the direction of establishing open, pluralistic, political regimes. It is striking to observe that the Middle Eastern NICs, on the whole, have been less successful than their Asian and Latin American counterparts, judged in terms of per capita income levels or "human development" indicators. Turkey is, perhaps, the only country (together with the rather unique case of Israel) that comes close to replicating the performance of the more successful NICs, with Egypt and Morocco finding themselves considerably behind in the league table of the emerging markets, in terms of both economic growth and the degree of political opening. This chapter attempts to uncover some of the systematic factors underlying these stylized observations.

## Development trajectories of the Middle East and North Africa: Divergence versus convergence?

Richards and Waterbury (1996), in their seminal study of the political economy of the Middle East, decompose the region into five distinct groups of nation-states with widely contrasting economic structures and performance levels along the following lines (Karshenas 1994; Richards and Waterbury 1996). Group A consists of small oil-exporting countries (e.g. Kuwait), characterized by substantial oil reserves and nothing else. Group B refers to "oil industrializers" (e.g. Iran, Iraq), which enjoy substantial oil revenues and possess large enough populations to render industrialization a real option. In many of these cases, however, pervasive political instability or mismanagement has prevented the realization of the type of economic performance that would be consistent with the countries' underlying natural base. Group C comprises a set of countries that are small and also lack oil or other natural resources (e.g. Syria, Jordan). The only real option for development in these countries is to create a substantial base of human capital which would, in turn, be instrumental in generating and exporting skill-intensive manufacturers. Group D refers to the NICs that have no oil (e.g. Turkey and Morocco), or not enough to provide a basis for a long-term growth strategy (e.g.

Egypt). These countries possess large populations, relatively good agricultural land, and a long history of industrial production. Finally, group E
covers the category of countries referred to as "agro-poor" (e.g. Sudan
and the Yemen), for whom agricultural development is the only option.

It is quite obvious, therefore, that the group of countries constituting
the MENA region display a considerable element of diversity. The degree of divergence in development trajectories and subsequent economic
performance is clearly evident from a broad examination of the data on
growth trends over time, as well as per capita income levels and population size of the countries making up the region.

Clearly, a number of Middle Eastern countries, notably countries in
group A, have managed to generate extremely high per capita income
levels, comparable to some of the highest in the world, by capitalizing on
their abundant supplies of oil in the context of small population size.
The three large Middle Eastern NICs, whose experiences are highlighted
in the present context, constitute an intermediate category among the
countries of the Middle East in terms of growth rates achieved and per
capita income levels attained. The choice of these three countries may be
justified by the fact that they account for a disproportionately large share
of the total population in the MENA region.[1] A comparison of the three
NICs with the remainder of the region points towards a marked divergence in development trajectories: the growth pattern of the three Middle
Eastern NICs appears to be more stable than that of the remaining set of
countries. All three have managed to maintain moderately high rates of
economic growth over the past thirty years. Given rapidly expanding
population size in these countries, however, growth rates generated have
clearly been inadequate in terms of closing the gap with the Asian NICs
and the more-developed countries of the West (table 6.1). In contrast to
the comparatively stable growth trajectory of the three Middle Eastern
NICs, a high degree of instability is evident concerning the growth of
countries dependent on exports of oil, following the decline in the fortunes of the Organization of Petroleum Exporting Countries (OPEC)
and the negative trends in the world market for oil. Many Middle Eastern
countries have experienced substantially lower rates of economic growth
in the post-1980 period, a trend that clearly highlights the vulnerability of
the countries involved in the vagaries of the global oil market.

It would be illuminating to place the performance of the Middle Eastern NICs in a broader context by comparing them with major Latin
American or Asian NICs as well as a similar group of "transition economies" in Central and Eastern Europe. The comparison is based on per
capita income levels, as well as on other broad indicators of development
including the Human Development Index and relative income equality
(table 6.2). Judged in terms of per capita income levels and the human

Table 6.1 Middle Eastern NICs: Growth performance, per capita incomes, population size, and manufactured exports

| | Growth of GDP (average percentage growth) | | | | Population 1999 | Per capita PPP[a] ($) 1998 | Manufactured exports (percentage of total exports) 1996 |
|---|---|---|---|---|---|---|---|
| | 1960–1970 | 1970–1980 | 1980–1990 | 1990–1998 | | | |
| Turkey | 6 | 5.9 | 5.4 | 4.1 | 65,599,206 | 6,114[b] | 74 |
| Egypt | 4.3 | 9.5 | 5.4 | 4.2 | 67,273,906 | 3,130 | 32 |
| Morocco | 4.4 | 5.6 | 4.2 | 2.1 | 29,661,636 | 3,120 | 50 |

Sources: World Bank. *World Development Report, 1994, 1999–2000*; for the population data: US Census Bureau. International Database.

a. PPP per capita is measured on the basis of GNP.
b. Observation is taken from OECD 1999.

167

Table 6.2 Middle Eastern NICs in comparative perspective based on real GDP per capita (PPP$), Human Development Index, and Gini coefficients

| Country | HDI value | HDI rank[a] | Real GDP per capita (PPP$) 1995 | Gini Index |
|---|---|---|---|---|
| Turkey | 0.782 | 69 | 5,516 | 50.36[b] |
| Egypt | 0.612 | 112 | 3,829 | 32.0 |
| Morocco | 0.557 | 125 | 3,477 | 39.2 |
| Argentina | 0.888 | 36 | 8,498 | NA |
| Brazil | 0.809 | 62 | 5,928 | 60.1 |
| Chile | 0.893 | 31 | 9,930 | 56.5 |
| Mexico | 0.855 | 49 | 6,769 | 53.7 |
| China | 0.650 | 106 | 2,935 | 41.5 |
| Hong Kong | 0.909 | 25 | 22,950 | 41.58[b] |
| Malaysia | 0.834 | 60 | 9,572 | 48.4 |
| Indonesia | 0.679 | 96 | 3,971 | 36.5 |
| Korea, Rep. | 0.894 | 30 | 11,594 | 34.52[b] |
| Thailand | 0.838 | 59 | 7,742 | 46.2 |
| Taiwan | NA | NA | 16,500[c] | 29.48[b] |
| Czechoslovakia | 0.884 | 39 | 9,775 | 26.6 |
| Poland | 0.851 | 52 | 5,442 | 27.2 |
| Hungary | 0.857 | 47 | 6,793 | 27.9 |
| Romania | 0.767 | 74 | 4,431 | 28.2 |
| Russia | 0.769 | 72 | 4,431 | 48.0 |

a. A positive figure indicates that the HDI ranking is better than the real GDP per capita (PPP$) rank; a negative indicates the opposite.
b. Observations are taken from Sarel 1997.
c. Estimation for 1998. Source: CIA 1999.
NA, not available.
Source: United Nations *Human Development Report 1998.*

development index, the performances of the three Middle Eastern NICs, on the whole, appear to be below the levels recorded by the leading representatives of the other three regions. In terms of per capita income levels, Turkey, the leading Middle Eastern NIC, appears to lag behind the NICs of Asia (with the notable exceptions of Indonesia and China) and Latin America, but displays a performance that is broadly comparable to an "average transition economy." Indeed, one could go further and place Turkey in a class of its own as a Southern European country without European integration and a minor civil war. Consequently, its development performance, although being way ahead of that of the Middle East, has been lagging with respect to the Southern European trio of Spain, Portugal, and Greece – countries that have benefited immensely from the EU's Mediterranean enlargement process (United Nations 1998). The per capita income levels of the two other Middle Eastern NICs – Egypt and Morocco – however, are considerably below the averages of countries located in the other three regions. It is also interesting, however, that an evaluation based on the human development index provides a somewhat different picture, with the transition economies recording superior performance with respect to Turkey, which itself is significantly superior to Egypt and Morocco. Ultimately, a key test of whether a country can be classified as an "NIC" or not is related to its capacity to generate manufactured exports on a significant scale. On the basis of this particular criterion, as well, Turkey has a significant claim to be classified as an NIC with a major share of manufactured exports (table 6.1). The corresponding ratios for Egypt and Morocco are considerably lower, suggesting that "potential" or "near" NICs would, perhaps, be more appropriate labels for these two particular cases.[2]

Finally, an interesting observation concerns the performance of the Middle Eastern NICs with respect to the objective of relative-income inequality. The Turkish development experience has been characterized by a longer period of sustained economic growth combined with high-income inequality, with levels of income inequality rather similar to those observed in large Latin American NICs such as Brazil or Mexico. In contrast, both the state-led authoritarian-populist model of Egypt and the considerably milder version of authoritarian state-led development in Morocco have been characterized by comparatively short periods of sustained economic growth, but at the same time by a substantially more even distribution of income (table 6.3). Furthermore, the claim that income inequality increases under neo-liberal reforms is not confirmed by evidence on patterns of income inequality over time in all three countries. In Turkey, household-income inequality has been persistently high and yet broadly stable over the import-substitution and neo-liberal periods. In Egypt and Morocco, income distribution has been consistently more even than in Turkey – indeed, there is some evidence of a decline in overall income inequality in the neo-liberal period in these two cases. None the less, it is important to point out that a significant gap between the rich and the poor has been very much a key characteristic of both of these societies (table 6.3).

Clearly, one has to be very careful in undertaking broad comparisons of income distributional profiles across countries and over time on the basis of aggregate indicators such as the Gini coefficient. In any event, observations concerning relative income inequality cannot negate the fact that poverty and unemployment, of varying degrees, are serious problems common to all three societies, especially in the presence of rapid population growth (although the birth rate has started to decline in recent years). Another striking dimension of income inequality deserves emphasis in this context: an element that sharply differentiates the Middle East in general, with the exception of Morocco and Tunisia, from

Table 6.3 Income inequality in Middle Eastern NICs

| Country | Survey Year | Gini Coefficient | Survey Year | Lowest 20% | 2nd Quintile | 3rd Quintile | 4th Quintile | Highest 20% |
|---------|-------------|------------------|-------------|------------|--------------|--------------|--------------|-------------|
| Turkey | 1973 | 0.51 | 1973 | 3.5 | 8 | 12.5 | 19.5 | 56.5 |
|  | 1996 | 0.50 | 1994 | 4.86 | 8.63 | 12.61 | 19.03 | 54.88 |
| Egypt | 1974 | 0.37 | 1974 | 5.8 | 10.7 | 14.7 | 20.8 | 48 |
|  | 1991 | 0.32 | 1991 | 8.7 | 12.5 | 16.3 | 21.4 | 41.1 |
| Morocco | 1965 | 0.50 | 1959–1960 | 7 | 11 | NA | NA | 43.4 |
|  | 1990–1991 | 0.39 | 1990–1991 | 6.6 | 10.5 | 15.0 | 21.7 | 46.3 |

Source: World Bank, *World Development Report* (various years); Richards and Waterbury 1996.
NA, not available.

other developing regions of the world concerns the presence of persistently high rates of gender inequality. The origins of this phenomenon
have been widely debated in the literature. Low labour force participation in the MENA region is explained by some as the outcome of religious and cultural factors such as the dominance of the patriarchal family
in the region. Others, however, tend to focus on purely economic factors
such as the capital intensity of production techniques and the resulting
low demand for labour (on gender inequality, see Karshenas and
Moghadam 1997).

## The Middle East as a distinct region in the global political economy: Common characteristics and challenges confronting the Middle Eastern and North African countries

Although an unusual degree of intraregional variation constitutes a
striking element of the "Middle East," it is, none the less, possible to
identify certain broad characteristics or challenges that are common to all
(or most) countries of the region, including the group of Middle Eastern
NICs identified. The first (and the most obvious) common element concerns the pervasive influence of oil on the economies of the region –
either directly, in the case of oil-producing and -exporting countries, or
indirectly (through mechanisms such as remittances, aid, or increased
trade flows) in the case of non-oil economies. During the past three decades, oil has been the key determinant of the region's economic performance (Richards and Waterbury, 1996; Wilson 1995). It is abundantly
clear, however, that petroleum can no longer provide sufficient resources
for sustained regional development in the future. In retrospect, the
availability of oil on a massive scale has proved to be something of a
mixed blessing for the region. At one end of the spectrum, its positive
impact in terms of raising living standards, notably (but not only) in the
oil-exporting economies, has been enormous. Many oil-rich countries
have registered remarkable improvements in socio-economic indicators
because of the substantial amounts of wealth invested in education.
There is, however, a negative side to the balance sheet originating from
the region's over-dependence on oil. Compared with other regions of the
world, the Middle East has been a focal point of superpower rivalry or
conflict.[3] The preference of the major powers involved for stability and
security of oil supplies has also meant support for authoritarian regimes.
Consequently, the impulse for democratization and political opening in
the Middle East has been, on the whole, far less pronounced than that in
other regions (such as Latin America, East Asia, and Eastern Europe) in
the post-cold-war context (Bromley 1994; Salame 1994).

The persistence of authoritarian structures and arbitrary forms of government in the current international conjuncture arguably forms a barrier against deeper integration of the Middle Eastern countries into the international economy and, hence, limits their exposure to the positive aspects of the globalization process. Over-dependence on oil has also helped to create a group of "rentier states," which, in a number of cases, have failed to translate the benefits of oil to generate a level of industrialization compatible with other parts of the developing world. "Rentier states," in many instances, have lacked the incentives to push intensively for industrial transformation and have failed to forge adequate links with their societies, with the consequence that significant resources have been diverted away towards unproductive or military activities. In retrospect, the persistence of structures associated with the "rentier state" perhaps constitutes the single most important barrier to effective development in the region (Ayubi 1995; Beblawi 1990; Chaudhry 1997).

Secondly, the Middle Eastern states have been characterized by an inherent sense of isolation and insecurity due to external strategic threats, contested boundaries, the perennial Arab–Israeli conflict, as well as the disputes over the position of ethnic minorities within the nation-states themselves. Arguably, the degree of insecurity felt by the individual nation-states within the Middle East runs deeper than that in developing countries in other parts of the globe. Empirical evidence in favour of this hypothesis can be marshalled by examining resources devoted to military expenditures in the Middle East compared with those in other developing regions of the global economy. Both as a proportion of central government expenditures and GNP, military expenditures in the Middle East are higher than those in other key developing regions.[4]

Thirdly, the Middle Eastern NICs have not distinguished themselves on the basis of domestic-savings performance, which is a key indicator of indigenous development capacity (fig. 6.1). Domestic savings have been unusually low in the Egyptian case, pointing towards a major deficiency. In the Turkish case, the savings ratios are somewhat higher and comparable to Latin American standards, with Morocco constituting an intermediate case. In all these cases, however, the savings ratios are considerably lower than those of the East Asian NICs, a factor that has clearly contributed to a marked divergence of economic performance between the two sets of countries.

Fourthly, the degree of regional integration in trade, investment, or monetary cooperation among different economies has been rather weak compared with other regions of the world (with the notable exception of East Asia). Furthermore, attempts to construct regional cooperative agreements have registered extremely limited progress in comparative terms, with economic links in most national cases being dominated by

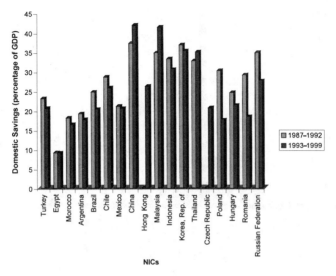

Figure 6.1 Domestic-savings performance of the Middle Eastern NICs in comparative perspective

external ties to countries located outside the region. Admittedly, there have been attempts to institutionalize regional cooperation through such mechanisms or agencies as the Arab Development Bank, the Islamic Development Bank, and other cooperative schemes in the Middle East; however, these attempts have made little impact in practice. Market-driven (as opposed to institutional-driven) integration has been a weak feature of Middle Eastern development.

Fifthly, the Middle East, broadly defined, has been marginalized in the distribution of global capital flows and notably in the allocation of long-term FDI, if one excludes exceptional cases in other parts of the world such as India. The region's share of global flows of foreign direct investment has remained strikingly low. Even the NICs (or the would-be NICs) of the Middle East have managed to attract unusually low amounts of FDI compared with their Asian, Latin American, and Eastern European counterparts (fig. 6.2).[5] Although capital flows have expanded to countries such as Turkey or Egypt in the context of the 1990s, the flows concerned have mainly assumed the form of relatively short-term and speculative portfolio or bank capital, the contributions of which to sustained economic growth in the long run are, by definition, open to serious criticism. Judged on the basis of "trade openness," however, the Middle East (in general) and the Middle Eastern NICs (in particular) appear to have displayed a high degree of openness in recent years following the

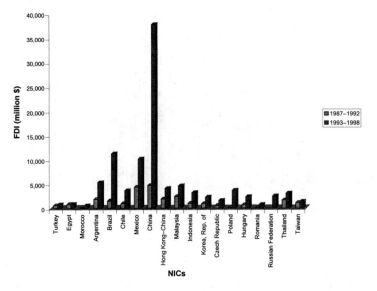

Figure 6.2 FDI performance of the Middle Eastern NICs in comparative perspective

implementation of neo-liberal reforms. It is rather paradoxical to observe that a region that tends to be marginalized in terms of the global allocation of long-term capital flows exhibits a greater degree of trade openness than does Latin America. Only Turkey has managed to expand its manufactured exports as a proportion of total exports on a substantial basis (table 6.4). A closer examination based on disaggregation of manufactured exports reveals, however, that even Turkey lags substantially behind East Asian NICs, for example, in terms of its ability to generate technology-intensive exports. Indeed, technology-intensive exports constitute less than 10 per cent of total manufactured exports in Turkey whereas the corresponding ratio is close to 40 per cent in the Korean case.[6]

In retrospect, these broad influences are interrelated with significant repercussions on the economic performance of the region. The availability of oil (even as a declining scale), the persistence of authoritarian political regimes, as well as the inherent weakness underlying the drive towards regional integration in the Middle East, have collectively produced an environment that is clearly not conducive to the expansion of trade and attraction of long-term foreign capital on a sufficient scale. This failure to expand trade and inflows of capital has, in turn, exercised a negative influence over the prospects of economic growth in the region.

Table 6.4 Export and foreign trade performance of the Middle Eastern NICs in comparative perspective (1997)

| Country | Exports (percentage of GDP) | Foreign trade (percentage of GDP) | Manufactured exports (percentage of total exports) | |
|---|---|---|---|---|
| | | | 1980 | 1996 |
| Turkey | 25 | 55 | 27 | 74 |
| Egypt | 20 | 45 | 11 | 32 |
| Morocco | 28 | 60 | 24 | 50 |
| Argentina | 9 | 20 | 23 | 30 |
| Brazil | 8 | 18 | 37 | 54 |
| Chile | 27 | 56 | 9 | 15 |
| Mexico | 30 | 60 | 12 | 78 |
| China | 23 | 18 | NA | 84 |
| Malaysia | 94 | 187 | 19 | 76 |
| Indonesia | 28 | 56 | 2 | 51 |
| Korea, Rep. of | 38 | 77 | 90 | 92 |
| Thailand | 47 | 93 | 25 | 73 |
| Taiwan | 34 | 66 | NA | NA |
| Czech Republic | 58 | 121 | NA | 84 |
| Poland | 26 | 56 | 61 | 74 |
| Hungary | 45 | 91 | 65 | 68 |
| Romania | 30 | 67 | NA | 77 |
| Russian Federation | 23 | 43 | NA | NA |

Source: World Bank, *World Development Report, 1998–1999.*
NA, not available.

Finally, as the sixth common denominator of the Middle Eastern states, the widespread influence or presence of "political Islam" in the region may be highlighted. Although a detailed consideration of this issue is beyond the confines of the present study, Islamism or political Islam in the Middle Eastern context signifies a protest movement that tends to emerge in response to inadequate and unequal development as well as limited participation in decision-making – the very features that constitute common tendencies in many countries of the region.

Setting the differences aside, attention ought to be drawn to the fact that the Middle East, in general, and the Middle Eastern NICs, in particular, share certain broad characteristics with the NICs of other regions. Indeed, the history of the Middle Eastern NICs, to varying degrees, is a history of state-led or state-dominated industrialization with a concomitant history of state domination and weak civil societies in the social and political spheres. This pattern of state domination has failed, however, to produce accountable states and effective state intervention. This history of state-led pattern of development also contains significant ramifications for the present-day prospects for economic performance, in terms of accomplishing the transition from clientelistic to competitive capitalism, as well for the prospects of authoritarian decline and democratic opening. Similarly, the Middle Eastern NICs have all experienced the familiar breakdowns of state-dominated models of development and the associated fiscal and balance-of-payments crises leading to the inevitable adoption of neo-liberal reforms. Furthermore, neo-liberal reform experiments have been introduced throughout the region, albeit with varying degrees of intensity and success. Reform experiences in the Middle East to date constitute a wide spectrum of cases involving relative success stories such as Turkey and Morocco, as well as a number of cases where the reform process has been more limited and the subsequent economic performance less impressive by international standards. None the less, it is fair to say that none of the three Middle Eastern NICs have been able to break away decisively from patterns of cyclical growth and periodic macroeconomic crises, resulting in frequent encounters with the IMF (Dervis and Shafik 1998; Pfeifer et al. 1999).

## Turkey: Fragmented developmental state and unjust growth

Among the non-oil economies of the Middle East, Turkey (together with the rather unique case of Israel) may be identified as the most successful NIC in terms of the rise in per capita income over time and the depth of industrialization achieved. Turkey has been one generation in advance of all its neighbours in the Middle East by starting the process of industrialization and state building in the 1920s that most other countries could not attempt before the 1950s. Significant steps have been taken towards industrialization in Turkey during the interwar period, following the achievement of independence in 1923, and notably during the étatist era of the 1930s. The étatist era marked the origins of Turkey's import-substitution drive, with the newly founded public enterprises playing a pivotal role in the process (Barkey 1990; Bromley 1994; Keyder 1987; Maxfield and Holt 1990; Owen and Pamuk 1998). In the post-war context, within the parameters of a novel international environment under the influence of the United States, Turkey experienced a shift in its development strategy away from import-substitution to a more open economy with much greater emphasis on agriculture, infrastructural development, and FDI. A similar radical shift occurred on the political front, with Turkey accomplishing a transition away from the mild authoritarian single-party regime of the interwar period to multiparty politics during the post-1946 era.

In retrospect, a crucial difference between Turkey and its Middle Eastern counterparts lies in the nature of the political regime. Turkey, in spite of periodic breakdowns and substantive limitations of its democratic order, has managed to combine a formally democratic regime with a process of rapid and sustained economic development. Following the economic and political crises of the late 1950s, Turkey has once again experienced a drastic shift in industrialization strategy. The early 1960s marked a new phase of étatism in Turkey with import-substitution in the context of formal development plans emerging as the dominant economic model. Key external actors such as the United States also favoured the continuation of ISI in Turkey rather than expediting a transition to export-led growth strategy. The Turkish development experience during the 1960s and the 1970s resembled a typical Latin American style of prolonged import-substitution, producing a reasonably rapid and yet rather unbalanced and distorted pattern of economic growth. The combination of heavy protectionism and export stagnation culminated with the inevitable balance-of-payments crisis of the late 1970s.

The Turkish experience with ISI has been associated with a substantial degree of industrial deepening. However, Turkey has faced similar problems when confronted with the Latin American NICs, such as Brazil. In the presence of stagnant exports and an inherent balance-of-payments constraint, rapid growth could not be a sustainable process. The development process in Turkey, which started in the interwar period and effectively built up momentum during the "liberal era" of the 1950s and the ISI era of the 1960s and the 1970s, has also been associated with the emergence of a strong entrepreneurial élite and a highly dynamic private sector, nurtured under the direct and pervasive influence of the state (Bugra 1994; Keyder 1987). Although the process of reasonably rapid development in the context of an open political system benefited all social groups in absolute terms, high relative-income inequality has been a persistent problem in Turkey, both in the context of the ISI process and during the more recent phase of neo-liberalism and reform.

Following the crisis of ISI in the late 1970s – a crisis that has been magnified by successive oil shocks in a country heavily dependent on imports of oil – a radical shift in development strategy occurred once again, this time in the direction of neo-liberalism and export-orientation. Given Turkey's important geostrategic position in the cold war context, the liberalization and structural-adjustment process has received significant international support from the OECD governments, as well as from international organizations such as IMF and the World Bank. In comparative terms, Turkey has managed to accomplish a relatively smooth transition away from the ISI model. Indeed, on the basis of its overall growth performance and ability to increase manufactured exports, Turkey was identified as one of the model cases or success stories by the Washington institutions in the early or mid-1980s (Aricanli and Rodrik 1990; Heper 1991; Kasnakoglu 1997; Öniş 1998, 2000).

Subsequently, however, the balance sheet of the reform experiment has been rather mixed. Growth has been reasonably sound and yet, at the same time, it has displayed a rather unstable, stop–go pattern. This stop–go pattern of economic growth has, in turn, been heavily dependent on continuous inflows of short-term foreign capital, a process that has been facilitated by full capital-account liberalization in 1989 as well as by the presence of high domestic interest rates. In fact, one of the striking elements of the Turkish development experience (rather parallel to other Middle Eastern NICs and in strong contrast to major Latin American NICs such as Brazil and Mexico) concerns the perennial inability to attract long-term foreign capital on a substantial scale (Öniş 2000). Although FDI to Turkey has increased in absolute terms during the neo-liberal era, the amounts involved have been considerably lower than those attracted by the NICs or the emerging markets in other key regions of the global economy. In spite of the fact that a liberal foreign-investment regime has been instituted in the early 1980s, investors have been deterred by a combination of macroeconomic and political instability. The civil war in the south-eastern part of the country, which has been in progress from 1984 onwards, has also had a negative role in terms of aggravating the fiscal crisis of the state, as well as providing unfavourable signals to foreign investors. The perception of a relatively insecure environment has clearly been influential in terms of creating a bias, on the part of external investors, towards short-term, speculative capital as opposed to FDI on a significant scale.

In a country where a disproportionate share of the population comprises young people on the verge of entering the labour market, social stability depends on the ability to sustain high rates of economic growth. In spite of the maturity and dynamism of its private sector, Turkey has failed to accomplish the type of hyper-growth characteristic of the first- or second-generation Asian NICs prior to the Asian crisis. The significantly superior performance of East Asia in terms of domestic savings has been a critical factor in this respect, as well as its superior performance in terms of labour productivity and development of indigenous technological skills. In retrospect, the diversion of resources away from civilian expenditures to military expenditures – a result of the continuation of internal conflict (as well as the protection of a hostile external environment) – combined with the failure to attract long-term investment on a substantive scale appear also to have played an instrumental role in Turkey's failure to shift from modest to consistently high rates of economic growth.

In the context of the 1990s, characterized by a fragmented political system and successive coalition governments, the Turkish state faced an important dilemma. On the one hand, strong pressures were placed on the state to perform the role of a "competition state" in terms of providing a favourable environment for domestic and international investors. Key interventions required in this respect involved the provision of human and physical infrastructure, generating a stable macroeconomic environment, as well as undertaking critical regulatory reforms in such key areas as the banking system and the capital markets. Pressures have also been exerted on the state, however, to take on an active role as a distributor of rents in an environment where relative-income inequality has been historically high by international standards. Clearly, these two types of pressures are increasingly in conflict, providing a fiscal crisis of the state. Furthermore, the environment of financial globalization and the high mobility of capital tend to place definitive limits on the redistributive capacities of the nation-state and its corresponding capacity to devote resources to the provision of social welfare. These pressures are, clearly, not unique but constitute a more general tendency that is also evident in the context of the Middle Eastern NICs, as well as that of NICs of other regions of the world economy.

## Egypt: Dilemmas of populism, late industrialism, and unjust growth

A crucial difference between Egypt and Turkey concerns the timing of independent industrialization and development of state institutions. The financial collapse of 1882 brought British occupation or control in Egypt, whereas a similar process of financial bankruptcy in Turkey did not produce direct control by an imperial power (Amin 1995; Owen and Pamuk 1998; Wahba 1994). Although Egypt has achieved political independence in the early 1920s, this independence has proved to be nominal. Imperial influence and the notable classes whose interests were tied to the interests of foreign powers were able to persist well until after the Second World War. Hence, the consolidation of state power in the context of the post-independent state in Egypt has occurred significantly later and in a very different international and domestic conjuncture to that of the Turkish case.

In contrast to the Turkish experience during the interwar period, which involved a significant take-off in the industrialization process, the Egyptian experience had been characterized by economic stagnation. The revolution of 1952 has marked a critical turning-point in the history of Egyptian economic development. A certain similarity could be identified between the "secularist" and "étatist" dimensions of the Kemalist regime in Turkey and the Nasserite regime in Egypt. Arguably, however, Egypt and other Middle Eastern states (including Algeria, Syria, Iraq, Tunisia, Sudan, and Libya) have proceeded well beyond the Turkish version of étatism since the 1950s by pursuing socialist and populist strategies characterized by a radical hostility against local and foreign capital and a rhetorical commitment towards redistribution of wealth within their societies. The legacy of the Nasserite regime in Egypt has been the presence of a much more extensive state presence and a considerably larger public-enterprise sector, with a correspondingly more limited development of private enterprise and the entrepreneurial élite than in the Turkish experience. The outcome, in retrospect, has been a pattern of development that has been far more egalitarian than those of Turkey and other Latin American NICs, but that, at the same time, has involved a shorter period of sustained industrialization.[7] Nevertheless, this "egalitarian" pattern of development has failed to prevent the emergence of a substantial gap between the rich and the poor segments of the Egyptian society (table 6.3). The extensive size of the state sector and state control over the economy, together with the relative weakness of the private sector, may explain why the authoritarian political structures have been relatively unchallenged. The degree of political opening has been extremely limited in Egypt, with the state élite groups clearly unwilling (in the absence of a sufficiently powerful opposition) to relinquish their discretionary control over considerable amounts of patronage resources (Hansen 1991; Waterbury 1993).

Egypt has also experienced the typical sequence of ISI, crisis, and neoliberal reforms characteristic of most developing countries. The timing, duration, and intensity of these processes have differed completely from those of Turkey or the Latin American NICs. In retrospect, ISI in Egypt, implemented through an extensive public-enterprise sector, appears to have been a relatively short process, with the defeat by Israel in the Six Day War of 1967 followed by a prolonged period of stagnation proving to be a decisive turning-point. It is also striking that the process of opening up or economic liberalization in Egypt, the so-called "Infitah" process, started earlier in Egypt (in 1974) than in Turkey, where the same process effectively commenced in 1980. A key objective of the "open-door economic policy" was to attract foreign investment, to encourage Western banks to operate from Egypt, and to promote joint ventures. In the early stages, the opening-up process was dominated by the liberalization of the trade and investment regime; however, it was soon followed by structural reform measures including privatization and industrial restructuring as recommended by the IMF (Bush 1999; Henry 1996). Reflecting the im-

pact of the liberalization process and the positive impact of the Organization of Petroleum-Exporting Countries (OPEC) on oil revenues, the
1970s emerged as the most successful phase in the post-war history of the
Egyptian economy. The same momentum could not be maintained, however, in the context of the 1980s, notably following the "bust" in the oil
market. On the eve of the Gulf War the Egyptian economy was clearly in
disarray, with growth rates declining steadily in the context of the 1980s;
this process of decline had reached a climax in 1990. By the turn of the
decade, the Egyptian economy had been characterized by large fiscal
deficits, major macroeconomic imbalances, as well as external indebtedness on a massive scale. A number of investigators have pointed out that,
in spite of the onset of the Infitah process in 1970s, Egypt has continued
to be characterized by significant microeconomic distortions, highlighted
by the presence of major divergences between private and social rates of
return in Egyptian industry (Barkey 1992; Harik 1997; Richards 1991;
Weiss and Wurzel 1998). This observation clearly suggests that the key
structures of the Nasserite order have largely remained intact in the context of the 1980s and the 1990s. In retrospect, the Egyptian case clearly
portrays the limitations of a "rentier state." Egypt has clearly benefited
from oil, both directly (although its reserves of oil were never on the
scale of the key Middle Eastern oil-exporting states) as well as indirectly
through the workers' remittances from the Gulf and Iraq. However, the
windfall gains generated through oil and other sources of income (notably
official development assistance as well as revenues from tourism or the
Suez Canal – revenues not directly related to the country's industrial or
productive capacity) also had some negative ramifications from a longer-
term perspective. These various types of "rents" enabled Egypt to experience growth without undertaking the necessary reforms or adjustment, which would have rendered the rapid growth of the 1970s a sustainable process.

The Gulf War, however, has proved to be a turning point in the
evolution of the Egyptian economy. Egypt has experienced a process of
stabilization and reform from 1991 onwards. Although the process has
been quite gradual, significant progress appears to have been achieved in
terms of macroeconomic stabilization, involving a radical reduction in the
size of the fiscal deficit and the rate of inflation. The positive role of the
United States and massive debt forgiveness following the Gulf War have
also produced an environment conducive to the implementation of the
structural-adjustment programme. Nevertheless, in spite of the success on
the stabilization front, the Egyptian reform process has been confronted
by major difficulties. First, very little success could be registered in terms
of privatizing the giant public-enterprise sector. Secondly, stabilization at

the macro level has failed to generate the type of boom in private investment in tradeables and economic growth that was clearly needed to absorb the rapidly growing numbers of young people entering the workforce. The supply response to stabilization has been this lacklustre because of inherent deficiencies in domestic entrepreneurship and savings. Furthermore, Egypt, like Turkey, has failed to attract long-term FDI on a substantial scale. Although foreign capital has been flowing into Egypt in recent years, the flows have been much more in the form of short-term, portfolio capital, the contribution of which to long-term development, in any case, is open to serious criticism.

## Morocco: Coping with cyclical growth and structural adjustment

Morocco is rather similar to Egypt, in the sense that the process of consolidating state power and independent industrialization effectively started roughly at the same date, namely 1951. Subsequently, Morocco has also progressed through the familiar phases of ISI, challenges to ISI, and crisis, followed by reform and structural adjustment. The political system of Morocco lies somewhere in between the authoritarian model of Egypt and the restricted or formally democratic model of Turkey. In fact, the Moroccan system has constituted a unique and rather strange blend of authoritarianism and pluralism (Hammoudi 1997; Layachi 1998; Van de Walle 1996; Zartman and Habeeb 1993) Indeed, Morocco has managed to combine elements of pluralism and restricted party competition under the centralizing control of the monarchy (Dillman 2000). The degree of pluralism should not be over-exaggerated, however, in the sense that, although the vote may be free for those parties admitted into the political arena, loyalty will be the price of opposition in a highly restricted political system.

Morocco has managed to attain modest rates of economic growth in the context of a prolonged import-substitution strategy based, as in the Egyptian case, on the development of a large public-enterprise sector. In spite of the fact that ISI started to reach its limits by the 1970s, the commodity price boom enabled Morocco to sustain economic growth by capitalizing on its major export commodity, phosphate. Morocco has also been able to sustain reasonably rapid growth through heavy recourse to international borrowing and was able to benefit, indirectly, from the boom in the oil markets. Hence, the typical "Dutch disease" problem has affected the Moroccan economy: easy access to foreign exchange in the presence of plentiful external reserves, although on a temporary basis, has stimulated consumption and imports and has helped, in the process, to postpone the much-needed adjustment in terms of the diversification of industrial structure and exports.

Morocco, however, like all countries of Greater Maghrib, started to experience a series of major economic and political crises during the course of the 1980s. The 1980s proved to be a decade marked by chronic governmental financial crises, severe shortfalls of food security, and violent civilian unrest. The Moroccan state increasingly had to perform a balancing act between economic accountability to foreign creditors and political accountability to domestic populations. The Moroccan state has faced a dilemma of the following kind: in the presence of sustained social pressures, economic growth remained crucial to the regime's survival; growth, in turn, required greater integration with transnational capitalism, with higher levels of external support necessitating radical economic reforms and a dismantling of the parastatal enterprises that had dominated the economy for years, as had been the case for other Maghrib countries such as Algeria, Tunisia, and Libya. In fact, violent opposition to the regime has occurred in 1981, 1984, 1990, and 1991. Clearly, the Moroccan state has faced certain crises of political legitimacy, although arguably the monarchy continues to enjoy considerable political support.

From the mid-1980s onwards, however, Morocco appears to have made significant progress in terms of undertaking stabilization and structural adjustment. Since 1993, Morocco has been considered by the World Bank as a highly successful case of economic reform (Karshenas 1996; Richards and Waterbury 1996; World Bank 1996) Adjustment and reform in Morocco has been accompanied by export expansion. Falling rates of economic growth in the 1990s reflected the impact of drought and not the failure of reforms themselves. Moreover, the privatization of the large public-enterprise sector has been steady and reasonably successful compared with that of Egypt (Khosrowshahi 1997). Further progress has been restricted, in a manner again rather similar to the pattern observed in the Egyptian case, owing to the fact that the highly centralized and authoritarian Moroccan state has not been willing to relinquish fully its patrimonial redistributive mechanisms. The corollary of this argument is that political liberalization is needed to overcome the monarch's patrimonial domination of the economy if further progress is to be accomplished with respect to the divestiture of the large public-enterprise sector. Finally, Morocco, rather like Turkey and perhaps more so than Egypt, has been attempting to develop close links with the EU in the form of a free trade agreement (as opposed to a Customs Union agreement in the case of Turkey) as part of the Barcelona Process in the context of the 1990s. The link with the EU has been conceived as critical for the expansion of Moroccan exports as well as a source of external anchor or discipline over the ongoing domestic reform process. The free trade agreement has so far failed to generate one major benefit, namely large inflows of long-term capital (Dervis and Shafik 1998; White 1996; Zartman 1993).

## A comparative perspective on the three large non-oil economies of the Middle East and North Africa: Similarities and contrasts

At a very broad level of analysis, the developmental trajectories of the Middle Eastern NICs display features that are rather typical of the majority of the developing world, with the notable exception of the East Asian NICs. The Middle Eastern NICs have also experienced the familiar sequence of prolonged import-substitution under pervasive state intervention and protectionism, the crisis of ISI, and subsequently attempts at reform in a neo-liberal direction with a rather mixed set of consequences. The variation in economic performance between the Middle Eastern NICs themselves may be explained, to a significant extent, by differences with respect to consolidation of state power and the process of independent industrialization. Turkey has been more fortunate than the other Middle Eastern NICs in the sense that the processes of consolidating state power and independent industrialization have been initiated in the early 1920s; consequently, Turkey has been able to experience a significant breakthrough in industrial expansion during the interwar period. This pattern of independent development, in which the state has performed a major entrepreneurial and supporting role, has facilitated the emergence of a highly dynamic, private, entrepreneurial élite. These rising entrepreneurs have subsequently challenged the monopoly of political power in the hands of the military–bureaucratic élite and have played an instrumental role in the country's transition to formal democracy in the post-war period. Turkey's democratic regime, in turn, provided a much more conducive environment for the private sector to flourish in terms of the application of the rule of law and protection of private property.

The consolidation of state power and independent industrialization could take place in Egypt only following the anti-imperial revolution of the early 1950s. Egypt and, to a lesser extent, Morocco have pushed the "étatist model" to its limits and have pursued ISI strategies in the context of authoritarian political regimes. The "authoritarian-populist" label particularly fits the Egyptian case, where the depth of industrialization has been lower than in the Turkish case, the latter being much closer to Latin American standards. The pattern of inefficient industrialization in Egypt in the context of an unusually large public-enterprise sector, however, has produced a relatively equitable type of economic development in contrast to Turkey or the principal Latin American NICs, which have been characterized by significant degrees of relative-income inequality.

All three Middle Eastern NICs have undergone significant reform experiences during the 1980s and the 1990s. Whereas substantial progress may be discerned in all three cases (and notably in the cases of Turkey and Morocco) in terms of liberalizing and integrating their economies to the external world, none of the three has been able to generate the consistently high rates of economic growth that are needed to absorb the disproportionate number of young people entering the labour market and, hence, to create a durable basis for social and political stability. Furthermore, all these countries, in spite of the differing degrees of their economic achievement, have encountered great difficulty in reforming their large public-enterprise sectors. Indeed, privatization as a process has proceeded much more slowly in the context of the Middle Eastern NICs than in Latin America (with the notable exception of Brazil) and much of Eastern Europe.

In retrospect, the three Middle Eastern NICs under investigation have been negatively affected by certain common regional characteristics. Certainly, the hostile and conflictive environment of the Middle East, as well as the inherent insecurity of the individual nation-states in the context of a "bad neighbourhood," have meant a significant diversion of resources from civilian to military expenditure. It is undoubtedly the case that peace and stability in the region would have substantial pay-offs in terms of both more rapid economic development and political liberalization. Stated somewhat differently, the "peace dividend" is likely to be high for the Middle Eastern NICs. The insecure environment of the Middle East has provided few incentives for transnational corporations to invest in the region. This, in turn, has had negative repercussions with regard to the region's growth prospects and its degree of integration into the international economy.

Even the most advanced NICs of the region, where the industrialization process is more deeply entrenched than anywhere else, have failed to attract long-term foreign capital on a considerable scale. The attempts by countries such as Turkey, Egypt, and Morocco to forge closer links with the EU, through a customs union agreement in the former case and a free trade agreement in the latter context, have hitherto failed to generate the expected benefits in terms of large inflows of FDI. In any case, one ought to take into consideration that all these agreements, although significant for the countries concerned, are comparatively loose forms of integration falling considerably short of full membership of the EU. The Middle Eastern NICs have been attracting volatile short-term capital but not FDI on a significant scale. Moreover, attempts at regional integration in the Middle East have remained far weaker than those in other regions (such as Latin America and South-East Asia) although, admittedly, regional integration in East Asia is also not very well developed. The very absence of regional integration, in turn, might also have exercised a negative effect in terms of attracting FDI and also accelerating the pace of economic growth in the group of countries concerned through expansion of intraregional trade.

Islamist social or political movements also constitute a common tendency and a significant challenge to the existing regimes in the Middle Eastern NICs, albeit with varying degrees of intensity. Political Islam appears to have the strongest roots in Egypt, where the process of secularization under Nasser has been implemented over a shorter period than in Kemalist Turkey and potentially represents the most serious threat in the Egyptian case. Turkey constitutes an intermediate category, where political Islam has some influence but not on the scale of Egypt; even in the Turkish case, however, the rise of political Islam has caused considerable political turmoil, resulting in a severe reaction from the secular state during the course of the 1990s. Morocco lies at the other extreme, where political Islam or Islamism is of marginal significance. Political Islam – which is a key distinguishing feature of the Middle East as a whole and which also has manifested itself in varying degrees in the Middle Eastern NICs – may be interpreted, at a very general level, as a reaction by those groups in society who are excluded from political power and decision-making as well as by those groups who are largely marginalized and excluded from the benefits of economic development and greater integration into the international economy.[8] In retrospect, political Islam is a complex and double-faced phenomenon: at a certain level of analysis it tends to be an obvious source of instability and tension, thereby limiting the progress of democratization and political deepening in Middle Eastern societies; from a somewhat different perspective, however, Islamist political movements or networks have tended to have a stabilizing role by performing a redistributive function in an environment where the individual states have been lacking in the provision of social welfare.

A major challenge facing the Middle Eastern NICs, again with varying degrees of intensity, is to accomplish a transition from "clientelistic capitalism" to "competitive capitalism."[9] The persistence of authoritarian and patrimonial political structures in much of the Middle East, however, creates barriers to progress and reform in this respect. A vicious circle is created, in the sense that authoritarian political structures are blocking reform and integration to the external world, with the state élite groups unwilling to relinquish control over large patronage resources. The slow pace of reform and privatization, in turn, limits the development of a mature private sector, largely independent from state influence, which would then be in a position to push faster in the direction of further political liberalization.

In retrospect, the state has had a critical role in the development process of the Middle East. It is worth highlighting the paradox, however, that the "Middle Eastern state" (even the states of the more advanced Middle Eastern NICs) is a "soft state" compared with the prototype "East Asian developmental state" at the peak of its influence or power. Compared with the East Asian developmental states, historically, even the most advanced Middle Eastern states appear to be fragmented, having failed to display similar "infrastructural power" to support as well as to discipline private capital. The size of the Middle Eastern state has been larger; however, its ability to direct an effective outward-oriented industrialization has been consistently weaker than the prototype East Asian developmental state in countries such as South Korea and Taiwan at the peak of its influence.[10]

## Conclusions

In comparative terms, the Middle East is the most heterogeneous and among the least integrated regions of the developing world. Its history has been shaped by oil, which has affected the development prospects of both the productive and the non-productive countries of the region. Given the significance of oil, the region has long been a focal point of interest for the leading nations of the world; yet, rather paradoxically, the Middle East has been a comparatively marginal region in the globalization process. Individual states of the Middle East feel less secure, owing to the presence of a number of external and internal threats in this part of the world. This explains the tendency of these nations to direct a greater share of resources towards military expenditure, resulting in underspending in such key areas as physical infrastructure, research and development, health, and human capital formation. With the exception of Turkey, the impulse towards democratization or political liberalization has been less pronounced than that in Latin America, East Asia, and Eastern Europe. It is also striking that the region appears to be highly marginalized from one of the major positive aspects of the globalization, namely significant inflows of long-term capital.

The large non-oil Middle Eastern NICs constitute an interesting subcategory of Middle Eastern states. In spite of acute resource constraints compared with other parts of the Middle East, these countries have managed to accomplish a significant degree of industrialization. The process of industrialization and integration into the world economy as exporters of manufactured goods has proceeded further in Turkey than in the other Middle Eastern NICs (excluding the notably exceptional case of Israel). Turkey's relative superiority may be attributable to the fact that the process of state building and independent industrialization had started in this country at a considerably earlier stage than in Egypt and Morocco; furthermore, Turkey has been able to develop stronger economic links with the EU since the 1960s.

The developmental trajectories of the Middle Eastern NICs, as a broad category, are quite similar to patterns observed in other regions – notably in Latin America. Prolonged import-substitution, followed by fiscal and balance-of-payments crises and, subsequently, protracted attempts at liberalization and reform, characterize the experiences of the Middle Eastern NICs (which, in substance, do not differ fundamentally from the experiences of the Latin American countries). However, whereas the sequence of development may be similar, the performance of the Middle Eastern NICs, on the whole, is less impressive than that of the Latin American NICs. Only Turkey, in recent years, has been approaching the per capita income levels of some of the key Latin American economies. In the cases of Egypt and Morocco, the difference may be explained, in part, by the fact that the processes of independent state formation and industrialization are comparatively recent phenomena. Ultimately, it is the domestic capacities of individual countries that emerge as key preconditions for development. The relative deficiency in the performance of the Middle Eastern NICs, compared with that of their East Asian counterparts, for example, may be explained by their limited capacities in terms of savings, entrepreneurship, and technology. In general, however, the Middle Eastern NICs have also been unfavourably affected by the region's salient characteristics. Historically, pervasive security threats, a weak regional integration process, and the relative exclusion in terms of global capital flows appear to have exercised a negative impact on even the most advanced non-oil economies of the region.

Looking towards the twenty-first century, none of the three Middle Eastern NICs under consideration are likely to accomplish a transition to the "high growth – just growth" trajectory in the foreseeable future. Although the three countries concerned are at quite different stages of industrialization, the pattern of cyclical and unjust growth – although to varying degrees – is unlikely to fade away over a short space of time. This rather unstable trajectory of unjust growth is, in turn, likely to act as a serious constraint on the full consolidation of liberal democracy in Turkey, as well as on further political opening in Egypt and Morocco.

## Notes

1. Arguably the list of Middle Eastern NICs could be extended to include Lebanon, Tunisia and Israel. However, these are relatively small states. Given their small popu-

lation size, industrialization based on the domestic market has been a much less significant element in their development experiences.

2. An additional test of qualifying as an NIC might be the ratio of technology-intensive exports as a proportion of total manufactured exports. On the basis of this criterion, even Turkey (with a share of 8 per cent) tends to lag behind countries such as Korea, Malaysia, and Mexico by a significant margin. Source: World Bank, World Development Indicators 1998, from *World Bank Development Reports 1998* and *1999* (World Bank, various years).

3. On the Middle East as a region of instability and conflict, see Guazzone (1997) and Abi-Aad and Grenon (1997). For a persuasive argument concerning the importance of insecure external environments, see Kenny (1999).

4. The share of military expenditures in GNP in the Middle East and North Africa for the period 1985–1995 has been estimated as 13.52 per cent. This is far higher than the averages recorded for other regions: the military expenditures in GNP for Turkey, Egypt, and Morocco for the identical period have been estimated as 3.79, 6.78, and 5.14 per cent, respectively (source: US Arms Control and Disarmament Agency: http://dosfan.lib.uic.edu/acda). One also ought to emphasize, however, that the Maghrib is a major exception to the broad claim that military expenditures tend to be much higher in the MENA region than in other regions of the world. Morocco itself is an exceptional case; high military expenditure in Morocco, in any case, does not reflect insecurity due to pervasive external threats. One should also emphasize, however, that isolation and insecurity are not unique to the Middle East: the fact that South Korea and Taiwan have managed to develop despite isolation and insecurity suggests that this variable is relevant only in combination with other factors accounting for variations in development performance across regions.

5. A brief glance at the distribution of FDI by regions highlights the marginal position occupied by the MENA region. In 1998, MENA attracted a total of 8,863 billion dollars of FDI: the corresponding figures for Latin America and the Caribbean; South, East, and South-East Asia; and Central and Eastern Europe emerged as $71,652, $77,277, and $17,513 billion, respectively (source: United Nations, World Investment Report 1999).

6. In 1997, exports of goods and services and foreign trade in total as a proportion of GDP in the Middle East, as a whole, constituted 33 and 65 per cent, respectively, figures broadly similar to those for Asia and the Pacific. In contrast, the corresponding ratios for Latin America and the Caribbean were only of the order of 15 and 31 per cent, respectively (source: World Bank, *World Development Indicators*, 1999). Comparative data on technology-intensive exports as a share of total manufactured exports are available in the *World Development Report 1999/2000* (World Bank 2000).

7. For a comprehensive overview concerning the nature of Egypt's post-war development experience see Waterbury (1993). For a comparative perspective on the development experiences of Egypt and Turkey see Hansen (1991). Hansen, however, seems to exaggerate the similarities and underestimates the starting points or the initial conditions in the two cases.

8. On the political economy of the Islamic resurgence in Turkey as a reaction or response to neo-liberal globalization, see Öniş (1997). (For a comprehensive discussion of the nature of political Islam in Egypt, see Sullivan and Abed-Kotob 1999 and Kienle 1998). Political Islam in Turkey appears to be moving in a more moderate direction during the most recent era. (For documentation and analysis of this phenomenon, see Öniş 2001).

9. The patrimonial nature of the state in the Middle East and the continuing significance of rent distribution in the presence of strong clientelistic ties have been frequently highlighted in the literature. Weaknesses pertaining to the application of the rule of law and low degrees of accountability by even the most advanced states such as Turkey, operating in a formally democratic environment, have also been investigated in some detail.

For a good discussion of these issues, see Waterbury (1998). For a penetrating discussion of the nature of private-sector development in Turkey and the problems concentrated in moving from "clientelistic" to "competitive" capitalism, see Atiyas and Ersel (1999).

10. For a comparison between the Middle Eastern states and the stylized model of the East Asian developmental state, see Pfeifer et al. (1999). Needless to say, for a variety of domestic and external reasons, the East Asian states have been facing serious challenges in recent years, resulting in the demise of the developmental state in its traditional form.

## REFERENCES

Abi-Aad, Naji and Michael Grenon. 1997. *Instability and Conflict in the Middle East: People, Petroleum, and Security Threats.* London: Macmillan Press.

Amin, Galal A. 1995. *Egypt's Economic Predicament.* Leiden: E.J. Brill.

Aricanli, Tosun and Dani Rodrik, eds. 1990. *The Political Economy of Turkey: Debt, Adjustment and Sustainability.* London: Macmillan.

Atiyas, Izak and Hasan Ersel. 1999. "Some Observations on the Role of the Private Sector in Turkey." Mimeographed, Department of Economics, Istanbul: Sabanci University and Yapi Kredi Bank.

Ayubi, Nazih H. 1995. *Overstating the Arab State: Politics and Society in the Middle East.* New York and London: I.B. Tauris Publishers.

Barkey, Henri. 1990. *The State and Industrialization Crisis in Turkey.* Boulder: Westview Press.

Barkey, Henri. 1992. *The Politics of Economic Reform in the Middle East.* New York: St Martin's Press.

Beblawi, Hazem. 1990. "The Rentier State in the Arab World." In *The Arab State,* Guicamo Luciani, ed. Berkeley: University of California Press, pp. 85–98.

Bromley, Simon. 1994. *Rethinking Middle East Politics.* Cambridge: Polity.

Bugra, Ayse. 1994. *State and Business in Modern Turkey: A Comparative Study.* Albany: SUNY Press.

Bush, Ray. 1999. *Economic Crisis and the Politics of Reform in Egypt.* Boulder: Westview Press.

Chaudry, Kiren. 1997. *The Price of Wealth.* Ithaca: Cornell University Press.

CIA. 1999. *The World Fact Book 1999 – Taiwan.* Washington DC: Central Intelligence, Agency. Also available at www.cia.gov

Dervis, Kemal and Nemat Shafik. 1998. "The Middle East and North Africa: A Tale of Two Futures." *Middle East Journal* 52(4): 505–516.

Dillman, Bradfort. 2000. "Parliamentary Elections and the Prospects for Political Pluralism in North Africa." *Government and Opposition* 35(2): 216–236.

Guazzone, Laura, ed. 1997. *The Middle East in Global Change.* London: Macmillan.

Hammoudi, Abdullah. 1997. *Master and Disciple: The Cultural Foundations of Moroccan Authoritarianism.* Chicago: University of Chicago Press.

Hansen, Bent. 1991. *The Political Economy of Poverty, Equity, and Growth: Egypt and Turkey.* Oxford: Oxford University Press.

Harik, Iliya. 1997. *Economic Policy Reform in Egypt*. Gainsville: University of Florida Press.

Henry, Clement M. 1996. *The Mediterranean Debt Crescent: Money and Power in Algeria, Egypt, Morocco, Tunisia, and Turkey*. Gainsville: University Press of Florida.

Heper, Metin, ed. 1991. *Strong State and Economic Interest Groups: The Post-1980 Turkish Experience*. Berlin: Walter de Gruyter.

Karshenas, Massoud. 1994. "Structural Adjustment and Employment in the Middle East and North Africa." SOAS Working Paper Series, No. 50.

Karshenas, Massoud and Valentine M. Moghadam. 1997. "Female Employment. Competitiveness and Structural Adjustment in the Middle East and North Africa." Paper presented at the Middle East Economic Association Meeting, 4–6 January 1997, New Orleans, USA.

Kasnakoglu, Zehra. 1997. "Income Distribution in Turkey: Who Gets What?" *Private View* 1/2(4/5): 56–62, Autumn.

Kenny, Charles. 1999. "Why Aren't Countries Rich? Weak States and Bad Neighborhoods." *Journal of Development Studies* 35(5): 26–47.

Keyder, Caglar. 1987. *State and Class in Turkey*. London: Verso Press.

Khosrowshahi, Cameron. 1997. "Privatization in Morocco: The Politics of Development." *Middle East Journal* 51(2): 242–255.

Kienle, Eberhard. 1998. "More Than a Response to Islamism: The Political Deliberalization of Egypt in the 1990's." *Middle East Journal* 52(2): 219–235.

Layachi, Azzedine. 1998. *State, Society and Democracy in Morocco: The Limits of Associative Life*. Georgetown: Georgetown University Press.

Maxfield, Sylvia and James H. Nolt. 1990. "Protectionism and Internationalization of Capital: U.S. Sponsorship of Import Substitution Industrialization in the Philippines, Turkey, and Argentina." *International Studies Quarterly* 34: 49–81.

OECD. 1999. *OECD Economic Surveys 1999: Turkey*. Paris: Organization for Economic Co-operation and Development.

Öniş, Ziya. 1997. "The Political Economy of the Islamic Resurgence in Turkey: The Rise of the Welfare Party in Perspective." *Third World Quarterly* 18(4): 743–766.

Öniş, Ziya. 1998. *State and Market: The Political Economy of Turkey in Comparative Perspective*. Istanbul: Bogazici University Press.

Öniş, Ziya. 2000. "The Turkish Economy at the Turn of a New Century: Critical and Comparative Perspectives." In *Turkish Transformation and American Policy*, M. Abramowitz, ed. Washington DC: The Century Foundation, pp. 95–115.

Öniş, Ziya. 2001. "Political Islam at the Crossroads: From Hegemony to Coexistence." *Contemporary Politics* 7(4): 281–298.

Owen, Roger and Sevket Pamuk. 1998. *A History of the Middle East Economies in the Twentieth Century*. London: I.B. Tauris.

Pfeifer, Karen, Marsha Pripstein-Posusney and Djavad Salehi-Isfehani, eds, with contributions from Steve Niva. 1999. "Reform or Reaction? Dilemmas of Economic Development in the Middle East." Special Issue, *Middle East Report*, Spring 1999.

Richards, Alan. 1991. "The Political Economy of Dilatory Reform: Egypt in the 1980's." *World Development* 19(12): 1721–1730.

Richards, Alan and John Waterbury. 1996. *A Political Economy of the Middle East*, 2nd edn. Boulder: Westview Press.

Salame, Ghassan, ed. 1994. *Democracy without Democrats? The Renewal of Politics in the Muslim World*. London: I.B. Tauris.

Sarel, Michael. 1997. "How Macroeconomic Factors Affect Income Distribution: The Cross Country Evidence." IMF Working Paper.

Sullivan, Denis J. and Sana Abed-Kotob. 1999. *Islam in the Contemporary Egypt: Civil Society vs. the State*. Boulder: Lynne Rienner.

United Nations. 1998. *Human Development Report 1998*. New York: Oxford University Press for the UNDP.

United Nations. 1999. *World Investment Report, 1999. Foreign Direct Investment and the Challenge of Development*. New York: United Nations.

US Census Bureau, International database ⟨http://www.census.gov/ipc/www/idbnew.html⟩.

van de Walle, Dirk, ed. 1996. *North Africa: Development and Reform in a Changing Global Economy*. London: Macmillan.

Wahba, Mourad M. 1994. *The Role of the State in the Egyptian Economy: 1945–1981*. Reading: Garnett Publishers.

Waterbury, John. 1993. *The Egypt of Nassar and Sadat: The Political Economy of the Two Regimes*. Princeton: Princeton University Press.

Waterbury, John. 1998. "The State and Economic Transition in the Middle East and North Africa." In *Prospects for Middle Eastern and North African Economies: From Boom to Bust and Back?*, ed. Nemat Shafik. London: Macmillan Press.

Weiss, Dieter and Ulrich Wurzel. 1998. *The Economics and Politics of Transition to an Open Market Economy: Egypt*. Paris: OECD.

White, Gregory W. 1996. "The Mexico of Europe? Morocco's Partnership with the European Union." In *North Africa: Development and Reform in a Changing Global Economy*, ed. Dirk Van de walle. London: Macmillan Press.

Wilson, Rodney. 1995. *Economic Development in the Middle East*. London: Routledge Press.

World Bank. 1996. *Growing Faster, Finding Jobs: Choices for Morocco*. Washington DC: World Bank.

World Bank. Various years. *World Development Report, 1994*, and *1999/2000*. New York: Oxford University Press for World Bank.

Zartman, William I., ed. 1993. *Europe and Africa: The New Phase*. Boulder: Lynne Rienner.

Zartman, William and William Mark Habeeb, eds. 1993. *Polity and Society in Contemporary North Africa*. Boulder: Westview Press.

# 7

# Democracy, growth, and poverty in India

*Atul Kohli and Rani D. Mullen*

India's record in the pursuit of just growth is mixed: democracy not only has survived but also has spread wide and deep; economic growth has varied from sluggish to modest; and although the gap between the rich and the poor is not as wide as, say, that in Latin America, nevertheless, at a per capita income below $400, India is home to the world's largest number of poor people. In this chapter we provide an overview of India's political economy, focusing particularly on three issues. First, we discuss India's democracy, commenting not only on its evolution but also on how efforts to stabilize it repeatedly endow the Indian state with a "softness" that undermines its capacity to promote socio-economic development. We then discuss India's growth experience, stressing its political determinants. Finally, we focus on the dark side of India's developmental experiment – its numerous poor. Here we underline the impact both of low economic growth and of failed efforts at deliberate poverty alleviation.

As in other chapters in this volume, the scholarly scope of this chapter is rather broad. This breadth necessitates a sweeping quality to the discussion that leads to a neglect of important controversies relevant for specialists. Although footnotes will alert the diligent reader to some related issues, it may also be helpful at the outset to note that India's political economy can be interpreted from two distinct standpoints, one of which is emphasized in this chapter. A more "neo-liberal" interpretation might suggest that India's massive poverty is mainly a result of its sluggish economic growth and that the latter, in turn, is a result of the relatively "closed" and "statist" model of development adopted by India's misguided nationalist and socialist leaders. According to this line of thinking, the last two "liberalizing" decades have been an improvement over the past, helping to explain both higher rates of economic growth and the lowering of the proportion of poor in India. Although there are valuable insights in such a perspective, this argument emerges from a world view that we do not share; it is also not wholly consistent with facts.

In this chapter we argue, instead, that the Achilles' heel of Indian political economy is not so much its statist model of development as the mismatch between that statist model and the limited capacity of the Indian state to guide social and economic change. Statist models have achieved important gains in other parts of the world, but they were generally directed by more efficacious states of either the left or the right. Trying to reconcile left and right political preferences, and that with a "soft" state, Indians failed both at radical redistribution and at ruthless capitalism-led economic growth. The "socialist" commitment of Indian leaders, for example, was rather shallow: although the rhetoric may have helped build short-term political capital, pro-poor policies were seldom pursued vigorously in India. Socialist commitments, however, not only were pursued via an inefficient public sector but also alienated private investors, creating difficult state–business relations and hurting economic growth. What has changed in India over the last two decades is not so much that it has become more "liberal," but that Indian politics has drifted right-ward, creating more harmonious state–business relations with a positive impact on growth. The problem of massive poverty, however, continues. Not only is growth not rapid enough to absorb the old and new poverty, but it is not likely that the new, right-leaning, religious and nationalist rulers are willing to incorporate India's poor or are capable of doing so. The path to just growth in India thus remains fraught with difficulties.

## State and democracy

India's leaders have nearly always put political goals ahead of economic ones; thus, India's economic policies often reflect, not only an economic calculus but also such underlying political considerations as ruling ideologies, interests of the economic élite, concerns of political stability, and, of course, the needs of the leaders to gain and maintain democratic power. Any full discussion of state–market interactions in India thus must begin by focusing on the changing nature of the Indian state and democracy itself, and then move to an analysis of the impact of chosen policies. Although this is a complex tableau, for the purposes of this volume one can divide modern India's political evolution into three phases: the Nehru era (approximately 1950–1964); the era of Indira Gandhi (approximately 1965 to the early 1980s); and the most recent two decades, during which institutional fragmentation and the rapid turnover of ruling élite groups have reinforced each other, but during which India's politics has shifted right-ward, and economic policies have aimed to "liberalize" the old statist model of development.

## The Nehru era

If the 1940s in India are best thought of as the decade in which India made the transit from colonialism to a sovereign, democratic republic, the Nehru era that followed is usefully viewed as the crucible of modern India: it is during this era that a stable democracy took root, and a statist model of economic development became dominant. Both of these important developments require comment, as does the critical fact of an early mismatch between political developments, on the one hand, and the state's economic ambitions on the other.

Indians take their democracy almost for granted, as if it was the most obvious way of organizing the politics of a poor, multi-ethnic, continent-sized country. Viewed internationally, however, as well as against the most popular theories that treat democracy as a function of economic advancement, India's democracy is a puzzle (for further discussion see Kohli 2001). At minimum, its survival suggests that, under specific conditions, a country's political structures and processes enjoy some autonomy from the underlying society and economy. The roots of Indian democracy thus need to be understood from the standpoint of institutional continuities, including India's British political inheritance. Among the significant factors that British colonial rule contributed to India's democratic evolution were a relatively centralized and coherent state, manifest most clearly in a well-developed civil bureaucracy, limited but real experience of elections and parliamentary government, and traditions of – again limited, but real – independent media and freedom of such associations as labour unions.

Since inheritance is seldom destiny, as in many other post-colonial countries, Indians could have readily squandered these valuable political resources; however, they did not. Besides colonial inheritance, therefore, one must underline the constructive political role of India's nationalist movement/party, the Indian National Congress (or Congress, for short), and India's leaders in the evolution of India's democracy. While demanding freedom from British rule, the Congress not only brought together a variety of Indian élite groups but also established numerous links between the élite and the masses. This relatively cohesive, mass-nationalist movement, in turn, provided the framework within which India's democracy advanced. India's leaders adopted mass suffrage, committed themselves to a parliamentary democracy, allowed a variety of political voices and organizations to emerge, and conducted the internal affairs of the hegemonic nationalist party in a democratic and inclusive manner (Kothari 1970).

A proto-democratic colonial inheritance and a democratically inclined, cohesive, mass-nationalist movement thus provided institutional preconditions for the emergence of democracy in India. As this democracy consolidated during the Nehru era, however, it also developed characteristics that made it difficult for India's political leaders to pursue their social and economic goals. Brief comments on a series of political developments of this period will help to clarify this point (Frankel 1978). First, although the colonial bureaucracy that sovereign India's leaders inherited was a fine professional force, it was mainly a "law and order" bureaucracy, not well suited to implement the ambitious developmental goals of Indian leaders. A major rehaul of the bureaucracy was contemplated but never really pursued, mainly because the well-trained civil servants were indispensable for governing the new state. When faced with the cruel choice of state as an effective agent of political order or as a successful facilitator of economic development, India's leaders opted (probably wisely) for the former. A longer-term trend, however, was also born – namely, prioritizing political needs over economic ones and thus initiating what would eventually become a substantial gap between the state's capacities and its developmental ambitions.

A similar mismatch came to characterize the Congress party as it sought to be simultaneously a popular ruling party and an agent of egalitarian "socialist" development. The majority of Indians lived in the countryside and a majority of these were enmeshed within a variety of patron–client relationships. One ready way to build political support in such a social setting was to cultivate the patrons – generally the highest, land-owing élite castes – who, in turn, could sway the political behaviour of their dependent clients, generally poor peasants. This is precisely what the Congress party did, building long chains of patronage that originated at the centre and stretched out to the periphery (Weiner 1967, particularly chap. 22). Although ensuring a popular base – at least for a decade or two – this strategy also led to a "capture" of the ruling party by the society's powerful members, thus undermining its more egalitarian ambitions (such as land redistribution).

Another significant political development concerned the evolution of Indian federalism. Soon after the nationalist struggle was won and India had gained sovereignty, its numerous ethnic groups started to demand a greater share of power within the new state. These struggles came to a head in the late 1950s, when a reluctant Nehru agreed to a linguistic reorganization of Indian federalism. This decision – again, probably wise – helped to accommodate ethnic demands and created a more stable political unit. At the same time, however, the central state lost some of the power that it needed to pursue its developmental agenda. To the extent that the developmental ambitions of India's leaders found institutional expressions (such as the Planning Commission), these were nearly all at the centre. By contrast, lower-level governments were mainly "machines," with significant powers and resources. Although India's central state continued to be quite powerful in relation to its constituent federal units, a federal reorganization also diluted the state's overall capacity to pursue a coherent developmental agenda.

The ruling ideology of the Congress party provides a final example of the mismatch between capacity and ambitions. Congress committed itself to "nationalism" and "socialism." This was the "creed" of Nehru's India and it helped both Nehru and the Congress party to gain substantial popularity and legitimacy in India. At the same time, however, these ideological commitments made it difficult to pursue vigorous economic growth – a goal that Congress and state élite groups also espoused. In spite of the socialist rhetoric, India was mainly a private-enterprise economy: if vigorous economic growth was to come, it would have to come mainly by encouraging private entrepreneurs. Nationalism, however, discouraged foreign enterprise in India, and the socialist inclination created difficult relations with Indian entrepreneurs. The Indian version of statism was thus, again, at odds with its espoused goals.

Taken together, these political developments during the Nehru era suggest two conclusions. First, Nehru and his colleagues put high priority on consolidating Indian democracy: they thus maintained a strong political centre and incorporated the society's powerful groups, on the one hand, and conceded some power to the demanding regional élite groups and maintained the hope of poor masses by promising egalitarian development, on the other hand. These strategies reflected political priorities and went quite a distance in institutionalizing India's fragile democracy. At the same time, however (and this is the second conclusion), the resulting political developments "softened" the Indian state in the sense of undermining its capacity to pursue developmental goals vigorously. This point becomes clearer after discussion of the economic policies and the record of Nehru's India. To anticipate the discussion, however, maintaining a "law and order" bureaucracy hurt the state's capacity to undertake economic tasks directly, a commitment to nationalism and socialism made it difficult to mobilize private capital's developmental resources, and the conservatizing developments within the Congress party sapped the political will to pursue egalitarian goals.

The economic model adopted during the Nehru era was, of course, the well-known model of state-led, import-substitution industrialization (ISI). Once adopted, this model became deeply enduring in India. Although significant efforts have been made in the recent years to move away from this model, India's economic policies exhibit a fair amount of continuity. Some of the policy details and their economic impact are discussed further below. For now, the main issue for discussion is the political nature of India's early economic choices (Nayar 1989). Economic policies in India, as elsewhere, were often legitimated in terms of economic and technical issues. The choices, however, were also quite consistent with dominant political values and interests.

Nehru's political preferences became India's dominant ideas via the Congress party, and stressed the following: (1) the importance of maintaining national sovereignty; (2) a belief in the state's superior capacity to steer progressive capitalist development; (3) the need to incorporate India's poor in the endowment of the fruits of development. Each of these requires a comment.

First, the nationalist commitments of India's leaders translated into both a suspicion of an open economy and a preference for heavy industry. In spite of low domestic savings, foreign investors were discouraged, mainly because they might have threatened hard-won national sovereignty. Over time, a variety of interests benefited from these ideological choices and helped to sustain them. A suspicion of an open trading regime is more difficult to understand in terms of underlying nationalism. Protectionism was, in any case, supported by prevailing economic ideas of "export pessimism" and "infant industry" arguments. However, in the Indian case, there was also something deeply experiential and political about these choices. Openness during the colonial era had been interpreted by nationalists not only as killing nascent industries but also as inhibiting the emergence of indigenous industrial capitalism. Indian businessmen and industrialists also stood to benefit from a relatively closed economy in which competition would be limited. Protectionism was thus seen as serving the interests of nation building, as was the emphasis on heavy industry. How else could a continent-sized country, with an ancient civilization, re-emerge as a powerhouse not easily manipulated by external powers?

The belief in the state's efficacy to guide social and economic change was "in the air" across much of the world in the middle of the twentieth century. In India, it was reinforced both by an admiration of the Soviet Union's developmental "successes" and by an affinity of Indian leaders

to the British, Labour Party type of socialism. These ideological procliv-
ities were also consistent with the concrete interests of India's political
class; the political élite at the helm could thus channel some of the fruits
of development to themselves and their offspring. The statist model
translated into both a significant, direct economic role for the state – as,
for example, in the widespread use of public enterprises – and into a
more indirect role in guiding activities of private capital via the "licence-
permit raj (or regime)." What is surprising in retrospect is not so much
India's affinity for statism but how little open discussion took place concerning what type of state could successfully undertake such ambitious
economic tasks. Whereas "market imperfections" were discussed ad
nauseam, there was no parallel discussion of "state imperfections" from
the standpoint of developmental capacity. One wonders if such a discussion was avoided because it would only have focused attention on the
shortcomings of the rulers.

Finally, a vague commitment to the poor and the downtrodden permeated much of India's nationalist political discourse. Gandhi and
Nehru, in their own ways, shared this commitment. It found expression in
socialist rhetoric, and in some such policy areas as land redistribution and
laws governing employment of urban labour. Unlike the commitment to
nationalism and statism, however, the commitment to the poor was relatively shallow: India's upper-caste rulers were no revolutionaries; they
meant well but Barrington Moore's apt description of Nehru as "the
gentle betrayer of masses" (Moore 1966) probably applies as well to a
fairly broad spectrum of India's political class, although not all of them
were always as "gentle." How else could one explain the limited political
energy devoted to land reforms or, for that matter, to a severe neglect of
such policies as the promotion of widespread access to primary education
(Weiner 1991).

## The Indira Gandhi era

If democracy and a nationalist–statist model of economic development
took root in India during the Nehru era, the Indira Gandhi era that followed is best viewed as one in which India's democracy became more
populist and deinstitutionalized, economic rhetoric moved further to the
left, and the gap between the state's developmental capacities and economic goals widened even further.

Nehru's death in 1964 marked the slow but steady departure of the
first-generation nationalist leaders from the political scene. As nationalist
legitimacy declined, numerous movements and parties opposing the hegemony of Congress emerged. The old ruling formula of Congress (a
mantle of inclusive nationalism and long chains of patronage, fed by

statism) was increasingly incapable of generating electoral majorities: Congress had to either come up with a new winning formula or give way to other parties. It was under such growing political vulnerabilities that Indira Gandhi stepped in and revived the flagging fortunes of Congress. Her winning strategy, however, involved populism and top-down deinstitutionalization of the polity, with long-run developmental consequences.

Under Nehru, India had undergone some industrialization and experienced modest economic growth. However, the poor in India had not benefited very much. The spread of commerce and democracy, moreover, had eroded patron–client ties, making the poor available for new forms of political mobilization. As a shrewd politician, Indira Gandhi understood these changes and capitalized on them. She made "poverty alleviation" her central political slogan, thus shifting India's political discourse further to the left. The short-term political dividends were handsome: she became a darling of India's numerous downtrodden and was rapidly catapulted to the top of the political pyramid. Unlike her father, Nehru, however, Indira Gandhi's popularity was not institutionalized: whereas Nehru presided over a nationalist party, Indira Gandhi found herself opposed by the old, entrenched Congress élite. Her solution was to label the old élite "enemies of the poor," to use the power of her popularity to undermine their power, and instead to appoint loyal minions into responsible positions. India's political system thus increasingly became personalistic, undermining not only well-established patterns of authority within the Congress Party but also derailing the broader process of institutional development in India's democracy (Kohli 1988, 1991).

In India, as elsewhere, personalization of power had an inexorable deinstitutionalizing logic. When confronted with power challenges in an increasingly contentious polity, Indira Gandhi not only eliminated the challengers but also weakened the institutions that enabled such challenges to emerge: she thus tampered with appointments in the civil service and the courts, dismissed "troublesome" chief ministers, and demanded complete loyalty from supporters. As a result, the professionalization of the bureaucracy was corroded, as were the independence of the legal system, the functioning of the national parliament, and the autonomy of the regional units within the national federation.

Indira Gandhi's political energies were focused less on matters economic and more on maintaining power amidst numerous challenges; the statist model of economic development adopted under Nehru thus essentially continued, without any deep changes. Within the framework of continuity, economic-policy changes during this era were mainly of two types – these were (a) a major shift in agricultural policy that was a result of domestic crisis and external pressure and that had a benign long-term impact on food production and (b) a variety of "left-leaning" changes that reflected Indira Gandhi's political calculations, and that helped neither economic growth nor redistribution. Discussion of the political underpinnings of the economic-policy choices follows immediately, and the economic impact of these policies is discussed in the subsequent sections.

What should also be noted as an aside here is that this was an era of missed economic opportunities in India. From the mid-1960s onwards, the global economy became more open to manufactured exports from developing countries (Lewis 1974, 1977). It was during this period that developing countries as diverse as South Korea and Brazil sought to take advantage of such global shifts. These countries, however, came to be ruled by military dictators who prioritized economic growth as a goal. By contrast, India moved in nearly the opposite direction, becoming more and more obsessed with "politics." Democracy in India was spreading and becoming more difficult to govern. Indira Gandhi discovered one answer to this conundrum – namely, personalism and populism. This answer led India down a path on which democracy was maintained but on which economic policies became further politicized and the gap between the state's economic rhetoric and implementing capacities grew wider.

A set of agricultural policies were adopted in the mid-1960s that eventually produced India's "Green Revolution." In so far as these policies sought to concentrate production inputs in the hands of landowning classes in some regions of India, they did not readily fit Indira Gandhi's populist designs. Why and how were these policies adopted (Lewis 1995)? First, they were adopted in the mid-1960s, just before Indira Gandhi's full embrace of "poverty alleviation" in the late 1960s. More important, India faced severe food shortages during 1965 and 1966: this made India both more willing to seek ways to boost food production and, temporarily, more dependent on food aid, especially from the United States. Green-revolution policies were favoured by the United States, who put pressure on India to adopt them in exchange for food aid. The adoption of these policies was thus quite politically sensitive; the sensitivity both of the issues of external dependence and of the possible maldistributional impact that the policies might have was underlined by the fact that these policies were adopted by a handful of the political élite, nearly as executive decisions, far from open political discussion.

The variety of social and economic policies that Indira Gandhi adopted in the 1970s were aimed at legitimizing populist politics. Although the significance of some of these was more symbolic, others turned out to be quite economically consequential. Among the more symbolic (but politically consequential) were the removal of privileges that the Indian government hitherto accorded to Indian princes. Moving up the scale of the economically consequential, Indira Gandhi intensified the rhetoric and, to an extent, the efforts to implement land reforms. Although the distributional impact was quite limited (more on this below), land redistribution was a fairly central component of the new "poverty alleviation" strategy. Similarly, nationalization of banks was supposed to "democratize" bank lending and was thus politically popular among Indira Gandhi's constituents.

Among the economically most consequential policy developments – that also had political roots but led to an adverse impact on economic growth – were the following. First, beyond rhetoric and symbolic politics, Indira Gandhi held her populist coalition together by channelling public resources to a variety of interest groups; this largess cut into public investment and hurt economic growth (Bardhan 1998). Second, radical political rhetoric, and real-labour activism that was part of the new politics, alienated private investors, both national and foreign. Third, closer political links with the Soviet Union and a parallel distancing of India from the West made it difficult for the Indian economy to derive benefits that might have come from further integration with more dynamic economies.

Moved more by political than by economic needs, Indira Gandhi added populism to India's statist model of development. The considerable gap between the state's ambitions and capacities (which already existed in Nehru's India) grew even wider during the Indira Gandhi era. For example, Indira Gandhi raised the expectations that her policies would help alleviate poverty. Aside from high rates of economic growth, this would have required some effective redistribution (such as land redistribution), which, in turn, would have required the capacity politically to penetrate and reorganize the rural society. This demanding task, in turn, would have required a well-developed political party and bureaucracy that responded to the centre while reaching out into the periphery. Indira Gandhi, however, further deinstitutionalized the Congress Party and undermined the professionalism of the bureaucracy. Second, higher rates of economic growth may have come in part from enhanced public investments in agriculture, infrastructure, and education and health. The state's resources, however, were increasingly being used to buy political support and the state's direct economic capacities were deteriorating with growing politicization of the bureaucracy and public enterprises. Finally, higher rates of economic growth may have emerged from state-supported private endeavours, in the manner of East Asia. Some such efforts were made in the agricultural sector with positive results. Elsewhere, India's statism was increasingly anti- rather than pro-capital, with predictable negative results for investment and growth.

## The most recent decades

Following Indira Gandhi's return to power in 1980, and especially following her assassination in 1984, Indian democracy entered a new phase – one that has been marked by a slow and steady decline of the hegemony of Congress over India and by numerous efforts to find workable alternatives (Kohli 1992, 1996, 1998). Whereas the last two decades have been characterized by a fair amount of governmental instability (and even political instability), especially through ethnic and communal violence, India's economic policies have exhibited more consistency, generally tending towards a more "liberal" direction than in the past. Both the political instability and the economic consistency require comment, as does the fact that, during this phase, the gap between governmental economic ambitions and capacities has narrowed somewhat – not so much as a result of enhanced capacities as by the scaling back of ambitions in both the productive and the redistributive spheres.

Indira Gandhi's departure from the political scene left India without a charismatic leader capable of holding together an increasingly mobilized and heterogeneous political society. Her failure to make a dent in India's poverty also clarified to her successors (and even to herself, in the early 1980s) the limits of class politics in India: without a well-organized social democratic party, appeals to lower classes in India quickly evolved into irresponsible populism that simultaneously hurt economic growth and failed to bring about effective economic redistribution. Subsequent attempts to discover new ruling formulas have moved in one of three directions, none of which has been totally successful: these are (1) maintaining the Nehru–Gandhi family rule; (2) forging new caste coalitions; (3) ethnic politics, especially mobilization of Hindu nationalism. The Congress Party has pursued the first strategy, and a variety of opposition parties the second and third strategies. As none of these strategies has readily translated into enduring national electoral victories, India's regions have also gained national political significance by joining coalition governments at the centre.

The most significant political development of the last decade has been the emergence of the Bhartiya Janata Party (BJP), a right-leaning religious nationalist party, as a major challenger to the Congress. The BJP currently rules India in coalition with a number of regional parties. The rise of the BJP needs to be understood in terms of filling a growing political vacuum in India. Following Indira Gandhi, her son Rajiv Gandhi (an heir-apparent of sorts) was also assassinated and deprived Congress of the opportunity to continue to capitalize on "dynastic popularity." With the aim of finding an alternative to the Congress, a series of opposition parties sought to mobilize hitherto unincorporated middle-caste groups of India, but failed owing to factionalism and rival leadership ambitions, not to mention the absence of any clear political programme.

The BJP, a better-organized party, stepped into this vacuum and sought to unite India's religious majority, the Hindus, into a nationalist political block. Reminiscent of European fascist movements, this party naturally sought politically convenient enemies, both within India (India's religious minorities, especially Muslims) and beyond India's borders. Reformulation of Indian nationalism along religious lines paid handsome political dividends for the BJP but not enough to win a national electoral majority. The party's appeal remained concentrated in those central areas of India where memories and symbols of rule by Muslims remain mobilizable. Coalition alignments, as well as experience of democratic governance, softened the more extreme elements of the BJP, enabling it to provide a viable alternative to the old Congress, at least over the short term. How the BJP will evolve in the future, however, remains an open question.

From the standpoint of this chapter, what is important to note is that shifting governments and coalitions of the last two decades have not translated into acute economic-policy instability. Although there have been fluctuations, economic policies over the last two decades have generally moved in a "liberalizing" (or, more precisely, in a pro-business) direction, both dismantling some of the inherited state controls on private economic activities and distancing the state from the rhetoric of redistribution and populism. How does one explain this shift, as well as its consistency, in spite of governmental instability? While a full account is not possible here, a few comments will help to round out the "story" (Jenkins 1999).

Neither state-led economic growth nor political efforts at redistribution and poverty alleviation have proved to be enormously successful in India. State capacity to push either the Korean type of high economic growth or the Chinese type of radical poverty alleviation was, simply, missing. The more this understanding of past failures seeped into the gestalt of India's political class, the more they embraced "market-oriented" solutions to problems of development. Even Indira Gandhi, in her later years, quietly de-emphasized poverty alleviation as a slogan and courted the business class that she had alienated earlier. Her son, Rajiv Gandhi, embraced fully the rhetoric of economic liberalization (although, in practice, his attempts to dismantle India's statism ran into numerous obstacles) (Kohli 1989). Subsequent national governments have, more or less, maintained a rhetorical commitment to liberalize the economy, moving in fits and starts, producing a type of incrementalism that suits a large, complex democracy. When questioned as to why, in spite of their nationalist orientation, the BJP sought to liberalize and open India's economy, India's current Prime Minister, Atal Bihari Vajpayee, replied: "Nehru Ji's approach was not all that successful. Indira Ji was never sincere. What else can we do now?"[1]

The growing sense among leaders that past strategies were not enormously successful, and that there is no other alternative but to liberalize, is probably the main driving force behind the shift in India's development strategy. A moment of reflection, however, suggests that past failures could have been interpreted differently, with different implications for policy change. For example, India's leaders could have embraced the model of East Asian "developmental states," or (less likely, but not totally out of the question) a more genuine social-democratic model that was an adaptation of what has been tried in some such Indian states as West Bengal and Kerala. The fact that they did not do this, in turn points to other pressing factors that have put pressure on India's new economic choices: the "liberalizing" trend is consistent with dominant interests and ideas, both within India and abroad.

In spite of its socialist flourish, India's statism provided a framework for the emergence of a largely capitalist economy in India. The more that Indian capitalism has matured over the last few decades, the more difficult has it become for India's leaders to maintain anticapitalist political positions. Even India's communist parties now accept "market realities" and seek to attract private investors. The shifting nature of the political economy has, thus, bounded the range of economic choices that India's leaders feel are available to them. International pressures have further reinforced these boundaries. Just as, at the mid-century, statism appeared to be a "natural" path to adopt worldwide, towards the end of the century virtues of markets became nearly hegemonic.[2] India's leaders could have put pressure on these national and international constraints, but that would have required considerable political cohesion around alternate values. Without such cohesion and imagination, however, nearly all of India's political parties have sought to work with – rather than against – powerful interests and ideas, especially business interests and anti-statist, pro-business ideas, thus narrowing the range of options within which economic discourse and policies may fluctuate.

It is important to note that, in spite of a commitment to economic liberalization, by global standards India's political economy still remains quite statist: for example, public enterprises remain very significant; tariffs have come down but are far from negligible; the role of foreign investment in the economy is minimal; numerous laws govern capital movements in and out of the country; and a variety of labour laws make the economy anything but a model of "flexibility." We are neither endorsing nor criticizing this state of affairs; what we wish to underline in-

Table 7.1 Some basic growth data, 1950–2000 (all figures as percentages per annum)

| Growth data | 1950–1964 | 1965–1979 | 1980–2000 |
| --- | --- | --- | --- |
| GDP growth | 3.7 | 2.9 | 5.8 |
| Industrial growth | 7.4 | 3.8 | 6.2 |
| Agricultural growth | 3.1 | 2.3[a] | 3.0 |
| Gross/investment/GDP | 13 | 18 | 23 |

Source: New Delhi: Government of India, *Economic Survey* (various issues). Owing to numerous complications, these figures should be viewed as broadly indicative, rather than as exact or definitive.
a. Figures are for 1967–1980. Inclusion of the two drought years 1964–1965 and 1965–1966 would make this average figure even lower.

stead is that, over the last two decades, India's leaders have sought to "liberalize" the statist economy that they inherited. This "liberalization," while real, has also been limited. Both the push towards, and the limited nature of, "liberalization" are consistent with powerful political forces in India: both business groups and labour have objected to some aspect or another of a radical policy shift. Weak governments have, in any case, been reluctant to undertake major policy restructuring. As noted below, however, limited liberalization has also coexisted very well with improved rates of economic growth.

## State and economic growth

An overview of economic growth in India (1950–2000) is provided by the values in table 7.1. Over the last five decades, the Indian economy has grown at an annual average rate of some 4 per cent. Whereas agriculture contributed more than half, and industry less than 10 per cent, of the national product at mid-century, the industrial sector now contributes nearly one-quarter and the service sector nearly one-half of the whole. This performance marks a dynamism that contrasts quite favourably with the nearly stagnant economy in the first half of the century under colonial rule, and underlines the constructive role of a sovereign, activist state over the last half-century. India's performance also compares favourably with numerous African economies over the same period. Juxtaposed against the needs of the teeming millions, however, or against the more impressive growers of East Asia, India's economic growth has, at best, been modest. When commenting on India's economic growth, therefore, one must ask both why it has done as well as it has and why it has not done better. What also require analysis are the fluctuations and changes evident in table 7.1: after a reasonable performance was recorded during the Nehru years, economic growth deteriorated during the Indira era but has improved considerably over the last two decades. Numerous factors underlie these trends; the discussion that follows provides only an abbreviated overview, focusing on the role of the state and of state policies (Jalan 1991).

## Nehru's statism

Nehru's economic approach was statist in intent and emphasized public investments in heavy industry. The modest economic success of the period poses the twin questions of why, in spite of India's "soft state," a statist model achieved some success and, of course, why the performance was not better. First, the agricultural sector: Nehru's approach to this sector was mainly "institutional," in the sense that he and India's economic planners hoped that, by tinkering with agrarian relations (via land reforms, for example), and by educating the peasantry (via extension programmes, for example), India's agricultural production would improve. After some significant initial public investments (especially in irrigation), therefore, the agricultural sector was more or less ignored at the expense of industry. The results reflected this neglect: agricultural growth managed to stay ahead of population growth, but barely. What was more serious was that much of this growth was "extensive" and not "intensive" (i.e. a result of bringing more land under cultivation rather than of improving productivity).

The modest increases in agricultural production thus reflected increasing labour input (growing population) and use of additional land, facilitated in part by new public investments in irrigation. Beyond this, abolition of a variety of taxes that the colonial government had imposed on agriculture may have also created better incentives for agrarian producers, contributing somewhat to higher rates of production. Conversely, the state's capacity to alter agrarian relations was extremely limited. As noted above, neither India's ruling party, the Congress, nor the bureaucracy was capable of such an intervention. As a result, the shifts in incentive structure that the political élite hoped would improve agricultural productivity never came to pass. The relative neglect of public investments in facilitating better irrigation and higher use of other agricultural inputs further undermined the prospects of rapid increases in food production. As the option of extensive growth increasingly closed by the mid-1960s, India's agricultural sector was on the verge of a crisis.

Nehru's emphasis was on heavy industry and this is where growth in production was considerable, suggesting the existence of some political capacity to translate goals into outcomes. Nehru enjoyed tremendous nationalist legitimacy and used it to pursue his priorities. Building infrastructure and heavy industry were also goals that could be more readily pursued from the political apex than, say, agricultural growth. Substantial tariffs and quotas provided a protected environment for industry to take root. Aside from the development of power, railways, and communication, industrial growth occurred in such industries as machineries and steel. The bulk of this growth was in the public sector and was facilitated by rapidly growing public savings and investment.

Growing public savings, of course, reflected both growing revenues and patterns of public expenditure. The main source of growing public revenues was indirect taxation, especially taxation of consumer goods. While progressive income tax laws were in place – consistent with India's socialist leanings – the government's capacity to collect them was limited. Over time, this incapacity would become quite consequential. Indirect taxation sufficed in this early period because the government's "non-developmental" expenditures at this stage were minimal. Not only did Nehru's government not spend much on health and primary education (underlining the superficial quality of India's socialism) but also his considerable legitimacy minimized the need to throw money at one group or another to buy political support. Public expenditures could thus stay focused on Nehru's priorities, especially the development of heavy industry, generating substantial production growth.

Critics of India's industrialization strategy have ably documented that this growth was quite "expensive," in the sense of being relatively inefficient (Bhagwati and Desai 1970; Bhagwati and Srinivasan 1975). Some of the underlying causes are inherent to the nature of public sectors (e.g. investment in industries that are not immediately profitable, or "social" pricing of output) but others were specific to India's "soft state" – the role of generalist bureaucrats, ill equipped to manage public-sector industries and/or the growing political interference by lower-level political élite groups, who treated public-sector industries as one more resource in their patronage networks. The highly protected environment within which these industries operated also contributed to their accumulating inefficiencies.

The Indian state's attempts to guide the private sector have also been roundly criticized (Bhagwati and Desai 1970). It is necessary, however, both to keep these criticisms in perspective and to understand their political roots. The role of private major capital in industry at this early stage was not all that significant. The prominent role assigned to the public sector at this early stage is thus better understood as providing a substitute for, rather than as a deterrent to, private sector-led industrialization. That said, however, the Nehruvian state in India sought more to "tame" than to "encourage" private-sector development. Unlike East

Asia, therefore, state intervention in India was less "developmental" and more "regulatory." Instead of asking business "what can you do?" and "how can the state help?" the state's approach in India was to list all that private business could not do and then to place numerous obstacles in the way of what business could do. The process of implementation was also both haphazard and inefficient: for example, priority industries were not always the ones that enjoyed maximum protection, and licensing of industry in the hands of overbearing bureaucrats often deterred private investors. Over time, these curbing political instincts and the mismatch between goals and the state's economic instincts created a maze of bureaucratic obstacles to private-sector development, leading to both corruption and the inefficient allocation of private sector resources.

## Indira's populism

India's economy did not perform very well between 1965 and 1980, as is evident from the data in table 7.1. The underlying causes were numerous, but what especially hurt industrial growth was Indira Gandhi's populism. The intervening links need to be clarified, after a few initial comments on the agricultural sector. As noted above, the new agricultural strategy that Indira Gandhi espoused was adopted under conditions of a crisis and external pressure. The new policies concentrated agricultural investments into providing better seeds and fertilizer to regions with assured irrigation, such as the Punjab. Price supports were also provided for food producers, thus shifting the terms of trade somewhat in the favour of the countryside. Although the distributional consequences were unquestionably mixed, the new policies did help to improve agricultural production.

On the face of it, the aggregate data in table 7.1 do not support this view: agricultural growth between 1965 and 1980 was lower than in the earlier period. However, much of this new growth was based on higher yields. With the possibility of bringing more land under cultivation more or less exhausted (certainly without major public investments to facilitate irrigation in dry-land areas), productivity-based food growth was essential to feed the growing population. Dramatic increases in wheat production undergirded this new growth, pulling India back from the brink of famine and mass starvation. The pattern of state intervention that generated this "Green Revolution" needs to be underlined. The state intervened massively to support those property-owning élite groups who were most likely to generate economic growth, with benign consequences for production. Although this was a product of a crisis and was concentrated in the agrarian rather than the industrial sector, there are shades of East Asia in this state-propertied class alliance for growth. Over time, India has moved in this direction, even in the industrial sector – but not before a significant populist interregnum and not without being pressed by yet other economic crises.

Industrial growth in India decelerated sharply during 1965–1980, leading some observers to dub this an era of "stagnation" (Ahluwalia 1985). The underlying cause was mainly declining investments but also accumulating inefficiencies; both of these, in turn, can be traced back to growing populism. While the rate of investment for this period (table 7.1) was higher than in the earlier period, a more disaggregated picture readily clarifies the apparent contradiction. The higher aggregate rate mostly reflected savings (and thus assumed investment) in the household sector, where the majority of non-consumed resources were maintained in physical assets and not readily translated into investments with high rates of return. More significant was thus the behaviour of public and corporate savings in this period, both of which decelerated.

Decline in public investments reflected failure to add to the revenue base (e.g. by taxing new agricultural incomes, or by generating surpluses in public enterprises) on the one hand and, on the other hand, growing public expenditures in such "non-developmental" areas as "subsidies" aimed at securing political support (Bardhan 1998). This pattern was a direct function of growing populism in which Indira Gandhi sought to mobilize the support of numerous groups and essentially threw public resources at them in return. Public investments thus declined, damaging industrial growth by effects on both the supply and the demand side (Ahluwalia 1985). For example, infrastructure development suffered, creating serious supply bottlenecks for industrial production. On the demand side also, given the weight of the public sector in India's industrial economy, reduced investments shrank the demand for a variety of industrial outputs, thereby discouraging production.

As public investments in India have not grown in recent years, but industrial growth has, it is also important to underline the role of corporate investments in industrial deceleration during the Indira era. Corporate investments also slowed down in this period, especially in fixed-capital formation. The underlying causes are hard to discern but are generally traceable back to declining profitability. Decline in demand in the overall economy was probably partly responsible; however, also at play were "political" factors. Populist politics led to steeper corporate taxes and to labour activism, industrial unrest, and higher wages, probably cutting into profitability. Finally, much harder to document would be the impact of a seemingly leftward turn in national politics on investor behaviour. It is not too far-fetched to suggest, however, that investors may have been discouraged by the growing talk of nationalizing business (and the reality of nationalizing some banks), of limiting their growth, and by adoption of a general anti-business tone during this period.

It is also important to underline that whatever investment was taking place was not always terribly efficient. As there is little evidence that productivity growth in this period was worse than that during the Nehru period (for data, see Ahluwalia 1985: 146), much of the industrial deceleration under discussion cannot be attributed to issues of efficiency. Nevertheless, one would have to forego common sense not to underline some possible links. A poorly managed and inefficient public sector repeatedly failed to generate investable surpluses, thus contributing to the slow-down of industrial growth. A policy framework that did not encourage domestic competition led to misallocation of resources, impairing growth. Although capital–output ratios are fairly rough indicators of efficiency, they increased during this period (especially in manufacturing), underlining the fact that, besides slowing of investment, investment was not being utilized efficiently.

Finally, a comment ought to be made about the continuing "closed" nature of the Indian economy. Irrespective of whether arguments of "export pessimism" or for the need to protect "infant industries" were ever technically supportable, the fact is that, given prevailing political values and popular economic doctrines of the time, they were understandable during the Nehru period. By the 1970s, however, many of these assumptions were being globally challenged, and countries such as South Korea and Brazil were turning aggressively towards export promotion and/or to the attraction of foreign investors. Indira Gandhi's political insecurity led her instead to adopt sharply anti-Western and nationalist political rhetoric, pushing India's economic policies in almost the opposite direction. As a result, India continued to embrace her import-substitution regime fiercely and to resist foreign investment, again impairing growth through a variety of bottlenecks. For example, limited exports remained a key area of vulnerability, creating periodic balance-of-payment crises. Moreover, by not promoting exports, India was not taking advantage of its key resource, "cheap" labour, and was also limiting imports of new technology and discouraging economies of scale. Enhanced foreign investment might also have facilitated growth, not only through the most obvious link of additional investments but also, more importantly, by contributing to better technology, management, and export promotion.

Populism may be politically expedient, and on occasion, even a political necessity to balance conflicting interests under conditions of weak political institutions, but its economic impact on growth is seldom benign. The Indian case was part of this broader pattern. A more genuine tilt to the left in India would have required a well-organized social-democratic party and a durable ruling coalition at the helm of a more effective state. Short of that, a charismatic and popular leader, promising radical redistribution within the context of a "soft state" and largely private-enterprise economy, was a recipe for failure. Below we discuss the issue of Indira Gandhi's redistributive failures. To sum up the present discussion, populism impaired economic growth by damaging public and private investments, on the one hand, and by further politicizing the statist and closed economic-policy regime, on the other hand.

## A pro-business tilt

India's rate of economic growth improved between 1980 and 2000 and averaged nearly 6 per cent per annum. This higher rate was, in part, a statistical artefact, in so far as it reflects the growing share of the faster-growing industrial and service sectors in the economy. Nevertheless, agricultural growth over the last two decades must be judged satisfactory, and both industry and services grew at nearly 7 per cent per annum, propelling India into a group of relatively fast growers in the world. How does one explain this superior performance, especially in the light of our focus on the role of the state and of state policies? The following discussion distinguishes between higher growth rates in the 1980s and in the 1990s: growth in the 1980s was debt-led, especially growing public debt, whereas growth in the 1990s was driven by higher rates of investment in the private corporate sector.

Before any comments are made on the political and policy determinants of improved economic performance, other underlying determinants that may have also contributed to this outcome ought to be noted. During the Nehru period, India invested in heavy industries and in higher technological education to feed this industry. Returns on these investments typically take time and India may now be benefiting from these earlier decisions. Relatedly, entrepreneurial and managerial skills have been slowly but steadily accumulating in India. There is also some evidence that the structure of industry is steadily shifting towards consumer industries where capital–output ratios are generally lower. Finally, India may have just been "lucky" over the last two decades, with a spate of good monsoons, growing contributions of overseas Indians, and better international terms of borrowing and trade.

In spite of such "non-policy" variables that may have been at work, there is still something significant to explain. It is clear from table 7.2 that higher growth rates over the last two decades were accompanied by higher rates of investment and that these increases originated in the public sector in the 1980s and in the private corporate sector in the 1990s. What factors help explain these higher rates of investment? Also, what role, if any, have attempts to "liberalize" the economy played in this improved economic performance?

Table 7.2  Patterns of capital formation, 1980–2000 (as a percentage of GDP)

| Period | Total gross capital formation | Private corporate sector | Public sector |
| --- | --- | --- | --- |
| 1980–1985 | 21.9 | 4.3 | 10.2 |
| 1985–1990 | 23.7 | 4.5 | 10.5 |
| 1990–1995 | 23.7 | 6.0 | 9.1 |
| 1995–1998 | 24.0 | 8.3 | 7.0 |

Source:  Adapted from Mohan 2000: 2028.

The Indira Gandhi who returned to power in 1980 was considerably less populist than in the 1970s. She thus initiated an era – marked especially by a much more pro-business "Industrial Policy Resolution" in 1982 – that has increasingly come to be characterized by growing silences on issues of deliberate poverty alleviation and greater public attention instead on promoting economic growth. The appropriate strategy for promoting growth has been evolving. There was much talk of "liberalizing" the economy in the second half of the 1980s, when Indira Gandhi's son Rajiv Gandhi was in power. Although some pro-business policy measures – such as reduction in corporate taxes – were, indeed, passed, overall "liberalization" was fairly limited: for example, the average rate of tariffs in India in 1990 was still over 100 per cent.

Following a balance-of-payments crisis in 1991, there was some significant "liberalization," especially of the internal economy from state controls, but the pace of change (especially of "opening" the economy to the world) slowed down in the second half of the decade. At the end of the century, tariff rates in India still averaged close to 40 per cent and foreign investment was miniscule compared, say, with that of China. What has changed steadily in India's political economy throughout the two decades, however, is a departure away from populism and towards a focus on economic growth, and relatedly towards a warmer embrace between the state and national business. The argument here is that this shift in the state's priorities and alliances is an important ingredient in improved economic performance.

As discussed above, there was substantial evidence in India in the 1970s of a link between declining public investments and deceleration of industrial growth. With changed priorities, subsequent governments decided that one way to improve growth was to boost public-sector investments. This is precisely what happened during the 1980s (Mohan 2000: 2028). Government channelled new investments into promoting infrastructure and industries that provided key inputs for intermediate and final goods, contributing to higher rates of growth. While the direct contribution of an increment of some three points in public investment to overall growth may be fairly small, given the significance of such bottlenecks as infrastructure, the indirect contribution of this new investment for growth may well have been more significant.

How was this new public investment financed? It is important to recall that the economic capacities of the Indian state during the Indira Gandhi years had deteriorated. Politicization of bureaucracy made it difficult to collect more taxes, or to improve the performance of public-sector enterprises. Some new public resources were found in further taxing international trade (hardly a route to improving economic performance) but, for the most part, the role of new resources was limited. The government also did not cut back on the variety of its "non-developmental" expenditures, such as subsidies. Given weak political parties – essentially, personalistic groupings – it was increasingly difficult in India to hold together ruling coalitions. The continuing role of public monies in buying and maintaining political support was essential. The government thus pursued the only option it thought it had – namely, to borrow, mainly internally but also externally. Because this borrowed money was being invested in areas with low financial returns and often through inefficient public firms, debt accumulated that created the twin crises of internal and external debt in 1991.

Meanwhile, the economy grew at a handsome rate of nearly 6 per cent throughout the 1980s. Increasing public-sector investment was one component of this growth. Private investments also grew, but not by much. There is, however, evidence of improvements in the productivity of investments, especially in private manufacturing (Joshi and Little 1994). The underlying causes are not readily evident. After much work, Joshi and Little conclude that "the high level of demand in the 1980s" may be an important part of the explanation (Joshi and Little 1994: 328). As we have just noted, the roots of this were also debt-led increase in public expenditure.

The Indian economy continued to grow at nearly 6 per cent per annum during the 1990s as well. It will be a while before all the relevant data for the most recent period is analysed and the underlying determinants of the continuing high growth become clear. Some of the trends, however, are already evident. The crisis of 1991, and the related agreements that the Indian government reached with the IMF, led to a pressure on government deficits. It is difficult for India's coalition governments to collect new taxes, or to improve the performance of public enterprises, or to cut back on the variety of supports and services that the state provides. The main strategy for debt management is thus evident in table 7.2 – namely, in declining public-sector investments. This is a worrisome trend, especially because of the woeful state of India's infrastructure, but also because of a pressing need in India to invest more in basic education and health (Mohan 2000).

In spite of a decline in public-sector investments, overall economic growth did not suffer. This is mainly because private-sector investments grew and the share of corporate investments in the GDP actually surpassed the share of public-sector investments (table 7.2). Private-sector investment in India in industry is generally quite productive. New investments, however, were only in part in new industries; the industrial sector, especially manufacturing, did not perform particularly well in the 1990s. Since most of the "liberalization" policies were aimed at industry, the link between policy reform and economic outcomes is not all that strong. The real locus of growth shifted instead to the less-regulated service sector, especially to exports of information technology. India's accumulating manpower resources in this area have finally found a niche in the global market, contributing to India's economic growth.

Among the factors that help to explain growing private-sector investment are the increasingly pro-business policies of the Indian state. Over the last decade or so, India's various governments have cut corporate taxes; have provided a variety of supports for business, especially for exports; have sought to tame labour (as shown by the decline of man-days lost due to strikes); and have relaxed public controls on entry, exit, and expansion. During the 1990s the private sector benefited specifically from tax reforms that have included an across-the-board reduction in rates and simplification of procedures for paying direct and indirect taxes; a lowering of import tariffs by almost one-third between 1990 and 1996; the dispensing with industrial licensing agreements for most industries; the allowing of new entrants – private, semi-private and foreign – into the banking system and capital markets; and the opening up of sectors such as power and telecommunications previously limited to the public sector.

Whereas champions of "liberalization" may see all these measures as evidence of a growing "free market" in India, it is important to underline that India's state still remains heavily interventionist and that the Indian economy still remains relatively closed to external goods, finance, and investors. The policy trend within India is thus better interpreted as a rightward drift in Indian politics in which the embrace of state and business continues to grow warmer, possibly leaving many others out in the cold.

## State and poverty

The democratic framework under which the Indian state has developed over the past fifty years has made many direct and indirect contributions towards India's development. The freedoms available under Indian democracy – such as free speech, free press, the ability to conduct public action, and the ability to hold elections – allowed the citizens to exercise their rights in many ways that are not available in other non-democratic, developing economies. To an extent, these actions of the public in turn influenced government policies and, ultimately, economic development. Personal freedoms and the nexus between public and state action thus helped to produce an Indian state that is more responsive – at least to disasters (especially famines) and possibly to other issues around which people have mobilized to demand state action, thereby helping make India's development relatively equitable.

At the same time, persistent poverty and a low quality of life has always been a problem associated with India. Prior to independence, the majority of the population lived in poverty, devastating famines occurred periodically, and social indicators of well-being (such as literacy and mortality rates) were abysmal. It was against this background and the mass nature of the Congress Party that eradication of poverty and improvements in quality of life became a main objective of the first sovereign Indian state from the outset. As noted above, Nehru's priorities included the ending of poverty and inequality of opportunity; universal access to education was enshrined in the constitution and these issues became recurrent themes of India's policy discourse. Indira Gandhi accentuated the sense of urgency of these issues with her slogan of *garibi hatao* (abolish poverty), and virtually every Indian government since then has repeated these promises of poverty reduction and improvements in well-being for all.

Despite much rhetoric and higher growth rates, the governments during the last two decades have obviously not been able to make any major progress in reducing poverty in India. One has only to walk city streets today or to go to a public health clinic or elementary school in rural areas to see that India is still far from fulfilling the dreams and promises articulated by Nehru, Indira Gandhi, and subsequent governments. One-third of India's population still lives below the poverty line, and many of those living above the poverty line are far from leading a life where their basic needs are adequately satisfied. Over one-half of Indian children below the age of 4 years are still moderately to severely malnourished, and high infant-mortality rates registered little progress during the 1990s. Basic educational attainment is still denied to about half of India's population: over two-thirds of Indian females and one-third of males were illiterate in the early 1990s. Furthermore, India is one of the few countries in the world to have had a low female–male ratio of 927 females per 1,000 males in the early 1990s – a ratio that illustrates its severe and persistent gender inequalities.

Moreover, these average statistics mask wide variations between different regions and states: disparities have increased since the Nehru era, when there was a greater percentage of the population living in poverty with less differential between regions. In the late 1950s the national poverty rate was around 60 per cent, with states from Kerala and Maharashtra to Bihar and Uttar Pradesh having similar poverty rates. However, by the early 1990s, less than 20 per cent of the rural population in Punjab and Haryana lived below the poverty line compared with nearly 60 per cent in Bihar. State performance in reducing poverty also differed widely: from the 1950s to the early 1990s, Kerala reduced its poverty rate by half, while Uttar Pradesh reduced its rate by 20 per cent, and Bihar's rates remained stagnant (mortality rates were only 12 per 1,000 live births in Kerala, but as high as 96 per 1,000 live births in Orissa). A recent study of basic education in the northern states of Bihar, Madhya Pradesh, Rajasthan, and Uttar Pradesh found that 45 per cent of males and 82 per cent of females in these states were illiterate (PROBE Team 1999: 9). This contrasts with illiteracy rates of around 7 per cent of males and 14 per cent of females in Kerala. In addition, although the female–male ratio is over 100 in Kerala, it is less than 90 in the higher-income and higher-growth states of Haryana and Punjab – states where there are also alarming signs of further deterioration of this ratio.

Indian governments since independence have accorded much importance to poverty reduction. Nevertheless, although national poverty rates fluctuated from year to year, the Nehru period began and ended with poverty rates of around 45 per cent, as did the period under Indira Gandhi. It was only during the late 1980s and 1990s that poverty rates decreased to below 40 per cent, with a rate of 35 per cent in 1990 – and there is evidence that this figure may have changed to some extent, but not greatly, by the turn of the century. Moreover, since India also continues to have a high population growth rate there are actually more poor people living in India today than ever before: the number of poor people has doubled from around 160 million in 1951 to 312 million in 1993–1994 (World Bank 1997: i). Those who are most likely to be poor today are the same people who were likely to be poor 50 years ago, at the beginning of the Nehru period – namely, women, those who are illiterate, the landless, the unemployed, and people of lower castes.

## Poverty

This widespread, enduring poverty and increasing inequality between states continues to be the Indian state's most obvious policy failure. Whereas slow growth rates up to the 1980s did not help the state's efforts to combat poverty, the increased growth rates of the past decades did not lead to dramatic decreases in poverty, either. The main cause of India's inability to decrease poverty and mitigate inequalities has been the state's limited institutional capacity and faulty policies at the central, state, and local levels. Neither the Indian state nor most of its individual regions have, during the last fifty years, followed through on their stated policies on poverty and social sectors by funding antipoverty programmes and social services to the extent needed to produce the stated results. This lack of following rhetoric with actions, or the "softness" of the Indian state, has been a major cause of India's continued poverty.

Another major cause of the slow rate of poverty reduction has undoubtedly been the state's growing incapacity to implement these programmes. India's antipoverty programmes are run mainly by the central government and therefore should be fairly uniform across states. Yet targeting of these programmes and their effective reach differs widely between states, underscoring that the capacity of state and local governments is important: for example, a recent study of villages in Uttar Pradesh, West Bengal, and Karnataka found that antipoverty programmes in villages in Uttar Pradesh were virtually defunct; in West Bengal, access to these programmes was good but correlated with Communist Party membership; and access was good and more egalitarian in Karnataka (Kohli 1987).

More development-oriented states, such as the southern states of Kerala, Tamil Nadu, and Karnataka, have consistently outperformed the laggard states of Bihar, Orissa, and Uttar Pradesh since the early 1970s of the Indira Gandhi period, and this trend has continued to this day. It is not only the rhetoric but also the capacity of state and local governments that underlies these differential rates of programme implementation and targeting. The governments of Kerala, for example, have shown strong commitment to reducing poverty by making antipoverty programmes and social sectors a high priority and allocating greater state finances to these areas. West Bengal has had a similar commitment since the Communist Party came to power in the 1970s, and this commitment was coupled with a strong local government system to help implement these programmes. In both states, there was commitment to an active antipoverty policy by the government, coupled with a well-organized and effective party system at the state and local levels, which helped to implement effective antipoverty programmes. Uttar Pradesh, on the other hand, has not had the same type of state commitment to poverty reduction over the past decades, and the recently elected local government bodies are virtually defunct. Without state and local government commitment and the greater accountability that comes with involvement of all levels of government and bureaucracy, antipoverty programmes cannot be run effectively. States with greater commitment and capacity to follow through on poverty-reduction programmes have made better progress, often despite below-average growth rates during the 1980s and 1990s. Poverty rates have thus stagnated for the last twenty years in populous states such as Bihar and Uttar Pradesh, whereas they have decreased significantly during the same period in states such as Kerala and West Bengal.

The lack of significant improvements in the lives of India's poor is evident not only in low incomes and in slowly declining poverty rates but also in the lack of progress in other indicators of poverty. India has moderate-income inequality, as reflected in its reasonable Gini co-efficients – coefficients that are significantly better than those of other large countries such as Brazil, Nigeria, or Malaysia. However, Gini co-efficients do not capture other aspects of inequality (such as caste, religious, and gender inequality) which, despite laws and rhetoric aiming to ameliorate the situation, have registered only slow improvements from the time under Nehru until the turn of the century.

## Land Reforms

Land inequality in India is not as high as that in many other parts of the world. Yet the failure to implement land reforms in a poor and still highly unequal country such as India is another example of India's larger state failure. Redistributive intervention in a low-income democracy such as India is a tool that can help to bring about more equitable development. In India, three-quarters of the population (and most of the poor) still live in rural areas, and control of land largely undergirds the political and social organization of rural society. Land ownership in rural areas is therefore still a good indicator of well-being; conversely, landless people are much more likely to be poor.

Land-reform programmes have been viewed as a tool for more equitable development since independence. Nehru tried to implement moderate land reforms, as did Indira Gandhi; however, again, government actions did not match the rhetoric. The initial stages of land reform – the abolition of landed intermediaries and consolidation of land-holdings – achieved only moderate success, largely because the ceilings on land-holdings failed to eliminate large inequalities in actual land distribution. Kerala and West Bengal were notable for their achievement of moderate land reforms that helped to disperse the concentration of political and economic wealth, thereby helping the poor to gain a means of survival and escape from poverty. The national Indian state and the majority of the individual states, however, failed to push through land reforms between the 1950s and the 1970s, when the government rhetoric and the global political climate were more favourable to carrying through these reforms. During the 1980s and 1990s, as the Indian state turned more to the right, it minimized pro-land reform rhetoric; indeed, virtually none of the states has implemented serious land reforms during the last two decades. Unequal land-holdings, insecure tenancy rights, absentee landlords, lack of access to land, and a situation where land ownership still equals power continues to characterize most Indian states today. The larger, northern states of Uttar Pradesh and Bihar today have the worst record on land reforms and equal ownership of land. Interestingly, these states are also the ones that continue to be among India's worst-performing states on social indicators and poverty rates.

The carrying out of land reforms is difficult for any state to accomplish, because restructuring social relations to benefit the poor at the expense of the rich is opposed by the powerful. Nevertheless, land reforms have been carried out by some Indian states, thereby illustrating that this is both possible and beneficial. Redistributive interventions such as land reforms are best carried out by strong states that have well-organized ruling parties with a commitment to poverty reduction and effective governments also at the local levels. As documented elsewhere, redistributive reforms were more successful in a state such as West Bengal, because the ruling party had a coalition of middle and lower classes as its social base combined with good party organization (Kohli 1987). West Bengal also had the longest history of functioning local governments, which was essential for carrying out land reforms on the ground. A few, strong states with effective government at state as well as at local levels have been able to carry through reforms, but the majority of Indian states have not. The Indian state has thus failed to lay down the material conditions for more equitable growth.

## Human capital development

Another obvious state failure has been the slow improvement in human development and quality of life. Promises to improve health and education opportunity for all have been repeatedly made and broken since they were enshrined in the constitution and reiterated by the first Indian government under Nehru. This is all the more surprising, given the widespread recognition that economic growth rates and improvements in well-being in East Asian countries have been (at least partially) due to their investments in human development. Investing in social sectors and education in particular was beneficial to many East Asian countries because it directly and indirectly improved the quality of life that people led. Being literate and healthier meant that people had the freedom and awareness to be able to make use of the increasing economic opportunities (Dréze and Sen 1995). Increased literacy also had other beneficial effects, such as improving health awareness and thereby producing a more healthy population; increased empowerment of disadvantaged groups, including women; and an increased awareness of rights, leading also to a more informed and potentially more active public. In addition, as pointed out by scholars, education also has an intrinsic value, directly affecting people's quality of life and degree of freedom. The Indian state, by having largely neglected the basic education of its citizens hitherto, has therefore directly decreased its citizens' quality of life, in addition to lowering their earning potential and India's growth rate. Persistent neglect of the health and education sectors has also characterized public policy in most states since independence. By not providing these basic social services for its citizens, the state has neglected to set the frame-work for achieving its own goal of increased growth and equitable de-velopment.

The failure of the state to provide effective health and education ser-vices has been a failure of both policy and implementation. On the policy side, the state has not allocated the resources needed to these sectors. Since independence, the Indian state's spending on education and health, in particular, has remained below recommended international norms, and allocations to these sectors have been fairly stagnant for the last decades. Even worse, India has failed to safeguard social-sector expenditures during times of economic adjustment, such as during the early to mid-1990s, when these expenditures were most needed to provide a safety net against the adverse impact of structural adjustment. Both union and most state government expenditures on health and education did not meet planned expenditures in the wake of the 1991 economic crisis, in spite of government promises of an "adjustment with a human face" (World Bank 1997: Statistical Appendix). At the same time, the government continued its policy of spending a disproportionate amount on higher education and tertiary health care at the expense of pro-poor spending on primary education and basic health care (PROBE Team 1999). Not only have government expenditures in the social sectors during the 1990s remained biased against basic health and education, public spending on these sectors has also remained significantly lower in the poorer regions and states, thereby exacerbating the neglect of disadvantaged regions and communities. The rightward shift of the Indian state thus may have benign consequences for growth but, by the same token, the impact on welfare provision has been adverse. Underfunding of health and educa-tion has resulted in the underprovision of facilities, inadequate mainten-ance, lack of resources and supplies at the facilities, high ratios of pupils to teachers and patients to health facilities, and increasing inequalities between richer and poorer regions, with the expected result on social indicators.

In addition to not providing an adequate infrastructure and not creating an environment conducive to better learning and health care, the Indian state has also shown a lack of interest and effectiveness in improving social-service provision. This general indifference towards social sectors in practice at the national level is mirrored in the attitudes of states. State officials tolerate widespread absenteeism of teachers and health workers, and extra payments for services that are supposed to be free of charge are an accepted practice throughout the country. National programmes designed to improve the access of the poor to health and education, such as the outreach programmes of the *anganwadi* (village health-care worker) and school feeding programmes, are virtually defunct in some areas of the country. The dismal functioning of these public services is exacerbated by lack of accountability in the education and health sectors. National and state governments have known of the shortcomings of these services for decades, yet only a few states have made a serious attempt to enforce the provision of effective social services. Moreover, local governments – the institutions that could ensure accountability of service provision on a daily basis – are not empowered to take action to enforce job performance of local civil servants, such as schoolteachers or health-care workers.

The net effect of this state inertia has been low (and only slowly improving) education and health indicators in India. Although the good social indicators in the state of Kerala and the recent spectacular progress in schooling in Himachal Pradesh are encouraging models, a large percentage of India's citizens remain illiterate and in poor health, with differentials between regions and states increasing. In order to change this scenario to accelerate improvements in the health and education sectors and thereby to enhance social opportunities, there will have to be a radical shift in public policy. Only through greater policy focus on social sectors, increased financial allocations, and increased accountability through better-functioning government from the national to the local level can any real change in these areas be accomplished. The lessons from other countries on investing in human resources are clear, and India cannot afford to miss this opportunity to ensure economic growth and more equitable development.

## Conclusions

Just development in India has been only moderately successful. It has neither grown as rapidly, nor has it been as equitable, as that in some East Asian countries; nevertheless, it has not been plagued by extremely low growth rates or by the exclusion from social development of all, as has been the case in large parts of Africa. Independent India has developed under a democratic framework, thereby providing its citizens with freedoms that some of its more economically successful East Asian neighbours lacked. However, with around 300 million people living below the official poverty line, India still has the largest number of the world's poor, while social indicators and other measures of equitable development have improved only slowly.

This poor record in achieving just growth has been independent India's greatest failure and needs to be understood in terms of the disparity between state ambition on the one hand and state capacity on the other. Growth and elimination of poverty have been part of India's development agenda since independence; state capacity to implement this agenda, however, has decreased, as has the motivation to carry through antipoverty programmes. On the economic side, growth rates were low during the decades immediately after independence, when capacity and pro-poor rhetoric were higher; higher growth rates during the past decades have, on the other hand, been accompanied by a political shift to the right. This move away from pro-poor, socialist ideology towards a more conservative political orientation has resulted in a decreasing antipoverty focus at a time when growth rates have been higher. Economic and political changes have thereby reinforced the mismatch between the statist model and the state's capacity.

India has pursued a statist model of development since independence. However, in contrast to some of its East Asian neighbours, the Indian state lacked the efficaciousness, and also the willingness, to follow through on its proclaimed policies. Democratic, and socialist-oriented, independent India set out many ambitious goals, among the most notable of which was the elimination of poverty. Not only were some of these social aspirations enshrined in the constitution, but also successive governments campaigned and were elected on bold social promises.

Although poverty reduction and redistributional policies have remained perennial campaign slogans, the Indian state has been less willing and able to follow through and implement these policies. That this has happened is largely due to the capture of political parties by powerful interest groups and, more recently, to the rightward shift in politics. As the main parties squandered their political capital and became more beholden to interest groups through an increasing web of patronage, they were less able to carry through pro-poor programmes, such as land reforms, that would have hurt these interest groups. Although antipoverty rhetoric continued to remain important to the stability of the state, dominant interest groups garnered the main benefits of welfare programmes by, for example, steering a disproportionate amount of the education budget to higher education and usurping a large amount of social benefits at the local level. In addition, the rightward political shift of the past decades undermined government willingness to carry through redistributional programmes. Recent higher economic growth rates – the result of policies of a more pro-business and less socialist-oriented government – had the potential greatly to improve poverty and social welfare but, in fact, led to few significant improvements. This rightward political shift and the mismatch between the statist model and state efficaciousness has resulted in the failure of the state's two main aims – achieving high growth and the eradication of poverty.

By failing to achieve these two main goals, the state squandered valuable capital. After independence, India had low growth rates but a strong and pro-poor state capable of achieving just growth – a state that did start to initiate land reforms and other antipoverty programmes. When the international context changed in the 1960s to allow for increasing growth through expanded export orientation, India (unlike many East Asian countries) missed the opportunity to take advantage of the changed international context and increase growth rates through expanded exports. The state's anti-business attitude inhibited investment; at the same time, it was increasingly unable to use available resources to carry through redistributional reforms that were unpopular with powerful interests. This pattern has continued: despite growth in India's service sector and a pro-business shift in the political environment in the context of increasing globalization, development policies have continued to have no dramatic effect on poverty rates and social indicators.

Given India's track record, it is unlikely that its capacity to foster equitable growth will improve radically. The increasing capture of the dominant political parties by powerful interest groups, the move away from its earlier socialist goals, and the "softness" of the Indian state, are not likely to increase its willingness or ability to ensure that future growth is more egalitarian. India's sheer size, together with the nature of its economy and current political framework, also suggest that it will remain less than receptive to global economic and political pressures for radical changes. At the same time, the state will continue to be critical for providing infrastructure, supporting private capital, developing human resources, and tackling poverty. India's record in achieving just growth has been mediocre and, unfortunately, the road ahead does not extend to sharply optimistic horizons.

## Notes

1. This is a translation of a conversation in Hindi between Mr. Vajpayee and Atul Kohli in Oxfordshire, England, 19–21 June 1992. Mr. Vajpayee at the time was a leader of the opposition in the Indian parliament and was attending a conference on "India: The Future," organized by the Ditchley Foundation.

2. This sweeping gestalt shift, which has an ideological quality, should give pause to thoughtful observers. The earlier embrace of statism led to some successes and numerous failures. The new commitment to markets is also likely to lead to a similar, mixed record that will be evident only in the future.

## REFERENCES

Ahluwalia, Isher Judge. 1985. *Industrial Growth in India: Stagnation Since the Mid-Sixties*. Delhi: Oxford University Press.

Bardhan, Pranab. 1998. *The Political Economy of Development in India*. Oxford: Oxford University Press.

Bhagwati, Jagdish N. and Padma Desai. 1970. *India: Planning for Industrialization – Industrialization and Trade Policies since 1951*. Oxford: Oxford University Press.

Bhagwati, Jagdish N. and T. N. Srinivasan. 1975. *India*. National Bureau of Economic Research. New York: Columbia University Press.

Dréze, Jean and Amartya Sen. 1995. *India: Economic Development and Social Opportunity*. Oxford: Clarendon Paperbacks.

Frankel, Francine. 1978. *India's Political Economy, 1947–1977: The Gradual Revolution*. New Jersey: Princeton University Press.

Government of India. *Economic Survey* (various issues). New Delhi: Government of India.

Government of India. 2000. *India: Reducing Poverty, Accelerating Development*. Delhi: Oxford University Press.

Jalan, Bimal. 1991. *India's Economic Crisis: The Way Ahead*. Delhi: Oxford University Press.

Jenkins, Rob. 1999. *Democratic Politics and Economic Reform in India*. Cambridge: Cambridge University Press.

Joshi, Vijay and I. M. D. Little. 1994. *India: Macroeconomics and Political Economy*. Washington DC: World Bank.

Kohli, Atul. 1987. *The State and Poverty in India: Politics of Reform*. Cambridge: Cambridge University Press.

Kohli, Atul, ed. 1988. *India's Democracy: An Analysis of Changing State–Society Relations*. New Jersey: Princeton University Press.

Kohli, Atul. 1989. "Politics of Economic Liberalization in India." *World Development* 17(3), March.

Kohli, Atul. 1991. *Democracy and Discontent: India's Growing Crisis of Governability*. Cambridge: Cambridge University Press.

Kohli, Atul. 1992. "Indian Democracy: Stress and Resilience." *Journal of Democracy*, January.

Kohli, Atul. 1996. "Can the Periphery Control the Center? Indian Politics at the Crossroads." *Washington Quarterly* 19(4), Autumn.

Kohli, Atul. 1998. "India Defies the Odds: Enduring Another Election." *Journal of Democracy*, July.

Kohli, Atul. 2001. *The Success of India's Democracy*. Cambridge: Cambridge University Press.

Kothari, Rajni. 1970. *India*. London: Little, Brown.

Lewis, John P. 1995. *India's Political Economy: Governance and Reform*. Oxford: Oxford University Press.

Lewis, W. Arthur. 1974. *Dynamic Factors in Economic Growth*. Bombay: Orient Longman for the Dorab Tata Memorial Lecture Series.

Lewis, W. Arthur. 1977. *The Evolution of the International Economic Order*. New Jersey: Princeton University Press.

Mohan, Rakesh. 2000. "Fiscal Correction for Economic Growth: Data Analysis and Suggestions." *Economic and Political Weekly* 10 June 2000.

Moore, Barrington, Jr. 1966. *Social Origins of Dictatorship and Democracy: Lord and Peasant in the Making of the Modern World*. Boston: Beacon Press.

Nayar, Baldev Raj. 1989. *India's Mixed Economy*. Bombay: Popular Prakashan.

PROBE Team. 1999. *Public Report on Basic Education in India*. Delhi: Oxford University Press.

World Bank. 1997. *India: Achievements and Challenges in Reducing Poverty*. Statistical appendix. Washington DC: World Bank.

World Bank. 1998. *India: Macroeconomic Update*. Washington DC: World Bank.

Weiner, Myron. 1967. *Party Building in a New Nation*. Chicago: University of Chicago Press.

Weiner, Myron. 1991. *The Child and the State in India*. New Jersey: Princeton University Press.

# 8

# Pragmatic neo-liberalism and just development in Africa

*Dickson Eyoh and Richard Sandbrook*

To choose "just development" as the issue for an essay on Africa may strike readers as a cruel joke. If just development is loosely defined as sustained growth with a degree of equity, resting on a foundation of political freedom, then few African countries have recently enjoyed any of these cherished states, let alone all three. Indeed, as the millennium dawned, many Africans would reasonably have aspired to much less than this lofty goal. Simple security, rather than "just development," might have sufficed for those tormented by climatic disasters, famines, civil wars, and bleak economic prospects.

Yet this chapter's focus is perhaps not as bizarre as it first appears. "Simple" security is actually not so simple: its attainment depends on many factors, including one or more of sustained growth, equity leading to reduced poverty, and political freedom. So a concern for human security returns us to the notion of just growth. Moreover, the currently dominant development doctrine in sub-Saharan Africa – pragmatic neo-liberalism, in our terms – has staked its intellectual claim to dominance on its ability to deliver something akin to just development on the basis of a comprehensive and integrated strategy. It is important to subject this claim to critical scrutiny.

We are sceptical that pragmatic neo-liberalism can deliver on its bold vision. Although this development doctrine is more sophisticated than the purer neoclassical model it replaced, pragmatic neo-liberalism does not offer a reliable guide to development that is sustained, poverty reducing, and democratic. In practice, this approach has achieved meagre results. Its proponents have attributed this poor performance to many factors: inept policies; poor or sporadic implementation; corruption; political instability; ethnic tensions; unanticipated shocks (droughts, insurrections, falling commodity prices); and difficult initial conditions, both physical and institutional. These impediments, which are mainly domestic in origin, are real. However, Africa's tragedy is that onerous external as well as internal constraints operate – and both types require attention. Pragmatic neo-liberalism, however, considers only domestic reforms within African countries. It counsels governments to adjust their policies and institutions to the imperatives of competitiveness within a supposedly inexorable global market economy, implicitly accepting the structures and inequalities of global capitalism as given. We argue, to the contrary, that globalization itself needs to be reformed, if poverty is to be reduced and other social goals are to be achieved. Just development requires major changes in policies and institutions at the global as well as national level (Mkandawire and Soludo 1999, 2000).

To support this argument, we turn in the next section (pp. 228–232) to explicate the pragmatic neo-liberal model. The section on pages 232–238 then diagnoses the origins of the economic crisis that engulfed most African countries from the mid-1970s, forming the basis for an evaluation of the national-level reforms subsumed under the rubric of structural adjustment (pp. 239–243) and the global-market assumptions (pp. 244–249) underpinning the dominant model. A brief concluding section (pp. 250–252) draws the implications of the analysis for the attainment of just development in Africa.

## The pragmatic neo-liberal development model

The World Bank, the most influential purveyor of development theory and strategy, has moved far from its austere and pure neo-liberalism of the 1980s to embrace a more pragmatic doctrine (World Bank 1981; Taylor 1997; Green 1998; Gore 2000). Under pressure to justify its very existence, the Bank has progressively broadened its approach to development. The disappointing performance of structural adjustment in the 1980s in Latin America (e.g. Gwynne and Kay 2000) and Africa (below) spurred mainstream development agencies and academics to innovate, mainly by absorbing popular concepts and challenges into a reinvented neo-liberalism. Of particular significance was the telling critique in 1987 (*Adjustment with a Human Face*) by the United Nations Children's Fund (UNICEF) and its extension by the UNDP in its annual *Human Development Report*, which first appeared in 1990. "Sustainable human development," as propounded by the UNDP and an array of NGOs, rejects an exclusive focus on the growth of GDP and a top-down, externally driven strategy. These organizations argue that "the ultimate test of development practice is that it should improve the nature of people's lives, and advocate that it should be founded on participation and a more equal partnership between donors and developing countries" (Gore 2000: 795). In the 1990s, first the World Bank and later the IMF and WTO supplemented their neoclassical doctrine with a declared commitment to poverty reduction, equity, enhanced participation, pluralism, human rights, and partnership.

Not accidentally, pragmatic neo-liberalism has much in common with the "Third Way," which now serves as a route map for major industrial countries within the new global economy. Both doctrines developed as a reaction to the limitations of the free-market fundamentalism of the Thatcher and Reagan era. The "Third Way," as advocated in particular by British Prime Minister Tony Blair (Blair 1996) and former US President Bill Clinton, urges a more forceful role for the state than that envisaged by old-style liberalism (North American neo-conservatism). However, this forceful role is largely limited to supply-side activities – especially honing the capacity of citizens, firms, and the national economy as a whole, to compete within an inexorably advancing global market economy. This priority directs governmental attention to improving universal education and technical training, as well as technological research and development. Additionally, the state assumes responsibility for providing minimally adequate safety nets for those individuals who cannot market themselves effectively. The Third Way's focus is to create equality of opportunity and minimal support for the market's losers, rather than to promote equality of outcomes by regulating markets (Westergaard 1999). That the Third Way parallels the dominant strategy for developing countries is hardly surprising, in light of the disproportionate influence of the US and British governments on the World Bank, and the Bank's influence on development thinking (Samoff 1996).

The pragmatic neo-liberal approach, culminating in World Bank President James Wolfensohn's Comprehensive Development Framework (Wolfensohn 1999; World Bank 1999a), was extravagantly touted as a new paradigm for development. Yet the elements of this approach appeared as early as 1989 (World Bank 1989, 1990, 1992, 1997). This "paradigm" features a market-based strategy with the following features:

- it is *holistic* – it encompasses political and social, in addition to conventional macroeconomic dimensions;
- it is *synergistic* – these dimensions are complementary and mutually reinforcing;

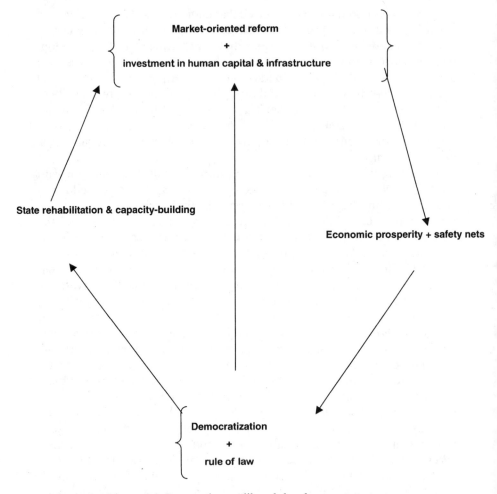

Figure 8.1  Pragmatic neo-liberal development strategy

- it is *complex* – efficient market systems are deemed to require the supportive action of effective national states.

  Figure 8.1 starkly portrays this model as a mutually reinforcing circle of development, based on the following assumptions.[1] Market-oriented reform has always involved, as is well known, three fundamental economic priorities.

- A commitment to maintaining macroeconomic stability.
- Deregulation and liberalization, including in particular the opening of the national economy to international trade and investment.
- Privatization of land and state-owned enterprises.

These changes are fostered by funnelling assistance to strong reformers by the international financial institutions, other multilateral lenders, and the donors. These reforms, together with increased investments in primary education and health care and physical infrastructure, should set the stage for growing economic prosperity. (A recent report by the World Bank and four Africa-based partners [World Bank 2000c: 15] estimates that Africa, to reduce poverty by half between 1999 and 2015, will require an annual average growth rate of at least 7 per cent.)

Of course, sustained growth will also require complementary social and political reforms. The prospect of economic betterment, combined with minimal safety nets to cater for those who lose out in market reform and for the chronic poor, will provide a conducive environment for the consolidation of the parallel processes of democratization and the refurbishment of the rule of law. Donors will assist by funding safety nets, providing technical assistance to electoral commissions and judicial reform, and promoting the organization and effectiveness of civil society. Democratization, according to this thinking, will directly support market reform in various ways. Elections not only should sweep from power the corrupt élite groups who were deeply implicated in the rent-seeking arrangements that initially stifled market forces but also will enable the new governments to undertake reform programmes by augmenting their legitimacy. Electoral democracy will enhance the political commitment to reform by allowing actual and potential beneficiaries to mobilize behind a reforming party, it is hoped. (This expectation rests on the assumptions that winners will form a majority, and that policy-based economic interests will prevail.) Finally, hardy democratic and judicial institutions will permit the regime to manage the tensions and conflicts that liberated markets will set in train.

Democratization will, in addition, indirectly support a vibrant market economy by promoting state rehabilitation. An ineffective and corrupt state is unable (and probably unwilling) to promote a market system. By introducing democratic rules, however, the state itself may be reformed. Democracy should augment accountability, transparency in decision-making, and informed debates over policy. It may enhance a government's (and its citizens') sense of ownership of reform programmes. Finally, political freedom and the rule of law should discourage corruption, arbitrary administration, and rent-seeking by political insiders. Accompanying this state reorientation are capacity-building programmes. A leaner, more expert, disciplined, and neutral public sector will enhance state capacity. The more effective a state, the more "market-friendly" tasks it should undertake. At a minimum, the state needs to provide the economic fundamentals (macroeconomic stability and basic services and infrastructure), the political fundamentals (the order and predictability that investors crave), and effective safety nets. The more capable states will also construct a conducive regulatory framework for market activities, particularly by ensuring prudence and probity in the crucial financial sector. If all works according to plan, this "virtuous" circle generates, in time, a pattern of just development.

In no region of the world is this development model more hegemonic than in sub-Saharan Africa. This dominance derives from the unusual degree of influence that the World Bank, the IMF, the bilateral donors, and other multilateral agencies exercise over governments in this region. These governments, however, play a contradictory role. The technocrats in their economic ministries and central bank are often more supportive of neo-liberal programmes than their political masters. Governments, although rhetorically committed to reform, often exhibit substantial backsliding in implementation, especially when reforms may undermine the regime's political support (by laying-off public employees, for example). Yet, for all the IFIs' and aid agencies' rhetoric regarding the need for "local ownership" of reform programmes, and governments assuming the "driver's seat" (Wolfensohn 1999), African governments have had little option but to acquiesce to market adjustment. "He who pays the piper calls the tune," as the old adage advises. Sub-Saharan countries have become heavily reliant upon foreign aid. The economic crisis of the 1970s and 1980s led to the drying up of commercial loans and foreign investment; governments were thereby forced into the arms of the IMF and World Bank. The flow of aid depends upon an IMF "seal of approval" – and this approval has required a government's adherence to a standard adjustment programme. Aid inflows to sub-Saharan Africa rose from 3.4 per cent of GNP in 1980 to 16.3 per cent in 1995, according to the World Bank (Mkandawire and Soludo 1999: 119), when the major donors cut their aid budgets. These official inflows typically funded basic government programmes, together with all or most of a government's development expenditures. This dependence explains why African governments have virtually ceded the shaping of economic and some social policy to external agencies (Mkandawire and Soludo 1999: 119), and why our focus on an externally generated development ideology makes sense.

Because remedies depend upon a sound diagnosis, we must now briefly probe the historical roots of Africa's contemporary travails. This survey provides us with a basis for assessing the efficacy of structural adjustment.

## Origins of the economic crisis, 1960–1980

At independence, Africa's ruling élite groups confronted the dual challenge of promoting nation-state building and economic development. On the one hand, nation-state building entails nurturing popular acceptance of the territorial boundaries inherited from colonialism, including a common national identity and a symbiotic relationship between the subjects and the rulers within those boundaries. On the other hand, economic development engenders new patterns of resource allocation that alter the distribution of benefits among social classes and ethnocultural communities. Tensions between these two processes were inevitable (Hawthorn 1991: 25–29).

Consider the challenge of economic development as it appeared at independence. Africans inherited economies that were reliant on the production and export of primary resources (Fieldhouse 1986: 1–66; Austen 1987: 155–223). With the exception of a few mineral-rich colonies (e.g. present-day Zambia and Democratic Republic of Congo) and settler colonies (such as Kenya and Zimbabwe) with large-scale agricultural sectors, these economies were dominated by rain-fed peasant agriculture. A few of the more prosperous colonies (e.g. Kenya, Nigeria, Ghana, Senegal, Democratic Republic of Congo, Zimbabwe) saw the beginnings of industrialization after the Second World War, but even in these instances the contribution of manufacturing to GDP was paltry. Colonial economic transformations thus failed to generate significant numbers of indigenous entrepreneurs who might have shaped post-colonial industrialization. The growth of such groups had been constrained by colonial policies favouring European businesses over African ones, and by colonial administrators' fears that African entrepreneurial success would disrupt political order by fomenting socio-economic divisions (Berman and Lonsdale 1979; Kennedy 1988: 28–59; Philips 1988). Consequently, the modern economic sectors of banking, insurance, large-scale commerce, and manufacturing were small and dominated by foreign capital at independence. The limited development of human capital, which was low even in comparison with other recently decolonized regions, was a further constraint.

Nation-state building was the second principal challenge at independence. Africans inherited states without nations. To successor élite groups fell the task of moulding weakly integrated territories into coherent national political communities. Colonial states were born of conquest and negotiations among imperial powers, and thus involved the haphazard and often brutal amalgamation of diverse communities within artificial boundaries. Coercion rather than consent was the operative principle of rule over subject populations. Colonial administrations were averse to the emergence of national political institutions under the tutelage of emerging urban-based indigenous middle classes. They were also reluctant to elevate "natives" to high posts in central administrations, preferring to administer the largely rural populations through indirect rule (a system Mamdani evocatively labels "decentralized despotism"; Mamdani

1997; Young 1994). Hence, pre-existing or newly invented traditional leaders often served as the local anchors of colonial authority. Indirect rule permitted colonial powers to administer vast territories with small corps of European officials; the result, however, was a mode of governance that stimulated ethnic divisions and consciousness by parcelling Africans into "tribes" for administrative convenience. Ethnic identities were further reinforced by the regionally uneven impact of new economic opportunities (through the cultivation of cash crops, for example) and uneven regional access to Western-style education. Hence, both uneven development and colonial administrative practices sharpened ethnic divisions. When competing indigenous élite groups vied to inherit control of the colonial states in the era of decolonization, they discovered that appeals to ethnic identities were a potent means of mobilizing support (Berman 1998: 312–333; Boone 1994; 109–119; Eyoh 1999: 268–278).

Following independence, governments gravitated to a state-led and élite-managed development strategy. Members of the local intelligentsia regarded themselves as the natural heirs of colonial states, and the state as the main instrument of their control and socio-economic progress. This approach accorded closely with the tenets of post-war paradigms of development, whether socialist or capitalist. At a time when Keynesian theory held sway, state intervention to correct market imperfections, mobilize domestic savings, and guide the development of human capital and technological change was regarded as essential (Toye 1993). In addition, Western-educated élite groups charged themselves with the task of promoting national integration and state-building in a top-down style. Students of comparative politics had, by the late 1960s, largely accepted the rationale of these élite groups for authoritarian regimes in developing societies. An advocacy of "strong states," capable of guaranteeing political order, replaced the earlier hopes of democratic development (Grendzier 1985; O'Brien 1979). Western powers, to defend their strategic interests in cold-war struggles, were quite prepared to support friendly dictatorial governments, in Africa as elsewhere.

During the 1960s and early 1970s, state-led and top-down development proved moderately successful. Sub-Saharan economies, in general, achieved steady (if unspectacular) economic growth. As table 8.1 reveals, this region's GDP per capita expanded at an annual rate of 3 per cent in this period. This aggregate statistic, of course, obscures annual and country variations in economic performance. Sub-Saharan Africa accounted for six of ten countries which experienced no growth (Senegal, Chad, Sudan, Madagascar, Niger, and Somalia), whereas five African countries featured among the world's 20 fastest-growing economies (Swaziland, Botswana, Côte d'Ivoire, Lesotho, Gabon, and Togo, with Kenya ranked twenty-first) (Rodrik 1999: 68–69). In addition, the degree

Table 8.1 Africa: Basic macroeconomic indicators, 1965–1996 (percentage increase per annum)

| Indicator | 1965–1973 | 1974–1979 | 1980–1985 | 1986–1990 | 1991–1995 | 1996 |
|---|---|---|---|---|---|---|
| Population | 2.7 | 2.9 | 3.0 | 3.0 | 3.0 | 3.0 |
| GDP growth | 5.7 | 3.5 | 2.1 | 2.8 | 1.7 | 4.8 |
| GDP percentage growth | 3.0 | 0.7 | −0.8 | −0.1 | −1.2 | 2.0 |
| Agriculture | 2.7 | 3.0 | 1.9 | 4.0 | 1.9 | 6.9 |
| Manufacturing | 7.3 | 6.7 | 3.6 | 3.4 | 0.5 | 3.2 |
| Export growth | 8.2 | 2.6 | 1.0 | 6.2 | 6.1 | 7.1 |
| Import growth | 7.4 | 6.2 | 2.5 | 6.8 | 6.1 | 7.1 |

Source: Mkandawire and Soludo 1999: 7; Mlambo and Oshikoya 1999: 29.

of economic diversification varied among countries. Foreign investment in manufacturing was insignificant in all but a handful of countries (South Africa, Nigeria, Kenya, Côte d'Ivoire). Economic nationalism spurred governments throughout the region to invest directly in production through state-owned corporations, and/or to subsidize and protect favoured indigenous producers (Adedeji 1981: 15–41, 383–394).

The first two decades of independence also witnessed significant investments in infrastructure and social services, especially education. Although Africa continued to lag behind other developing regions, primary and post-secondary education expanded at an impressive rate. Between 1965 and 1985, primary-school enrolments rose from 41 per cent of the eligible population to 68 per cent, while enrolments in post-secondary institutions increased at a similar pace (Mkandawire and Soludo 1999: 16). Tertiary education also grew steadily, although with low enrolments in the natural sciences and science-based professions such as engineering and medicine (Brautigam 1996: 92–93).

The top-down, statist approach served political as well as economic ends. Nation-state building strategies often degenerated into desperate attempts on the part of the governing élite to centralize and consolidate their political power. At independence, attention shifted from a common struggle to end colonial rule to competition within the élite for control of the successor states. In the ensuing power struggle, élite groups tried to mobilize ethnoregional constituencies. This pattern of political competition was fostered, if not predetermined, by prevailing socio-economic structures. Not only did the limited class differentiation discourage politicians from relying on workers or other classes for support, but the grouping of the preponderantly rural populations in ethnically demarcated constituencies encouraged ethnic appeals. Opposition to the incumbent government, therefore, usually assumed the form of communally based challenges. In response, new regimes expanded and personalized state power, co-opted rivals, and often violently repressed both dissenters and nascent civil societies. Patron–client networks, sutured by ties of kinship and community, emerged as the political foundation of state–society relations.

State-led economic development, coupled with this neo-patrimonial strategy of regime/state consolidation, spawned social differentiation and regional inequality. By the mid-1970s, income inequality in this region ranked second only to that of Latin America (World Bank 2000c). The vast income gap between upper- and lower-level public-sector employees, and between employees in the modern sector and non-waged urban and rural groups, accounted in part for this inequality (Nafziger 1984: 21–34). In addition, the small private sector grew wealthy because of its access to state-controlled resources. Senior civil servants filled the ranks of the post-colonial entrepreneurial élite in countries such as Côte d'Ivoire (Rapley 1993), Nigeria (Forrest 1994), and Kenya (Himbara 1994), which welcomed the growth of indigenous private enterprise. The economic gulf between the rural and urban people was widened by the excessive taxation of agricultural producers and by the urban bias of public and private investment. Women, especially rural women, composed the majority of the poor because of discriminatory cultural attitudes, including unequal access to education. Finally, historical regional inequalities persisted because post-colonial regimes failed to transform colonial economic structures. These spatial inequalities, which often coincided with ethnic boundaries, reinforced inter-ethnic tensions.

During the "Golden Years" of capitalism (1950–1975), the rapidly expanding global economy and the concomitant strong demand for primary commodities stimulated modest economic success. However, even then, several factors impeded substantial economic progress. Since African economies were dependent on rain-fed peasant production, they remained vulnerable to external shocks such as negative climatic changes and lower international commodity prices. Dependence on external forces was further exacerbated by import-substitution industrialization (ISI), the viability of which ultimately depended on primary resource exports to finance the needed imports of machinery, inputs, and management. Manufacturing was also limited by small domestic markets for consumer goods and weak linkages to other sectors. Restrictions on the quantity of imports and overvalued currencies, as well as other measures intended to protect infant industries, created inefficiency. Although ISI made sense as an initial stage, no policies encouraged shifts to export-oriented manufacturing and the development of domestic technological capabilities. Agriculture also suffered reversals: agricultural growth by the mid-1970s tumbled below the rate of population growth, owing to high levels of taxation on farmers and the paucity of public investments to improve the productivity of smallholders.

After 1975, most economies declined. In the second half of the 1970s, GDP per capita growth fell to less than 1 per cent annually. Moreover, the "lost decade" (1980s) witnessed Africa's GDP per capita decline annually by rates of up to 1 per cent, with the notable exceptions of Botswana, Lesotho, and Mauritius; this growth rate was well below the average of other developing regions. In the early 1990s, the negative growth trend worsened: per capita GDP declined by an annual average of 1.8 per cent while the growth differential between this region and other developing regions widened to 6.2 per cent (Collier and Gunning, cited in Mkandawire and Soludo 1999: 7). Economic collapse magnified Africa's marginality in the global economy. Between 1975 and 1990, the region's share of agricultural and food exports as a percentage of developing-country exports, and its share of manufactured goods, machines, and equipment exports as a proportion of developing-country exports, plummeted from 21 per cent to approximately 8 per cent, and from 7.8 per cent to 1.1 per cent, respectively (Sahn, Dorosh, and Younger 1997: 3–6). This downward economic trend affected self-proclaimed socialist states (Congo-Brazzaville, Madagascar, Tanzania, etc.) as well as capitalist-oriented states such as Kenya and Côte d'Ivoire – countries which were then regarded as African examplars of "developmental states."

The causes of this economic crisis were several. Despite disagreement on the weight to be attributed to domestic and external factors, analysts agree that exogenous shocks played a significant role. These factors included severe droughts (in 1973, the early 1980s, and again in the 1990s), coupled with negative international economic circumstances such as hikes in oil prices (1973 and 1979), the global recession of the late 1970s and the ensuing decline in demand for primary commodities, and rising interest rates. African governments' inability or unwillingness to implement countervailing policies exaggerated the negative effects of these external shocks. For example, faced with declining export earnings and rising international interest rates, most countries increased external borrowing to finance both rising oil bills and food imports. Indeed, the few countries such as Botswana, Lesotho, and Mauritius that maintained a high growth path appeared to have succeeded because they implemented measures that ensured a quick return to macroeconomic stability (Rodrik 1999: 105–107).

In addition, the weaknesses of African states contributed to economic decline. That politics is a prime domestic factor in the origins of economic crisis is widely accepted. Political shortcomings, which stemmed from institutional weaknesses inherited from colonial rule, were reinforced by the mode of neo-patrimonial regime consolidation. Effective developmental states were, and remain, rare in Africa, because they demand an unusual combination of features: a professional and autonomous bureaucratic administration; a social embeddedness of political leaders and bureaucrats who exercise considerable discretion; and a singular commitment to national development on the part of governments, bureaucrats, and the populace (Evans 1992). Not surprisingly, few states achieved these exacting requirements.

State deficiencies were manifested in numerous ways, ranging from inefficiency and instability to corruption. As bureaucracies ballooned to cater to expanding state functions, they were rapidly Africanized; inexperienced personnel in managerial positions undermined administrative efficiency. Even more damaging to the developmental capacity of states was the personalization of power and the use of state institutions as the main means of social regulation. Political loyalty to ruling élite groups, not merit, became the criterion for advancement. Erasing the divide between politics and public administration permitted short-term political expedience to shape public policy. Organized interest groups, which could have anchored national development strategies, failed to gain influence. Relations between the political and business élite, for example, were characterized by ambivalence: the political élite were wary that the business élite might use "private" wealth to undermine their power; the dependence of the business élite on states rendered their economic interests vulnerable to political caprice. Safeguarding one's business interests turned on maintaining good personal relations with incumbent regimes or having the "right" persons in control of the state (Throup and Hornsby 1998: 7–46). Lastly, regimes were prone to instability, which in turn discouraged investment and lowered the rate of growth. Governmental legitimacy was always tenuous, given their composition – multiethnic coalitions of élite groups cemented by patron–client networks (see e.g. Berman 1998: 332–341; Chabal 1992: 136–142; Eyoh 1999: 283–294). As patronage played a central role in the acquisition and maintenance of power and goods, regimes alienated groups that were excluded from the spoils.

Economic and political crises thus reinforced each other. Lacking the resources to finance neo-patrimonial networks, ruling élite groups intensified repression to maintain their grip on power. The resulting attenuation of the limited social accountability of these regimes kindled a growing hostility to authoritarianism among mainly urban groups; they blamed economic hardships on the abuse of power by the ruling élite groups. The end of the 1980s and early 1990s saw this hostility culminate in the rise of urban-based pro-democracy movements.

## Era of economic and political adjustment, 1981–2000

Led by the IMF and the World Bank, the Western powers' response to Africa's crisis has taken the form of structural-adjustment programmes. These programmes initially required fiscal and monetary policies to reduce inflation and budget deficits, wide-ranging market-oriented reforms, and an opening of economies to foreign trade and investment. Their scope, however, has continually broadened since adjustment's inception in 1981 – to embrace measures to rehabilitate infrastructure, privatize state-owned corporations, alleviate poverty ("social dimensions of adjustment"), foster human capital, restructure financial institutions, enhance state capacity, and improve governance and the rule of law. Consequently, the time horizon for successful adjustment has steadily lengthened.

One legacy of this lengthy crisis is an acceptance on the part of Africa's policy makers and intellectuals of the need for new approaches to development. Economic nationalist ideology no longer appeals: African intellectual opinion is now aligned with the new neo-liberal ideology – at least to the extent of rejecting heavily state-led development, loose monetary and fiscal policy, and arbitrary governance, and of acknowledging the indispensability of macroeconomic stability and market mechanisms (Ndulu and van de Walle 1996: 3–31). However, this agreement has not dampened criticisms of the effectiveness of Western-sponsored adjustment policies and political reform since the early 1980s.

According to the predominant assessment, structural-adjustment programmes have enjoyed only limited success or have failed outright, especially in light of the extraordinary level of external financial support (Collier and Gunning 1997; Killick 1998; Mkandawire and Soludo 1999, 2000). Stabilization measures certainly slowed the downward economic spiral from the mid-1980s through the mid-1990s. Although adjustment measures have contributed to the restoration of a modicum of macroeconomic stability, their impact has been uneven across countries, time, and sectors. Reforms have been most effective in the liberalization of prices and foreign-exchange regimes; progress in fiscal adjustment and institutional reforms (especially the privatization of state enterprises) has been limited.

In the mid-1990s, sub-Saharan economies at last grew modestly, posting an average 2 per cent increase in per capita GDP (table 9.1). However, the long-term sustainability of macroeconomic growth and stability is not guaranteed, predicated as they are on levels of aid that shrank after 1995. This resumption of growth (at least until the 1997–1998 East Asian economic collapse) has failed to reverse the widening performance gap between this region and other developing regions. A common justification for liberalization was the need to create an economic environment that would attract foreign investors; however, a foreign investment boom has not occurred, despite the apparent lure of higher rates of return on investments.[2] Structural-adjustment programmes have also done little to improve the weak production structures, high external dependency, and institutional weaknesses that are at the root of African economies' slow growth. As well, the negative social and economic impact of adjustment reforms has impeded nation-state building because central governments cannot deliver essential social services and hope of progress to the people.

Poverty rates have not improved much. Even the most optimistic analysts are hard pressed to deny that reforms have done little to improve the precarious welfare of most people. Sahn and associates (Sahn, Dorosh, and Younger, 1997), for example, report that these policies had achieved, by the mid-1990s, a neutral effect on, or had led to a slight (1 per cent) increase in, the incomes of rural producers – those who comprise the most vulnerable population segment. In the cities the picture is even bleaker, as poverty has intensified and the middle class is forced into the expanding ranks of the near poor. The factors contributing to this process include job losses from the closure or privatization of state enterprises; the contraction of state budgets; and the rising cost of living due to currency devaluations, the removal of subsidies on social services, and the elimination of price controls. Poverty is, of course, created by factors other than national policy – natural resource endowments, inequalities in assets among social groups, shifts in international prices, political instability, and civil strife. The precise contribution of structural-adjustment policies to the suffering of the African people is, therefore, not easy to ascertain.

State rehabilitation has also not proceeded far. State capacity-building measures are intended to enhance a state's institutional capability to design and implement policy. Yet state capacity, like the related and equally nebulous concept of governance, is multidimensional, the outcome of a long-term historical process (Brautigam 1996: 83–84). Under structural adjustment, bureaucracies' limited technical capabilities have been addressed through administrative reforms (concerning the selection, promotion, and remuneration of employees) and training. The negligible success is understandable, in light of the extensive problems plaguing African states. For example, socio-economic conditions since the 1970s have devastated public employees' morale and productivity. The tightening of state budgets, coupled with other components of adjustment programmes, have diminished the purchasing power of civil servants. In response, many of them have redirected their energies to alternative sources of income, including corruption. The most skilled and experienced among them continue to desert the civil service for lucrative opportunities in consultancy, the expanding NGO sector, and foreign countries. The vast gulf in salaries and perquisites between local bureaucrats and the burgeoning number of foreign technical advisors, together with the exclusion of the former from policy-making, have fuelled the demoralization of public-sector employees (see e.g. Brautigam 1996: 86–88; Mkandawire and Soludo 1999: 76–77).

The late 1980s and early 1990s witnessed the mushrooming of pro-democracy movements across Africa, a sudden and largely unanticipated development. This process has been shaped by a confluence of domestic and international forces. At the domestic level, pro-democracy movements were fostered by economic decline and the subsequent weakening of neo-patrimonial systems. At the international level, a new global order, that not only is hostile to dictatorial rule but also regards democracy as an integral precursor to development, was spawned by various factors. These included the implosion of the Soviet Union and Eastern European communist regimes and the rise of anti-authoritarian movements across the developing world. The post-cold-war erosion of sub-Saharan Africa's former geo-strategic importance permitted Western powers to spurn friendly dictators. The World Bank and the donors have, therefore, felt free to stipulate political reform as another condition of aid, or at least to abandon their tacit support for repressive client regimes.

Donors assisted in the construction of democracy in several ways. The dominant development model adopts a limited, procedural conception of democracy. It is a system of rule in which periodic multiparty elections are the mechanism for the selection of political leaders and in which the respect of certain basic rights prevails. Hence, since 1990, the Western governments and international development institutions have promoted democracy by aiding multiparty elections, the buttressing of the rule of law, and the strengthening of civil society through the funding of NGOs. Support for NGOs as the bastion of civil society is cast in the rhetoric of empowerment. These associations will, it is hoped, circumvent the degraded state apparatus to deliver social services and development directly to deserving clients; as well, they will fortify the organizational infrastructure of democratic participation and accountability.

Democratic experiments have varied in their timing and depth, reflecting different historical traditions and objective conditions. Democratic consolidation, if it occurs, is inevitably a lengthy and tumultuous process. Democracy, as Richard Sklar (1987) reminds us, does not emerge in pure form: democratic values, institutions, and practices evolve discontinuously, with progress in some spheres not matched by progress in others. None the less, the euphoria that greeted the rebirth of multi-party elections had largely dissipated by the end of the 1990s. Although multiparty electoral competitions have redefined the context of élite competition for power, successive cycles of elections in the 1990s have not altered inequalities of power, whether structured by class, gender, region, or ethnicity. These elections have, moreover, confirmed the resilience of neo-patrimonial networks as the institutional foundation of political power (Bratton and van de Walle 1997; Sandbrook 2000: chap. 2).

Western governments and international development institutions both facilitate and impede democratization. By the early 1980s, most African states were bankrupt (or close to it). They have been propped up by infusions of aid that long ago ceased to be considered a discretionary item in state budgets. Indeed, aid in the 1980s and 1990s accounted for virtually all investments in infrastructure and social services in many sub-Saharan countries. In return, Western governments and international development agencies have demanded economic and political reform. In most cases, the political élite have bent to some restraints on their power. However, they have also used the aid to refurbish patronage networks, resisting popular demands for more substantive changes in the distribution of political power. Heightened aid dependency thus serves to reinforce the historical lack of accountability of African governments (Chabal and Deloze 1999: 111–118; Moore 1998: 102–109). Minor democratic concessions more often reflect the need to comply with the new requirements of the international aid regime than the desire to appease the citizens, whose actual contribution to state coffers is often low.

Post-colonial regimes have depended on patron–client networks to maintain power. Differences in ideologies and policies have mattered less in shaping political loyalties than the distribution of material rewards, often to individuals and groups bound by ties of kinship and community. The ability of leaders to represent these constituencies effectively is the main criterion for the public's evaluation of their political representatives. For many analysts, the much-touted resurgence of civil society and the aid-driven proliferation of NGOs was the fountain of hope for democratic transitions in Africa. However, civil associations have been inconsequential in political life: like opposition parties, they have failed to offer visions of alternative futures (see e.g. Sandbrook and Oelbaum 1997; Widner 1997: 65–81).[3] Infatuated with power, opposition leaders succumb to factional rivalries and co-optation by government. This self-serving behaviour, together with the opposition's failure to follow through with populist promises on the rare occasions that they displace incumbent regimes, have soured popular enthusiasm for opposition politics.

However, it is the resurgence of ethnoregional conflict that most threatens national cohesion and the prospects for democratic development. Of special significance are two overarching and related factors: the élite's predisposition to political manipulation of cultural differences, and the endurance of "kinship ... as the most significant local principle of social organization" in African society (Eriksen 1999: 60). Accustomed to ruling without popular mandate, élite groups are compelled by multiparty politics to seek the support of ordinary citizens. Appeals to kinship and communal solidarity become the quickest path to success. The freer political environment exposes politicians to the long-repressed grievances of those who had lost out in the post-independence distribution of the spoils. Although many of these grievances are legitimate, they provide fertile soil for ambitious political leaders. Furthermore, citizens had retreated into kinship and ethnic networks to cope with economic adversity and escape state-sanctioned violence that followed the collapse of post-independence nation-state building projects (Chazan and Azarya 1988; MacGaffey 1987; Rothchild and Chazan 1988). In sum, ordinary people see the effective political representative as someone who can access state resources for individual and community benefit.

The outcome of these attitudes and behaviours is a fraying of state authority and accountability and the weakness of a sense of national purpose. A sense of kinship is central to African conceptions of selfhood. Identification with ethnocultural communities is often more highly valued by people than the abstractions of national citizenship.

The consolidation of democratic and effective states therefore poses, as necessary conditions, two long-term challenges. One is the forging of multi-ethnic approaches to nation-building that separate the sense of citizenship from nationality. The other task, no less important, is to nurture institutional arrangements that balance the expression of local communities' political values and traditions, on the one hand, against the universal political and civil rights of individual citizens, on the other. Needless to say, in countries where neo-patrimonial governance prevails, shifting the rules of political engagement in these directions will require nothing less than the concerted action of enlightened leadership and patriotic civil associations over many years. To substitute a virtuous circle of political development and economic growth for the existing vicious circle demands a herculean effort.

Adjustment has focused on the reform of national economic and political processes. Many of these reforms, though attainable only in the longer term, make good sense in light of the prevailing conditions. Globalization, however, poses a further set of challenges; this process, too, needs adjustment to create a propitious external environment for just development, in Africa as elsewhere.

## Adjusting globalization

According to pragmatic neo-liberals, globalization is not only an irreversible outcome of technological progress but also an impetus to improved economic performance. Opening up economies will augment developing countries' growth, it is argued, which in turn will reduce poverty and improve living standards (World Bank 2000a: 3). In the words of the associate director of the IMF's Africa Department:

Globalization is proceeding inexorably and sub-Saharan Africa must decide how to live in a more complex and more competitive world ... Africa has little to lose from globalization ... and much to gain, provided it is accompanied by policy changes in several areas. (Hernández-Catá 1999: 11)

This assertion is dubious on both counts. The first doubtful proposition concerns the benefits that the prevailing form of globalization – neo-liberal globalization[4] – allegedly offers Africa, after one or two decades of progressive trade, investment, and capital-account liberalization. Ironically, one reason for scepticism stems from a book subtitled *Making Openness Work*, the analysis of Harvard economist Dani Rodrik (1999). Rodrik contends that Africans, like everyone else, can benefit from opening up their economies. Even "export pessimism" is unwarranted, he claims; not even the region's weak infrastructure, unfortunate geographical features, or reliance on a limited number of primary products will hold Africa back if its governments correct policy errors (overvalued currencies, high trade restrictions, etc.) and maintain the policy and institutional "fundamentals" (Rodrik 1999: 104–105). Yet the terms of Rodrik's argument actually lead to a more pessimistic conclusion than that which he offers. Essentially, he argues that openness offers potential benefits to all participants – imports of technology, capital goods, foreign savings, ideas, and institutions – but that their achievement requires governments to adopt a set of complementary policy and institutional reforms. These reforms are crucial, he states, because openness also introduces heavy potential costs – growing social inequalities, the marginalization of some groups, and local turbulence and insecurity occasioned by external shocks. To control these destabilizing side-effects and thereby reap the benefits of globalization, governments must scrupulously construct macroeconomic stability, attractive investment conditions, and "sound" institutions of conflict management. The last institutional condition – essentially, complex democratic and judicial systems and safety nets – is needed to channel peacefully the strains and conflicts inevitably generated by global markets.

Thus, African countries will benefit from neo-liberal globalization only if they possess what most of them manifestly lack – sound institutions. Rodrik's case suffers from an overly voluntaristic cast: if sound institutions are needed, then governments must provide them. But institutions cannot simply be willed into existence; they are generally the outcome of lengthy struggles. It is significant that all of Rodrik's African "success" cases are micro-states – Mauritius, Botswana, Lesotho, Swaziland, Seychelles – where conflicts can be managed and accommodations made through face-to-face interactions. In contrast, virtually all of Africa's large countries, excluding South Africa, are convulsed by disorder and instability. This pattern is not accidental; it reflects the greater challenges of nation-state building in large, heterogeneous countries.

To premise the benefits of globalization on strong institutions is implicitly to accept that populations lacking such institutions will derive few advantages from it, at least in the decades required for them to forge such institutions. But why must societies and governments do all the adjusting to global economic forces? Simply allowing global markets to determine the allocation of resources is unlikely to solve Africa's problems. Why should not market forces themselves be adjusted, via international treaties, to suit better the needs of people throughout the world, including Africans in particular? Unregulated global markets should not be treated as a given. Since they produce such negative tendencies as growing inequalities, increased insecurity, and turbulence, globally negotiated rules should limit these pernicious trends. This project may be labelled a "social-democratic" globalization.[5]

Certainly, the deepening integration of Africa's economies into the global market system since the early 1980s has not yet promoted much development. Africa, with some exceptions, has accrued very few benefits from global integration, and its economic prospects remain bleak. The gap in per capita incomes between the richest countries with one-fifth of the world's population and the poorest countries with an equal population share (including most of sub-Saharan Africa) has yawned wider – from 30 to 1 in 1960, to 60 to 1 in 1990, and to 74 to 1 in 1999 – and is still widening (Jolly 1999: 5). In sub-Saharan Africa, the number of people living on less than a dollar a day grew by almost 50 million between 1990 and 1998, with the poor population constituting just under half of the region's population in 1998 (World Bank 2000b).

Benefits, such as they are, have come largely in the form of aid and the promise of debt relief. Foreign aid might act as a mechanism to offset the growing inequalities on a North–South basis and to assist marginalized groups. Africa has received ample aid, although experts question its effectiveness (Lancaster 1999). Official Development Assistance in 1997 represented 12.4 per cent of sub-Saharan Africa's GNP, whereas it represented only 1.1 per cent for all low- and middle-income countries combined (*Economist* 13 March 1999). Many countries were heavily dependent on aid: for instance, aid accounted for 37 per cent of GDP in Mozambique and 13 per cent in Uganda and Tanzania. Sub-Saharan governments have had to rely on official sources of credit because private banks have been unwilling to lend to countries with threatening debt overhangs, bleak economic prospects, and unstable governments.

Aid, however, has declined, as have development grants from NGOs. Total aid to all recipients, which peaked at $59.6 billion in 1994, stood at $49.7 billion in 1998 (OECD 1999). The United States registered the sharpest reduction in 1996–1997 – 28 per cent – which reduced its contribution to only 0.09 per cent of its GNP. Japan, the largest donor, announced a cut of 10 per cent in 1998, although some of the funds were later restored. Only the Scandinavian countries and the Netherlands continued to devote at least 0.7 per cent of their GNP to aid transfers. Aid to sub-Saharan Africa remained constant at about $17.3 billion between 1990 and 1995, but then declined sharply – by almost $4 billion over two years (World Bank 1999b: table 12-1). Not only are Western governments unlikely to restore earlier aid levels, but a growing share of existing aid is devoted to handling burgeoning emergency relief efforts in Central America, Eastern Europe, and Asia, as well as in Africa.

Debt relief is a necessary condition for economic recovery in Africa.[6] By the 1990s, many sub-Saharan countries were insolvent, in the sense that they were unable to service their debts. Therefore, external debts were periodically rolled over, thereby compounding the long-term problem by expanding the capital owed. Thirty-three sub-Saharan countries were classified as Highly Indebted Poor Countries (HIPCs) in 1998; these countries struggled to service their debts by curtailing expenditures in infrastructure, health, education, and other key services. High debt burdens also discouraged private investors.

In 1996 the donors agreed on a debt-relief scheme, but this plan delivered limited benefits to few beneficiaries. Highly indebted countries required six years of consistent market reform to qualify, and even then received only enough relief to reduce their external debts to twice their export earnings. Only Uganda and Bolivia had benefited somewhat from the scheme by 1998. Massive demonstrations organized by a coalition of civil associations (Jubilee 2000) at the G-7 summit of industrial countries[7] in Birmingham in 1998 and the G-8 Finance Ministers' meeting in 1999 pressed for more substantial debt relief as a key to recovery in the poorest countries. This protest apparently succeeded: in June 1999, the G-8 agreed to a debt-relief package said to be worth $50 billion. Countries eligible for debt relief expanded from 29 to 36, most of them in Africa, and the qualifying time for debt relief was reduced to three years (*Guardian Weekly* 20 June 1999).

Jubilee 2000 supporters, however, argued that the new deal was only a slight improvement. Almost half of the advertised $50 billion cost of the initiative involved writing off irretrievable debts. Moreover, those who received aid under the agreement would still be expected to devote as much as one-fifth of government revenue to debt service. Debt relief, in any case, has been slow to materialize. The 1999 initiative stalled in early 2000, owing to Japanese indifference, the US Congress' refusal of President Clinton's request for full funding of the US share of the HIPC Trust Fund, and the EU's unwillingness to release its major contribution until the United States complied.

In light of Africa's continuing debt burden and declining aid, virtually all commentaries agree that foreign trade must be Africa's main engine of growth (see e.g. Sharer 1999). Export-led development, however, has not fulfilled its promise. Sub-Saharan Africa's share of world trade has steadily declined over 40 years – from 3.1 per cent of world merchandise exports in 1955 to just 1.2 per cent in 1990 (Yeats et al. 1996: 38). By 1997, the entire continent of Africa accounted for a lesser share of the world's exports than Belgium (2.3 per cent against 3 per cent) (World Trade Organization 1999). Further, in 1998, Africa's exports fell by 15 per cent over the previous year, as a result of the East Asian financial collapse. Africa's weak export position will probably continue because the region's comparative advantage, owing to its relatively abundant natural resources and its scarcity of skilled workers, lies in agricultural and mineral production and related unskilled activities (Helleiner 1997: 69).

The long-term market prospects for Africa's traditional primary exports are bleak, however. According to the World Bank's projections, real non-oil commodity prices will fall by an average 2 per cent per annum over the period 1995–2005. Tropical beverages, which contribute more than a third of total exports in 10 African countries, will see price declines of 5–6 per cent per annum. World Bank data suggest that these projections were on target: the unit value of sub-Saharan exports had fallen by 1998 to 86 from an index of 100 in 1995 (World Bank: 1999b). Further, commodity exports lack dynamism because "unskilled labour-intensive activities can be a technological 'dead-end', unconducive to the productivity enhancement and indigenous learning upon which development is now generally believed to depend" (Helleiner 1997: 69).

Global trade rules have recently created further impediments to African development (Mshomba 2000). The Uruguay Round of GATT and the WTO have not favoured African interests. Trade rules have limited the preferences that the region has enjoyed under the EU's Lomé Convention and the Generalized System of Preferences, and barred significant protection of infant industries. Furthermore, the North, and the EU in particular, have been allowed to prolong high tariffs on textiles and agricultural imports that compete with local production – as well as cascading tariffs that rise the higher the value added to imports (Dunkley 2000; Kaplan and Kaplinsky 1999). In March 2000, the WTO, the IMF, and the World Bank proposed the removal of tariffs on exports from the world's 48 least-developed countries; this initiative, however, was blocked by the Clinton Administration, which feared endangering US producers of textiles, clothing, shoes, and agricultural products (*New York Times* 9 April 2000). How then will an export orientation spur sustained growth in Africa? Considering the limited development of non-traditional exports during 15 years of adjustment (Helleiner 1997: 67–68), one cannot be sanguine that Africa will reap gains from international trade, even in the longer term.

Sub-Saharan Africa also did not experience a major increase in foreign investment until the mid-1990s, despite the fact that many governments had undertaken policy and institutional reforms in the 1980s to attract investment (Helleiner 1997: 78–81). Foreign direct investment, which fell to an abysmal 1 per cent of the developing countries' share in the 1980s (Anonymous 1992: 51), stagnated in the early 1990s. At its high point in 1997, FDI had risen sixfold (to $5.2 billion) from its 1990 level, while gross portfolio investment had grown from an outflow of $31 million in 1990 to a respectable $1.2 billion inflow in 1997 (World Bank 1999c). The following year, however, panicked investors withdrew their funds from all emerging markets in the wake of the East Asian and Russian financial crises. New investments, moreover, have flowed largely to South Africa and Nigeria and mainly into the mining and petroleum sectors. Despite periodic panics, foreign investors perceive superior opportunities in East Asia, Central Europe, and Latin America. Investors still regard Africa as a risky place in which to do business. The thinness of capital markets in sub-Saharan countries, together with capital-account liberalization, suggest that portfolio investments in Africa will be as volatile and disruptive as in other developing regions.

How can one claim that Africa has "little to lose, and much to gain" from this pattern of globalization? Neo-liberal globalization is unlikely to generate sustained growth in that region. As even billionaire Ted Turner notes: "[e]ven as communications, transportation and technology are driving global economic expansion headway on, poverty is not keeping pace. It is as if globalization is in fast forward, and the world's ability to react to it is in slow motion" (UNDP *Human Development Report 1999*).

If it is true that "globalization is proceeding inexorably" (Hernandez-Catá 1999), then those who suffer high costs and few advantages from the global economy have no alternative but to adjust to its harsh imperatives. This second neo-liberal claim also appears dubious. There are two contending perspectives on globalization (Friedman and Ramonet 1999: 110–127). One is the technological–determinist perspective that globalization is driven by unstoppable forces of technology – information processing, satellite communications, fibre optics, digitalization, rapid transport, and the Internet. The other viewpoint sees neo-liberal globalization as a societal choice that technological developments have facilitated, though not determined. We follow this view that the new global economy, far from being an inexorable outcome of technological change, has been *constructed*, largely by means of negotiated intergovernmental agreements; in principle, therefore, it can be reconstructed to suit human needs better, in Africa and throughout the world. Although space does not permit us to establish this position, our argument must reject the claim that there are no alternatives to the prevailing global order (Boswell and Chase-Dunn 2000; Korten 1999; Martin and Schumann 1997).

African countries and their global allies *do*, in principle, have options other than adjusting their economies and societies to the exigencies of competition within a global free-market economy. The options are not the neat dichotomy of globalization or protectionism, as they are often portrayed; rather, the choice is that of neo-liberal globalization or a more regulated form of global integration – social-democratic globalization. This pattern involves reconstructing the rules of global economic exchange to minimize the destructive side-effects of unregulated markets: to reduce the massive international and intranational inequalities, to tame the turbulence and insecurity created by footloose capital, to halt the competitive devaluation of national environmental standards, and to protect basic labour standards. Because the most powerful states are aligned with neo-liberal policies, this alternative will depend on the forcefulness of a transnationally organized protest movement.

Such a movement has, in fact, gathered momentum since the early 1990s through a variety of effective campaigns: the "50 Years is Enough" campaign directed at the Bretton Woods Institutions in the mid-1990s; the coalition against the Multilateral Agreement on Investment (1998); Jubilee 2000's programme on debt relief for the HIPCs (1998–2000); the protests in 1999, 2000, and 2001 against the WTO, the World Bank and IMF, and the Asian Development Bank; and the various environmental and health actions, especially those directed against genetically modified food. Although this diverse group of organizations and protesters do not adhere to a unified agenda, they share a common antipathy to the sway of untrammelled global market forces. This protest is likely to gain momentum in the context of a global economic "bust" or environmental calamity. Faced with xenophobic–protectionist demands, the regulatory-market approach of a social-democratic globalization may appeal even to the avid free-traders of the US Congress.

## Conclusions

Although the rhetoric of pragmatic neo-liberalism is "people-friendly," it retains its "fierce" neo-classical core (Sen 1997: 533). Since 1990, the World Bank and the IMF have adopted a broader and gentler approach, which reflects the meagre success of their development doctrine in the first decade of adjustment. Faced with growing criticisms from both the right and the left, including proposals to downsize or abolish both agencies, the Bretton Woods institutions repositioned themselves. The World Bank reinvented itself as a champion of the world's poor in the early 1990s, and the IMF followed suit after its bungling of the East Asian financial crisis in 1997–1998: the latter's Enhanced Structural Adjustment Facility, for instance, was reborn as the Poverty Reduction and Growth Facility in early 2000. Both organizations undertook to build partnerships with recipient governments, opinion leaders, and NGOs; to enhance participation in the design of adjustment programmes; to augment human capital; and to address problems of governance, corruption, and human rights. Nevertheless, the dominant doctrine – although kinder, gentler, and more complex – did not abandon the core principles of the earlier Washington Consensus, which assumes that the greater good is served by adjusting firms, governments, employees, farmers, and citizens in general to the exigencies of competition within increasingly deregulated and global markets. The pragmatic extensions of neo-liberalism, therefore, supplemented this core notion: they presented neo-liberalism with a human face.

But will pragmatic neo-liberalism prove people-friendly? Neo-liberal policies and institutional reforms aim to engineer a capitalist transformation in developing countries. The early stages of these transformations typically involve intense exploitation, inequality, and oppression. The poor may eventually gain, as capital accumulation augments employment opportunities and this process, in turn, builds demand for agricultural and mass-consumption goods – the "trickle-down" effect.

Neo-liberalism offers the African peasantry, for example, the prospect of increased vulnerability and dislocation. A characteristic feature of African agriculture is the preponderance of smallholders who possess, not freehold title but communal rights to use land and transfer such rights to their children. This system of communal land-tenure maintains not only a considerable degree of equality in the countryside of most sub-Saharan countries but also an anchor for a set of reciprocal arrangements that provide "safety nets" for members (Mkandawire and Soludo 1999: 113–114). To disrupt these arrangements by creating private property in land is to heighten the vulnerability of rural populations. Such a transformation may also sow political instability and violence in some regions, as conflicts instigated by overlapping traditional rights pit one clan or ethnic group against another. Conflict between "indigenes" and "strangers" have flared in various countries, notably in Northern Ghana and the Rift Valley of Kenya in the past few years. Yet neo-liberals seek to create a land market, on the grounds that communal land-tenure impedes agricultural production. Private landownership will allow innovative rural entrepreneurs to accumulate land, to secure credit for investment in their land, and thus to raise agricultural productivity.

Although pragmatic neo-liberalism intends to ease the pain of this and other adjustments to market exigencies, it is doubtful this strategy has the means to accomplish this goal. Not only do underfunded safety nets reach few individuals in societies where half or more of its members are poor, but the priority placed on balanced budgets squeezes the resources available for productivity-enhancing public education and health care. One 1999 survey of 16 African countries following IMF prescriptions discovered that 12 had *cut* their spending on basic education (*Globe & Mail* [Toronto] 13 April 2000).

This harsh and inegalitarian phase of capitalist development is not inevitable; it can be mitigated by a proactive state, as the recent record of Taiwan, Korea, and Singapore shows. To combine growth with equity, a "developmental" state will orchestrate incentives to ensure that firms adhere to a broad industrial strategy, and will manage the distribution of assets and income to advance such goals as equity, an adequate labour force, and agricultural production. Pragmatic neo-liberals do not envisage such a deeply interventionist role for the state; instead, they advocate a lean state with a "market-friendly" mandate – to maintain macroeconomic and political stability, ensure the supply of human capital and infrastructure, and mount minimal safety nets. In any case, the recent experience of sub-Saharan countries does not suggest that development states are likely to emerge in the next decade or two. Whereas microstates such as Botswana and Mauritius have forged effective – even developmental – states, the record elsewhere in the region is discouraging. Even Côte d'Ivoire and Kenya, which were lauded in the 1960s and 1970s for their effective states and growth-oriented policies, have undergone political decay in subsequent years. Hence, Africa cannot realistically now rely on the state to underpin just development, although programmes to prevent state collapse and rejuvenate state apparatuses must be a key part of any long-term strategy.

These reflections lead to certain sobering conclusions. Despite the disappointing results of structural adjustment, we must not simply discard the neo-liberal model. Developmental challenges in many countries are so intractable as to defy any short-term solutions: progress will be measured in decades, not years. An important task is to "unpack" the adjustment packages by separating those measures that address real problems from those that derive more from liberal faith than reasoned argument. On the one hand, it is generally true, as neo-liberals hold, that heavily state-led development in most African countries has proved disastrous: there is, in the World Bank's words, a "crisis of governance." Hence, much of market-oriented adjustment and macroeconomic stabilization makes good sense as a long-term programme. Even many sceptics support policies and programmes to reduce inflation and fiscal deficits, shrink the role of incapacitated states in economic management, expand the responsibilities of decentralized communities and voluntary organizations in social provisioning, promote democratic governance and the rule of law, and rebuild state capacity. On the other hand, the neo-liberal model links these adjustments to Africa's deeper integration into the prevailing global market economy. It assumes that all participants in self-regulating global markets will eventually benefit. However, the current pattern of globalization is proving unfavourable to African economies in various ways. Hence, just development in Africa surely entails a struggle to reform the existing pattern of neo-liberal globalization, as well as domestic policies and governance.

## Notes

1. It would be wrong to leave the impression that proponents of this model are in full agreement. Those within the fold disagree strongly at the level of tactics – that is, on the proper bundle of policies and institutional changes at a particular time, their sequencing, and the timing (whether rapid or gradual) of the reforms. None the less, at the level of strategy, a fair amount of agreement is evident. See Helleiner (1994) for agreements and disagreements, over economic policy in particular, by the mid-decade.
2. Collier (1997: 95) puts much of the blame for this on the inability of Africa "to live down its past" as a high-risk environment for investors.
3. The enthusiasm for NGOs as harbinger of political democratization in the literature of the late 1980s and 1990s has given way to more sober assessments; see e.g. Dicklitch (1998) and Van Rooy (1998). A credible, if somewhat cynical, view is offered by Chabal and Deloze (1999: 18–26), who maintain that the recent proliferation of indigenous NGOs is less about the flourishing of civil society and more to do with the generation of new opportunities for gaining access to resources by the political élite as they creatively adjust to the changing requirements of the international aid regime.
4. That is, a pattern of transnational economic integration animated by the ideal of creating self-regulating global markets for goods, services, capital, technology, and skills.
5. Social-democratic globalization refers to a pattern of transnational economic integration that is animated by the ideal of harnessing global markets to social ends – that is, treating markets as the servants of society rather than its master. The negative side-effects of free markets include growing inequalities within and among countries, heightened personal and societal insecurity as a consequence of financial volatility and turbulence, environmental degradation, and the dilution of democracy by restricting the sovereignty of governments and accentuating the power of capital. A social-democratic form of global-

ization would tackle these problems by setting negotiated limits to the operation of markets. Enforceable social, environmental, and cultural charters would probably require new forms of global governance and, to gain the adherence of the South, new mechanisms of North–South redistribution.
6. A. K. Fosu (1999) uses World Bank data to show that sub-Saharan Africa's growth would have averaged nearly 50 per cent higher in the absence of its crushing external debt payments.
7. The G-7 includes the United States, Japan, Germany, France, the United Kingdom, Italy, and Canada. The G-7 became the G-8 with the addition of Russia.

# REFERENCES

Adedeji, Adebayo, ed. 1981. *Indigenization of African Economies*. London: Hutchinson.

Anonymous. 1992. "Recent Trends in FDI for Developing Countries." *Finance and Development* 29(1): 50–51.

Austen, Ralph. 1987. *African Economic History*. London: James Currey.

Berman, Bruce. 1998. "Ethnicity, Patronage and the African State: The Politics of Uncivil Nationalism." *African Affairs* 91(388): 305–341.

Berman, Bruce and John Lonsdale. 1979. "Coping with Contradictions: The Development of the Colonial State in Kenya." *Journal of African History* 20(4): 287–305.

Blair, Tony. 1996. *New Britain*. Boulder: Westview.

Boone, Catherine. 1994. "State and Ruling Classes in Postcolonial Africa: The Enduring Contradictions of Power." In *State Power and Social Forces: Domination and Transformation in the Third World*, eds Joel Midgal, Atul Kohli, and Vivian Shue. New York: Cambridge University Press.

Boswell, Terry and Charles Chase-Dunn. 2000. *The Spiral of Capitalism and Socialism: Toward Global Democracy*. Boulder: Lynne Rienner.

Bratton, Michael and Nicholas van de Walle. 1997. *Democratic Experiments in Africa: Regime Transitions in Comparative Perspective*. New York: Cambridge University Press.

Brautigam, Deborah. 1996. "State Capacity and Effective Governance." In *Agenda for Africa's Recovery*, eds Benno Ndulu and Nicholas van de Walle. New Brunswick, NJ: Transaction Books for Overseas Development Council, pp. 81–108.

Campbell, Bonnie. 2000. "New Rules of the Game: The World Bank's Role in the Construction of New Normative Frameworks for States, Markets and Social Exclusion." *Canadian Journal of Development Studies* 21(1): 7–30.

Chabal, Patrick. 1992. *Power in Africa: An Essay in Political Interpretation*. New York: St Martin's Press.

Chabal, Patrick and Jean-Pascal Deloze. 1999. *Africa Works: Disorder as Political Instrument*. London: James Currey; Bloomington: Indiana University Press.

Chazan, Naomi and Victor Azarya. 1988. "Disengagement from the State in Africa: Reflections on Ghana and Guinea." *Comparative Studies in Society and History* 29(1): 107–131.

Collier, Paul. 1997. "Living Down the Past: How Europe Can Help Africa." In *African Development Perspectives Yearbook, Vol. 6*, eds Karl Wohlmutt, Hans Bass, and Frank Messner. Hamburg: Lit Verlag Munster, 89–110.

Collier, Paul and J. W. Gunning. 1997. "Explaining African Economic Performance," Working Paper WPS97-2, Centre for the Study of African Economies, Oxford University.

Dicklitch, Susan. 1998. *The Elusive Promise of NGOs in Africa: Lessons from Uganda*. New York: St Martin's Press.

Dunkley, Graham. 2000. *The Free Trade Adventure: The WTO, the Uruguay Round and Globalisation*. London: Zed Books.

Eriksen, Thomas. 1999. "A Non-ethnic State for Africa?" In *Ethnicity and Nationalism in Africa: Constructivist Reflections and Contemporary Politics*, ed. Paris Yeros. New York: St Martin's Press, 45–64.

Evans, Peter. 1992. "'The State as Problem and Solution: Predation, Embedded Autonomy, and Structural Change." In *The Politics of Economic Adjustment*, eds Stephan Haggard and Robert Kaufman. Princeton: Princeton University Press.

Eyoh, Dickson. 1999. "Citizenship, Community and the Politics of Ethnicity in Postcolonial Africa." In *Public Spaces and Private Quarrels: Space, Culture and Society in Africa*, eds Ezekiel Kalipeni and Paul Zeleza. Trenton, NJ: Africa World Press, 263–301.

Fieldhouse, David. 1986. *Black Africa, 1945–1980: Economic Decolonization and Arrested Development*. London: Unwin and Hyman.

Forrest, Tom. 1994. *The Advance of African Capital: The Growth of Nigerian Private Enterprise*. Edinburgh: Edinburgh University Press for International African Institute.

Fosu, A. K. 1999. "The External Debt Burden and Economic Growth in the 1980s: Evidence from Sub-Saharan Africa." *Canadian Journal of Development Studies* 20(1): 307–318.

Friedman, Timothy and Ignacio Ramonet. 1999. "Duelling Globalization: A Debate between Timothy Friedman and Ignacio Ramonet." *Foreign Policy* 116: 110–127, Fall.

Gore, Charles. 2000. "The Rise and Fall of the Washington Consensus as a Paradigm for Developing Countries." *World Development* 28(5): 789–804.

Green, Reginald H. 1998. "Cloth Untrue; The Evolution of Structural Adjustment in Sub-Saharan Africa." *Journal of International Affairs* 52(1): 207–232.

Grendzier, Irene. 1985. *Managing Political Change: Social Scientists and the Third World*. Boulder: Westview.

Gwynne, Robert N. and Cristobal Kay. 2000. "Views from the Periphery; Future of Neoliberalism in Latin America." *Third World Quarterly* 21(1): 141–156.

Hawthorn, Geoffrey. 1991. "Waiting for a Text?: Comparing Third World Politics." In *Rethinking Third World Politics*, ed. James Manor. London: Longman, 24–50.

Helleiner, Gerald K. 1994. "From Adjustment to Development in Sub-Saharan Africa: Consensus and Continuing Conflict." In *From Adjustment to Development in Africa*, eds Giovani C. Cornia and Gerald K. Helleiner. New York: St Martin's Press, 3–24.

Helleiner, Gerald K. 1997. "External Constraints and Prospects." In *Towards Autonomous Development in Africa*, eds Roy Culpeper and Charles McAskie. Ottawa: North–South Institute, 65–92.

Hernández-Catá, Ernesto. 1999. "Sub-Saharan Africa: Economic Policy and Outlook for Growth." *Finance & Development* 36(1): 10–12.

Himbara, David. 1994. *Kenya Capitalists, State and Development*. Boulder, CO: Lynne Rienner.

Jolly, Richard. 1999. "Global Inequality." *WIDER Angle* (Helsinki) 2 December, 5–6.

Kaplan, David and Raphael Kaplinsky. 1999. "Trade and Industrial Policy on an Uneven Playing Field: The Case of the Deciduous Fruit Canning Industry in South Africa." *World Development* 27(10): 1787–1801.

Kennedy, Paul. 1988. *African Capitalism: The Struggle for Ascendancy*. Cambridge: Cambridge University Press.

Killick, Tony. 1998. *Aid and the Political Economy of Policy Change*. London: Routledge.

Korten, David. 1999. *The Post-Corporate World: Life after Capitalism*. West Hartford: Kumarian.

Lancaster, Carol. 1999. *Aid to Africa: So Much to Do, So Little Done*. Chicago: University of Chicago Press.

MacGaffey, Janet. 1987. *Entrepreneurs and Parasites. The Struggle for Indigenous Capitalism in Zaire*. Cambridge: Cambridge University Press.

Mamdani, Mahmood. 1997. *Citizens and Subjects: Contemporary Africa and the Legacy of Late Colonialism*. Princeton, NJ: Princeton University Press.

Martin, Hans-Peter and Harald Schumann. 1997. *The Global Trap: Globalization and the Assault on Democracy and Prosperity*. London: Zed Books.

Mkandawire, Thandika and Charles C. Soludo. 1999. *Our Continent, Our Future: African Perspectives on Structural Adjustment*. Trenton, NJ: Africa World Press.

Mkandawire, Thandika and Charles C. Soludo, eds. 2000. *African Voices on Structural Adjustment*. Trenton, NJ: Africa World Press.

Mlambo, Kuukile and Tempitope Oshikoya. 1999. "Investment, Macroeconomic Policies and Growth." In *The African Economy: Policies, Institutions and the Future*, ed. Steven Kayizzi-Mugerwa. London: Routledge, 28–49.

Moore, Mick. 1998. "Death without Taxes: Democracy, State Capacity and Aid Dependence in the Fourth World." In *The Democratic Developmental State*, eds Mark Robinson and Gordon White. Cambridge: Cambridge University Press, 84–121.

Mshomba, R. E. 2000. *Africa in the Global Economy*. Boulder: Lynne Rienner.

Nafziger, Wayne. 1984. *Inequality in Africa: Political Elites, Proletariat, Peasants and the Poor*. Cambridge: Cambridge University Press.

Ndulu, Benno and Nicholas van de Walle, eds. 1996. *Agenda for Africa's Economic Renewal*. New Brunswick, NJ: Transaction Books for Overseas Development Council.

O'Brien, Donal. 1979. "Modernization, Order and the Erosion of a Democratic Ideal." In *Development Theory: Four Critical Studies*, ed. David Lehman. London: Frank Cass.

Organization of Economic Cooperation and Development (OECD) 1999. *Development Cooperation Report 1999*. Paris: OECD.

Philips, Ann. 1988. *The Enigma of Colonialism: British Policy in West Africa*. London: James Currey.

Rapley, John. 1993. *Ivorien Capitalism: African Entrepreneurs in Côte d'Ivoire*. Boulder: Lynne Rienner.

Robinson, Mark and Gordon White, eds. 1998. *The Democratic Developmental State*. Oxford: Oxford University Press.

Rodrik, Dani. 1999. *The New Global Economy and Developing Countries: Making Openness Work*. Washington, DC: Overseas Development Council.

Rothchild, Donald and Naomi Chazan, eds. *The Precarious Balance: State and Security in Africa*. Boulder, CO: Westview.

Sahn, David, Paul Dorosh, and Stephen Younger, eds. 1997. *Structural Adjustment Reconsidered: Economic Policy and Poverty in Africa*. Cambridge: Cambridge University Press.

Samoff, Joel. 1996. "Chaos and Certainty in Development." *World Development* 24(4): 611–634.

Sandbrook, Richard. 2000. *Closing the Circle: Democratization and Development in Africa*. London: Zed Books.

Sandbrook, Richard and Jay Oelbaum. 1997. "Reforming Dysfunctional Institutions Through Democratization?: Reflections on Ghana." *Journal of Modern African Studies* 35(4): 603–646.

Sen, Amartya. 1997. "Development Thinking at the Beginning of the 21st Century," In *Economic and Social Development into the 21st Century*, ed. Louis Emmerihi. Baltimore: Johns Hopkins University Press.

Sharer, Robert. 1999. "Trade: An Engine of Growth in Africa." *Finance & Development* 36(4): 26–29.

Sklar, Richard. 1987. "Developmental Democracy." *Comparative Studies in Society and History* 29(4): 686–714.

Taylor, Lance. 1997. "The Revival of the Liberal Creed: The IMF and the World Bank in a Globalized Economy." *World Development* 25(2): 145–152.

Throup, David and Christopher Hornsby. 1998. *Multiparty Politics in Kenya: The Kenyatta and Moi States and the Triumph of the System in the 1992 Election*. Oxford: James Currey; Athens, OH: Ohio University Press.

Toye, John. 1993. *Dilemmas of Development Discourse: Reflections on the Counterrevolution in Development Economics*, 2nd edn. Oxford: Blackwell.

Van Rooy, Allison, ed. 1998. *Civil Society and the Aid Industry*. London: Earthscan Publications.

Westergaard, John. 1999. "Where does the Third Way Lead?" *New Political Economy* 3(4): 429–436.

UNDP. 1999. *Human Development Report 1999*. New York: Oxford University Press.

Widner, Jennifer. 1997. "Political Parties and Civil Societies in Sub-Saharan Africa: Conflicting Objectives?" In *Democracy in Africa: The Hard Road Ahead*, ed. Marina Ottaway. Boulder, CO: Lynne Rienner.

Wolfensohn, James D. 1999. "A Proposal for a Comprehensive Development

Framework." Address to the Board, Management, and Staff of the World Bank Group, January 21. Washington DC: World Bank.

World Bank. 1981. *Accelerated Development in Sub-Saharan Africa: An Agenda for Action*. Washington DC: World Bank.

World Bank. 1989. *Sub-Saharan Africa: From Crisis to Sustainable Development*. Washington DC: World Bank.

World Bank. 1990. *World Development Report 1990*. New York: Oxford University Press.

World Bank. 1992. *Governance and Development*. Washington DC: World Bank.

World Bank. 1997. *World Development Report 1997*. New York: Oxford University Press.

World Bank. 1999a. *The World Bank Group: 4 Years of Change and Renewal: A Progress Report*. Washington DC: World Bank, September.

World Bank. 1999b. *African Development Indicators 1999*. Washington DC: World Bank.

World Bank. 1999c. *World Development Indicators 1999*. Washington DC: World Bank.

World Bank. 2000a. "Assessing Globalization: Does More International Trade Openness Increase World Poverty?" *Briefing Paper*, Washington DC: World Bank.

World Bank. 2000b. *Global Economic Prospects and the Developing Countries 2000*. Washington DC: World Bank.

World Bank. 2000c. *Can Africa Claim the 21st Century?* Washington DC: World Bank.

World Trade Organization. 1999. *International Trade Statistics 1999*. Geneva: WTO.

Yeats, A., A. Amjadi, U. Reincke, and F. Ng. 1996. "What caused Sub-Saharan Africa's Marginalization in World Trade?" *Finance & Development* 33(4): 38–41.

Young, Crawford. 1994. *The African Colonial State in Comparative Perspective*. New Haven: Yale University Press.

# Conclusion: The prospects for just growth

*Chung-in Moon and Georg Sørensen*

This volume has examined the interaction of states and markets in an effort to determine how their interaction can facilitate just growth, i.e. economic growth that is consistent with the pursuit of fair economic distribution and open polities. Whether just growth is achieved depends on a combination of domestic and international conditions. As to the latter, the present period is characterized by globalization in a climate dominated by liberal political and economic values. As to the former, domestic conditions must vary between countries; in order to establish the more general trends, we have focused on distinctive regional patterns and the resulting variations between regions.

## Recasting globalization, democracy, and just growth

Given this starting point, Atul Kohli's introduction to the volume raised several important research questions. What are the implications of the globalized political economy for development? More specifically, how do constraints of global capitalism alter the challenges of poverty, inequality, and democracy? What are the distinctive regional profiles of democracy and development? How does one best understand patterns of regional variation? In this conclusion we briefly outline the major answers to these questions as they were given in the chapters above. Turning to the implications of our results for the role of international organizations, and especially the United Nations, we outline a "policy brief" containing the task that the UN system must confront in order better to further the promotion of just growth.

Globalization is a complex and contested concept: in the broadest sense it involves the expansion of social relations (economic, political, social, cultural) across borders. Barbara Stallings's contribution stresses four aspects of globalization of particular importance for developing countries. The first is the macroeconomic aspect, i.e. the growth in trade and finance flows, both of which have outstripped the growth in production. Second, there is the microeconomic aspect, i.e. technological changes and the development of new global processes of production. They are reflected in the increasing dominance of TNCs, the expansion of which is combined with the development of new global networks of trade and production that do not necessarily involve direct foreign investment or ownership. Third, the globalization of culture and media tends to create a global middle class demanding universal access to a range of goods and services, including news, entertainment, and travel. Finally, values associated with liberal, Western models of economic and political development are increasingly dominant. This is strengthened by the demands from international institutions for liberalization of economies and polities as a condition for economic and other aid.

It is clear that these patterns of globalization present new opportunities as well as new constraints for developing countries. Focusing on the economic aspect of globalization, the opportunities include better possibilities for economic growth via improved connection to global exchange; this is promoted by improved access to external capital and technology. The constraints involve much-increased vulnerabilities to fluctuations in global trade and financial markets; they also involve a narrower set of policy options because the priority of economic openness creates the need to pursue macroeconomic stability in ways that are acceptable to global markets.

The chapter by Barbara Stallings contains a detailed analysis of the more precise nature and composition of opportunities and constraints. She particularly emphasizes the importance of the composition of capital flows: FDI is better for growth, whereas short-term flows sooner increase volatility. Less inequality may or may not be tied in with economic globalization. The poorest countries must rely on declining official flows; private flows, by contrast, are more volatile and can result in increased inequality through the unequal employment patterns that they generate. Economic globalization has had a constraining effect on government policies, but not to the extent that is sometimes claimed. The main constraints are the principle of inviolability of private property and the requirement for certainty about the rules of operation for economic actors.

Democracy and development are as salient as globalization in the developing world. In chapter 2, Atul Kohli presents a comprehensive overview of correlates of democracy, governability, and just growth. His observation shows that the developing world as a whole has made some progress in democratization in the 1980s, after going through fragile democratic experiments of new nations through the late 1940s to the early 1960s, as well as authoritarian setback throughout the 1960s and the 1970s. However, the third wave of democratization in the 1980s has been uneven across the regions. Whereas some countries in Latin America (e.g. Brazil) and East Asia (e.g. South Korea) have undergone profound democratic changes, numerous developing countries (China, North Korea, Indo-China, much of South-East Asia and the Middle East, and a significant number of North and sub-Saharan countries) are still under authoritarian rule, defying the global trend of democratization.

Kohli argues that most of the new democracies are currently having a hard time in ensuring democratic consolidation and providing effective governance, both of which are essential for just growth. The crisis of governability in new democracies has been precipitated by the dynamic interplay of deformed institutional foundation and rigid policy choices. An élite-dominated democracy and personalistic rule, coupled with weak political parties, have blocked the training and socialization of new leaders, escalated factional conflict among leaders, and blurred lines of authority, deepening the dilemma of governability. Equally critical are the political problems generated by misdirected state intervention, which not only has politicized social cleavages by failing to differentiate the public from the private sphere in social life but also has intensified conflicts over the state's scarce resources. Rigid policy choices wrapped in the neo-liberal orthodoxy have also critically undercut the governability of new democracies. The neo-liberal mandates of economic stabilization and structural reforms have produced considerable tension with forces of democracy. While the process of democratic transition has heightened expansive popular expectations on the spread of power in society and subsequent economic gains, the contractionary consequences of the neo-liberal reforms have forced the managers of new democracies to stabilize the system, often by limiting the scope of democracy. Likewise, new democracies encounter numerous obstacles to democratic consolidation and governability.

What, then, are the correlates of democracy and just growth? Kohli contends that cross-national evidence on the impact of democracy on just growth (namely, economic growth with equity) is highly inconclusive. Nevertheless, a stable democracy can be compatible with moderate rates of economic growth. In a similar vein, no linear causal relationship can be delineated in linking democracy to democratization of power and ultimately to socio-economic democracy. As advanced industrial democracies have demonstrated, however, democracies could generate more pressures towards greater equalization. Yet Kohli warns that "improvement in equity may be compatible with democracy if, and only if, the design of new democracies consciously aims to strengthen social-democratic institutions such as social democratic parties, peasant-labour organizations, careful decentralization, and restructuring of the role of the governments" (chap. 2).

Growth is an important mandate for most developing countries. Judged from the perspective of just growth, however, poverty and inequality are the most pressing issues. Despite five decades of international and domestic efforts, poverty has become an inseparable part of the developing world. In chapter 3, Mick Moore and Howard White present a rather gloomy picture of poverty and inequality in today's developing world. They divide poverty into income poverty (i.e. household or individual income or consumption or purchasing power) and non-income dimensions of poverty such as famine, malnutrition, and the level of access to basic health services and education. According to their findings, only two regions – East Asia and the Pacific, and the Middle East and North Africa – have performed better in reducing poverty, in that the number of people below the poverty line has declined between 1987 and 1998. In other regions – such as Latin American and the Caribbean, South Asia, and sub-Saharan Africa – however, the number of poor has increased. In South Asia, for example, the number of people under the poverty line rose from 480 million in 1987 to 510 million in 1998, while those in sub-Saharan Africa grew from 220 million in 1987 to 290 million in 1998.

Undernourishment has become an equally critical issue. As with poverty, East Asia and the Pacific has performed better than other regions in the developing world. Share of the undernourished as a percentage of population in East Asia and the Pacific was 32 per cent in 1979–1981 but was reduced to 17 per cent during 1995–1997. While the Middle East and North African states have shown virtually no changes (9 per cent) during both periods, Latin America and the Caribbean and sub-Saharan Africa have revealed only slight improvements. In terms of relative size, however, undernourishment in sub-Saharan Africa seems most problematic: over 33 per cent of the population was undernourished during 1995–1997 in sub-Saharan Africa, posing a major national and global challenge. What is more troublesome is the proportion of children under five years of age who are undernourished. In the case of South Asia, the proportion was reduced from 37.5 per cent in 1979–1981 to 23 per cent in 1995–1997; however, in sub-Saharan Africa, 33 per cent of children under five years were estimated to be undernourished. Apart from overall poverty and undernourishment, numerous people in the developing world are suffering from famine and lack of access to basic human needs.

Income inequality is another salient issue in the developing world, but it also varies by region. Incomes are more equally distributed in Asia than in Latin America and Africa. The Gini index of income inequality in the various regions of Asia ranges between 0.31 and 0.38; however, in Latin America and Africa it is close to 0.50. In particular, income inequality in sub-Saharan Africa is estimated to be the worst in the world (Moore and White, chap. 3).

Moore and White ascribe a dismal performance in poverty reduction primarily to lack of growth. Thus, although growth is necessary for poverty reduction, they argue that "going for growth alone is not enough." They assert that "if poverty is to be reduced, economic growth needs to be more pro-poor and governments need to intervene more directly" (Moore and White, chap. 3). In view of this, economic growth without corresponding human development is bound to fail to satisfy basic human needs and just growth. Contrary to neo-liberal prescriptions, thus, solutions to poverty lie not solely in markets, economic growth, price signals, and competition, but in carefully devised strategies and public action for poverty reduction and human development.

According to Moore and White, effective poverty reduction depends on governance and the capacity and accountability of the state. They argue that the states in the developing world should be reconstructed in order to deliver basic human services and to have sufficient stability and coherence. Essential to this process is the creation of political parties and movements that embody and advance the interests of the poor. In this regard, Moore and White suggest three vital links between governance and poverty reduction. First, democracy matters, because it opens venues for the creation of organizations of the poor that can ultimately lead to poverty-reducing government interventions. In reality, however, democracies may not necessarily guarantee pro-poor policies, not only because of the exclusion of poor people from the political process but also because of issue cleavages – such as ethnic, linguistic, and regional identities – and difficulties of effective organization of the poor (as in the case of rural populations). Participation serves as the second vital link between governance and poverty reduction. The voice of the poor should be organized and articulated in such a way as to generate poverty-reducing policy outcomes through the creation of effective, encompassing, programmatic political parties and social movements. Finally, accountable states are indispensable: programmatic and effective opposition parties, open policy debates, and contending lobbies from different quarters of society are essential ingredients of accountable states. In addition, active mass media and a concerned middle class are critical in drawing domestic and international attention to the problems of famine and poverty.

## Just growth and regional variations

What are the results of these new opportunities and constraints when combined with domestic conditions as they prevail in the major regions of Latin America, East Asia, the Middle East, South Asia (India), and sub-Saharan Africa? As we briefly review the major results of the regional analyses in the following, it rapidly becomes apparent that just growth has *not* been achieved on a significant scale in most regions. We indicate some of the main reasons why this is the case. Against this background, an agenda for international and domestic change can be set forth.

### Latin America

Latin America has undergone dramatic changes over the last two decades. Plagued by a debt crisis connected to the previous development strategy of ISI, the region began, during the 1980s, to pursue neo-liberal policies of economic openness, market competition, financial reform, and privatization. Overall, Latin America displays a "dramatic convergence toward liberal market economies," making the region "distinctive in its embrace of 'neo-liberalism'" (Kaufman, chap. 4).

The economic growth results of these dramatic changes have not been impressive. The nine largest Latin American economies achieved a 2.3 per cent GDP per capita growth average during the first half of the 1990s and a mere 0.8 per cent during the second half. The comprehensive financial crises in Mexico and Brazil are important factors in this deteriorating performance. These crises had both international and domestic causes; as Kaufman explains, they have upset the "Washington Consensus" and led to increased debates over the proper economic policies, even if the basic consensus on an open, liberal, economic course remains in place.

The economic crisis of the 1980s involved recession, high inflation, and sharply decreasing social expenditures. The result was a substantial increase in both poverty levels and inequality. During the 1990s, the number of households under the poverty line remains high, but has gone down somewhat, from 41 to 36 per cent (in Chile, Brazil, Panama, Costa Rica, Peru, and Columbia, see Kaufman, chap. 4 in this volume). But the income gaps that widened so sharply during the 1980s have continued to grow, so there is not much hope for major progress in reducing inequality.

Welfare reforms are, therefore, needed in order to achieve just growth on a sustainable basis. It is not surprising that the issue of appropriate measures is hotly contested. At the same time, narrow fiscal constraints reduce the medium-run capacity for reform. Kaufman points out that the prospect for reform and thus for just growth is narrowly connected to the major political question in most Latin American countries, i.e. whether there can develop "a system of representation that provides the basis for the negotiation of stable compromises over development and welfare policies and that allows citizens to hold governments accountable for their implementation" (Kaufman, chap. 4 in this volume). Macroeconomic stability is desirable, of course; steady economic growth will hardly be possible without it. However, if such stability is not achieved in a way that also considers social investment, welfare goals, and less inequality, it will be much less sustainable in the long run. Already, Latin American voters are increasingly alienated from the established political system, including its political parties.

## East Asia

The East Asian countries have undergone profound economic transformations and emerged as dynamos of the world economy in a relatively short period. The East Asian miracle was not everlasting, however: forces of globalization are radically altering the regional economic terrain; most noticeable are impacts of financial globalization. The economic crisis that plagued East Asian countries since 1997 was a product largely of failure to cope with vulnerability embedded in financial globalization. South Korea and South-East Asian countries fell prey to the crisis, not only because they were not able to handle the burden of controlling the volatility in exchange-rate regimes and short-term financial inflow and of containing the contagion effects but also because they were not properly equipped with domestic-banking and financial-regulatory mechanisms to minimize negative impacts of movements of speculative money.

However, Taiwan was an exception. It remained intact from the spiral of regional economic crisis. Proactive policy choices prior to the crisis have helped Taiwan avoid the spread of the contagion effects. While low dependence on foreign portfolio investments and minimal exposure to short-term foreign borrowings reduced its margin of vulnerability to international financial instability, emphasis on domestic savings significantly enhanced its resilience in coping with external turbulence. The Taiwanese example clearly suggests that adverse effects of financial globalization are not fatalistic but can be managed through a mix of right and precautionary policy measures. Chu (chap. 5 in this volume) concurs with Barbara Stallings (chap. 1) in suggesting countermeasures to avert risks of financial globalization: proper sequencing of capital-market liberalization; development of domestic capital markets; priority on domestic investors over global ones; and appropriate banking and financial institutions, with more emphasis on prudential regulation and supervision.

Another important challenge of globalization is technological changes and impacts on the structure of industry and export. East Asian countries have long benefited from export-oriented industrialism in which manufactured exports have served as an engine of growth. However, Chu questions the long-term sustainability of the export-oriented industrialization (EOI) in East Asia. World-wide excess capacity in manufactured goods, plus intensified international competition and the loss of wage competitiveness, are signalling the exhaustion of the EOI strategy through shifting comparative advantage. Moreover, the trend of deverticalization and fragmentation in the global production process and the unprecedented time compression in technological innovation (both of which are the defining features of revolution in IT technology), are exerting constant pressures on East Asian countries to upgrade their industrial portfolio and levels of technological sophistication. Unless they move from the current status of OEM to ODM and to OBM, their export-driven economies are most likely to be stalled. According to Chu's analysis, the first-generation NICs are gradually catching up with such technological changes through human resources development, technological upgrading, and overseas sourcing, but the second-generation NICs are facing enormous difficulties in adjusting to these changes, portending an uncertain future.

Forces of globalization have not only dampened economic growth but also precipitated a crisis of social policy. During the period of rapid economic growth, East Asian countries were able to cope with poverty and inequality, partly through the dynamics of growth and constant employment creation and partly through a social safety net based on a traditional-values system such as the extended family. However, the recent financial and economic crises have critically deteriorated equality and social welfare, adding around 10 million more people to the ranks of those living below a dollar-a-day income between 1996 and 1998 (Chu, chap. 5). Crises, and the mandates of neo-liberal reforms, have produced an unprecedented number of unemployed, and the myth of lifetime-employment guarantees in the corporate sector (an East Asian trademark) has disappeared. Yet existing social safety nets in East Asia are not sufficient to handle the worsening social inequality, causing a major distributional dilemma. Another important distributional consequence of globalization is the "digital divide"; the uneven spread of knowledge and skills in information technology has resulted in a growing inequality in income and status, further complicating the problem of social inequality. Likewise, globalization has brought about severe adverse effects on just growth in East Asia.

To cope with the dual challenges of globalization and just growth in East Asia, Chu suggests, there should be a radical realignment of state–market relations. The old version of the East Asian developmental state – where the state prevails over the market through central coordination of production activities, strategic allocation of resources, and insulation of economic decision-making – is no longer suitable for dealing with the complex and delicate process of globalization. The role of the state should be reinvigorated in tandem with changing economic realities. What is needed is not an all-out intervention and orchestration but an effective monitoring and prudent regulation of economic activities. It should also play a guiding role in upgrading technology and diffusing technological innovation. More importantly, in order to cope with the tasks of sustaining growth and distributive justice, the East Asian states should transform themselves into "a 'democratic developmental state'" under which "participatory forms of democracy and broad-based development can be mutually re-enforcing under the right political and institutional circumstances" (Chu, chap. 5 in this volume).

## China

China deserves special attention, not only because of its sheer size and market socialism but also because of its remarkable performance in the past two decades. Indeed, the economic transformation of China has been most impressive. Before undertaking the open-door policy in the late 1970s, China was one of the poorest countries in the world, with 80 per cent of its population living on an income of less than a dollar a day and only a third of all its adults able to read or write. Within less than two decades, however, China has made a dramatic ascension in the world economy: its economy grew by 10 per cent per annum on average between 1978 and 1988 and its exports jumped to 4.6 per cent in the 1990s from less than 1 per cent in the pre-reform period; furthermore, about one-third of all FDI flows from the OECD to the developing world went to China. The Chinese performance in poverty reduction and human development has also been profound (Chu, chap. 5 in this volume).

The Chinese success was a product of a prudent strategy that has reduced risks by preserving vested interests through the maintenance of a socialist political and economic template, while creating new incentives through market channels and the devolution of economic decision-making power to local governments and to professional management of the enterprises. The prospects for growth seem good: vast natural and human resources; market size and economy of scale; high domestic savings ratio; and technological progress can be seen as valuable assets for sustaining its economic growth. But realization of just growth can be problematic, not only because of an increasing regional, generational, and gender gap in income and wealth inequality but also because of a dismal social safety net, authoritarian governance, and pervasive corruption. Chu contends that China should carry out the dual tasks in meeting the challenges of globalization and just growth. On the one hand, it should expedite the process of extensive reforms in the public sector, public financing, and the banking and financial sector; otherwise, China could face an acute economic crisis and protracted economic stagnation. On the other hand, it should undertake more bold political reforms in the direction of open, democratic governance through institutional changes and the nurturing of civil society.

## Middle East

The Middle East has followed divergent paths to growth and development. Whereas oil exporters and oil industrializers have achieved relatively high growth rates, agro-poor countries such as Sudan and the Yemen are still trapped in a vicious circle of protracted poverty and underdevelopment. There is also another category of Middle Eastern countries, such as Jordan and Lebanon, which have attempted to manage economic hardship by taking advantage of human resources. Only a limited number of countries (such as Turkey, Egypt, and Morocco) have emerged as NICs. The divergent paths to economic development make it difficult to delineate common regional denominators.

However, an overall profile of just growth in the Middle East seems quite bleak. The spectre of economic stagnation and chronic inequality has haunted countries in the region. Ziya Öniş attributes the regional predicament to such structural features as oil dependency and the rise of rentier economy, poor domestic savings and weak indigenous development capacity, and perpetual insecurity amidst "bad neighbours" and a heavy burden of defence spending. Furthermore, while lack of globalization has delimited the potential for economic growth, pervasive authoritarian governance has deepened poverty and inequality throughout the region. According to Öniş, the Middle Eastern dilemma consists of under-globalization rather than over-globalization. Weak market-driven integration of Middle Eastern economies into the world economy, coupled with marginalization in the distribution of global capital flows and the allocation of long-term FDI, has profoundly undermined the regional dynamics of economic growth. As Kohli points out in the Introduction, open politics is the fundamental prerequisite for just growth. However, democracy is rare in the region, and the proliferation of political Islam and subsequent domestic instability have posed major barriers to just growth.

Turkey, Egypt, and Morocco demonstrate an inherent contradiction between globalization and democratization in the pursuit of just growth. Economic growth is crucial to the survival of political regimes in these three countries, but it cannot be achieved without deepening integration of their economies into transnational capitalism through extensive structural-adjustment measures. None the less, efforts toward structural reforms have encountered enormous domestic political resistance, delaying the process of globalization and obstructing the inflow of much-needed long-term foreign capital. Thus, political leadership in the Middle Eastern NICs is burdened with "a balancing act between economic accountability of foreign creditors and political accountability of domestic population" (Öniş in this volume). Managing the inherent contradiction between the two mandates will ultimately determine the nature and direction of just growth in the region.

The tasks for most countries in the Middle East, according to Ziya Öniş, are manifold. They should liberalize and integrate their economies into the world capitalist economy in order to ensure economic growth; however, this cannot be done without overhaul of the existing state structure. Clientelistic rentier states, endemic to most Middle Eastern countries, should be dismantled and "hard states" with entrepreneurial capacity should be institutionalized to cope with challenges of globalization and economic growth. At the same time, globalization should be managed effectively by minimizing the inflow of volatile short-term capital and attracting long-term foreign investment. State capacity and globalization are, however, only a necessary (but insufficient) condition for just growth. Growth with redistribution cannot be attainable without a fuller democratization. A democratic polity is the best way to mitigate negative externalities of globalization while fostering equitable growth.

## India

India presents another interesting regional variation for the understanding of democracy and just growth. India is the oldest democracy in the developing world, but its performance in just growth has been rather mixed. Economic growth has varied from sluggish to modest, and the inequality gap between the rich and the poor has been less pronounced than in other parts of the developing world such as Latin America and the Middle East. However, the perennial question of poverty has not been ameliorated: around 300 million people are estimated to live below the official poverty line. The democratic framework under which the Indian state developed over the past fifty years has not made any significant contribution to alleviating poverty and improving the quality of life.

Kohli and Mullen (chap. 7) attribute India's mixed performance to the mismatch between state ambition and state capacity. Since independence, Indian leaders and political parties have ambitiously pursued economic growth and poverty reduction. Despite rhetoric of state-led growth and emphasis on redistributional politics, neither of the two mandates has materialized. The adoption of a more pro-business and conservative political orientation has recently enhanced the potential for economic growth. However, such reorientation, which was initiated at the expense of its traditional pro-poor, socialist ideology, has gradually eroded its antipoverty focus, to the detriment of the quality of life. The social capture of political parties by powerful interest groups; the soft nature of the Indian state (with a lower degree of effectiveness in policy implementation); and the rightward shift in politics and ideology, account for India's dismal performance in just growth. The problem of massive poverty continues, not only because growth is not rapid enough to absorb the old and new poverty but also because the new right, or right-leaning, political leaders are neither willing to incorporate India's poor, nor capable of doing so. As Kohli and Mullen succinctly point out, "the path to just growth in India thus remains fraught with difficulties," clouding the future of just growth in India.

Likewise, neither state-led economic growth nor political efforts at redistribution and poverty alleviation have proved to be successful in India. Prescriptions to the Indian dilemma seem self-evident – freeing political parties from social capture by vested interests, revitalizing social democratic ideology aimed at removing poverty, and enhancing capacity of the Indian state in policy formulation and implementation. Given the structural rigidity of Indian politics, as Kohli and Mullen note, such realignment might not be easy.

## Sub-Saharan Africa

Sub-Saharan Africa is characterized by weak states at low levels of economic development. These countries are highly dependent on aid flows, the conditions for which are, to a large extent, formulated by the IFIs, i.e. the World Bank and IMF. Therefore, the terms of Africa's involvement in economic globalization are set by the model of development recommended by the IFIs. That model, according to Eyoh and Sandbrook (chap. 8 in this volume), can be labelled "the Pragmatic Neo-liberal Development Strategy." It consists of market-oriented reform together with investment in human capital and infrastructure, supported by progress in political democratization and the rule of law. These changes should help improve both state capacity and state transparency and accountability. Economic growth with "a human face," provided in part by social safety nets, both will be the result of such measures and will itself provide positive feedback to further progress.

In per capita GDP terms, economic growth in Africa was negative in the −0.1 to −1.2 per cent range from between 1980 and 1995; 1996 growth rates averaged a modest 2 per cent. The already high level of poverty in Africa has remained in place or even increased. The number of people on less than "a dollar a day" increased by 50 million between 1990 and 1998; close to one-half of the region's population lives in poverty.

Liberal reforms cannot take all the blame for these meagre results; environmental conditions, including severe droughts, have led to crisis and famine in many cases. More importantly, weak and inefficient states continue to rely on patronage and clientelism. Serious efforts at nation-building and economic development have not been a primary goal for most state élite groups. However, even if this were the case, Eyoh and Sandbrook argue that "pragmatic neo-liberalism" does not constitute a viable strategy for Africa's development. The countries are plagued by large debt burdens and continue to rely heavily on foreign aid, which is declining. Prospects for increasing exports are bleak because of stagnating demand and falling price levels for non-oil commodities. Finally, there has been no major increase in FDI, with the exception of the period 1995–1997.

The achievement of just growth, Eyoh and Sandbrook assert, will require a kind of globalization that differs from the one expounded by "pragmatic neo-liberals"; these suggestions for change are summarized below. Just growth will also require domestic change, in particular in the political institutions: "The consolidation of democratic and effective states therefore poses, as necessary conditions, two long-term challenges. One is the forging of multi-ethnic approaches to nation-building that separate the sense of citizenship from nationality. The other task ... is to nurture institutional arrangements that balance the expression of local communities' political values and traditions, on the one hand, against the universal political and civil rights of individual citizens, on the other" (Eyoh and Sandbrook, chap. 8, this volume).

Examination of the five regions – Latin America, East Asia, the Middle East, India, and sub-Saharan Africa – reveals several interesting regional patterns of convergence and divergence. First, spread of globalization is not uniform across the regions. Whereas countries in Latin America and East Asia have been overexposed to the process of globalization, India and those in the Middle East and sub-Saharan region have been rather under-globalized. Such a pattern underscores an uneven distribution of international capital across the developing world.

Second, regardless of the degree of integration into the world economy, the ideal of just growth in most developing countries has been adversely affected by forces of globalization. East Asian countries used to enjoy a relatively high growth and high equality, but the economic crisis since 1997 has severely threatened their performance in both categories. Africa continues to suffer from low growth and high inequality, whereas countries in Latin America reveal an interesting combination of a relatively high growth with high inequality. The Middle East in general falls into the category of low growth with high inequality; however, Middle Eastern NICs resemble Latin American countries – with the exception of Egypt, which has shown a low growth pattern but with a relatively high level of equality. India displays a combination of moderate growth and massive poverty. The regional variations can be accounted for by a number of factors – resource endowment and historical initial conditions, trajectory of developmental sequencing, the level of globalization, state capacity, patterns of interactions between the state and market, and underlying coalitional dynamics. A timely shift from ISI to an export-oriented industrialization, a more aggressive pursuit of globalization, a high level of state capacity, and organic links between the state and market appear to be conducive to high growth and high equality.

Third, there seem to be close correlates between open polities and distributional patterns. Whereas countries with democratic governance tend to perform better in delivering social equality, those with authoritarian governance or illiberal democracy have turned out to be poor performers in poverty reduction and social equality. However, democracy does not necessarily lead to social and economic equality. As Kohli argues in chapter 2, satisfaction of equality and basic human needs depends on political institutional arrangements (e.g. social-democratic arrangement) that can enhance social empowerment of the poor through their effective organization and participation. State capacity and accountability are equally important in resolving poverty and inequality.

Finally, all contributors have emphasized the importance of state capacity, but its operational meanings vary by the region and the stage of development. Whereas middle-income countries of East Asia and Latin America have needs of state capacity such as market regulating and welfare providing, the needs in the low-income countries, such as India and much of the Middle East and the sub-Saharan region, might require state capacity that can generate growth and channel the fruits somewhat equitably. Likewise, state–market relations need to be contextualized by the region and the level of development. Nevertheless, the findings in this volume clearly indicate that neither the state nor market alone can meet the mandates of just growth; both should be wisely conjugated in a way to produce synergy effects for the promotion of just growth.

## Domestic changes and just growth

We have reviewed challenges of globalization and the interactions of states and markets in the major regions of the developing world. Although there are positive developments in some countries and also some general tendencies that are promising (including movement towards macroeconomic stability and the creation of more open polities), the dominant trend is not encouraging: just growth has not been achieved in most cases. The analyses in this volume point to major political and economic areas where domestic and international change is needed if just growth is to be achieved on a larger scale in developing countries. The domestic agenda is addressed briefly first, but our main focus is on the agenda for international change, i.e. the task that must be confronted by international organizations, including the United Nations.

Our analyses point to the need for domestic political and institutional change in order to develop democracy and effective governance. Latin America lacks a system of representation capable of negotiating stable compacts on development and welfare which have something to offer all major groups in the population. The Middle East also needs a fundamental realignment of domestic political and institutional structure. States in the Middle East region should overcome their social capture by vested interests through the enhancement of state capacity and the demolition of rent-driven "clientelistic capitalism." At the same time, a democratic mode of governance should be actively sought in order to secure just growth. East Asia also needs to make a transition from the old version of a developmental state to "a democratic developmental state" that is based on the devolution of power and more inclusive state–market relationships. A deeper and more extensive democratic consolidation is vital to the transition. Africa is in need of multi-ethnic approaches to nation-building that can provide a solid basis for democratic development. As with countries in other regions, India also needs to realign its domestic political structure as well as to enhance governability.

Common to all these regions are the three institutional prerequisites for just growth. First is democratic governance: open polities; a viable, encompassing political party system; and effective citizen participation and social empowerment are the critical requirements for just growth. Second, state capacity and accountability matter. State actions are still required in meeting the challenges of growth and equality; nevertheless, the state should be able to balance its entrepreneurial and legitimizing functions in order to deliver just growth. Finally, market forces need to be harnessed through new institutional arrangements pertaining to effective monitoring and regulation. Thus, inducing domestic political and institutional changes will be the most challenging task for just growth in the twenty-first century.

The domestic political changes must be accompanied by changes in economic policies. As emphasized by Barbara Stallings in chapter 1, such policies must be much more effective in (a) offsetting the inequality stemming from economic globalization, (b) improving regulation and supervision of the financial sector, (c) controlling foreign capital surges and conducting anticyclical macroeconomic policies, and (d) setting up regional arrangements that can help to strengthen domestic policy initiatives.

Apart from Stalling's prescriptions to cope with challenges of globalization, several additional measures should be taken into account. For most regions, structural reforms need to be implemented continuously. Despite their temporal backlash, the reforms can facilitate developing countries' adjustment to changing comparative advantages, while enhancing international competitiveness and efficiency in the management of national economy. In this regard, macroeconomic stability, microeconomic reforms in the corporate as well as the banking and financial sectors, privatization of state enterprises, investment in human resources, and constant technological upgrading and changes in industrial production strategies constitute the critical steps. Along with this, domestic savings should be more aggressively encouraged. As several contributors to the volume have argued, long-term foreign investment is much more desirable than short-term borrowings or inflow of speculative funds. Attraction of long-term foreign capital is in turn contingent upon macroeconomic stability, deregulation, and provision of a variety of policy incentives. At the same time there should be renewed and systematic efforts to alleviate poverty and to satisfy basic human needs.

## International changes and just growth

There is thus no doubt that domestic political and economic change is needed in order to obtain just growth; however, international change is direly needed as well and in the present context it is relevant to focus on the international level. The starting point for such reflections is the basic insight that globalization is a constructed and not a given entity (Eyoh and Sandbrook, chap. 8 in this volume). There are several possible versions of a global free-market economy – that is to say, it is possible to make changes in the current model of economic globalization in order to create an improved framework for the achievement of just growth. The choice for developing countries is not one of integration versus protectionism; radical protectionism is not feasible or desirable. The core issue concerns the precise terms of market integration and there is no doubt that improvement of the current model of economic globalization is needed for the realization of just growth.

What kind of international change is needed? Unsurprisingly, our analyses do not come up with a fixed master plan; this is a complex issue requiring further reflection. Nevertheless, there is a consensus in our group that a model of economic globalization is needed that relies less on market forces – that is to say, a model that is regulated in order to be able better to meet the requirements of just growth. Various propositions for such further regulation have been set forth in the chapters above. Eyoh and Dickson speak in favour of a "social-democratic" model of globalization. Such a model would involve "reconstructing the rule of global economic exchange to minimize the negative side-effects of unregulated markets: to reduce the massive international and intranational inequalities, to tame the turbulence and insecurity created by footloose capital, to halt the competitive devaluation of national environmental standards, and to protect basic labour standards" (Eyoh and Sandbrook, chap. 8, this volume).

A number of more concrete proposals for economic regulation are set forth in Barbara Stallings's chapter. They include (a) consistent macroeconomic policies at the global level, including a commitment to stable growth rates in developed countries; (b) enhanced financial supervision and regulation and improved information flows in order to create a more level financial playing field for developing countries; (c) reform of the IMF to provide adequate international liquidity in times of crisis; (d) sharing the costs of adjustment so that lenders share in the costs rather than letting borrowers be responsible for all the consequences; (e) debt alleviation for the least-developed countries.

These proposals aim at changing the framework for economic globalization. Changes in the political framework are needed as well, concerning two core areas. One is related to the promotion of democracy and human rights in the developing world. Developed countries have pushed for free and fair elections and for "good governance." These efforts need to be strengthened in a way that better takes the specific political and institutional problems in the regions into account. Some of those major problems were identified earlier in this Conclusion. That is to say, rather than a "one-size-fits-all" standard model of Western liberal democracy, the distinct problems faced by the regions must be taken seriously. Liberal democracy has developed in many different variants in the developed world. Democratic development in the developing world will surely have to add new diversity to the democratic tradition. It is quite clear by now that the mere holding of elections, even if they are relatively free and fair, is not sufficient to provide substantial representation and accountability in many countries.

The other core area for change concerns the international institutions themselves. Debate on global governance for just growth is not new. Since the early 1960s, the United Nations has taken the leadership in deliberating on just growth and effective international institutions. The Group of 77, the creation of the UNCTAD, and negotiations over New International Economic Order, were a result of international debates initiated by the United Nations. Along with this, the World Bank and other multilateral lending institutions have also paid attention to just growth by campaigning growth with redistribution, basic human-needs strategy, and human development. The recent advent of the "post-Washington Consensus," emphasizing international activism toward social empowerment and human development, also underscores the efforts of international institutions in promoting growth, reducing social inequality and poverty, and nurturing human development. As the findings in this volume reveal, however, such efforts have not been successful. New global governance that can not only harness galloping forces of globalization but also promote just growth is the mandate of the twenty-first century. There is no other candidate than the United Nations to take the leadership in restructuring global governance.

However, the current United Nations system cannot effectively initiate and sustain new global governance for just growth, and should be reformed and reinvigorated. Three important types of change can be conceived of, the first being extensive institutional reform. The existing Social and Economic Council is unfit for addressing and redressing salient issues of just growth; it should be given much more power and authority, comparable to that of the Security Council. Second, the United Nations should take a more proactive leadership in addressing and enhancing just growth. As the episodes of New International Economic Order illustrate, the United Nations system, lacking an effective enforcement mechanism, has been turned into an intellectual debating place rather than the centrifugal point of international activism toward just growth. Such passive leadership cannot warrant the resolution of unjust growth that is pervasive throughout the developing world; the United Nations needs to be realigned to ensure more actions and enforcement. Finally, the United Nations should take initiatives in forming an epistemic community toward just growth; it should be the leader, not the follower, in setting the agenda, spreading knowledge, and forging collective actions on just growth. The United Nations should lead the World Bank, not vice versa. Indeed, leadership of the United Nations will be vital to tackling the tasks of achieving just growth in the twenty-first century.

We also want to emphasize the need for a change of perspective in these matters, both in the North and in the South. The global issue is not so much the level of economic aid, i.e. the amount of resources committed by the rich countries to the poor: the global issue is that market forces have achieved too much dominance in the present model of globalization, to the disadvantage of states in both North and South. The better harnessing of market forces that is required must be constructed in a way that creates a much better framework for just growth everywhere. The dividing line in this respect is not between North and South, but between the groups in both places that want to continue the present model of globalization and the groups that want to reform it. This is a complex situation, but it also opens up possibilities for cooperation that cut across traditional North–South divisions.

Regional-level efforts should be made in tandem with those at international level. Intraregional cooperation to minimize negative externalities of globalization and to enhance the potential for common prosperity should be encouraged. Most regions in the developing world lack intraregional economic cooperation and coordination and are less effective in utilizing such integrative schemes where they are available. Intraregional macro- and microeconomic cooperation and coordination, as well as regional economic monitoring and regulation, will serve as a useful tool for promoting just growth on the regional level.

In sum, the current interaction of states and market does not sufficiently secure the goal of just growth in the developing world. Significant international, regional, and domestic change is needed in order to realize that goal. It is clear that a world order geared to achieve just growth is very different from the present one, in both economic and political terms.

# Acronyms

| | |
|---|---|
| APEC | Asia-Pacific Economic Cooperation (Conference) |
| ASEAN | Association of South-East Asian Nations |
| BIS | Bank for International Settlements |
| BJP | Bhartiya Janata Party |
| DFID | Department for International Development |
| E(S)CLA | Economic and Social Commission on Latin America |
| EAEC | East Asian Economic Caucus |
| ECLAC | [UN] Economic Commission for Latin America and the Caribbean |
| EG | economic growth |
| EOI | export-oriented industrialization |
| EU | European Union |
| FDI | foreign direct investment |
| GATT | General Agreement on Tariffs and Trade |
| GDP | gross domestic product |
| GNP | gross national product |
| HD | human development |
| HDI | Human Development Index |
| HIPC | Highly Indebted Poor Countries |
| IC | integrated circuit |
| IDB | Inter-American Development Bank |
| IDS | Institute for Development Studies |
| IDTs | International Development Targets |
| IFIs | international financial institutions |
| ILO | International Labour Organization |

| | |
|---|---|
| IMF | International Monetary Fund |
| ISI | import-substitution industrialization |
| IT | information and telecommunications |
| LCD | liquid-crystal display |
| MENA | Middle East and North Africa |
| NAFTA | North Atlantic Free Trade Agreement |
| NGOs | non-governmental organizations |
| NICs | newly industrialized countries |
| NIEs | newly industrialized economies |
| NT | New Taiwan |
| OBM | own-brand manufacture |
| ODA | official development assistance |
| ODM | own-design manufacture |
| OECD | Organization for Economic Co-operation and Development |
| OEM | original-equipment manufacture |
| OPEC | Organization of Petroleum-Exporting Countries |
| PAN | Partido Acción Nacional |
| PBEC | Pacific Basin Economic Council |
| PECC | Pacific Economic Cooperation Council |
| PPP | purchasing power parity |
| PRD | Partido de Revolucion Democratico (Party of Democratic Revolution) |
| PRI | Partido Revolucionario Institucional (Institutional Revolutionary Party) |
| PRONASOL | Programa Nacional de Solidaridad (National Solidarity Program) |
| R&D | research and development |
| SIDA | Swedish International Development Cooperation Agency |
| SOEs | state-owned enterprises |
| TNCs | transnational corporations |
| UNCTAD | United Nations Conference on Trade and Development |
| UDHR | Universal Declaration of Human Rights |
| UNDP | United Nations Development Programme |
| UNICEF | United Nations Children's Fund |
| WTO | World Trade Organization |

# List of contributors

**Yun-han Chu** is a professor of Political Science at National Taiwan University and serves concurrently as Vice-President of the Chiang Ching-kuo Foundation for International Scholarly Exchange. Professor Chu received his PhD in political science from the University of Minnesota and joined the faculty of National Taiwan University in 1987. He was a visiting associate professor at Columbia University in 1990–1991. He served as Director of Programs of the Institute for National Policy Research, Taiwan's leading independent think-tank, from 1989 to 1999. He has been appointed to the Advisory Board of the Division of Humanities and Social Sciences, National Science Council since 1998. Professor Chu specializes in politics of Greater China, East Asian political economy, and democratization. He is a three-times recipient of an Outstanding Research Award from the National Science Council. He currently serves on the editorial board of *China Perspective*, *China Review*, *Journal of Contemporary China*, *Journal of East Asian Studies*, and *Journal of Democracy*. He is the author, co-author, editor, or co-editor of ten books. Among his recent English publications are *Crafting Democracy in Taiwan* (Institute for National Policy Research, 1992), *Consolidating Third-Wave Democracies* (Cornell University Press, 1997), and *China Under Jiang Zemin* (Lynne Rienner, 2000).

**Dickson Eyoh** is Associate Professor of Political Science and Director, African Studies Program, University of Toronto. He is co-editor of, and contributor to, *Ethnicity and Democratic Nation-building in Africa*, eds Bruce

Berman, Dickson Eyoh, and Will Kymlicka (Oxford: James Currey, forthcoming).

**Robert R. Kaufman** is a professor of Political Science at Rutgers University. He received a PhD from Harvard University in 1967, and specializes in comparative politics with an emphasis on Latin America. Kaufman has written extensively on the politics of economic reform and democratic transitions. He is author of *The Politics of Economic Stabilization in Argentina, Brazil, and Mexico* (1988), co-editor of *The Politics of Economic Adjustment* (1992), and co-author of *The Political Economy of Democratic Transitions* (1995), winner of the 1995 Leubbert Prize for the best book in comparative politics, awarded by the Comparative Politics Section of the American Political Science Association. He has also contributed articles to the *American Political Science Review*, *Comparative Politics*, and *International Organization* and is a co-editor of, and contributor to, *Reforming the State: Fiscal and Welfare Reform in Transition Economies* (Cambridge University Press, 2000).

**Atul Kohli** is Professor of Politics and International Affairs at Princeton University. His principal research interests are in the area of comparative political economy with a focus on the developing countries. He is the author of *The State and Poverty in India* and of *Democracy and Discontent: India's Growing Crisis of Governability*. He is also the editor of five volumes: *The State and Development in the Third World*; *India's Democracy*; *Stated Power and Social Forces: Domination and Transformation in the World*; *Community Conflicts and the State in India*; and *The Success of India's Democracy*. His current research project is a comparative analysis of the politics of industrialization in South Korea, Brazil, India, and Nigeria. He is an editor of *World Politics* and has been the recipient of grants and fellowships from the Social Science Research Council, Ford Foundation, and Russell Sage Foundation. He has a PhD degree from the University of California, Berkeley.

**Chung-in Moon** is Dean of the Graduate School of International Studies and Professor of the Political Science Department in Yonsei University, Seoul, Korea. Previously, he taught at the University of Kentucky, Williams College, Duke University, and the University of California at San Diego; he was also a Public Policy fellow at the Woodrow Wilson Center, Washington, DC in 1999. He has many publications, including articles in *World Politics*, *International Studies Quarterly*, and *Millennium*. Most recently he has written *Economic Crisis and Structural Reforms in South Korea: Assessments and Implications* (2000), *Emerging Threats, Force Structures, and Role of Air Power in South Korea* (2000), *Kim Dae Jung Government and Sunshine Policy: Promises and Challenges* (1999), *Democratization and Globalization in Korea: Assessments and Prospects* (1999), *Democracy and the Korean Economy* (1999), and *Arms Control on the Korean Peninsula* (1996).

**Michael P. Moore** is Professorial Fellow of the Institute of Development Studies at the University of Sussex. His professional interests are in political and institutional aspects of economic policy and performance, and antipoverty policy; the politics and administration of development; political authority and governance in "the South"; markets and economic transactions. He is the author of *The State and Peasant Politics in Sri Lanka* and *Agriculture and Society in the Low Country (Sri Lanka)*; and is the editor of *Development and the Rural–Urban Divide* and *The Disintegrating Village? Social Change in Rural Sri Lanka*, etc. He is a member of the editorial boards of *Democratization* and the *Journal of Development Studies*. He has been the recipient of five major research grants from the Economic and Social Research Council, the Economic and Social Committee for Overseas Research of the Overseas Development Administration, and the Gatsby Foundation.

**Rani D. Mullen** is a doctoral candidate at Princeton University's Woodrow Wilson School of Public and International Affairs. Her dissertation research is on the relationship between local governance and social welfare, based on field research in villages in three states in India. She has an MA degree from the Johns Hopkins University School of Advanced International Studies and has worked on poverty and development issues at the World Bank, the Asian Development Bank, and the US Agency for International Development.

**Ziya Öniş** is Professor of International Political Economy at Koc University, Istanbul, Turkey. He was previously a professor of Economics and International Affairs at Bogazici University, Istanbul. His primary fields of interest are comparative and international political economy and the political economy of development. His most recent publications include "Political Economy of Islamic Resurgence in Turkey: The Rise of the Welfare Party in Perspective," in *Third World Quarterly* 18(3) (September 1997); *State and Market: The Political Economy of Turkey in Comparative Perspective* (Istanbul: Bogazici University Press, 1998); "Turkey, Europe and Paradoxes of Identity: Perspectives on the International Context of Democratization," in *Mediterranean Quarterly* 10(3) (Summer 1999); (with A. F. Aysan) "Neoliberal Globalization, The Nation State and Financial Crises in the Semi-Periphery: A Comparative Analysis," in *Third World Quarterly* 21(1) (January 2000); "Neoliberal Globalization and the Democracy Paradox: Interpreting the Turkish General Elections of 1999," in *Journal of International Affairs* 54(1) (Fall 2000); "The Turkish Economy at the Turn of a New Century: Critical and Comparative Perspectives," in Morton Abramowitz (ed.) *Turkey's Transformation and American Policy*, Washington DC: The Century Foundation (2000); and "Luxembourg, Helsinki and Beyond: Towards an Interpretation of Recent Turkey–EU Relations," in *Government and Opposition* 35(4) (Autumn 2000).

**Richard Sandbrook** is a professor of Political Science and a Fellow of the Munk Centre for International Studies at the University of Toronto. He has published and edited eight books on the political economy of Africa and development studies. His most recent book is *Closing the Circle: Democratization and Development in Africa* (2000).

**Georg Sørensen** is Professor of Political Science, University of Aarhus, Denmark. His recent books include *Introduction to International Relations* (Oxford University Press 1999, with Robert Jackson) and *Changes in Statehood: The Transformation of International Relations* (Palgrave 2001).

**Barbara Stallings** is Director of the Economic Development Division of the UN Economic Commission for Latin America and the Caribbean (ECLAC). Before arriving at ECLAC in 1993, she was Professor of Political Economy at the University of Wisconsin-Madison (USA) for 15 years. She was also a visiting professor or researcher at Harvard, Yale, and Columbia universities in the United States and at several research centres in Latin America and in Japan. Ms Stallings holds doctorates in Economics (Cambridge University, UK) and in Political Science (Stanford University, USA). As a specialist in development economics and international finance, she has published eight books and some fifty articles on these topics. Her latest book is *Growth, Employment, and Equity: The Impact of the Economic Reforms in Latin America and the Caribbean*, Brookings Institution Press, 2000 (with Wilson Peres).

**Howard White** is an economist whose main areas of research have been aid effectiveness and poverty analysis. Recent publications include "Growth versus distribution" in *Development Policy Review*, "Redistribution: the missing link in the World Bank's policy agenda" in the *Journal of International Development* and "What do World Bank poverty assessments tell us about poverty in Africa?" in *Development and Change*. He has worked in Africa and Asia on behalf of several agencies including DFID, SIDA, and the World Bank. He is a Fellow at the Institute of Development Studies, University of Sussex.

# Index

# Catalogue Request

Name: _____

Address: _____

_____

Tel: _____

Fax: _____

E-mail: _____

To receive a catalogue of UNU Press publications kindly photocopy this form and send or fax it back to us with your details. You can also e-mail us this information. Please put "Mailing List" in the subject line.

 **United Nations University Press**

53-70, Jingumae 5-chome
Shibuya-ku, Tokyo 150-8925, Japan
Tel: +81-3-3499-2811  Fax: +81-3-3406-7345
E-mail: sales@hq.unu.edu  http://www.unu.edu